Developing Talent
in Young People

Benjamin S. Bloom
EDITOR

CONTRIBUTORS
Lauren A. Sosniak
Kathryn D. Sloane
Anthony G. Kalinowski
William C. Gustin
Judith A. Monsaas

Developing
Talent
in Young People

BALLANTINE BOOKS   NEW YORK

Library of Congress Catalog Card Number: 84-90809

ISBN: 0-345-31951-6 (hdcvr)
ISBN: 0-345-31509-X (pbk)

Manufactured in the United States of America

First Edition: January 1985

10 9 8 7 6 5 4 3 2

Designed by Ann Gold

Contents

We dedicate this book to the talented individuals and their parents who gave much of themselves to this study so that succeeding generations might learn from their experiences.

★ ★ ★ ★ ★ ★ ★

Acknowledgments

This work is the outcome of the combined efforts of many people—most especially the talented individuals and their parents who talked about their lives at length and with great candor.

A number of University of Chicago students and recent graduates worked on the project. Several conducted parent interviews. We are especially grateful to Susan Bloom, who interviewed a substantial number of the parents, and who was always available to share her insights with others on the staff. Thanks also to Jean Carney, Paula Sorbello, and Rita Sussman.

Sheila Smith initiated the study of the research neurologists and conducted interviews with this group of talented individuals. Other commitments kept her from completing the data analysis and writing the chapter on the research neurologists.

Inagrace Thoms Dietterich, project secretary, kept our files and our thoughts both straight through many years of work on the project. She did all of our typing, and never hesitated to remind us when something didn't seem quite right. It was our good fortune to have a secretary who was also a doctoral student.

We express our gratitude to Dr. H. Thomas James, President of the Spencer Foundation, for the financial support of this study as well as for his encouragement and faith in us. We hope the results of the project justify the Foundation's support.

We also express our thanks to David Krathwohl who made funds in our joint Taxonomy royalty account available for the pilot studies as well as for the overruns in our expenses when we so desperately needed them.

Finally, we wish to thank the University of Chicago and Charles Bidwell, Chairman of the Department of Education, for the encouragement and support so necessary for this kind of research. We hope that this study of the most extreme examples of learning and achievement will further our understanding of the educative process.

Developing Talent
in Young People

1

★ ★ ★ ★ ★ ★

The Nature of the Study
and Why It Was Done

Benjamin S. Bloom

Over the past four years a team of research workers under my direction at the University of Chicago has been engaged in a study of the development of talent in children. We have examined the processes by which individuals who have reached the highest levels of accomplishment in selected fields have been helped to develop their capabilities so fully. The subjects of our study included concert pianists, sculptors, research mathematicians, research neurologists, Olympic swimmers, and tennis champions.

The study has provided strong evidence that no matter what the initial characteristics (or gifts) of the individuals, unless there is a long and intensive process of encouragement, nurturance, education, and training, the individuals will not attain extreme levels of capability in these particular fields. This research has raised questions about earlier views of special gifts and innate aptitudes as necessary prerequisites of talent development.

Most of the individuals selected for this study attained these high levels of accomplishment in their field before the age of thirty-five. Our investigation was concerned with the talent development process and the role of parents, teachers, and others in teaching, motivating, and supporting these individuals until they reached the highest levels of learning and capability in their field.

We limited our study to individuals born and reared in the United States, since we wanted to be certain that the long teaching and learning process was within the American context. We had earlier found that countries differ in the value placed on particular types of talent, and they differ in their methods of identifying individuals to receive special training in particular talent fields, as well in their methods of developing these talents.

PREVIOUS RESEARCH
ON SCHOOL LEARNING

After forty years of intensive research on school learning in the United States as well as abroad, my major conclusion is: What any person in the world can learn, *almost* all persons can learn *if* provided with appropriate prior and current conditions of learning. This generalization does not appear to apply to the 2% or 3% of individuals who have severe emotional and physical difficulties that impair their learning. At the other extreme there are about 1% or 2% of individuals who appear to learn in such unusually capable ways that they *may* be exceptions to the theory. At this stage of the research it applies most clearly to the middle 95% of a school population.

The middle 95% of school students become very similar in terms of their measured achievement, learning ability, rate of learning, and motivation for further learning when provided with *favorable learning conditions*. One example of such favorable learning conditions is mastery learning where the students are helped to master each learning unit before proceeding to a more advanced learning task. In general, the average student taught under mastery-learning procedures achieves at a level above 85% of students taught under conventional instructional conditions. An even more extreme result has been obtained when tutoring was used as the primary method of instruction. Under tutoring, the average student performs better than 98% of students taught by conventional group instruction, even though both groups of students performed at similar levels in terms of relevant aptitude and achievement before the instruction began.

While this theory and the research done so far have been limited to school learning, they raise some very important questions about the ways in which special talent develops in many areas. How were the outstanding persons in art and music, in athletics, in various fields of scholarship, and in industry, government, and other areas of human endeavor discovered, developed, and encouraged? Do these very talented individuals achieve because of innate and rare qualities and/or as the result of special training and encouragement?

The central thesis of *Human Characteristics and School Learning* (Bloom, 1976) is the potential equality of most human beings for school learning. We believe that the same thesis is likely to apply to all learning, whether in schools or outside of schools. At least, it leads us to speculate that there must be an enormous potential pool of talent available in the United States. It is likely that some combinations of the home, the teachers, the schools, and the society may in large part determine what portions of this potential pool of talent become developed. It is also likely that these same forces may, in part, be responsible for much of the great wastage of human potentiality.

A METHOD OF STUDYING
TALENT DEVELOPMENT

The Development of Talent Research Project began with the speculation that there must be a very large pool of potential talent available in each society that can either be developed or neglected, depending in large measure on environmental conditions. By talent we mean an unusually high level of demonstrated ability, achievement, or skill in some special field of study or interest. This is in contrast with earlier definitions, which equate talent with natural gifts or aptitudes. We assumed that the development of both excellence and standards of excellence in a society is dependent on the extent to which there are opportunities and encouragement for individuals to find meaning and enjoyment in one or more areas and fields of development. The project also began with the belief that the development of talent provides a sense of fulfillment for individuals as well as a source of great contributions to the society at large.

We have briefly considered various methods of trying to answer some of the major questions we raised about talent development. For example, a longitudinal study of thousands of children over ten to twenty years of development would have been a possible method if one could be certain that many of them would reach high levels of talent development. However, at this point we know of no method by which one could predict which young children (under the age of ten) would eventually become outstanding musicians, athletes, mathematicians, and so on.

We did some pilot studies in which we tried to answer some of our questions about talent development by reading biographies of unusual mathematicians, musicians, athletes, writers, and scientists. However, we found little information on the developmental processes by which these individuals were enabled to reach high levels of attainment in their respective field because most of the biographical material dealt with the lives and work of these people *after* they had reached adulthood and a high level of attainment. It became evident to us that the kind of information we needed on the formative years could only be secured by *interviewing* people who had already attained these high levels of capability in selected fields.

We then did some pilot studies with a small number of mathematicians, pianists, and athletes who had met particular performance criteria. We interviewed these individuals and found that they could tell us a great deal about how they became interested in the field, the role their parents and others in the family played in some of the early years, the kind of instruction they received from teachers and coaches, and some of the factors they believed helped them reach their present level of capability in these fields.

On the basis of these exploratory studies we decided to select as subjects of our study some people who had reached
world-class levels of accomplishment in particular fields and
to interview them to get a *retrospective* picture of the process
of talent development. We assumed that the patterns of development would emerge most clearly in the individuals who had
reached the highest levels of talent development in each field.
Although it is likely that no two individuals would have had
identical talent development experiences, we believed that
the clearest picture of what is required for full development in
a talent field would emerge from studying a sizable number of
individuals (twenty to twenty-five) who had reached very high
levels of talent development in that field.

SELECTION OF FIELDS
OF TALENT DEVELOPMENT

As we began to search for the fields of talent to be studied, it
became clear to us that there were literally hundreds of fields
we might study. Since we decided to study approximately
twenty-five highly talented individuals in each field, we
needed to restrict our study to no more than six to eight fields,
given our time and budget limitations.

It became apparent in our pilot studies and from our reading that the fields could be grouped in such a way that each
field studied would have implications for related fields. For
example, in the psychomotor or athletic fields we could study
many different types of athletes. We believed that the study of
a few well-chosen athletic fields would have implications for
other athletic fields. Similarly, in other areas of talent development, we believed that the particular fields studied would
have relevance for many other related ones.

We decided to study talent fields that were representative
of four distinct areas of talent. The area that includes the
many athletic fields we labeled *athletic* or *psychomotor* fields,
since these involve fine motor coordination, skills in the use of
the body, and training to develop strength or endurance. A second area includes the many *aesthetic*, *musical*, and *artistic*

fields, which involve sensory and aesthetic perception, particular types of motor coordination, and the training of eye and/or ear to respond to particular sights and sounds. A third area includes the many fields that emphasize *cognitive* or *intellectual* development. These fields typically require emphasis on a large knowledge base as well as the learning of particular skills, ways of thinking, and approaches to social, technical, and scientific problems. Many of these also require creativity in attacking a range of problems and difficulties within each field.

A fourth area we planned to investigate included talent fields that emphasize *interpersonal relations*. By this we meant fields that emphasize the quality of interactions with other people. We were of the view that there is a relatively large number of occupations in which sensitivity to interpersonal relations is a central factor in the work. Initially, we thought of school teachers, social workers, psychiatrists and psychologists, administrators, foremen and other supervisors, and other occupations in which much of the work is dependent on relations with others, the ability to empathize with others (to be sensitive to the feelings and difficulties others are experiencing), and skills in helping others to solve personal as well as professional problems.

Thus, we defined a broad spectrum of talent fields, from athletics to interpersonal fields. We regarded this spectrum as a useful schema for identifying fields that require different types of abilities, learning experiences, and development. We decided to select two talent fields in each area that would involve distinctly different types of activity, that are well defined, and for which there are relatively objective criteria (such as competitions, achievements, and awards) for selecting the outstanding twenty-five persons in the United States.

We decided to study two fields of athletics with the hope that we would find some similarities in the patterns of selection, development, and encouragement. We finally chose Olympic *swimmers* and world-class *tennis players*. For each of these we could find clear criteria that assured us that the individuals selected for study had reached the highest levels of talent development in that field. We chose athletic fields in which the individual's own attainments were central. In athletic fields primarily involving team sports we could not be certain of the attainments of the individual, since in some cases the team's support might, in part, account for the success of selected individuals on the team.

A second area of interest was the aesthetic fields, which include many types of musicians and artists. We believe that all these fields are likely to involve aesthetic development of some type and should yield some similarities in developmental patterns. After much searching we decided to limit our study to *concert pianists* and *sculptors*. Again, these are fields in which individual accomplishment is central and there are clear criteria for selecting the twenty-five individuals in each field who have reached very high levels of attainment. It was our assumption that the study of these two fields would yield findings that are in some ways relevant to the very large number of possible aesthetic fields.

A third area of interest was the cognitive or intellectual fields, which include the largest number of subjects and professions dependent on the entire system of education, from the home and elementary education through college, university, and professional education. In these fields we finally decided to study *research mathematicians* and *research neurologists*. Again, we believe that the findings here are likely to have some relevance for other scholarly and professional fields that emphasize cognition as a central concern in the developmental and educational process. Here again, these are highly individual pursuits in which there are criteria for the identification of individuals who have reached very exceptional levels of development in the field.

Finally, we began with a fourth area that we planned to investigate—fields that emphasize interpersonal relations. But try as we might, we could find no criteria or method of selection that would assure us that we were including individuals who had reached the extremes of development in this area. Awards, special honors, particular selection procedures, and so forth are rarely primarily based on talent in interpersonal relations. We consulted with experts in these special fields, but they could not help us in the same way as the experts and informants in the athletic, aesthetic, and cognitive fields. We reluctantly decided that, at this time, we are unable to locate criteria in these fields that would assure the selection of individuals who had attained national or international levels of capability in interpersonal relations.

We recognized that none of these talent areas is pure, since it is likely that other characteristics are involved besides the class or types of thinking, acting, and behaving believed to be central in the classification. Clearly some athletics involve a great deal of thought as well as action. The aesthetic fields are likely to involve some elements of muscular or psychomotor development as well as intellectual considerations. The intellectual or cognitive fields undoubtedly require aesthetic judgments. All of which is to say that in the cognitive, aesthetic, and psychomotor areas, none of the specific talent fields can be restricted to only the specific characteristics of the area under which it is classified. Although each talent field does *emphasize* the types of processes under which it is classified, it is likely that other qualities and characteristics are also included to some extent.

METHODS OF SELECTION
OF TALENTED INDIVIDUALS

In each of the six fields, we contacted a number of outstanding experts, teachers, and scholars in the field to find criteria that could be used for identifying individuals who have reached world-class levels of attainment in that field. They helped us to find contests, awards, and existing selection methods that could be used to identify the top twenty-five persons in each field. In some instances, we also made use of expert ranking of a list of persons as a way of ensuring that the individuals finally selected met the criteria of talent development as well as national recognition by experts in the field.

The swimmers were selected because they had earned a place on an Olympic swimming team in a sprint event. The tennis players had been identified as top-ranking players at the international level by a rating method developed by the major tennis organizations and publications.

The concert pianists had been finalists in one or more of six major international piano competitions. The sculptors had won both a Guggenheim Fellowship and one of the National Endowment for the Arts awards.

The research mathematicians were the winners of Sloan prizes in mathematics who were also judged to be the most significant contributors to mathematics by mathematical faculty members of six of the major universities. These research mathematicians were also cited most frequently in the Science Citation Index. Each of the research neurologists had been awarded a five-year special grant for research from the National Institute of Health. In addition they were cited most frequently in the Science Citation Index and were rated highly for their research contributions by the chairmen of the neurology department of five major universities.

We are not suggesting that the talented individuals selected are the absolute top twenty-five in each field. Others might have been found who were equal to or even better than some of the individuals finally included in the study. Any set of criteria for inclusion in a study such as this undoubtedly misses other highly qualified individuals who did not participate in the contests and awards or were not included in the rating methods. Although we may have missed a few very talented individuals, all those we did include were clearly among the top persons in their fields.

In addition to these criteria of excellence in the field, we set an age criterion. With a few exceptions the individuals finally selected were below the age of thirty-five when interviewed. We used this age criterion because we hoped that the talented individuals would remember some of their early experiences.

It also made it more likely that one or both of the parents might be alive to help us with information about the early years as well as to help us understand the changing role of the home relative to the talent development over the years.

We are pleased with the responsiveness of the talented individuals. Initially, we were fearful that a substantial portion of our carefully selected sample might refuse to participate in the study. We had selected top individuals in each field, and the refusal of many of these could have seriously damaged our study because we could not hope to find equally talented individuals to replace them. Fortunately, in each field we lost only about three or four individuals from our original sample. A few did not participate because they were abroad for several years, some because they could not be contacted by phone or mail, and some because they were not interested in taking part in the study.

METHODS OF DATA COLLECTION

As was pointed out earlier, we decided to do this as a retrospective study. We proposed to identify individuals who had attained world-class levels of competence in each field, then, by interview methods, attempt to understand the developmental and educational processes that were important in enabling them to reach these high levels of competence in their field. This is a study of the process of development, and we needed to secure information about these individuals at each of the major stages in their development. Our long experience in the field of education and human development led us to assume that there are identifiable stages in the development of each individual.

We proposed in each case to determine each of the following:

- The special physical, intellectual, or other relevant characteristics evident in the individual at an early developmental period

- The role of the home in the guidance and support of the talent from the early years to later stages in the development
- The type and quality of instruction and guidance in the talent field available to the individual at different stages in his or her development
- The sources and types of motivation and reward and the special circumstances that gave encouragement and support to the individual at different stages in his or her development of the talent
- The amount of active learning time, practice, and other learning effort invested by the individual at each stage of development
- Any other factors the individual regarded as relevant to his or her discovery, development, and encouragement in relation to the particular field
- Finally, the ways in which these individuals developed habits, interests, and values that increasingly committed them to their special talent field and brought them to what we believe are the limits of learning in each of these fields

Before interviewing the talented individuals in our study, we tried our interview methods with other talented individuals who did not quite meet our final criteria. Discussions among the staff about the results of these interviews helped to train staff members. In these semi-structured interviews, we tried to get the individual to tell his or her own story with questions raised at various points in order to ensure that we obtained much of the information we sought. These interviews typically took two to three hours and were held at a time and place convenient to the talented individual. In some cases, when we needed additional information, we telephoned the individual for it at a later time.

Most of the talented persons interviewed expressed great interest in the study and a very positive reaction to the interview. We believe that most of them were very proud to be included in the study. Some of them especially welcomed the opportunity to talk about the people who contributed to their development and to tell about some of the difficulties and problems they encountered.

In each case, we asked the talented individuals for permission to contact their parents and their major teachers. Many of the major teachers and coaches we contacted were very cooperative. They helped us to understand some of the developmental processes in the talent field generally and their special role in encouraging and supporting these individuals, especially in the later stages of the talent development process.

We planned to interview the parents primarily as observers to verify particular points in our interviews with the talented persons, to describe some of the early experiences of their child, and to describe some aspects of the home environment during the child's early years as well as later. In the case of the parents, we realized that the time and costs were prohibitive if we had to travel to more than a hundred different communities to interview them. Because we were interviewing parents primarily as observers, we were of the opinion that telephone interviews might secure the information we needed. In order to test the effectiveness of telephone interviews, we tried face-to-face interviews with the Chicago-area parents of selected individuals who did not quite meet our final selection criteria for the talent field and compared them with telephone interviews of the parents of other individuals in this group. As far as we could determine, for our purposes the telephone interviews were as effective as the face-to-face interviews.

In any case, our telephone interviews with parents have been very useful as a supplement to the face-to-face interview with the talented individuals. We had planned for one-hour interviews of the parents, but many of these were extended to two hours or more because the parents had so much they wanted to say about their successful child. Only a few of the parents refused to be interviewed. A few called us back after the interview to tell us about something they regarded as especially important. In almost all cases, the parents expressed some satisfaction at being included in the study. Most of them answered our questions in a very open way.

In order to guarantee our subjects' anonymity, we have used a coding system for quote attributions that works as follows: Each talent field is assigned an appropriate initial letter, such as *P* for Pianist or *S* for Swimmer. The talented individuals are thus referred to as P-2 (for Pianist 2) or S-3 (for Swimmer 3). Similarly, the parents are coded as follows: M of P-2 (Mother of Pianist 2) or F of S-3 (Father of Swimmer 3).

THE RESEARCH STAFF
The staff of researchers on the Talent Development Study consisted of seven major research workers in addition to the principal investigator (Bloom). Each of the researchers took primary responsibility for a single talent field. This researcher met with teachers, coaches, and other expert informants in order to determine the criteria for selecting the twenty-five top individuals who would constitute the sample of highly talented individuals for the field. The same researcher interviewed the talented individuals in a single talent field. This researcher also interviewed the master teachers and coaches, who helped us understand what was required of an individual to be selected for advanced training in the field as well as some of the developmental processes they regarded as important for these persons to achieve at the highest possible level.

Other researchers took responsibility for the interviews with the parents of these talented individuals. Since the home interviews came after the interview with the talented individual, these researchers read the interview with the talented individual and consulted with the researcher who wrote this report. These meetings ensured that the parent interviewer was aware of the report on the talented individual and that particular questions and problems raised in the interview with the talented individual could be probed further in the parent interview. However, this researcher was careful to maintain the confidentiality of the earlier interview with the talented individual during the interview with the parents.

All the interviews were tape-recorded (with the consent of the interviewee), and these were the basis for the summaries of the interviews with the individuals and their parents.

In preparation for the interviews, the staff worked out a series of topics or questions to be covered. These included the major points raised on pages 12–13 of this chapter. However, the intent of the interview was to enable the talented individual (and the parents) to tell their story with a minimum of interference. The topics or questions were referred to as necessary to ensure that the interview covered the salient points in each of the stages of talent development.

Periodically, the summaries of these interviews were reviewed with the researcher by the project coordinator and by the principal investigator. Staff meetings were held regularly to discuss the work, the problems being raised, and the plans for further interviews. At the staff meetings we attempted to delineate some tentative generalizations as we saw them emerging in each talent field and we discussed particular cases that were most representative of these generalizations, as well as the cases that were the most striking exceptions to them. In preparing for these discussions, the researchers made charts to summarize the salient features and the frequency with which they emerged in the different cases.

TALENT DEVELOPMENT RESEARCH

As we proceeded from one talent field to another over these four-plus years, we acquired greater and greater confidence in the value of the retrospective-interview approach to the study of talent development. Some of the talented individuals initially expressed doubts about what they could remember over the ten- to twenty-year period of their talent development. However, once they began talking, most of them appeared to have little difficulty remembering details, events, and persons they regarded as significant in their development. Also, their parents responded with considerable detail and enthusiasm about their child's development. With few exceptions, there was good correspondence between the two interviews, thus providing some corroboration of the two independent interviews.

As we summarized the interviews of the different individuals within each talent field, we were especially fascinated by the striking similarities in the process of talent development. In addition, although we found many detailed differences across the talent fields, there were many similarities in the underlying processes of talent development.

It is our hope that our work will be of interest to other researchers and that others will extend this type of research to many different talent fields.

PREPARATION OF THE FINAL REPORTS

The researcher assigned to the interviews with the talented individuals in a field was responsible for the final report on that field included in this book. He or she began the analysis with a few summaries of the interviews with the talented individuals and with their parents and began outlining the salient features in each case and then compared these from case to case to determine the common features as well as the major exceptions. These were discussed at staff meetings and were also discussed among the different researchers within a talent area (e.g., swimming and tennis) as well as across talent areas (e.g., athletes, musicians, mathematicians) where possible.

The final reports that appear in this book were discussed in some of these meetings and especially with the principal investigator and the project coordinator. For each of the talent fields, we found it convenient to summarize the evidence relating to the years in the home before formal instruction began, the early years with the first teacher(s) in the talent field, the middle years (typically with one or more advanced teachers), and the final years of talent development (typically with one or more master teachers or coaches).

We have also written up a case study of one talented individual who we believe best represents the typical pattern in each of three fields.

In addition to the descriptive chapters about each of the six talent fields, we have included four chapters in which we summarize the role of the home in talent development, the changes in the learning over time, some of the reasons for the long-term commitment to the talent field, and some major generalizations about the process of talent development.

Some of our findings contrast sharply with present conceptions about talent development. Perhaps the major value of this study is that it documents many new insights into human potential and the means by which it is translated into actual accomplishment. This applies not only to talent development but, to some extent, to all *learning* in or out of the schools.

Underlying the entire study is our belief that the quality of life is dependent on individuals having a sense of fulfillment in one or more roles and fields of human endeavor. The development of both excellence and standards of excellence in a society is dependent upon the extent to which the society offers opportunity and encouragement for the majority of individuals in it to find meaning and enjoyment in one or more areas and fields of human development. We believe that societies that emphasize only minimal standards of competence are likely to produce only minimal levels of competence and talent.

REFERENCE

Bloom, Benjamin S. *Human Characteristics and School Learning.* New York: McGraw-Hill, 1976.

2

★ ★ ★ ★ ★ ★

Learning to Be a Concert Pianist

Lauren A. Sosniak

Twenty-four American concert pianists under the age of forty were invited to talk with us about their development. Each had been a finalist in one of six international piano competitions[1] that are recognized by experts in the field as being the most important for identifying exceptionally accomplished young musicians. Twenty-one of those invited agreed to take part in this study. Two who live in Europe could not join the project because they seldom visit the United States. The third never responded to our attempts to contact him.

At the end of each interview the pianist was asked for permission to contact his or her parents in order to request their participation in this study. All but one gave that permission. Most seemed pleased that we were interested in learning more about their development. We were able to interview parents of sixteen pianists for corroborating and supplementary information.

---

[1] The Chopin International Piano Competition, The Edgar M. Leventritt Foundation International Competition, The Leeds International Pianoforte Competition, the Queen Elisabeth of Belgium Competition, the Tchaikovsky International Competition, and the Van Cliburn International Quadrennial Piano Competition.

The typical pattern of learning for the group of concert pianists will be presented in four parts. The first part consists of information that provides a context for understanding the pianists' experiences. This includes demographic data about the sample and a discussion of the musical background of the pianists' families.

The other three parts divide the chronological narrative of the pianists' development into early, middle, and later years of learning. These three broad periods are, generally speaking, related to the age of the learner, but they are not defined by age. Instead, they reflect the amount of experience the person has with music and with a piano; his or her psychological perceptions of the activity of music making and the future of the activity; and the nature of the pianists' interactions with parents, teachers, the instrument, and the world of music.

There are two reasons for using these periods to describe the pianists' development. First, the age at which the pianists had certain experiences varies widely. For example, first experiences with a piano in their own home came anywhere between infancy and age seven, and first experiences with formal instruction occurred between ages three and nine.[2] Age does not seem to be nearly as useful a touchstone for describing the process of learning as the type and amount of the learners' experiences.

The second and perhaps more important reason for using the three broad periods to describe the learning process is that they emerge from the pianists' recollections of their years of

---

[2]Other examples of how age varies include: the pianist (P-24) who had already had a professional debut and was practicing four hours a day three years before another (P-15) had his first piano lesson; the pianist (P-5) who, at fourteen, was attending a music conservatory full-time and studying with perhaps the most noted living pianist in the country while another (P-4), also fourteen, was juggling practice time—in preparation for weekly lessons with a good local teacher—and high school work and other traditional adolescent activities; and the pianist (P-28) who had a first international success of note at nineteen while still another (P-8), at nineteen, was just making a formal commitment to the world of music.

learning. The periods are relatively easy to identify from the pianists' talk about something "changing" or "being different." The description of the learning process will thus still be chronological. Ages will be noted where appropriate, but the broad periods to be used actually refer to qualitatively different sets of learning experiences.

The early years of learning to be a pianist—those years from first exposure to music to the first major change in the pianists' perceptions about music and behaviors while studying and practicing—will be described at greater length and in greater detail than will subsequent years of learning. The pianists' and parents' perceptions and behaviors vary most from family to family in the beginning of the learning process. In the later years of learning, the pianists become much more similar in their thoughts and actions, as does the role the parents play in the learning process.

A CONTEXT FOR THE
PIANISTS' HISTORIES

The twenty-one concert pianists call into question almost any stereotype one might hold of classical musicians. Although they share a profession and have demonstrated similar very high levels of expertise at the keyboard, in most other ways they are as different from one another as they are different from people in general. The pianists are tall and short, heavy-set and slight, reserved and affable, athletic and sedentary, analytical and emotional. The hobbies they pursue in their spare time range from climbing mountains to cooking gourmet meals to just puttering around the house.

Sixteen of the twenty-one pianists are male. All are Caucasian. There is a tendency for them to be only children (six; the other fifteen were equally likely to be the oldest, youngest, or a middle child) from middle-class families. Their parents were professionals (35%), white-collar workers (45%), and blue-collar workers (20%).

Five of the pianists were raised in the New York metropolitan area. Philadelphia and Los Angeles were each the home-towns for three. The remaining ten pianists were raised in separate cities and towns across the country.

At the time of the interviews the pianists ranged in age from twenty-four to thirty-nine; all but two were between twenty-seven and thirty-seven. At the time of their first international achievement, the pianists ranged in age from nineteen to thirty-one; all but one was under twenty-eight. They had been studying piano for an average of seventeen years (see table 1).

TABLE 1
Years of Study until International Recognition

	RANGE	MEAN	S.D.
Begin Lessons	ages 3–9	5.71	1.93
Win Major Competition	ages 19–31	22.86	2.83
Elapsed Years	12–25 years	17.14	3.73

FAMILY MUSICAL BACKGROUND

The families the pianists were born into varied widely in musical interest and expertise. They can be crudely divided into four groups: (I) families whose livelihood depended on music; (II) families with an active avocational interest in music where one or more members were amateur musicians; (III) families with a passive avocational interest in music where one or more members frequently listened to music; and (IV) families with no apparent involvement with music before the child we interviewed began playing the piano. As table 2

TABLE 2
Family Musical Involvement

		N	
Group I	Family earned living through musical activity	4	19%
Group II	Active avocational instrumental musical activity in home	5	24%
Group III	Passive avocational listening musical activity in home	8	38%
Group IV	No musical practice/involvement in home before child's involvement	4	19%

shows, the musical background of the pianists' families was quite diverse.

Parents in two of the four families who earned their living through musical activities did so as professional symphony orchestra members, neither as pianists. In these homes there was a tremendous amount of musical activity. The performers supplemented their income by giving lessons in the home. Symphony-member colleagues were close family friends who played together formally and informally in chamber music groups. Visiting conductors and performers were frequent guests in the home. Music was a regular topic of serious discussion and light conversation. In the other two homes in this category music performance and discussion were not of the same exceptionally high quality, but still, music was abundant.

In five of the homes, a parent was actively playing music as a hobby. None of these "musicians" performed professionally, but they did take their hobby very seriously. They practiced regularly, sometimes arranged informal chamber music groups, and generally found a great deal of pleasure and relaxation in their music making.

The category containing passive listeners—eight families—is admittedly fuzzy. Although no one in these families played an instrument, there was music in these homes to varying degrees. Some families were FM radio listeners; classical music was on all day. Some families had large record collections, which they listened to often. These collections often featured classical music, although sometimes they were more general. Some were quite focused, concentrating on, say, opera selections. Some families listened to music "regularly," others did so "avidly" or "with a passion." The depth and extent of the musical involvement of these families varied considerably, but music was definitely present to some degree in each of these eight homes.

In four homes there was apparently no interest in music at all prior to the child's involvement. In one of these homes a piano that had been inherited was left untouched. The adults could not play, and the piano was *not* allowed to be a toy for the children. Only because of a baby-sitter did the pianist from this family have her first opportunity to touch the keyboard.

But even in homes with no apparent involvement with music, and especially in the others, music lessons of some sort became matter-of-fact for the children. It was assumed that everyone would have some basic musical experience. Music lessons were "a good thing" for the children.

While it may seem from table 2 that the percentage of musically oriented families is high in our sample, the numbers come close to matching those of a 1974 Market Facts study.[3] Almost 44% of the 848 households surveyed included an amateur musician, approximately 79% of all the families said they listened to records often, and about 69% agreed with the statement that "every child should learn at least one instrument."

The Early Years

Music was a natural part of most of the pianists' lives almost from birth. One mother reports singing to her son from the time "I first held him in my arms" (M of P-7). One father sang musical intervals and patterns to his infant, and eventually the child began repeating them back (M of P-22). Another mother reports,

> There was music played when she was an infant in the crib. I would have the radio on. She went to bed with the music on . . . on the good station only. I just left it on for her to fall asleep to (M of P-24).

---

[3]Information about the 1974 Market Facts survey, conducted under the direction of Dr. William Wells of the University of Chicago Graduate School of Business for the American Music Conference, comes from *Music U.S.A. 1974: Review of the Music Industry and Amateur Music Participation*, a publication of the American Music Conference.

Or, as was true for several of the pianists,

> My mother belonged to a record club, so we had all kinds of really
> wonderful records. So there was always music going on in the
> house. So I grew up with that in my ears (P-28).

Many of the pianists spoke of waking to music, being fed to
music, or being put to sleep to music as infants.

As already noted, 81% of the homes were engaged in at least
some musical activity before the child was born, although in
38% of these instances the activity was strictly listening, not
playing, and the music listened to was not necessarily high in
quality. Music was introduced, then, as a family activity, not
something just for the children. And the children were exposed to music whether they were "paying attention" or not.

A piano was present in fifteen of the twenty-one pianists'
homes (71%) before the child was born. (In most of these
homes the piano was only played by older brothers or sisters
who were already taking lessons.) "One had a piano" (P-8).
"The piano was there . . . the piano was simply the cultural
baggage" (P-10). Several of the pianos were inherited from
grandparents.

The available piano was a toy for all but one of the pianists.[4]
Some children were propped up at the piano as infants and encouraged, or at least allowed, to play at the keyboard. Others
began by toddling to the piano and "plunking on the keys as
much with the palms of my hands as with my fingers; and then
running to Mother and saying, 'Was that a nice song?' " (P-2).
One "played around on the keyboard making sound effects.
Thunder, lightning" (P-29).

Most would work at picking out tunes of songs they sang or
music they heard. As more than one mother told us, "At age
four she would go to the piano and with one finger try it . . . she

---

[4]One mother reports, "I made a mistake, I guess, because we had a piano,
but I didn't think little two- and three-year-olds should bang on pianos and
bother things. I trained them not to bother things" (M of P-13).

would find the tune by herself" (M of P-8). "Happy Birthday" and most of the Christmas carols were the first musical pieces played by the pianist who reported,

> By the time I was five I was able to pick out melodies that I'd heard, with my right hand, and my father showed me how to put some simple chords to it with my left (P-2).

A few of the pianists had parents who would write down the tunes the child composed.

Some parents taught their preschoolers to play simple tunes or scales. One mother, who kept a diary of her son's activities and accomplishments, told us that when he was three and a half, she noted that they were sitting at the piano together and he was playing simple tunes. "I thought, 'How nice. Mother and son can sit here . . .' " (M of P-15). Another mother recalls that "I showed him how to do a scale, and he learned immediately. He was about five years old" (M of P-2). One pianist reported that when he was about six, his mother played little tunes with him; he would play the melody and she the left hand, and the next time they would switch parts (P-23).

Several parents were able to play simple tunes for their children. "I would play simple things for him . . . we always had music books of children's songs . . . and long before he could talk, he would identify songs by the pictures in the music books" (M of P-7). "I would play [nursery rhymes] and we'd sing" (M of P-23).

Parents took the children to musical performances "from the time they were very young" (M of P-25) and "even though she was only two or two and a half" (M of P-24). Many families bought children's phonographs and the children learned to "pick out records and name them" (M of P-15). "Children's records and symphony records—I exposed him to everything" (F of P-22). One family bought "records chosen for different age groups by psychiatrists and educators. These were fun records, records to educate them, music appreciation records" (M of P-28).

"ALL CHILDREN SHOULD HAVE MUSIC LESSONS"

The majority of the pianists we spoke with (16 of 21, or 76%) were taking piano lessons by the time they were six. One started as young as three; one as late as nine. All but two of the pianists began instruction because a parent decided that the child ought to do so.[5]

The parents report a variety of reasons for deciding to find a piano teacher for their child. These reasons fall into two broad categories: (1) a belief that all children should have some formal musical training; and (2) a perception that their child had demonstrated some musical talent (or at least interest) that warranted attention. The categories are not mutually exclusive. All but one of the pianists' families held the belief that children should have some musical education.[6] Some of the parents who were predisposed to giving children music lessons also reported starting lessons in response to a child's interest or ability.

One mother, when asked why she gave her children piano lessons, expressed sentiments shared by almost all:

> Because I liked music. Because I felt the kids needed it. I sent them to church for the same reason. I wanted them to have experience. I never pressed them one way or the other . . . but I don't believe you can learn anything until you're exposed to it (M of P-29).

---

[5]The two who initiated their own lessons also had to wait for a parent to make a decision, but they did a lot of cajoling to force the issue. One child, whose father and older cousin played the piano recreationally, and who often listened to an extensive family collection of piano recordings, "wanted it very much, kept begging for lessons" (P-18) before his parents acquiesced when he was five. The other youngster spent three years, from age four to seven, virtually living at the house of a neighbor with a piano, playing whatever he could by ear, before a piano became a fixture in his house and lessons became an acceptable "hobby" (P-6).

[6]The exception was the child who persuaded his nonmusical mother because of his three years of experience with some musical neighbors. Note also that according to the Market Facts study cited on page 24, about 69% of families in general report that "every child should learn at least one musical instrument."

This matter-of-factness about at least minimal musical instruction for children is also reflected in the fact that, with the exception of one family with a very large number of children, all the siblings of the pianists we interviewed also took music lessons.

> It was just understood that the children would be musical, since we both were. . . . It was just so much a part of our lives. . . . We didn't know to what extent, but we wanted them to be exposed and to do whatever they wanted to do with it (M of P-7).

Not all parents were adamant about the importance of music, but all had some interest in having their children learn to play a musical instrument.

> I had a friend who was very good on the piano and organ, and I think somewhere that may have had something to do with it. I loved her music and I loved to hear her play. I've always told her that she had something to do with it. . . . It just seemed the thing to start ——— on the piano (M of P-4).

> I just thought this is nice for someone to have music as well as other things . . . so I know I never planned this or pushed for it. Never in my wildest dreams did I think he'd be a concert pianist. . . . I thought he'd be something like a physicist or an engineer (M of P-15).

The fact that some parents felt their child or children were musically talented only strengthened the parents' commitment to the children's musical training. These parents' perceptions were usually generalized to all the children in the family. "All our children were musically inclined" (M of P-23).

> Music talent has been in my family for six generations that we know of [although there are no professional musicians in the family], so we know when a child is born in our family he's going to be talented in music (M of P-28).

The perception of musical talent may have hastened the start of instruction for some of the pianists. For example, a kindergarten teacher told parents in two homes (P-4 and P-5) that their child was very good with rhythm instruments. This prompted both families to purchase pianos (for one "it was *very* expensive") and to find piano teachers for the children. Of course in one of these homes the mother "always wanted to play the piano" and in the other the mother "had taken piano myself [as a child], so I suppose that entered into it."

The pianists' parents obviously valued music and music making, although it was neither a very intense nor a very focused value.[7] The vagueness of the parents' focus is further reflected in the ways most of the parents chose a piano teacher for their children. Most did so on the basis of the proximity of the teacher to the home. Just as most children go to the kindergarten down the street, most of the pianists we spoke with went to the teacher down the street for their first formal instruction. For eighteen of the twenty-one pianists (86%), first teachers were selected just because they were known by parents or friends of parents to give lessons to children in the neighborhood.

The first teacher was likely to be the teacher across the street who was already teaching the child's older brother (P-12), or "a neighborhood teacher who lived down the street from my aunt and uncle at that time" (P-10). One pianist told us,

> I think it was because she was an organist at our church. . . . She was close by, in the neighborhood, lived about ten blocks away. She was also a person that we knew of (P-4).

---

[7]In three instances (14% of cases) there was much more than a general value for music. Three parents had a strong interest in seeing their children grow up and become professional musicians. The early years of learning were much more intense in these homes than in the other eighteen.

His mother confirmed this:

> [The teacher] knew him well, and I knew her, and I felt like that
> was probably the place to start. And she was fairly close to home,
> so he could walk there (M of P-4).

In two instances, the fact that a parent found a better than
average teacher at a local music conservatory was again a
matter of happenstance. One family found a music conservatory "very convenient . . . we started him down there and we
got ———. He happened to get a good teacher from the beginning" (M of P-23). The other mother who went to a nearby conservatory discovered that she had to sign a one-year contract
for lessons. She decided to do so, figuring "If ——— doesn't
like it, then I'll take up lessons" (M of P-15).

The parents did not choose a first teacher on the basis of
musical expertise, but they did not leave their children in the
hands of just anybody. The parents monitored the first lessons—either by sitting in or by observing their children's re-
actions—making sure that the child and teacher "got along."
In two or three instances a parent quickly arranged for a different "first" teacher when something felt amiss. One pianist
explained such an occurrence this way:

> My mother did the traditional motherly thing. She came in and sat
> in on the first lessons and she decided after three lessons that [the
> teacher] and I were just getting nowhere. . . . She stormed to the
> director. . . claimed this was not working. He tried to talk her out
> of it, but she insisted on a switch. So we switched to [another
> teacher]. After ten minutes she just left the room because she saw
> that we were getting along like a house afire (P-15).

It seems from the pianist and parent reports that what was
most important was to find a teacher who liked children and
worked well with them. Whoever the lady (or man) "down the
street" was, whatever his or her musical ability or teaching
skills, the first teacher was almost always a warm, maternal,
"nice" person.

"She was really great with young kids" (P-5).

She "was very kindly, very nice" (P-10).

[She] liked young people, and she was very nice to ——— and he liked her (M of P-2).

He was very good with kids, liked kids instinctively and had a good rapport (P-15).

She was "very kind and very patient" (P-28).

He was "enormously patient and not very pushy" (P-22).

[She] carried a big basket of Hershey bars and gold stars for the music and I was crazy about this lady. All I had to do was play the right notes in the right rhythm and I got a Hershey bar (P-24).

Are these fond memories overly romanticized due to more recent comparisons with more intense and demanding teachers? Or did our sample of pianists truly have the good fortune to have first teachers who made piano lessons an enjoyable experience? It is impossible to know for sure, but the ease and pleasure with which these first teachers later turned over their promising students to more experienced and expert teachers does suggest that they were, in fact, nice, kind, patient, and nurturing.

BEGINNING LESSONS

The quality of the first piano teacher was a matter of chance. The local teacher may or may not have been a fine pianist. The local teacher may or may not have had concert experience, have been schooled to teach piano, or have ever worked with an aspiring concert pianist. As chance would have it, most were nice people but not very fine musicians or expert music teachers. Table 3 categorizes the quality of the pianists' first teacher.[8]

---

[8]One pianist studied with his mother, a local piano teacher, until he was about nine. He will not be included in this discussion.

TABLE 3
Quality of First Teacher

LOCAL, AVERAGE	BETTER THAN AVERAGE	VERY GOOD
62%	24%	10%

The majority of the pianists (13/21, or 62%) began instruction with "a local teacher," "a neighborhood teacher," often "a good beginning teacher," but "definitely not a musician." These teachers have been categorized as "average."

Five of the pianists (24%) (P-1, P-2, P-15, P-23, and P-29) began instruction with someone "better than average." These teachers were affiliated with a local conservatory or department of music at a local university. These teachers had some relatively good musical training themselves and they were more knowledgeable about music and the world of music making than the local neighborhood teachers the majority of the pianists began with. Two of these teachers were chosen by parents specifically because the parents were looking for someone "decent" (P-29) or better than "the first piano teacher next door" (P-15).

Finally, two of the pianists (10%) began formal instruction with very good teachers, far better than average. In one instance the teacher was selected by a musician father after consultation with his musician friends (P-22). In the other instance the mother thought her child "should be handled by a pro," so she contacted one of the top music schools in the country for recommendations (P-28).

Lessons for the very youngest pupils (ages three and four) lasted about a half hour. By the time the children reached age six, lessons lasted one hour. From the start, and throughout the learning process, the pianists generally took one lesson each week. Only when preparing for a performance might the pianists get more instruction than that.

Since about half of the pianists we talked with came from homes where a parent had some practical musical ability, in a literal sense the first instruction these children received came from a mother or father. "I helped him a little bit. . . . He knew the notes and everything before he started taking lessons" (M of P-23). However, with only one exception, the parents viewed themselves clearly as parents, not teachers.[9] One pianist's comment about his mother's early intervention echoes the sentiments of most. "She just wanted me to have a little head start" (P-15). Much like middle-class parents who teach their children to count and to recognize the letters of the alphabet in preparation for the first day of kindergarten, these musical parents sometimes taught notes on the keyboard in preparation for their child's first piano lessons.

Learning the basics of reading music—translating symbols on paper to notes, to particular keys on the piano, to certain sounds, in certain rhythms—was basically what the early lessons were all about. "She had these flash cards that would have a note. You would say immediately what that was, and then she'd go on to the next one" (P-4). "All I had to do was play the right notes in the right rhythm and I got a Hershey bar" (P-24).

The pianists tended to "go through" the John Thompson series of music books. They learned to play pieces from beginning to end. The teacher was likely to "indicate when a piece was finished by putting a star at the top of the page" (P-26).

Lessons were designed to teach some technique (scales, exercises) and some music. The teachers were gentle—"just pointing out my carelessness . . . in a very unconstricting way" (P-28). One pianist noted that when he would play a high note, for example, the teacher might say, "Doesn't that note just feel so good that you'd just want to hold it a little longer?" (P-2)

Instruction also included playing in recitals that the teachers held regularly. The students recall being "thrown in recitals" "right off." "I was taught to perform right along as I was taught to play" (P-29). There was at least one recital at Christmas and another at the end of the academic year.

---

[9]At most, the instruction they gave was "in preparation" for formal lessons with someone outside the home. Some parents taught their child the names of the notes. Some taught the children simple tunes.

The pianists remember very little about their early lessons beyond the positive effect connected with going to lessons and working with a teacher who was sometimes thought of as "a second mother."[10] "I really enjoyed the lessons. I looked forward to them" (P-28). "I was crazy about this lady" (P-24). "It was an event for me to go to my lessons" (P-4).

Seven of the pianists (33%) had a parent who sat in on most of the early lessons and took notes—"more interested to know not what I was doing bad but also what we needed to do to follow up" (P-4). "I had to know what she was to do . . . I supervised and saw that she practiced" (F of P-1).

> Because she was so young the teacher would have to teach me to teach her. I mean [the teacher] taught her, but I was absorbing it. I would take notes, or [the teacher] would call me over and show me exactly what she wanted to do" (M of P-24).

"I would sit through that lesson and learn how to prorate the [practice] time" (M of P-13). Parents generally stopped going to lessons, or were banned by the teacher, when the children were about ten.

PRACTICE

The time the twenty-one pianists spent practicing in the early years of learning varied tremendously. Some of the pianists spent "every free minute I had" at the piano, partially preparing for the next lesson and partially playing for fun. Others spent only as much time practicing as was required by a parent or teacher. The children who were "playing all day long" and those who did as little practicing as possible were rare. From age six, preparing for the next lesson typically involved spending somewhere between forty-five and ninety minutes a day, six days a week, at the keyboard.

In the interviews the pianists tended to make little of the

---

[10]Three of the pianists (P-7, P-8, and P-20) did *not* enjoy their early lessons. They thought of lessons as a chore or requirement. They went because they had no choice.

time they spent practicing as youngsters. A typical comment when asked about practice time was "Oh, very little. Not much at all. Maybe four or five times a week for about an hour each time." The average of five hours a week practice plus one hour of instruction time at the age of six, seven, or eight seems like a lot to this researcher. Perhaps it seems insignificant to the pianists because they now tend to practice more than four hours a day.

Reported times cannot be accepted as hard facts. Eighteen or twenty-two years after the fact, memories are unreliable about regular day-to-day events. However, if inaccuracies exist, our information is likely to err on the side of underestimating the time the youngsters really did invest. There is evidence that practice time during the early years was enforced, either by a parent or a teacher, often with an eye more to the clock than to the keyboard. One hour of practice time per day was likely to be a required minimum, with only a secondary emphasis on musical objectives. It was not always possible for parents or teachers to insist on and supervise a certain quality of music making, but it was possible for them to enforce a certain amount of time at the piano. Lessons were one hour long, and practice was likely to be one hour a day as well.

There was about an even split between those pianists who practiced with a parent at their side on the piano bench and those who practiced by themselves. The parents who went to lessons and took notes were obviously in the group of parents who scheduled practice and sat with the child. Several other parents who were not going to lessons *did* work with the child during practice.

> Children get to the point where they don't want their parents to go with them [to lessons], which is all right. But I would always sit down with him and make sure he did what I thought she wanted him to do. And I think that helped, especially when they're young. Because it's pretty hard to just sit down and practice without someone there beside you (M of P-4).

More than one mother "was always there to show [the child] what she needed to know" (M of P-28).

Those parents who did not literally sit by the child's side during practice still played a major role in practice, keeping the child at the piano and listening often (from another room perhaps) to make sure practice was going well. The parents were there—overhearing, praising, encouraging, and instructing—although they didn't do these things every single day from a seat on the piano bench.

> If I didn't like something, I would scream. If he was having trouble with something . . . we'd go in and figure it out. He wasn't allowed to play mistakes. My ear was good enough so I'd know if something was wrong (M of P-29).

"I wouldn't sit down and give him a lesson, but . . . if he was doing something wrong, I would correct him" (F of P-22). The same parent, among others, added, "When he was younger I listened to him more, because there was much more correcting to do, more steering."

Daily practice was "the rules of the arrangement" (P-10). A mother might pretend to go to the telephone and call the piano teacher to stop lessons if she thought the child wasn't practicing enough (P-24 and P-19). Most pianists remember hearing, "Have you practiced today?" One recalls hearing, "If you don't practice, we'll sell the piano" (P-1).

The pianists seldom missed daily practice and more often than not they were not allowed to practice "mistakes" (or what the parents thought were mistakes). The latter was possible because almost all of the pianists recall having notebooks in which the teacher recorded each week's practice routine in detail. The parents could use these notebooks to help the younger children work properly and to keep track of whether the older children were doing what they were supposed to be doing.

EARLY REWARDS

The pianists got considerable attention for their early musical efforts. Because music was valued by their parents, the pianists' singing and picking out tunes at the piano elicited attention and applause. The more musically involved the children got, and the better they got at singing and playing the piano, the more approval they got from the family. "I always praised them and showed them how thrilled I was when they learned a new piece" (M of P-28).

> My mother liked to hear me play. I knew it gave her pleasure. So when she would come home, I would sometimes run over to the piano as she was coming in the door and play her favorite piece (P-20).

The pianists were shown off a lot, that is, asked to play for the extended family or parents' friends who came to visit.

> There was an awful lot of praise and an awful lot of attention. Play for the family, play for this one, play for that one. There was so much reward for performing that I've always loved it (P-24).

The attention encouraged the children to take their lessons and practice more seriously.

The pianists seemed to be "quick learners." They "picked things up quickly," responded well to the teachers' directions, and were quickly able to translate newly acquired knowledge into action.[11] "I was very quick at learning whatever he asked

---

[11]Whether or not the pianists were "quick learners" is an interesting question. We might well be a little skeptical about the label "quick learner," given the head start the pianists had before they began lessons, the enforced daily practice, and the parents' efforts to make sure the children never practiced mistakes. Nonetheless, in any comparison of speed between two or more people, one will be faster than the others, and the pianists we interviewed were typically the fastest in their comparison group. The actions and effects resulting from the labeling seem more important, however, than the actual characteristic.

me to do. I used to come prepared" (P-8). And for this they caught the teachers' eyes.

The pianists report that the teacher "told me I was her favorite student" or "told me I was his best pupil." The teachers placed the pianists we talked with at the end of recital programs, a placement taken to be a significant sign of ability. The teachers spoke with the parents about the pianists' progress, and the circle of rewards grew larger.

> I knew [the teacher] was very delighted with me. I got lots of approval from him, and lots of approval from my parents after they talked to him because they felt very good about that (P-15).

Elementary school teachers and principals found out that these children were studying the piano and invited the children to play for talent shows, Christmas shows, or end-of-the-year class shows. One pianist recalls that at the end of the third-grade school year, a teacher encouraged, almost cajoled, him to play for a talent show. At the end of his performance "[the children] just stamped their feet and screamed and howled and hollered and suddenly I felt welcome" (P-15). Classmates began to acknowledge the children as pianists, and usually as the best pianists of their age.

The pianists report that they began to feel special. They were different, somehow, from other children. They could do something that other children were not doing. One pianist recalled that at a very early age

> I think I knew I was special. I think I knew I had an unusual talent. There wasn't anybody else my age who played, that I knew, and it was something that was mine. My way of getting approval, my way of getting attention (P-24).

Another pianist who did not think she had any unusual talent recalls being persuaded that she did:

> I was a little kid and here were my parents and all my teachers in school and the principal of my school telling me that I was going to be great and famous and how unusual I was (P-13).

There is a striking consistency in the pianists' reports of being special or the best, but how special were they? They were clearly the best pianists in their families. A few were the best by virtue of their age. (They could play better than a younger sibling or better than a sibling or a parent could at the same age.) A few were the best because they were more interested or involved than their siblings.

The pianists were perhaps the best in their neighborhood, even in their town, *for their age.* Yet if these children who were raised in neighborhoods and towns across the country had been in competition with one another, or just with a larger group of children their own age who also studied the piano, few would have looked very special. One pianist, who was in fact among the more accomplished youngsters, remembered discovering that he was not as unusual as he had thought himself to be when, at age sixteen, after nine years of instruction, he went to live and study at a school of music.

> It was a shock. It's not easy to find out that there are other people who really play very well when you've been isolated and made to think you're something. You may very well be, but you're not alone (P-6).

A small number of the pianists accomplished something extraordinary—such as winning an important youth competition—before age nine. In two of three instances these were the children of the parents who were intensely devoted to the child's musical education, who had aspirations for their child's musical success before the child was born, and who went to lessons and sat with the child for two hours of daily practice sessions. However, most of the pianists look special only when comparing one child with others in the family or neighborhood. Nevertheless, the perceived specialness seems important, perhaps critical, in the pianists' development for its effects, namely, that of increasing the pianists' motivation to study and practice and increasing the parents' involvement in the process.

Unfortunately, one of the early rewards for a few of the pianists was also that they could escape from the noise and fighting in their homes, or from their loneliness, by practicing the piano.

> I used the piano as an escape from a lot of things. Piano practicing and reading were the two things I did. There was just so much noise and fighting, just from the proximity more or less, and I would shut myself off from reality by sitting down and practicing (P-28).

Again, time at the piano seems to have been translated into learning, which resulted in positive attention from teachers and others, better feelings about oneself, and an increased commitment to learning.

THE PIANIST IS RECOGNIZED

For reasons that cannot be explained by the data, one child in a family "took to" music more eagerly than the others. That child was recognized, either by a parent or by a first teacher, as someone to concentrate one's efforts on. Eventually someone realized that if the child was to have an opportunity to reach the highest possible level of performance, it would be necessary to have the best possible instruction.

All but one of the pianists switched teachers at least once, usually twice (N = 11) before they finished high school. In nine cases out of twenty, the person who recognized that the child needed a better teacher was the local teacher with whom the child had started instruction. The teacher noticed "there was something there after about six months" (M of P-24). Or, after about a year the teacher "sensed that he was a student of exceptional ability, and she passed him off to ———" (M of P-26).

Another parent reported that after about a year and a half of lessons, the first teacher

> said herself that he needed another teacher because he was getting along too fast to go on with her. She didn't feel that she was good enough (M of P-2).

In instance after instance the teacher contacted the pianist's parents and told them it was time for the child to work with someone else. "Mrs. ——— seemed to think I needed to have some other influence" (P-4). According to the pianists, the teachers often added a note of excitement when they evaluated the child's potential. "She decided I needed a really top-quality teacher because I was showing so much promise" (P-28). Or, noting that her pupil's knowledge of music seemed far superior to hers, she insisted "you've got to do something important with him" (P-6).

If the teachers didn't decide that higher quality instruction was necessary, the parents eventually did. In ten cases of the twenty-one, the local teachers did not seem to feel that the child needed any more than they had to offer, even though the teachers knew they were not expert musicians. Although the pianists' parents always seem to have taken seriously a teacher's excitement about their child's progress, they were not as accepting of a teacher's complacency.

> My father felt that if he's going to be paying for lessons, even if it's not going to go anywhere, I've got to be doing better than what I was doing. I needed somebody to teach me how to practice, for example. I had just been playing any old way and it was fine (P-22).

> My mother also realized that I was by far the biggest fish in ——— and that I was playing better at thirteen than most of the students. . . and she figured that there comes a point where you outgrow the teacher (P-15).

Usually the transition to a higher quality teacher was then made with the guidance and support of the first teacher.

As might be expected, the higher the quality of the first teacher, the longer it took before the switch to another teacher was made. But in all but one instance, changes in teachers were made. Table 4 illustrates the relationship between the quality of the first teacher and the time it took to move to a higher level teacher.[12] The better the first teacher, the longer the amount of time before it was "necessary" to make a move to another teacher. The less expert the first teacher, the more quickly the pianists moved to better instruction.

TABLE 4
Looking for Better Instruction

YEARS WITH FIRST TEACHER UNTIL SWITCH	Quality of Teacher		
	AVERAGE	BETTER THAN AVERAGE	VERY GOOD
1	6		
2	3		
3	4		
4		1	
5		2	
6			1
7			1

DEVELOPING A COMMITMENT

Over a period of four to seven years, all but one of the pianists switched teachers once, and 50% switched twice.[13] The shifts in instruction reflect other changes in the direction of an in-

---

[12]The chart is based on only eighteen cases, because (a) as noted, one student did not switch teachers until graduation from high school; and (b) two students had many teachers for short periods of time in the beginning and were unable to reconstruct confidently the moves they had made.
[13]The number of teachers the pianists worked with regularly in the average seventeen-year period of development varied from three to seven. Some pianists moved to better instruction in gradual increments, and others made big leaps. Some pianists moved laterally once or twice before they found a much higher quality teacher to work with.

creasing commitment to a musical education on the part of both the pianists and their parents. In the same four- to seven-year period, for example, most of the pianists began either attending concerts or listening to piano recordings regularly, or both. Several read children's books about performing musicians or composers.

Parents started music lessons and played with their children. "Mother started taking piano lessons again when I started taking them" (P-4) . . . "because of working with him" (M of P-4).

> I remember one period of a year or two when both my parents decided to take lessons on other instruments so they could play along with me in a chamber situation. It was completely misguided because they had no idea what they were doing. And they chose all the wrong instruments (P-5).

Music lessons, which had been matter-of-fact, began to become more serious business for the children and their parents. The children were not extraordinary pianists, but they were committed to a learning routine that their parents were committed to as well. Careers as concert pianists seem to have been set in motion before the children finished elementary school. The children were labeled "pianists," and they began to think of themselves as such.

SUMMARY OF THE EARLY YEARS

During the early years of learning, the foundations were laid and the stage was set for the musical successes the pianists would realize many years later. Certain actions and conditions emerge repeatedly:

• Music was an integral part of these children's homes. They heard recordings and/or live performances regularly and naturally. Music was not only pervasive, it was also highly valued. It was deemed to be important, beautiful, worthwhile.

• The children had no choice about getting involved with music. Lessons were forced upon them. The children were expected to learn at least the rudiments of instrumental music. It was not special for the child, it was one of the normal experiences for children in these families.

• The children had very positive experiences with their first lessons. They made contact with another adult, outside their home, who was warm, supportive, and loving. At an age when children are beginning to spend a substantial part of their time each day away from home, if for no other reason than they are beginning to go to school, the pianists had someone to go to outside their home who made them feel good. They also had a variety of opportunities to feel good about being able to do something.

• The children spent a lot of time at the piano compared with others their own age. They were focusing their attention on the piano and building both interest and ability. These children spent more time on music than most children spend on any activity, except perhaps watching television. And there was no choice about it.

• The children were almost fully initiated into weekly lessons and daily practice *before* they had the opportunity to engage in a variety of other activities, either school related or social. Lessons and practice were not fit into a busy schedule of homework or scouting or playing with friends after school. All of the other activities were fit around an already routinized lesson and practice schedule.

• These children were labeled as pianists. They were called pianists and told they could become professionals someday— first by parents and then by teachers who took a special interest. These children were labeled pianists by their peers, their community, and sometimes even larger audiences before they reached their teens. And the children were rewarded over and over again for being what everyone told them they were, or could be.

The early years of learning seem critical in at least four ways:

1. They were a time for beginning to develop an identity as a pianist and finding value in one's self through that identity.

2. They were a time for developing a routine. Lessons and practice were integrated as a natural part of life, and the groundwork was laid for the potential of a more intense involvement.

3. They were a time for developing motivation for subsequent learning. In the early years, when most of the activities a child engages in are those provided and supported by parents, the desire to do something may not be as important as the fact of its availability. But if strong reasons for pursuing an activity are not developed, in later years as other opportunities arise, weak interests are easily abandoned.

4. The early years were a time for developing increasing aspirations. Children built dreams and hopes that seemed reasonable to them. Parents were excited and encouraged to expand their own previous aspirations for their children. With so many years ahead, and so few wasted behind, both parents and children could easily generate energy for increasing work with a minimal amount of qualms. These are four themes important to keep in mind as we follow the pianists' development and later analyze why they continued to work at learning to be concert pianists for as long as they did.

The Middle Years

Somewhere along the line, the child must become possessed by music, by the sudden desire to play, to excel. It can happen at any time between the ages of 10 or so and 14. Suddenly the child begins to sense something happening and he really begins to work, and in retrospect the first five or six years seem like kinderspiel, fooling around.

Isaac Stern
in *The New York Times Magazine*
(December 23, 1979)

The age range may not be quite accurate, but the pattern that Stern identifies seems consistent with the reports of the pianists studied. At some point along the road to outstanding development, the budding pianist began to think differently about music and music making. The sheets propped on the stand became more than notes on a printed page. Music making became more than striking those notes and then looking for the resulting gleam in someone else's eyes. Although the young child may have been quite serious about playing *the piano*, and may have been practicing an hour or more a day for five years, the adolescent found a new seriousness in playing *music*.

One pianist noted that what music meant to her and how she thought about it changed when she was about twelve years old.

> Up until then it used to be very easy for me. I would practice and I'd be able to play pieces. But I never really thought about them that much. I never thought that much about the structure of the work and how it's put together and the way that you go about learning it. And from that time on I was much more aware of the work and of its construction. And I would start to analyze it harmonically (P-1).

This pianist came to understand that music could be *studied*. Another pianist found that by fourteen or fifteen he "had something special to say through at least specific works of music if not in a general way" (P-5). Still another found himself discovering music, developing a sense of mission, and believing in the value of what he was doing for the first time at age eleven, although he had been playing the piano since age five.

One pianist recognized a turning point at age fifteen when he had the opportunity to hear an outstanding older pianist in concert from the unique vantage point of sitting about three feet from the instrument.

> I remember feeling inundated and overwhelmed with the dynamic range, with the expressive potential, with hearing the real

bite of the sound, the real softness of the sound. . . . I realized suddenly that my pianissimo wasn't pianissimo, my fortissimo wasn't fortissimo, my options were sloppy compared to his, my sense of phrasing primitive. . . and at that point I became serious like I never had before. I cut out horsing around at the piano. I cut out sightreading for two hours a day just for the pleasure of it. I worked (P-15).

The time the pianists spent at the piano increased dramatically in this period of learning. Those who had been practicing forty-five minutes to an hour a day began spending two hours a day at the piano. Those who had been practicing two hours a day found themselves working as many as four.

The subtle change in the quality of practice sessions is more striking than just the increase in hours. Practice was no longer just a matter of "putting in time." Thoughts about the passage of time faded, and the requirements of the music loomed larger. As more than one pianist stated, "The practice just grew naturally and organically out of what I had to do, what I had to prepare" (P-28).

The question of whether a new and better teacher inspired these changes in perceptions and behaviors or whether the changes sent the pianists and parents in search of better instruction is a bit like asking, "Which came first, the chicken or the egg?" The pianist and parent reports divide equally into two groups: those for whom changing perceptions led to finding a better teacher and those for whom a new teacher provoked the changes. Regardless of who or what triggered the changing attitude, the circumstances the pianists found themselves in—the kinds of lessons, practice time, and other musical experiences they engaged in—were unusually similar.

LESSONS AND PRACTICE

By the age of twelve or thirteen, the pianists typically were working with teachers who were recognized experts in at least their part of the country, well connected and well respected in music circles and well versed musically. A few of the teachers, but not most, were performers as well. For most of the pianists, these were their second teachers, though some pianists had already changed teachers two or three times.

As occurred when lessons were begun, the move to a better teacher was usually monitored by the parents to ensure that teacher and child "get along." Sometimes it took some doing to find a second teacher who would provide the necessary expertise in a manner that was appropriate for the child. For example, one pianist reports,

> We made the wrong choice first. We went to this other teacher and it was a terrible situation. We didn't react well together. I just wanted to stop taking piano lessons. Didn't want to have anything to do with the piano. It was a pretty disastrous situation (P-5).

Both the pianist and his mother recalled that the teacher "was awfully harsh. He would hit [the child's] wrist with a ruler. I could see that this was going to ruin anything that [my son] wanted to do" (M of P-5). "After three or four lessons or something, that was immediately terminated and we went to [another teacher] which was just more than the opposite. Immediate chemistry" (P-5).

The more musically knowledgeable teachers "expected perfection of me constantly" (P-6) or "wanted everything just so" (P-1). And they were very specific about what they wanted. "The minutest movement would be discussed. Just how you held your hand. This way, that way; this finger, that" (P-26).

> [Lessons] were very long. Very, very detailed. Always working on the shape of my hand and all these little tiny things. She had me phrase things. Had me do things over and over and over to make them as beautiful as possible. With great attention to detail (P-13).

> The training was fairly thorough. He gave me basic technical studies I still use. Hannon and Czerny and Brahms exercises and Moszkowski and Chopin études, which I think you go on playing till you die. These are so hard. . . . Essentially excellent technique (P-10).

Fingering, phrasing, sound quality, the shape of the hand, articulation, and other technical aspects of piano playing were discussed in detail. For some of the pianists this was a first conscious exposure to piano technique. For others, the concepts were familiar, but the emphasis, their importance, was new.

Most of the pianists reported that they learned technique through good music.

> He believed in giving hard music to his talented younger students and having that develop technique rather than giving a lot of exercises and getting your technique developed and then giving harder pieces (P-28).

> I would bring the same piece nine, ten, eleven, twelve weeks in a row sometimes. [Lessons were] very intense. Very, very detailed. Lots of technical things. Lots of individual problems. See, I would approach new pieces as new problems then. Like this would be a piece that would be my first piece that had a lot of octaves, or a lot of double notes of some sort, or a certain kind of digital problem. So we'd work on that, and he'd give me exercises or suggest ways of practicing, things like that (P-25).

Many of the pianists talked about working on one piece for perhaps as many as eight or ten lessons, going over it note by note, phrase by phrase, "until I got it right."

Technical expertise was not the only focus of a lesson, nor even, perhaps, the most important. Over and over the pianists stressed that a new musical dimension was being made available to them. As one put it, "[The teacher] sort of imbued me with a feeling of music and the arts" (P-23). Another pianist explained how this happened to him:

> We talked about when this composer lived, and what kind of things were going on. Cultural attachments and the like in the other arts. What this represented, what this went along with, or what was parallel to this. Significance on the spiritual level. Very detailed. Very intense (P-25).

Or, according to still another,

> He continually stressed that there was something behind the notes
> or underneath the notes that one must respect. That there's some-
> thing bigger than respect for just the literal facts on the page, and
> that's the heart of the matter, what the music has to say, the con-
> tent (P-7).

The pianists worked on technical details, but were asked to
think about the music they were playing as well. Building a
repertoire started to become very important.

The essence of instruction during the middle years seems to
be a combination of building a foundation of a set of musical
skills and developing a structured way of studying music and
music making.

> You've got to build a foundation. And you build a tonal founda-
> tion, you learn theory, interpretation, musicianship, technique,
> all at the same time. . . . And this is what she did. And she told me
> how to work. She *taught* me to work. She taught me how actually
> to practice (P-29).

Another pianist summarized work with his teacher by explaining that instruction was designed

> to give me a technical base. Also a basic approach to music. How
> to draw good sound out of the piano. Proper rules for phrasing and
> interpretation of musical passages. . . . He gave me a very struc-
> tured way of looking at the music (P-26).

The pianists learned how to practice. "She would very
clearly outline practice methods. . . . She would write it down
in a book" (P-5). "I remember him actually setting a practice
minimum. Three hours, I think it was. So you're starting into
serious stuff. He did have high standards" (P-10).

> [Practice] became very scheduled, because ———— would have a
> way to practice things. X amount of time on this and that, x num-

ber of metronome speeds on this and that. You practiced this slowly, and then faster. Very, very detailed (P-13).

The pianists no longer needed, nor wanted, parents practicing with them, although they still needed to be reminded and prodded to practice intermittently. They practiced because they were interested in what they were doing, because they enjoyed working with the teacher, "as a matter of survival" (P-5) because the work they were given in each lesson required it, because the teacher insisted on it, out of "fear of being unprepared" (P-8), and in preparation for recitals and competitions.

In large measure they seemed to practice because "when you're studying four or five years. . . habit has taken over quite strongly, I think" (P-10).

I would get up and practice just like you would get up and wash your face in the morning and brush your teeth. It was a very natural thing to do and you just accepted it as something very normal (P-4).

RECITALS, COMPETITIONS, AND PERFORMANCES
Performances were an important part of the pianists' education during the middle years of learning. There were a variety of kinds of performances the pianists engaged in, from small recitals to major concerts. The teachers' regularly scheduled class recitals, which had seemed so important and exciting earlier, were now routine. The pianists were also playing solo recitals for school programs, community organizations, women's groups, and the like, even receiving pay for some. The most exciting and challenging experiences during these years were youth competitions. These were opportunities to play before large and musically sophisticated audiences, and perhaps to earn the privilege of playing with a full orchestra.

One of the pianists played an important performance at age six, which led to a regular schedule of performances thereafter. Another pianist did not play a major event until eighteen. The majority of the pianists began performing regularly, and in some especially significant events, between the ages of thirteen and fifteen.

Most of the performances were suggested or arranged for by the pianists' teachers. The teachers told their pupils about the competitions, and sometimes drove the students to the events as well. If a community group called the teachers in search of a performer, the teachers eagerly sent their students. If no one in the community sought a young performer, the teachers arranged solo recitals on their own. One pianist recalls that "everything was done in a gradual way. It was methodically well thought out" (P-6). First he played a short program for a small audience. Then he played a longer program, then a still longer program before a much larger audience.

The kinds of significant performances the pianists had were determined, in part, by the section of the country they lived in. For example, in several cities the resident symphony orchestra held yearly competitions for young pianists. These competitions were important experiences for the pianists who entered, whether they won or lost. In addition, winners in each of usually three age groups earned the opportunity to give a performance with a full orchestra.

In sections of the country where symphony orchestras did not hold such competitions, the Young Musicians Foundation or the National Music Teachers Association held similar kinds of events. The National Music Teachers Association conducted what they call adjudications every year. (These are music "examinations" assessing the child's competence against standards set by judges who are themselves musicians.) Depending on the local association, there were "best performers" in different age groups each year, or one could accumulate points toward being a "winner" in each age division after a number of years. Again, through these adjudications the pianist might earn the chance to perform with an orchestra. The pianists entered a variety of local competitions as well. These were sponsored by large companies or universities in the area.

Recitals and competitions were motivation for working day after day at difficult and often boring tasks. They gave the pianists a chance to try out their skill before an audience, doing what they had practiced endlessly on their own and with teachers and, hopefully, reaching or saying something to the listeners. Recitals and competitions also gave the pianists the chance to meet other musicians—both recognized adult musicians who came to judge or just to listen, and child performers such as themselves. Finally, the performances and competitions gave the pianists the chance to gain the attention of and be recognized by people they had never met, some of whom would turn out to help them directly.

Some of the pianists won every contest they entered from about age fourteen on. Others lost more than won. The winning or losing does not seem to have been as important as the doing. Even those who were not winners found something worthwhile to take away from the experience.

Teachers and parents pointed out the progress the youngsters were making year by year. Whether they won or not, the pianists often got recognition from local newspapers, people in their schools and communities, and so forth. "We lived in a small community. . . . Everything that a child does a little better than the others at school gets into the paper, so she had the reputation. I have dozens and dozens of clippings" (M of P-8). Most important, whether they won or lost, the pianists seem to have learned to walk away from the performances thinking about what they had to work on next in order to do better next time.

FAMILY INVOLVEMENT

The pianists were labeled special by the time they reached their early teens. At home, "Of course I was top dog. I always got to play whenever I wanted to and [my sisters] kind of had to fend for themselves" (P-5). "I got out of a lot of chores. . . . I was really indulged. . . . I got away with murder" (P-28). "[My father] would excuse me from having household chores because I had to practice. He would say ——— has to practice and so she doesn't have to help with the dishes" (P-8).

> We did give him special privileges. We didn't interfere in his music. We didn't feel that he should have little chores around the house because it cut into his music time. When we realized he did have this talent, we let him have full rein of time and not force him to do things that other children have to do. We realized that he was special and that he should not be asked to wash the car (M of P-15).

Parents made many more sacrifices than just giving up a helping hand around the house. If necessary, they drove their child miles (eighty, in one instance) in order that he or she might study with the best teacher available, "which speaks very well for them. . . . They were eager to support any kind of ambition I had" (P-7). More typically, a parent would drive an hour or so, sometimes in heavy traffic, and wait while the child had a lesson. Three families actually moved their entire household many miles in order that their child might get the best possible instruction.

Even in homes where money was tight, no sacrifice was too great in order that the child have whatever he needed to learn to become a musician. "[My parents] didn't have nickels to rub together. Those were bad days. But there was always money for music" (P-10). "We weren't rich, but we were frugal. We always got along fine. There was no doubt that he should get the best teacher and so on" (M of P-2). "I tried with my very small financial means to give her the best" (F of P-1).

When a grand piano became necessary, as it inevitably did, the money was found to buy one. "We just had to sacrifice, that's all. Because we wanted him to have another piano. He was progressing and doing real well" (M of P-23).

> [My teacher] told my mother I had to have a decent piano to practice on. It had to be a grand piano. . . . The piano was twenty-five hundred dollars. My father was driving around in a beat-up old car that he was hoping to trade in for a new car that year. Instead of buying the new car, he bought me a grand piano (P-26).

BUILDING A COMMITMENT
TO MUSIC

The youngsters began building their lives around music. They practiced every day, no matter what else they had to do. Some practiced mostly out of habit, and some with a determination to prove something.

> I think there's a tremendous force. The psychological effect that operates when you've done something for so long. You feel that it must have incredible value to you simply by virtue of spending so much time. . . . It would take, I think, a trauma to break that and have something else take precedence (P-10).

"I was so ambitious. I felt I had to prove I was worth something, and the best way to do it was through the piano" (P-7).

Every available music activity was capitalized upon. The pianists played in school concerts, for school musicals, and in bands at school socials. By the end of high school the majority of the pianists had spent one or more summers at one of the three or four serious music camps across the country. (This, again, was usually at the suggestion of and was arranged by a teacher.)

The summer camps had a powerful effect on the pianists. There they met other people their own age who were doing what they were doing: people with whom to compare experiences, compete, and exchange information. The youngsters also met some of their idols at the summer camps. "The people who mean the most to me, outside of my family, are the people I met at [one such camp]" (P-1). Those summer experiences were instructive, challenging, and motivating.

Although the pianists spent a great deal of time learning to become musicians, that did not necessarily mean that they had no friends and were socially isolated, although for some that was indeed so. The pianists were almost evenly divided between those who had friends and were active in junior high and high school and those who spent most of their time alone at a piano keyboard. Some tell us, "I had no friends because I didn't have time" (P-6), and others were class presidents or yearbook editors. Some were never able to play ball or go bowling, for example, for fear of hurting their hands, while others "always managed to play in the neighborhood" (P-10). But whether they were social or isolated, physically active or cautious, their attention to music making was so great that they effectively sealed off other options for themselves.

> We did not encourage enough other activity. Indirectly, I think, we encouraged the music. . . by not pushing the other things. And also seeing that there would be enough time [for practice and the like]. . . that her time would not be too loaded by other things (M of P-8).

For their ages, the pianists were very good at making music. They were also much better at making music than they were at anything else. So whatever their conscious commitment to becoming musicians (which varied from those who knew they would do so at five and those who were unsure until eighteen), they all tended to value everything else less and let other things slide. There was always music to fall back on. "Since I had the piano on the side, I never could be really *as* ambitious [about schoolwork] as a lot of the other kids in the class" (P-15).

The time it took for the pianists to make conscious commitments to music, and to make notable progress as pianists, varied widely. Sometimes proper music guidance was missing for a while and the youngster wasn't prodded to higher levels of aspiration and ability as quickly as he or she might have been. Some youngsters resisted commitment and expanding horizons for a while, remaining content to practice and play as they were doing, temporarily without new goals or aspirations. Some pianists climbed the ladder of accomplishment steadily and evenly, whereas others made progress in spurts. But by the close of the middle years of learning (which again took anywhere from four to seven years), each of the pianists was almost irreversibly headed toward a career in music.

Decisions had been made, by the parents and the pianists, which were no longer easily alterable. For example, once an entire family had relocated many hundred miles so that one child could study with a particular teacher, it seems unlikely that a year or two later the child could declare himself to be tired of the piano and choose instead to be an architect or something. Once a child had been allowed to dismiss usual high school subject matter requirements and to attend only classes that appealed to him, it becomes impossible for him to apply to most colleges and universities in the country, save for schools interested in his musical ability. Those children who were taken out of regular schools entirely and were tutored to meet state requirements while devoting the majority of their time to music (N = 3) had their fates effectively sealed by such action. So set was the course for all but three of the pianists that toward the end of their high school years there was no consideration of possible colleges to attend other than a few select music schools. The three exceptions were people who chose to go to music conservatories or departments within larger universities, with the conscious intent of exploring other worlds before they "fully" committed themselves to music.

SUMMARY OF THE MIDDLE YEARS

The middle years in the pianists' lives were a time for learning how to do one thing very well and for closing the doors to most alternatives.

• Habit had clearly taken over with respect to lessons and practice. Parental motivation and monitoring became much less important. The piano, and an identity as a pianist, were now matter-of-fact to the child, taken for granted.

• A tremendous amount of time was devoted to learning to be a musician. In general, this was at least equivalent to a half-time job. For some, it was much closer to a full-time job. More and more of this time was spent preparing for and trying out the role of pianist in increasingly more sophisticated and significant ways.

• There was a striking shift in the pianist's vision of the activity. As a very young child he or she "played the piano." It was play. With lessons, practice, and a routine developed in the early years, the pianist got involved playing "the music," and was enticed by the possibility of "making music."

• The pianists studied weekly with teachers who were knowledgeable about and dedicated to music. They talked, played, and lived with the music. It was an intense and highly valued experience for the student. The student was pushed to the highest levels of precision and given the opportunity to explore the wider world beyond the mastery of mechanics.

• The pianists and their parents made decisions in favor of learning music that removed many of the options that most of the pianists' age-mates still had. A family long-distance move and a limited general education were two of the more dramatic examples of this. Subtle decisions to put a lot of time and energy into music and much less into school classes were equally limiting.

• Families made intensive and extensive commitments to the pianist. Time, money, and life-styles were directed in ways that would help one child become a good musician, at the possible expense of other family members.

• The evaluation of and rewards for music making moved from the family to a more musical world. The teacher's opinion of the student and his or her music making became critical. Pianist peers provided competitive motivation and signals of worth.

Success, or the perception of success, during the middle years of learning essentially set the pianist's course. He or she was one of the teacher's best students, a finalist in youth competitions, and well received in recitals. The question of where one was heading was never really asked. Music was to be one's life, even though the youth really didn't understand what it might mean to "be a pianist."

I'm sure she didn't really realize at fourteen or fifteen or sixteen the wear and tear, the traveling, the motels. It all looked very glamorous. She was playing in concerts, she was applauded, she would get flowers. . . . You only see one side of it (M of P-8).

The world of music did seem glamorous to many of the teenage pianists; and this, too, was enticing.

The Later Years—
Into Adulthood as a Musician

The most critical step in the transition from being a talented teenage pianist to becoming a professional performing soloist seems to be that of moving to a master teacher. By their eighteenth or nineteenth birthday, *all* of the pianists were studying with professional musicians who were fully aware of what the life of a touring soloist entails. (In fact, sixteen of the pianists studied, at different times, with one of five master teachers.) The master teachers were part of the inner circle of professional pianists. Some were still touring regularly; others had retired or had but limited engagements. All were among the most respected faculty at professional schools of music. These teachers played a critical role in introducing the young pianists to the innermost sanctum of the music world.

Not everyone who would like to study with one of these teachers can do so. First, the teachers do not work with beginning pianists. Second, they do not work with pianists who, although technically accomplished, are not extremely motivated and disciplined. As one of the teachers told us, "If they don't come with [discipline and motivation] already built in, I just don't keep them." Third, a pianist is not likely to be able to audition for one of these teachers simply on his or her own initiative. The teachers seem to rely on a network of acquaintances and fellow musicians to send them applicants, who are then further weeded for subjective qualities of talent, potential, and determination.

Good music teachers around the country, who have had opportunities over the years to meet and perhaps come to know one of the master teachers, channel their best students to those teachers. They do so through letters and telephone calls or by sending the student to a special summer camp where he or she will be able to audition for the master teacher informally. It is understood that middle-echelon teachers will only do these things for very special students. If they were to recommend too many pupils who were unacceptable to the top teacher, their credibility would soon be lost.

A few students find their way into a master teacher's class by way of their performing and competition experiences. A musician in the audience might have been impressed by the performance and suggested so and so. The master teacher might have been in the audience, or judged the occasion, and might then recognize the applicant and accept him or her on that basis.

The mere opportunity to audition for a master teacher requires at least an intermediate standing in the music community. The teenager, the parents, or the student's teacher must know someone or someplace to go. But one doesn't have to be born into a family of professional musicians to know the right people or places. The pianists and their families spent seven to ten years learning about the music world, meeting people and being heard, before the pianist was ready to study with a master teacher. Even those families who were not involved with music at all before their children began playing seem to have learned where to go.

It is interesting, though, that the pianists themselves did not seem to pursue the great teachers aggressively. They might have dreamt about studying with him or her one day, and they did take a risk in auditioning and possibly being rejected, but primarily the pianists were carried forward by their more aggressive teachers and parents.

> [The pianist] just felt that he was in good hands, I think. It would have been different if [those discussing where he should study next] were not in the business and didn't know what the score was.

But he was talking to people who knew what the whole field was about (F of P-22).

INSTRUCTION WITH MASTER TEACHERS

The pianists began studying with master teachers somewhere between the ages of twelve and nineteen. The majority began between ages fifteen and seventeen. The significance of this experience cannot be overestimated.

Being accepted into one of these teachers' classes was seen as the highest honor. The pianists often spoke with awe about beginning lessons with these great teachers. "The idea that this man was willing to teach me, to give me his time, overwhelmed me" (P-6). "Who was there after Serkin?" (P-5) "Van Cliburn went to Juilliard, so did I. Van Cliburn studied with Lhevinne, so did I" (P-7). "What she said to me was like the voice of God" (P-13).

The teacher's presence alone motivated, inspired, and instructed. The teachers already were what the young pianists had only dreamed of becoming. First and foremost the teachers provided role models of the highest order. The young pianists studied how the teacher sat at the piano, how the teacher looked at the page of music, how the teacher prepared himself to play a particular piece or style of music, how he marked the music, and how he moved his body. They listened for his pauses, his crescendos, his trills. They observed his attitude toward other musicians, musical styles, performances, and competitions. The pianists learned attitudes and habits and ways of working that they often were not even conscious of learning, simply by being in the presence of the master.

He doesn't just teach you how to play the piano, he teaches you— every word he said was as though it was coming from God and through Mr. ———'s mouth to me. And I absorbed it, every word, like a sponge. . . . I learned integrity, devotion, and a complete dedication to making music and being an artist (P-6).

I am positive that certain things she got from ——— she could not get from anybody. . . . He's very experienced from those twenty-five or thirty years of concertizing. . . . Certain suggestions he gave her I think nobody could give her (F of P-1).

He didn't want to teach me as a pianist so much as to become a musician. That's really the criterion he had. . . . A person's attitude in a wider sense, and yet a more inclusive sense too is much preferable than just learning to play the piano (P-4).

One was studying with the whole composite musician, not just a piano teacher. His way of looking at a piece of music was therefore much broader than probably most other people's. . . . His whole attitude about making music was very special. It was a great privilege to work with someone like this (P-22).

Fortunately, the master teachers had a lot more to offer than merely "show." They knew a tremendous amount about their craft. They knew the great and not so great repertoire. They understood the complexity of works, their elegance, their drama, their simplicity.

She had a very strong sense of how a piece was put together and she could take literally the weakest piece from the repertoire and somehow make it hold together, which I thought was one of her great things in teaching. So there was that enormous knowledge I absorbed from her of just being able to see in the most complicated pieces . . . why it gets from here to there and there. You see the hills and valleys (P-23).

He worked with me technically as a pianist, but the distinction of becoming a musician became clear every time I took a lesson because we talked about music. We began to try to become more intellectual about how phrase structure [worked] and what it meant and what you were trying to say, rather than how do you accomplish this at this instrument (P-4).

They knew which works the young pianist needs to be familiar with and which works require intensive study.

The master teachers assumed that their pupils were serious and that nothing would stand in the way of their studies. They assigned an enormous amount of material and they expected it to be learned to the high standard they set.

> He was an impossible task master. It was incredible. He would just intimidate you out of your mind. He would sit there. . . . You played a concert, you didn't play a lesson. You walked in prepared to play a performance. . . . You would get torn apart for an hour (P-5).

The teachers did not tolerate sloppiness or laziness. The work they assigned required a tremendous amount of time and attention from the pupil, a minimum of four hours a day. The teachers did not hesitate to let their disappointment be known when a student did not meet their standards for any given lesson. In turn, when the teachers thought a student had played well, their satisfaction and pleasure were apparent.

Studying with a master teacher required patience, inner strength, and self-discipline. Frequently, the teachers were away on tour, so lessons tended to be long (two hours) and irregular (every third week, for example). The teachers valued music above the musician, so they were likely to be short and curt with their students. Feelings were not spared. The teachers had carefully selected the most promising and serious students and they expected the students to be capable and self-motivated. They assigned works and expected the student to return for the next lesson with a nearly polished performance.

Finally, the master teachers knew much more than how to make music. They knew how to perform. They knew other musicians, managers, and conductors. They also knew the musical opportunities available to and important for an aspiring solo pianist.

LIVING AMONG MUSICIANS

Part of working with a master teacher involved working with other extremely competent young musicians. Previously, the aspiring pianists had been part of a "class" only in a loose sense. They heard their teachers' other students in recitals, and they met other young musicians at competitions. But it wasn't until they began working with a master teacher that they shared the company of others with aspirations and abilities similar to theirs day after day.

When I got to Curtis, I realized there were other kids who played the hell out of the piano; I wasn't the only one. It was a shock. It's not easy to find out that there are other people who really play very well when you've been isolated and made to think you're something. You may very well be, but you're not alone (P-6).

The "group" of young pianists provided exciting comradeship and frightening competition. The pianists used the group to compare notes about what they were being asked to do and how they were going about learning to do it, and occasionally to commiserate with each other about the abuse they were taking from their teachers. They shared gossip and tidbits of knowledge about competitions, performances, and other such experiences. They went to hear important performances together, and they went to movies or played cards together.

The young pianists also competed with one another. On the light side, they sometimes competed to see who could play the Chopin études the fastest. There was also "a competitive thing set up when people are practicing: 'who can do more?' And it's stimulating" (P-8). The pianists also competed for school honors, teachers' and managers' attention, and "to prove I was somebody, too" (P-13).

Perhaps the most anxiety-provoking situations were the "master classes" the teachers held. At each master class one student played for and was criticized by the teacher in front of the teacher's other students. The pianists were always very conscious of "performing" for and being evaluated by their peers. Fear, of being inadequate or just not very good, motivated many of the pianists to practice "as many hours as I could fit in without losing my mind" (P-6).

PRACTICE

Practice was motivated by more than fear or competition. By virtue of working with an outstanding teacher at a well-known school of music the pianists reported that they were "expected to practice anywhere from a minimum of four to seven hours [a day]" (P-23). The teachers assigned a lot of work. In addition, there were master classes, recitals, and competitions to prepare for. One pianist, among others, noted that he practiced all day because he was eager

> to get good enough that you would make a career—give concerts, become famous, continue to play the music the way you want to hear it, and make a lot of money and all those things (P-2).

One of the most important changes in attitude in the later years was that "I took charge rather than [music] kind of being there" (P-10). Music making became very personal. "While you've heard other people play it better than you can play it, still they never did exactly what you wanted" (P-2). Again, this was something the pianists learned from their teachers.

> He made me think and he made me experiment and he made me understand that you have to find your own way. You have to know what's right [and] what's wrong, but the possibilities and tonal color are absolutely endless. And he made me do that (P-24).

Did they ever think of giving it all up? Some say, "Never!" Others say, "Of course!" The real issue, though, was the question of what else there was for them to do. "I was ready to give up several times, but I didn't know what else to do" (P-8). "There was nothing to take equal interest with music, which I had been doing so much longer than anything else" (P-10). "It's the easiest way I know to make a living. It's what I know how to do. It's what I've been trained for. I don't know how to do anything else as well" (P-24).

THE FINALE

The parents' role in the later years of learning was small. Once the pianists were working with a master teacher, it was limited to being supportive—mostly in a financial way. They paid for school, paid to hire halls for debuts, sent the pianists to Europe for competitions, and so forth. They were also always an enthusiastic audience. The parents' ability to help their children was taken over by others who knew from personal experience what the music world was like and what had to be done.

Through their teachers and schools the pianists gained an increasing understanding of the roles and types of established piano competitions. Music schools run a series of internal competitions, generally for the opportunity to play a solo recital or with the school symphony. There are regional, national, and international competitions, usually focusing on specific types of music. The pianists tried their hands at different levels of competition, with the music they were most comfortable working on. They also chose competitions in search of a variety of different prizes. Some of these the pianists entered for financial reward, others for the opportunity to play certain solo or symphony engagements, and still others to be heard by a jury of valued and influential musicians and managers. Of course each competition was an opportunity for increasing success and visibility, as well as for learning the skills necessary to be accepted as a concert pianist.

The pianists began taking increasing responsibility for their own professional development. They became more independent in their lessons, listening to teachers but not necessarily agreeing with them or following their suggestions. They began to identify and develop personal musical styles, with the encouragement of the master teachers.

The pianists began finding and solving their own musical problems, rather than those posed by the teachers. "Teachers" became "coaches."

He sets the standards and provides an artistic ear. . . . A coach is somebody who will not work over little passages and won't go into details—They will give you feedback. . . . They'll give a reaction. . . . It's a very mature kind of thinking.

Teachers who were previously seen as "gods" lost some of their omniscience, and the pianists sought suggestions and interpretations from a variety of experts. Finally, the pianists began to pursue careers aggressively.

Few of the pianists we talked with are yet well known to the general public. While for our research purposes they have attained the highest levels of accomplishment, they are also just beginning lifelong careers. It is impossible to know how many, if any, will be eminent pianists thirty years from now, or even how many will still be performing soloists.

Though our interviews were designed to focus in depth and detail on the years culminating with the pianist's award-winning performance at a major international piano competition, we did get glimpses into the years that have followed. We heard about how finding professional management became an all-consuming endeavor for some of the pianists. We heard about how securing concert dates in quantity and quality also became a full-time job. Some pianists were preoccupied with arranging debuts and making connections. Some were starting to learn how to travel, how to practice in the midst of hectic schedules, and how to perform consistently week after week in city after city, all the while maintaining their enthusiasm and energy. Having reached professional status, the process of learning continues.

3
★ ★ ★ ★ ★ ★

One Concert Pianist

Lauren A. Sosniak

Although in an earlier chapter all of the pianists were given many opportunities to speak for themselves, nowhere would the reader find any one pianist's story. This is because the study of the development of exceptionally accomplished young concert pianists was the study of a group of individuals. The analysis was concerned with identifying the patterns common to all or most of them. Two or three stories were studied for similar and dissimilar patterns, another two or three were studied separately, the two sets were compared and contrasted, and so forth. Of course the details were different in each pianist's story, but the search was for a broad set of conditions, most of which are present in all of the selected instances of exceptional development.

This chapter, however, presents the story of one pianist's development, with the detail of a life that just one person can live. It is intended to highlight the uniqueness and dynamic nature of successful learning.

Dan Greene's* story was chosen to illustrate the development of the group for several reasons. First, if an "average"

---

*The pianist's name has been changed to protect his identity, as have all names used in the chapter.

story could be identified, Dan's would most likely be it. His story neither overemphasizes nor overlooks any of the general patterns and processes identified earlier. In other words, his was not an extreme case. Second, Dan's story has few, if any, dramatic moments or critical turning points. No single incident could deceive the casual reader.

Finally, Dan's story was chosen because it was possible to present it without revealing his identity. All of the pianists would find much of themselves in the case, because Dan's development is so much like all of the pianists' development. Dan's story highlights most of the issues in the development of all twenty-one pianists. But it is also personal and unique.

BACKGROUND

Dan was raised in Turnersville, a midwestern town with a population of 35,000. Both of his parents were born and raised in small towns nearby and had somehow gravitated to Turnersville, the "nearest large city," where they met and married. Mrs. Greene was a housewife who occasionally did secretarial work for the extra money it provided. Mr. Greene was a repairman with an excellent reputation for miles around. He worked slowly, but "he was a real perfectionist about his work."

According to Mrs. Greene, even before Dan was born, she and her husband talked about

> want[ing] Dan to do something. Whatever it was, I wanted him to do it well. . . . I wanted him to be like a man should be . . . able to do and talk to people. I didn't want him to be backward.

Dan confirms this report.

> I think my parents both realized that as children their opportunities had been extremely limited, and maybe even as adults they felt that to some extent. . . . So . . . they were probably very keen to do everything they could do to keep their child doing something if they could. . . . I'm not sure they thought it through that way, but it was just an instinct.

They weren't unhappy with their lives. I never once sensed that. But they felt always that here's our chance now to have someone do something that we might not have had the chance to do.

I think their expectations were of quality rather than of any one direction. Now obviously, as I grew up and they saw that the piano was an area that I excelled in and loved. . . . It was more or less just natural.

Dan was born into an environment that was similar in many ways to that of most of the pianists.[1] Working hard and doing something well were both preached and practiced. "Honesty and forthrightness was something [my parents] always admired and knew was good." And the biggest hope was that the child be able to live an even better life than his parents. Eventually the piano would provide Dan with the opportunity to work hard and succeed and to realize his parents' dreams. But music was not a priority in the household when Dan was born.

Mrs. Greene's experience with music included piano lessons for four or five years when she was a young girl. She also "had an uncle who played the fiddle. He just loved it and of course I loved to hear it. . . . That was about all we had." Mr. Greene grew up in a home with "an interest in music, particularly singing. . . . His brothers and sisters sang, . . . and a few of them even played some instruments." Mr. Greene would also collect records when he could afford them.

He used to occasionally buy RCA Red Seal records and I would hear pianists like Iturbi and Rubinstein, and some singers too. I

---

[1] It must be noted that Dan is an only child. However, our experience indicates that the large amount of attention he received from his mother was no different from the attention the "musical" child received in larger families. We were told repeatedly that the pianists were the favored children in the household and that the other children had to fend for themselves. Both the pianists and their parents were in agreement about this. For instance, one mother of three commented, "My daughter thinks we favor [the pianist]." When asked, "And did you?" she quickly responded, "Yes, I guess it does happen."

know we did after I started the piano. . . . And they also had classical music too. And [Mr. Greene] would listen to that. Daddy would just sit back and close his eyes and listen.

INTRODUCTION TO MUSIC

In his preschool years, Dan

enjoyed his sandbox, he was always building little towns. He enjoyed blocks, would spend hours working with blocks, Silly Putty, and he loved to study the phone book.

Mrs. Greene read to him every night at bedtime.

Dan's kindergarten teacher "discovered that I loved to play the rhythm instruments—the wood blocks, the tambourine, the triangle. I loved these instruments," and she mentioned this to his parents. "So that started the procedure of beginning to take [lessons on] a musical instrument, and somehow the piano was it." Mrs. Greene recalls thinking, "Well, this is certainly the time to think about the piano." "I had taken piano myself [for four or five years when she was a child] so I suppose that entered into it."

We got a piano . . . a beautiful piano, and we got it for seventy-five dollars. It was a big upright and it had ivory keys and most importantly, a very beautiful tone. So that's what I always remember, the tone of that piano.

Mrs. Greene comments: "I think piano is the thing to start with, regardless of what you play. It's so important to have that background. We never thought of anything else.[2]" She also notes,

I had a friend who was very good on the piano and organ, and I think somewhere that may have had something to do with it. I

---

[2]Dan did take violin lessons for a short time in fourth grade. According to his mother, "It was alright, but he just seemed to like the piano better."

loved her music and I loved to hear her play. . . . It just seemed the thing to do to start Dan on the piano. I loved what she did, and she was doing what I would have liked to have done. . .

Mrs. Greene arranged for Dan's first piano lessons with the choir director and organist at their church. Dan began lessons with Mrs. A. "a month before I was six." "She was close by, in the neighborhood, lived about ten blocks away. She was also a person that we knew. We knew her as a person, as a friend of the family."

For Dan, piano instruction "always was something to do. It was an event for me to go to my lessons." Dan learned to read notes with Mrs. A.

She had these flash cards that would have a note. You would say immediately what that was, and then she'd go on to the next one. . . . We even had a set at home, which Mom used [with me].

Mrs. Greene attended Dan's lessons and supervised his practice.

[Mother] did come to my lessons. I don't think always that she would sit in on them, but I know that she did come to some of them. More interested to know not what I was doing bad, but what we needed to do to follow up. Now, all of my beginning teachers I remember always would have a notebook, and they'd write down what to do for the next week specifically. But I know Mother would also take note of it, too.

[Mother] would sit down and practice with me for the first several years. We would read notes always, every new piece I would take we would read the notes. We would clap the rhythm, and she would work right with me.

Mrs. Greene explained why she worked with Dan this way:

Children get to the point where they don't want their parents to go with them [to lessons], which is all right. But I would always sit down with him and make sure he did what I thought [Mrs. A.]

wanted him to do. . . . Because it's pretty hard to sit down and practice without someone there beside you. And of course he'd love to play duets. . . . That was a big item. It was just more fun than anything. And of course Mr. Greene loved to hear us play together. That brought the whole family together.

The Greene family interest in Dan's work is further reflected in the fact that both parents began to engage in more musical activities for themselves. Mrs. Greene took lessons with the same teacher after Dan started studying the piano—"to help him, because we wanted to do everything we could . . ." Mr. Greene took singing lessons for a while. Dan reports,

I think that as a youngster it made a great impression. One, that they would take that kind of activity—I mean real activity—themselves. And two, they also directed a great deal of interest toward my own work.

Performing was a regular part of Dan's life from the beginning of his studies.

Very soon after I started taking lessons I evidently did well enough that I also played in recitals. So I always remember performing, from early on. . . . Maybe six months after I started taking lessons I played in my first recital. It was in [Mrs. A.'s] home, so it was never like going to another place to perform, but nevertheless there were always a lot of chairs and you had a piano.

Dan explains, though, "I was not a wunderkind. I didn't play, go to the piano immediately and sit down and sound like Beethoven or Mozart."

Dan's mother practiced with him for the first three or four years of his musical development. And practice was a *daily* routine. "We always had our vacations," Mrs. Greene reports, "but never any break time from [lessons and practice]. I don't think it should be curtailed unless it is something very, very important." At first Mrs. Greene arranged practice times twice a day, for fifteen minutes each sitting. Soon Dan was able to sit for longer periods of time. By the time Dan was ten or eleven, "he got to the place where he wanted to do it on his own."

> I would always practice before school. My family always got up at six o'clock and by six-thirty I would practice. At least, I would try to get about forty-five minutes before I had to go to school. And I was always told that's because if I don't get it done after school, at least it's done. And I always believed that that was the way you do things. It is sensible. So it was always done. . . . Generally speaking, I would also practice after school, too. It wasn't always so easy. . . . I lived in a neighborhood with lots of kids. . . and [I was] normal, wanting to play. . . .
>
> I would get up and practice just like you would get up and wash your face in the morning and brush your teeth. It was just a very natural thing to do and you just accepted it as something very normal.

When Dan was in the fourth grade, he began taking lessons with a different teacher.

> I think both my mother and father probably decided that they felt that I needed someone else. Maybe Mrs. A. also suggested it, too. We never had any breach or schism of relationship with these people, as I recall. I think they probably mutually decided that now was a good time to change, because I think my three teachers were always very honest about it, what they thought they could accomplish. And I think . . . Mrs. A. seemed to think I needed to have some other influence.

Mrs. Greene reports that the decision to switch teachers

> was mine, I'm sure. I just felt like they do need a change. And while they were all very good teachers, I think one teacher can take them so far and then they need another one to create more interest. And that's why I changed.

"I felt Mrs. B. could do more for him, and she did—she did an awful lot for him."

**SUMMARY OF THE
INTRODUCTION TO MUSIC**

As Dan notes, his parents' interest in his developing musical ability "was not just a peripheral interest." Mr. and Mrs. Greene were actively involved in Dan's musical education. The Greene household was exceptionally child-centered, as were most of the pianists' homes. Family life was made to fit around the child's activities, rather than the child's activities being fit into family life. And the parents were willing to change their own activities and lives to follow the child as he or she got more and more involved with music.

Dan spoke of one aspect of his life that he thinks of as both very unusual and extremely important for his ultimate successes:

> I had a very special background that I think is important. And that is, parents who had no motives other than just fantastic interest in their son and what he could do, and enjoying that. It wasn't anything that, "Well, he's going to have to learn to grow up to be a concert pianist". . . . They were happy this was happening, [but] it wasn't that they were bound and determined that this was going to happen. . . . I do think that's part of why it worked, perhaps, where [for] other people [it] didn't.

Dan may think of his parents as being unusual in this way, and to many people they may seem unusual indeed. But for the concert pianists we interviewed, Dan's "special background" seems to have been typical.

The initial structure and discipline for Dan's musical education were created by Mrs. Greene, under the guidance of the piano teacher. The teacher was not notable for her expertise, but as a family friend, she was a person the Greenes could trust and feel comfortable with. Dan needed the structure and discipline, because as Mrs. Greene notes, "It is pretty hard [for a youngster] to sit down and practice [consistently] without

someone there beside you." It may have been just as important for Dan's development that his first teacher was a person
with whom his mother could work. If Mrs. Greene had not
been comfortable sitting in on lessons, taking notes, and su-
pervising practice, Dan might not have learned to make practice a habit.

Dan had no choice at all about taking piano lessons. His
parents made the decision, as they also decided, for example,
that he would join the Cub Scouts. Dan started Cub Scouts,
but according to Mrs. Greene,

> He wasn't interested. I was a little unhappy about that, but he just
> wasn't and that was it. I don't know [what he didn't like about it],
> he just didn't take to it. Of course I wasn't there, but his leader told
> me that he just sat in the house, he wouldn't go out with the rest
> of them.

Some parents *do* get involved with Cub Scout troops; Mr. and
Mrs. Greene obviously did not. Mrs. Greene *did* attend Dan's
piano lessons, though many mothers would never think to do
that.

DEVELOPING SKILL

Mrs. B. was the second of three piano teachers Dan studied
with before he went to college as a music major.

> Now, not one of these three, not one, was an artist-teacher. They
> had no background as a performer themselves. They were just fine
> hometown teachers. I'm not going to say that they were better
> than usual. I will say this, that I know they were above average.

Mrs. B., who was a schoolteacher as well as a piano teacher,
had a little more musical expertise, a better reputation, and
more advanced pupils than Dan's first teacher. Also, "she was
much more demanding, and my folks felt that I needed a
teacher who was a little stronger." When the decision was

made to switch to Mrs. B., Dan and his parents were not yet familiar enough with the regional music community to have heard about the even more advanced teacher he would move to in two years.[3]

Despite their lack of musical sophistication, all of Dan's hometown teachers set high standards for his work.

I never felt that there was an opportunity to skip over anything. In other words, if something was not quite to a point, they didn't say, you know, "Well, we'll go on and catch that next time." I never felt that was a possibility. I always felt it had to be finished, to whatever met with their approval.

With Mrs. B.,

I think she insisted on what she felt needed to be learned in a piece of music. She wanted it that way, period. It had to be done. It wasn't just getting the right notes, but . . . she wanted to phrase there and make that softer and that louder—very general things. Who knows, maybe [her interpretations] were good and maybe they weren't. But she insisted upon that. . . . I thought it was something very good. I think I thought that was quite the way it should be.

All of Dan's hometown teachers "would have a notebook, and they'd write down what to do for the next week specifically." What would they note? "If I had to repeat a piece for the following week, watch that this is done that you did not do.

---

[3]Dan's work with Mrs. B. very nicely demonstrates the transition from the early years of playful learning to the middle years of learning the rules of music making. Mrs. B. did not know enough about music making to give Dan the solid foundation of skills he would need for subsequent work, but she introduced him to what she did know, which was more than Mrs. A. knew. Perhaps more important, she introduced the Greene family to a larger world of musical training than they had ever known. Two years later they would easily be able to make the move to an appropriate middle-level teacher and middle-level musical activities (competitions, for example).

It was always a critical thing as well as an advancing thing too."

Dan reports that the notebooks "didn't look different" as he moved from teacher to teacher.

> They all more or less did the same thing. If you got a piece well, they put a sticker up there in the book, or a star, maybe even two. And I think Mrs. B. would sometimes add pluses.

> [Mrs. B.] would write down somewhere down the piece MEM.—memorize to that point for the next week. So certainly memorization began to be a part of my training.

> I always remember that if [Mrs. B.] assigned you a piece, she would put a line through the title. That meant that the piece was assigned for the next week. . . . I think they add up to something. It's the specificity that told you that was assigned for you next week. That belonged to you, and whatever you were going to make of it.

About the time that Dan was in fifth grade, he and his parents started attending concerts. There was a concert series in his hometown, and "that was the only [live] music I heard. [I heard] what we had on records, what I heard on radio, and what we had in community concerts." Dan's fifth-grade teacher [in public school] was very strong on the concert series also.

> She gave me an artist's book that she had, with a little record and all the pictures of everybody who played in the community concert series. And that sort of gave me the idea that this was something beyond, you know. I loved that. I studied that book and read all about everybody.

Mrs. B. was a member of the National Guild of Piano Teachers. When Dan began studying with her, he also began entering the National Guild's yearly auditions as one of her students.

It's not a competition as such. You are graded by a judge just on your own performance and on the standard that that judge sets in his or her own mind. Then there are various [musical] studies on a certificate that they mark a plus or minus on, and then all of those are counted up. . . for your final grade. It was a goal to work for. . . . Many teachers joined, and all their pupils would go and play. You paid a fee to play to the judge.

Dan continued practicing daily, although his mother no longer sat with him while he practiced. "But she knew what was happening. She could read the notebooks, make sure I was doing [what I was assigned]. It was really my responsibility by that time." Still, his parents played a strong role in maintaining his continual effort.

I'm sure there were times when I didn't want to [practice]. I was never punished for not practicing, but I think I realized: one, that they were disappointed that I would not do this—they sort of expected it—and two, that they would show their interest. You would sort of feel like maybe this might be something happy for them. Also, they would soon tell me that this had to be done. If you didn't work, nothing would be accomplished. Lessons won't be ready and so on. And also I think another thing would be brought up—that there would be something else come up tomorrow and you would want to do that too and you won't get [practice] done tomorrow, so why not get it done today. I don't think those times [not wanting to practice] were that often. I was pretty reliable.

Dan was further motivated to practice by his schoolmates and his developing identity as a musician.

I was interested. And then being in the neighborhood had its advantages too. Because the kids would show their interest. They knew I played the piano and they didn't—not one other in the whole neighborhood played the piano. So sometimes they showed something of an interest. . . . Quite often they'd come up and sit on the front porch and listen while I practiced. And of course we had to be careful that they didn't bother, make sure they were quiet.

And I'm sure that made an impression on me, that my contemporaries were interested too.

Two years after Dan began lessons with Mrs. B., when he was twelve, he made a move to the most expert teacher in the area. By this time both he and his mother were familiar enough with the local music community to know who was the best teacher in the area.

[Mrs. B.] quite often turned her pupils over to Mrs. C. when they reached a point when they needed her. Mrs. C. always had the top-notch students in [the town]. And [Dan] was reaching that teenage time, so I felt if anyone could take care of it, Mrs. C. could. And she certainly did.

I think we probably made that decision more than Mrs. B. I think she was very willing to just continue to teach me. But I think my mom felt, well, honestly, I began to be noted in [town], and we heard about other teachers as I began to play more. And we heard that Mrs. C. had always had the best students.

Lessons and other music-related activities and materials became more expensive. Unlike several of the pianists we interviewed, Dan was never given free instruction. Mr. and Mrs. Greene did not have much money, but they always found money for Dan's musical development. "We'd always see to it that he had those lessons. We managed it somehow." Dan added,

I had an aunt, my mother's sister, who would help us some too. Sometimes she would give my mother some money for my lessons. She wasn't wealthy, but she was by herself. . . . She would help out.

Dan noted about his parents,

They would see that I was successful at what I was doing. In other words, when I was playing, people would enjoy it. They would appreciate it. Somehow I just had a talent to do this. That was enough to satisfy their sacrifice in some ways, and enough to satisfy their interest to keep me at it.

Lessons with Mrs. C. were different than they had been before.

We always had to decide what to do with phrasing. We had to decide what the music was saying. . . . I think she brought more attention to an expressive quality of music. Not just playing right notes and mechanical aspects. That had to be there. That had to be basic, not the final result. In other words, the final result of what you're wanting to express musically began to be more heightened and more, perhaps, complex, one might say. Although it was certainly a very elementary complexity.

Piano practice required at least an hour and a half a day. "There were not weeks that would go by that I didn't practice. There weren't even days that would go by that I didn't practice. I always practiced."

I do remember learning that I had to concentrate every time that I sat down. I finally discovered that if I only had an hour and a half a day to practice, then I've got to really concentrate. And I still see the value of that, of course. . . . You hope that what you want to accomplish happens. If you also have an idea of what you want to accomplish. . . . I was concentrating on learning the piece, or trying to get behind the piece to do what I would hopefully think the composer wanted, and that was pointed out to me.

Dan's parents never seemed to tire of his work at the piano.

When Daddy would come home at night, he would be very tired. . . . But he would sit or lie down and rest while I would be practicing. There was nothing that he would let interfere if I was going to practice. He wouldn't say, "Look, Dan, I'm too tired. I don't want to hear this." There wasn't anything like that that I can remember. The only thing I can remember is the opposite, that there was always a decided interest.

Mrs. Greene was not only involved with Dan's work, she also began to make music her own work. Dan taught beginning pupils for a while when he was fourteen or so. But eventually high school activities and other part-time jobs became more important. Mrs. Greene took over.

> He just got to the point where he didn't want to anymore. So it fell to my lot to take over. So I taught them, and gradually other students would come in. I just took beginners. If they showed any real talent, I'd send them to another teacher, because I don't think they should be held back.

Mrs. C. encouraged Dan to enter a yearly regional competition when he was in ninth grade.

> It was a cumulative kind of competition. You would enter the first year. If you won, you would get a certificate. If you won second prize, you would get a credit slip, which meant you could advance on to the second year. And then the second-year repertoire changed. They always got a little more difficult.

Dan did very well, and the competition became a yearly event for him.

> Usually I would go with Mrs. C. and some other students who were entered, so we would share the cost. Or sometimes, as I recall, I think [Mrs. C.] would just do it. Maybe my folks would give her a few dollars to help with the gas.

Mrs. C. began arranging a variety of performing opportunities for Dan. According to Mrs. Greene, local organizations would "call [Mrs. C.], and she would think of a student to take and have them play." Mrs. Greene doesn't recall whether the organizations ever asked specifically for her son. She recalls,

> Of course I was always in the background—pushing it along. I'm sure he was a little concerned [about competitions], but he always went ahead and did it and he came out fine. Of course he didn't win always, but it's just good practice to do these things.

In addition, Dan created his own opportunities to perform. He said he was always "making my own production for a chance at accomplishment. . . . I wouldn't just wait to play when I was asked. . . I would always be willing to play at church or at school."

Dan summarizes this phase of his development quite simply: "There was always progress being made. It was demanded, and it happened."

SUMMARY OF THE YEARS
OF DEVELOPING SKILL

Dan became increasingly more expert as a musician in a number of ways. Most obvious, he developed skill at some of the basic techniques of piano playing. The "standard that the judge sets in his or her own mind" at the National Guild yearly auditions was a standard of performance that Dan could meet yearly. Whatever it was that Mrs. B. "insisted . . . be learned in a piece of music" and that Mrs. C. "brought more attention to," whatever it was that constituted the "detail" of lessons and the "specificity" of the homework, the teacher's instruction was congruent with other musicians' evaluations.

Dan and his parents were also developing an increasing understanding of music making beyond the practical "know-how." As they watched professional musicians who came to town to perform in a concert series, the Greenes began to listen to music differently and to think about music making differently. Now playing the correct notes in the proper tempo was assumed; playing with "style" and "interpretation" was something to think about. Playing for fun, for family and friends, was assumed; playing for a livelihood was something to ponder. Attending live musical performances by professional musicians who were literally touchable, and whose lives could be studied for models, changed everyone's understanding of what they were involved in.

The Greenes also began learning the "rules" of the music world. They learned to distinguish the more expert teachers from the less expert teachers, and the better piano students from the more average students. They learned about the National Guild of Piano Teachers auditions and the Federated Studies Club competition. They learned about the people, places, and repertoire important to those established in the music community across the country. Mrs. Greene made a commitment to getting "the best" instruction for her son. And Dan met people, such as the university musicologist who evaluated him in his second National Guild audition and who would become important in moving him along the road to musical success.

The self-discipline that Dan needed for exceptional achievement was being reinforced continuously by Mrs. Greene and Dan's piano teachers. Mrs. Greene no longer physically supervised Dan's practice, but psychically she still did so. Dan was aware of what his parents "sort of expected," what would be a serious disappointment, and what "had to be done." Each teacher Dan studied with conveyed greater seriousness and concern about "the music" than the teacher before. Each set increasingly more demanding requirements for lessons and public events. To meet these requirements Dan had to work harder and make a greater investment in music.

Finally, through the years of developing skill, Dan also began developing an identity as a musician. "No one [else] in the whole neighborhood played the piano." Dan's peers began to think of him as a pianist, his mother thought of him as a "top-notch" piano student with potential that required the best instruction available, and Dan "began to be noted in [town.]"

BECOMING A MUSICIAN

Dan was gaining attention as a pianist from quite a few people in town. Mrs. Greene reports, "It seemed like everyone was interested in what Dan did or what he had to say." Among the interested were the parents of a professional pianist who is many years older than Dan, and the family minister and his wife.

Dan has vague recollections that there were several people in his hometown who suggested that he attend a special music school rather than the public high school in town. This would have involved moving almost a thousand miles. Mr. and Mrs. Greene vetoed the idea (unlike several other of our pianists' parents, who acted on similar suggestions), but they did allow Dan to attend a special summer music camp in another state after his junior year in high school. The summer experience, working and studying with musical peers and experts from around the country, "really was an awakening time for me." Among other important benefits from this experience, Dan got to know several students of the well-known pianist and teacher with whom he would study after high school.

Mrs. C. took a special interest in Dan's development. According to Dan, "Comparing my ability (with her other students and with people she'd heard before too) made her think that I had something unusual." She encouraged Dan to enter the Federated Studies Club competition, which was a yearly, cumulative competition for high school musicians. In his third year Dan won "overall in the state," the following year he won "overall top winner." In fact, it seems possible that without Mrs. C.'s serious commitment to Dan's musical career during his high school years, Dan might have gone to college and later become a lawyer, a politician, or any number of things other than a concert pianist.

Dan was very involved in extracurricular activities during high school. He was class president his junior year, student-body president his senior year, and was always engaged in campaigns, making buttons and posters, and so on. He loved his classes in math, civics, and history, and for a period of time in high school he entertained thoughts about other careers. "Not so much politics, but I thought about something like diplomacy or something like that." Of course he also played piano for a lot of school assemblies. And he always held a part-time job, one of which was in the city library in the music department.

Dan looked forward to going to college. He had some friends with whom he thought he would continue to be "buddies" at college, and they all talked about joining fraternities and so forth. His high school involvement with politics and debating led to thoughts of pursuing a career in politics or statesmanship.

But Mrs. Greene was no longer just interested that Dan "do something . . . well"; by now she was committed to his career in music. "He had just gone so far that I felt it was ridiculous to stop. . . . Dan's becoming a concert pianist just seemed like one of those things that had to be."

"The decision," to continue to study piano after high school and try to become a concert pianist, "was not made just one day . . . but it had to finally be concluded." "Sophomore, junior, and senior year [in high school], this was something for us all to start thinking about." The "big turning point," according to Dan,

> was when I won a big symphony competition in [city] as a senior in high school. That gave me the opportunity to play with [an] orchestra and it came at an [important] time. I know my teacher was very upset because she really wanted me to go ahead with music. And she still tells people about when she was fighting for me to do this and I said, "No, I'm going to go ahead with political science, history, and that kind of thing." Then I won this competition, and of course that played into her hands. It was also interesting to me because no high school person had ever won that competition. It had always been a college person. That also made a great impact, of course.

Mrs. Greene tells a slightly different version of the same story, and of how Mrs. C. "handled" her son. According to Mrs. Greene, Dan was becoming much more interested in politics than piano and was debating about whether or not to enter this competition.

> And I was just frantic because I thought he was not going to enter. And this is the way she works. She said, "Well now, Dan, let's go ahead and register so if you decide at the last minute that you wish you had entered, at least you'll be entered." So he did. . . . [He won the competition] and I guess that's what did it [made the decision

for music over politics, at least as a college major]. But anyway, it all worked out. I talked to her [Mrs. C.] about it and she took care of it.

Several people had a strong influence on Dan when he had to decide with whom he would study music after high school: Mrs. C., of course; a musician judge for the National Guild evaluations who was impressed enough by Dan's performance to talk with him personally and remain available when Dan needed guidance; and some of the young pianists Dan met during his summer at music camp. Dan had enough experience with the music world by now to know that it was important to study with a particular teacher at this stage of his development rather than simply to choose a music school and study with whomever he was assigned. And he had access to enough teachers and students from different music schools to help focus his choice.

Dan auditioned for several music teachers who then indicated their interest in working with him. He weighed his own level of expertise and the advice he'd been given by musicians more advanced than himself and chose to study with the teacher Mrs. C. recommended most highly.

I felt a real vitality of interest musically I hadn't felt with the others. I also felt the great interest on his part in my own talent, too.

Dan adds about his choice, this teacher "didn't want to teach me as a pianist so much as to become a musician. That's really the criterion he had."

My repertoire was terribly deficient, terribly deficient, and [Mr. D.] knew that. . . . From the standpoint of just the basic material that I had to have repertoire-wise, and also experience-wise of interpretative talent, I had a great deal to learn. So he determined that I was going to accomplish that, and he was a great disciplinarian. And we had to really work like hell. He demanded it.

He worked with me technically as a pianist, but the distinction of becoming a musician became clear every time I took a lesson. Because we talked about music. We began to try to become more intellectual about how phrase structure [worked] and what it meant and what you were trying to say, rather than how do you accomplish this at this instrument.

As soon as Dan began studying with Mr. D., he reports that "my sights were always very high. First of all, I didn't want to just be a pianist, I wanted to be a musician." Thoughts about joining a fraternity, continuing debating, or whatever, were abandoned. "[Mr. D] would have none of that. If I was going to come there to work, there wasn't any possibility that I was going to start depleting my time and my interest."

Dan immediately began practicing about four or five hours a day. "[The teacher] gave me enough to accomplish that that was the only way to do it." Dan also had to prepare for the recital his teacher expected him to give at school while still in his first year of study there. "Also, we had juries . . . every six months. . . . So I had some very decided goals that had to be accomplished."

What he offered me was that he would teach me if I would be serious. And of course I knew of him as being a great teacher, which he was, and a great pianist, which he also was. And if I could somehow muster enough maturity at that point to see that, that what he demanded would be necessary, if I also thought and demanded of my own talent what was going to be necessary, then there might be a coming together.

I also realized that I was behind, and if there was any hope of being able to join a rather small group of people . . . that had anything to offer, and hopefully develop over a lifetime, that I would have to do this kind of work.

The boy who had been so popular and active in high school began to close himself off from almost everyone except his piano teacher. "I didn't really have a lot of time to socialize very much." Dan still had to find the time to work; he needed the money. He found a steady job playing the piano for ballet classes. "Then of course there were the competitions. I started winning all those, and that gave me some funds too, which I always saved."

Dan told the following story to demonstrate his commitment to music making and his teacher's demands:

> At the time I entered school, the school was not open for practice late at night or on Sundays. He [teacher] would come in and let me in and then lock me up [*laughs*] and then come back and let me out, on the weekends. And late at night too, sometimes. Although sometimes he would give me a key, which was not supposed to be done.

He added,

> I really threw myself into it. . . . It was just like being compelled into something immediately. You were on a course, and the course was good, it was right. And it really worked.

Five years later, both student and teacher could only be pleased with their work. Mr. D. "insisted" that if Dan wanted some minor finishing touches, he had to go study elsewhere. Mr. D. sent Dan to work with an old friend of his, also a very well-respected and accomplished musician. Dan was both pleased and surprised to find "the same kind of attitude toward music from an entirely different perspective." Shortly thereafter Dan established himself as a young musician worthy of considerable attention.

Dan has had enormous professional and personal successes in the short time since he officially stopped "studying" music and began "being" a musician. He now also has time once again for interests and activities that go well beyond the world of music.

Mrs. Greene reports, "We just became a whole lot more interested in music. If it hadn't been for Dan, life just wouldn't be worth very much. Isn't that awful to say that? But it's made a lot of difference."

4

★ ★ ★ ★ ★ ★

The Development of Accomplished Sculptors

Kathryn D. Sloane and
Lauren A. Sosniak

T he sculptors interviewed for this study met the standards of excellence suggested by experts in their field. All received either a Guggenheim Fellowship or the Rome Prize for their work. In addition, they have been granted the largest of the Individual Artist Awards from the National Endowment of the Arts.

Twenty-five sculptors met these criteria and were under the age of forty when the sample was being selected. Twenty (twelve men and eight women) agreed to talk with us about their development. We also interviewed parents of fifteen of the sculptors for supplementary and corroborative information.

The Context in Which the Sculptors Were Raised

The sculptors were raised in different cities and towns across the country. Five were only children. The others were equally likely to be the oldest or youngest of their siblings, or a middle child in families with three to six siblings.

The sculptors' families were quite different from one another. Several were well-to-do. Some were extremely poor. Two fathers had earned M.D. degrees. Both also enjoyed high social status in their involvement in community affairs. In contrast, one father "was a slum [land]lord" and a few had only elementary school educations.

Slightly more than half of the sculptors' fathers (55%) had earned college degrees. The fathers worked at jobs so different from one another that there is no useful system of classification. (For example, one was the editor of a trade journal, two were salesmen, two were manufacturers, one a blue-collar worker, two were college deans, and so on.) Slightly less than half of the mothers (40%) had earned college degrees. Most of the mothers were said to have been housewives, at least while their children were living in the house. The five who worked did so because their income was important for their families. Two had no choice at all: their husbands had died and they were the sole support of their families.

PARENTS' VALUES AND HOPES
FOR THEIR CHILDREN

Although there was a very wide range in the social and economic status of the families, and in the amount of formal education the parents had received, as a group the parents were remarkably similar in their values and in their aspirations for their children. Working at something one was truly interested in and pursuing it to the best of one's ability were the dominant messages communicated to the sculptors. One sculptor reported,

My father spent a lot of time and a lot of energy, and my mother as well, talking to us about . . . how one did things. About doing things in such a way that you enjoy doing them, and that you did them well. About developing yourself as a person. . . . [My parents] were much more interested in the quality of the way I was living my life, not in what I was doing particularly (A-6).

Another sculptor explained, "[My parents] wanted me to be ambitious and they didn't really care what I was ambitious about as long as it wasn't a life of crime" (A-3).

The emphasis was on the way one lived, rather than on the specifics of what one was doing.

> [My father] wanted from all of us one thing; and that was that we be good people. That would probably have been more important to him than that we were successful people. . . . [Being good meant being] productive, functioning to your best capacity . . . principled (A-18).

Another sculptor was certain that her father would have been happy with almost any vocational choice she made,

> as long as it was what I wanted to do. As long as I didn't say, "I wanted to do so and so but I couldn't do it." I don't think he could have tolerated that (A-20).

From another sculptor we heard, "My mother was always saying [that] if I was happy, [then] she was happy" (A-14).

The parents' reports about what they wanted for their children confirm the impressions they left with their children. "I just wanted them to be happy and fulfilled and go to college and all that" (M of A-4).

> We really didn't have too many [specific aspirations], I mean like many fathers wanted their sons to carry on in their footsteps. There was none of that at all. We just wanted him to, you know, have a good life, and work up to his ability if possible, and that sort of thing (M of A-5).

There were three additional aspects of the good life that the parents tried to communicate to their children. It was important to the parents that their children be educated, financially secure, and, especially for the women, happily married.

A college education was taken for granted by all but one of the sculptors. "It was always understood that we would all go to college" (A-4). "There was never any question in my mother's mind that I would go to college. . . . By God I would have gotten it if I had wanted it or not" (A-8).

In some instances this was so well understood that it was never discussed. "I think my parents assumed that I was going to college so absolutely that it never occurred to them to give me any counseling whatsoever" (A-18). In other instances a college education was discussed frequently, and plans for it were begun in advance. "This college thing was something my parents took very seriously. We were set up all along to go to good schools, to go to the East Coast" (A-3).

The parents had equally varied reasons for wanting their children to go to college. Some parents stressed the importance of a deep and broad-based liberal arts education for a rich life, others stressed the importance of a college degree "to get a good job" (A-14). No matter what the reason, however, the desire was strong. Continuing one's formal education beyond college, however, was rarely mentioned.

Although the parents also reported a deep concern for their children's financial security, they clearly did not communicate this as well to their children as they did the other concerns just discussed. In fact, inadvertently perhaps, the parents taught their children that economic attainments were not the standards by which to measure accomplishment.[1]

[There was] a disparagement of the materialism of those around us. [My family was] never interested in making money; partly because my parents were well off enough that you didn't have to be constantly thinking about it, and partly that was not a value of theirs (A-3).

Even in the poorest of the families the sculptors never learned to link enjoyable and fulfilling work with work that

---

[1]Some parents were to regret this. When it became obvious that their child was thinking seriously about a career as an artist, they suddenly expressed concern about how their child would earn a decent living. See pages 131–133.

would provide a comfortable income. The former was essential for a good life, and if the latter followed, that made life especially nice indeed.

The sculptors' parents also expressed hopes that their children marry and have families of their own someday. The sculptors themselves seem to have interpreted their parents' remarks about this as a clichéd way of expressing their general concerns for their child's happiness.[2] "They just wanted me to marry a nice man and be happy" (A-19), one sculptor told us while struggling to express her parents' lack of specific expectations for her. A male sculptor reported that his parents "would have expected me to go to maybe [a college well known for parties] and have a good time, get married, and start my life in [my hometown]" (A-7).

The absence of career directions from the parents while the children were growing up was mentioned again and again. "I think [my parents'] ambitions [for me] were pretty vague. They were just within the parameters of [raising] this kid to be a nice, respectable, upper-middle-class kid" (A-2). "[My mother] wanted us to do very much what we wanted to do. . . . I think that was a real priority for her. That somehow we make a choice and she would support it" (A-17). For the most part, the parents made no attempt to suggest possible careers. Some parents reported taking special care that this be true because they resented the pressures they felt when they were growing up.

> I really didn't remember thinking, you know, doctor, lawyer, merchant, chief. I think my husband and I both felt, coming from . . . homes where there was so much of the attitude of growing up to be a doctor or lawyer . . . we sort of, not resented but didn't like this idea that that's what people ought to do. And I guess we both had the feeling that people ought to be free to be whatever they

---

[2]Several of the parents, however, seem to be truly concerned about their child's marital status even today. They talk with pride about successful marriages, and with dismay about children who have not yet married or who have married and divorced.

wanted to be. . . . I don't really think I had any [specific] ideas that I can recall. And my husband has always been even less directive of what they do than I (M of A-3).

FAMILY INVOLVEMENT WITH ART

The father of one of the sculptors we interviewed was a commercial artist. None of the other parents earned a livelihood through artistic activities. There were some artistically enthusiastic families, however.

In slightly more than half of the homes, one (or both) of the parents was fairly knowledgeable about or appreciative of fine art. Some of these parents had taken art classes in college or began painting or sketching later in life. Although they were strictly amateurs, they found artistic pursuits to be an enjoyable pastime. "My father did watercolors. . . . He'd always done it, as long as I knew. Not incredibly seriously, but I was aware that he did that from time to time" (A-9). "I remember [mother] sketching, doing our portraits, which were quite good" (A-1).

Other parents in the same group visited museums frequently, actively supported local art activities, or maintained friendships with artists or art collectors. "On Wednesdays, in the afternoons were [father's] days off. We'd usually . . . go to the galleries or go to visit artists who were friends of his. He'd take me along" (A-6). "My parents were very respectful of the arts and were interested in going to museums and that sort of thing" (A-3).

In another 25% (N = 5) of the homes, the parents themselves were not highly interested in or knowledgeable about the field of art. They did, however, view the arts as a worthy—although unfamiliar—area of pursuit. These were parents with "a sense of culture" (A-11).

> [My mother] doesn't really understand art. She took us to museums. She did all the right things. . . . She always supported culture in general terms. In the way a nineteenth-century woman would support culture, as one of the finer things in life (A-8).

Parents in the remaining 20% (N = 4) of the homes stand out as being much less supportive of the arts than the other parents. In these homes, the parents were either unaware or unappreciative of the arts and artistic activities.

> There was no "high culture" going on in my family. We did not go to museums. We did not go to musical events. There was not a sensitivity of either of my parents when I was growing up to any of the arts (A-7).

The Early Years

The sculptors' early behavior seems to have been as commonplace and varied as we would expect from young children. A little boy was said to have played with his older brother, "a lot like little boys usually play. With trucks and cars and cowboys" (M of A-3). A few of the women remembered "little-girl games," such as "dress up in costume, [put] makeup [on] people" (A-1).

For the most part, the sculptors seem to have played in much the same way regardless of their sex. "I played with my neighbors. . . . We rode bicycles and played in an area that at the time wasn't developed" (A-9). "You play games with your friends, you read comic books or go to the movies or go down for a soda. Absolutely ordinary, no different from what anyone else was doing" (A-2). A woman remembered that she and her younger sister "would play adventure games. I would cast myself into some heroine role" (A-6). A male sculptor with an older brother told the same story from the point of view of the younger child. "We'd put on performances. . . . He would be Superman, I would be stuck doing Jimmy Olson" (A-3).

LEARNING TO DRAW AT HOME
The majority of the sculptors (75%) liked to draw as children. They "drew all the time" (A-4), not just on rainy days or when

they had the measles. Some drew cartoons or copied pictures from books, magazines, and newspapers. Two were particularly interested in animals and drew horses, bees, or dinosaurs. Others drew pictures to illustrate stories their parents told them or they made up themselves.

About one-third of the sculptors had an adult role model for art activities. A parent or relative enjoyed sketching occasionally or was learning to do watercolors or to make pottery.

> I grew up in a house that was full of painting and music. From the time I was little, I was involved in one of those things, either watching it or playing around with it or whatever. It was something that [father] did, it wasn't for the benefit of anybody else. So I got to experience it as the way somebody spent their time. A lot of people don't get to do that . . . it just seemed natural to me if I wanted to make art to just begin to make art (A-6).

These sculptors began to learn basic techniques either by watching the adult or through occasional, informal "lessons."

> [Relative would] show me how to draw. When I was with him I probably did lots of drawings and he would gently explain to me where I was going wrong. He did spend time helping me. It was something mutual . . . that brought us closer together (A-5).

> [Grandmother] would take the newspaper and have me copy things . . . she would draw certain things too. . . . I didn't really imitate her, but I'd pursue that and she would help me or something like that . . . just spending time with your grandmother (A-14).

Most of the sculptors, however, did not have parents or relatives who were amateur artists or who worked on art projects with the children. Nonetheless, the youngsters found approval and attention from adults for their own work.

> I knew I drew as a child. And I knew that these drawings were probably made a great deal of fuss over. *I* was made a great deal

of fuss over. . . . And I would try and do it as much as possible. I mean I really wanted to gain everybody's approval (A-17).

When I was very little, I would do a drawing and then run around and show it to everybody. . . . That was great fun and I would get a lot of response (A-4).

The parents bought their children sketch pads, watercolors, or colored paper. They displayed their children's drawings around the house and saved them.

At the very least, we were told, the individuals who liked to draw were never discouraged. Even if the parents did not make a "great deal of fuss" over the child's artwork, drawing was considered an appropriate and acceptable way to spend time. "I think they sort of didn't know what to do, where to encourage me. But they never discouraged me" (A-10). "They encouraged me, I think, by not hindering me. They didn't put a stop to it, they didn't question my doing it" (A-5).

A striking communality in these individuals' early attempts at making art is the purposeful nature of the artwork. There was a reason behind these activities, a desired end or effect. Rarely were they scribbling or doodling or coloring in coloring books. They were creating a product.

The purpose, or goal, of making these products was to represent a "subject" accurately. The standard was "realism" in the sense of accurately reproducing an object or scene, or copying the style or form of others. Thinking back to her earliest work, one sculptor chuckled and referred to herself as a "conformist artist. You know, trees were always green, the sky was always blue" (A-19).

The sculptors copied pictures from books, magazines, or newspapers—trying to reproduce a cartoon character, for example. Two recall being particularly interested in animals, and they practiced sketching pets or from picture books until they could create a facsimile. Two others compiled sets of drawings to tell stories—picture books.

BUILDING AND CONSTRUCTING

An activity cited as frequently as drawing—and to which the sculptors often attached more significance—was creating physical objects. At least 65% of our sample have always enjoyed working with their hands. This included "building model planes, carving soap" (A-15) and many other kinds of constructing activities. "I liked to work with my hands from the very beginning. A major moment was when I was five and it was decided that it was okay for me to have a jackknife so I could carve things" (A-2). "I remember from when I was very little making models and forts. Always building with my hands" (A-10). "I built stuff. Treehouses and that kind of thing. . . . More from a building sense than a sense of this is art, but always liked putting stuff together. Hammering and nailing stuff" (A-9).

Again, some of the youngsters observed adults engaging in similar activities and were guided or informally instructed by these adults. The boy with the jackknife at the age of five was taught how to use the knife, and many other tools, by his uncle and his uncle's partners in an antique shop.

Experience with tools was generally gained by "helping" a parent or relative with the adult's project. At first the child watched and fetched tools or held the work light. Soon the child was assigned simple tasks. One sculptor, whose father enjoyed cabinetmaking and remodeling as a hobby, recalled her first experience with carpentry this way:

> There were some old buildings on the land, so we tore down the buildings and saved the wood. My job was to take the nails out, straighten the nails on this rock, stack everything up . . . and he'd build worksheds out of the wood. . . . He'd put a board up with two nails, and I'd get to put all the other nails in (A-12).

For the most part, the children did their constructing on their own, or at least without the help of an adult. If they had a model, it was a model "kit" for building an airplane or a car. And they were more likely to work with cardboard and glue than with hammer and nails.

> There were enormous amounts of cartons, and we [the artist and a friend] would build things. . . . We were sort of the set designers. We would make all kinds of games and we would build structures (A-11).

> There were some old books that my mother had from her childhood about fairy kingdoms and things like that. So we [artist and sister] would make . . . stand-up fairies and castles and clouds (A-4).

Art and constructing activities were only a small part of the children's lives, as we will see in the following pages. But the children did a lot of such work, they enjoyed it, and they usually enjoyed doing it alone. "Copying things out of books . . . was a way to amuse myself" (A-5), according to one sculptor, an only child. Another sculptor amused himself with models and forts.

> The more intricate [the model] the longer it could captivate me. . . . It used to amaze people that I could go into my room for three or four hours and just be totally wrapped up in this battleship . . . not go out of my room, not watch Mickey Mouse on TV (A-10).

One art project led gradually to another. The children developed skills, and learned lessons from their mistakes. The sculptor who learned to hammer and straighten nails while helping her father chose to build a birdhouse as her first independent project.

> I seemed to be particularly enthusiastic about hammering nails. . . . I made my birdhouse, and it was all very cute. It had shingles on it and all that. I put it up outside the kitchen window. All these birds would come and sit on it, look inside, and fly away

and never come back. So finally I took it down and looked inside and [realized] there were so many nails, there was no place to go (A-12).

The "structure" builder reported,

If it fell down, we'd find another way to build it. It was really quite interesting. . . . If it works, fine. If it doesn't work, then you just do it another way (A-11).

A youngster who was fascinated with model airplanes graduated from putting together store-bought models to creating his own.

I'd take a model that I had and do a cardboard [version] that looked totally different. I'd fashion it in a way that I'd get the shapes by scoring the cardboard. Very intricate, very complex designs. . . . It was like carving construction. . . . I spent a lot of time doing those things, too. That was my free time, and I wanted to do that (A-14).

OTHER OUT-OF-SCHOOL ACTIVITIES

The amount of "free time" the children had to do those sorts of things varied considerably when they were of elementary school age. Some had little if anything formally scheduled between the end of one school day and the beginning of the next. Others regularly had a "lesson" of one sort or another after school.

If they had a regularly scheduled after-school activity, it was likely to be a music lesson. Half of the sculptors played a musical instrument when they were children, typically beginning when they were nine or ten years old and ending two or three years later. More sculptors took music lessons than the combined number of those who had religious instruction and those who were active in the Scouts.

About one-quarter of the sculptors were what we might call lesson takers, that is, children who are regularly sent for instruction outside of school in any activity of interest to their parents or, more generally, when some sort of instruction is easily accessible. These children were given tennis lessons, dance classes, horseback riding lessons, and French instruction. Instruction in these areas usually continued for between one and three years.

The one out-of-school activity that is conspicuously absent is regular art instruction. Four sculptors of the twenty went to some sort of art class outside of school during their elementary school years. The nature of the experiences, however, and their very short duration, makes it difficult to think of them as classes for art instruction. One artist explained the classes he attended at the age of seven this way:

> My father took me to a couple of classes where one made art. . . . I don't think there was any direction. You had a little table and clay and you made what you wanted to make and they fired it for you (A-6).

A mother gave this account of the art instruction she found for her two sons:

> I found this man who did give lessons on Saturday. And they were just really very unstructured, kind of creative classes, where the kids would be given wood and told to do something with it. Or different shapes. He then moved to New York, and those classes stopped, and I didn't see any that were available until [years] later on (M of A-3).

We speculate that the absence of regular art instruction outside of school had more to do with the nature of art instruction and the art world than with the parents' conscious or subconscious decisions or the children's desires. If art instruction had been as easily available as, say, music lessons, at least the lesson takers in our sample might have been enrolled in art classes. But such was not the case.

Private art instruction for young children is rare. Even group art instruction—at a community center, for instance—

is not readily available. If the parents had wanted special art instruction for their young children, they would have been hard pressed to find it. (Whether this is ultimately "bad" or "good" for the artistic development of an individual or a society is a separate issue.) Furthermore, art instruction is thought to be a regular part of the school curriculum for young children, unlike religious instruction, tennis, or even music. Therefore parents seldom feel the need to make sure their children have some experience with art.

ELEMENTARY SCHOOL

The sculptors did, in fact, encounter art in elementary school. They don't think of these experiences as instructional, however, nor even as having much to do with art. One sculptor speaks for many with this comment on the classes: "They are for amusement. . . . I don't think it was even about art. I think it was about having somebody draw something in a room" (A-5). Another explained that art in elementary school was treated as though it were "a *craft*, and art is not a craft, it is an intellectual discipline" (A-11).

Teachers generally dictated the subject to be drawn and often the method by which to draw it. "You'd get to build a robin out of an ellipse, a circle, and a triangle" (A-2). Everyone was expected to produce the same product, which was frequently determined by the season. The class colored mimeographed drawings of pumpkins at Halloween, turkeys at Thanksgiving, Santas at Christmas, bunnies at Easter. "There were all these little windows [in the classroom], and every occasion you would paint some little design on the window—tulips in the springtime" (A-12).

The sculptors were divided in their reaction to such activities. For some it was a pleasant part of the school day or week, "always a lot of fun" (A-8).

It was a free period basically. It was nice. . . . I think that my main concern was looking at what someone else was doing and trying to copy it (A-7).

For others, it was sometimes a frustrating experience.

> I had problems at times with teachers who said I didn't follow directions. I would do things that had nothing to do with the assignment. I guess they thought I had a problem understanding (A-14).

For better or worse their elementary school teachers' response to their artwork did not seem to have had much effect on the youngsters. They had been doing artwork for quite some time, usually with encouragement and approval from their family. Their behavior was not affected by the infrequent remarks a teacher made about their artwork. We heard stories like this one about a fifth-grader whose teacher thought his "elegant tracings ... were morally incorrect" just because they were tracings:

> I got put down a lot for [tracing] and I hated it. And I was very glad that at that point my mother was collecting these drawings and treasuring them. That felt really good, to have this validation at home when the teachers were just dumb as doornails (A-2).

Elementary school in general was remembered with indifference. Some of the sculptors were always among the best students in the class. Others were B or C students. Either way, for the most part they were not strongly invested in their school achievement. They reported that they met their parents' expectations without much trouble, in large measure because their parents didn't expect any more than they could produce easily.

Little time was spent on homework. It was said that little was assigned. Nor did the majority of the parents monitor the time spent doing homework or the product of the child's effort. Homework, the parents reported, was the child's responsibility.

In three instances the parents did have to get involved with their child's schoolwork for a while, because their child was said to be a "discipline problem," "looking for attention," by one or more schoolteachers. Those problems seem to have taken care of themselves by the time the children were in fifth or sixth grade.

The sculptors dismissed any talk of elementary school with comments like these:

> I was happy [in school]. . . . I wasn't the slowest kid in the class and I wasn't the fastest. . . . I largely got along with everyone (A-9).

SUMMARY OF THE EARLY YEARS

In these early years, no one—neither the parents nor teachers nor the children themselves—foresaw that the children would someday become exceptional artists. "It *never* entered my mind" (M of A-10) was a comment we heard again and again from the parents. According to one mother,

> [My two sons] were both good in school in almost everything they took. They were good students and they didn't seem to have any, at a young age, any real strong predispositions that I can recall. In fact, I thought they might have a hard decision as to careers because they were so good at all subjects. It really wasn't until high school that ——— showed a lot of interest in art (M of A-3).

But with hindsight we can see the seeds that were being sown for careers as artists.

First, the children produced a lot of artwork and/or constructions. They did so in their free time and even, sometimes, in school when they were supposed to be doing something else. For the most part, they were learning to reproduce pictures or an art object, or transfer a three-dimensional object into a two-dimensional representation of that object. They "copied," they "traced," they "drew from" animals (living and preserved) and from other aspects of their lives. They built objects to resemble things they saw and things that were functional. The children were developing the kinds of visual perceptiveness and hand-eye coordination necessary for such activities, and, just as important, they were developing confidence in their abilities.

Second, drawing and constructing were encouraged and well-supported activities in the sculptors' homes. Nearly half of the children saw parents or relatives doing such things, clearly for personal pleasure. With the possible exception of two individuals in our sample, the children's early "art" efforts were noticed and praised (lavishly at times) by their parents.

The extent of parental encouragement for their children's art activities can be better gauged, perhaps, by noting that parents saved a considerable amount of the children's earliest artwork. "I have everything he ever made. . . . It was out [on display in the house] all the time" (M of A-10), many parents told us. Special works were given special attention. "When [my daughter] was five or six, . . . she saw a piece of holly . . . and she made a drawing of it which really took my eye. . . . It just looked so realistic to me and so artistic that I framed it. And we had it hung up for quite a few years" (M of A-4).

The sculptors supported their parents' claims. "[My drawings] were saved, they were preserved with great care. . . . The only things that have ever been thrown out are the things that I threw out" (A-8). When this same artist was asked whether her parents saved any other work of hers—stories she wrote, for instance—she hesitated for a moment before she answered, "No, I'm sure they didn't. I'm sure they didn't" (A-8). Then she started to laugh. She had never before realized the disproportionate amount of attention given to her art activities, and she was reasonably certain that her mother had never been consciously aware of this either.

A further consideration in the development of these sculptors is the absence of direction from their parents. None of the experiences they were thrust into—school, music lessons, dance classes—seems to have been especially compelling. Nor was there any strong encouragement for the youngsters to invest themselves seriously in any of these activities.

The youngsters were rarely praised for their achievements in music, academics, or the like. They were not guided to quality teachers. No one noticed "latent talents" waiting to bloom. Neither their teachers nor their parents fired their dreams and goals in these directions. The youngsters were neither noticeably bad nor noticeably good at any of these activities. They may have enjoyed one or more "well enough" for a while, but they never became fully involved or committed. In fact, it seems as if the youngsters were never expected to get very involved with anything provided for them by others. The message they received from their parents was that they were supposed to find something for themselves, on their own.

Adolescence

As the sculptors grew older and had more opportunities to act independently of their families, they moved in many different directions. As adolescents they were different from one another in many more ways than they were alike.

About five of the twenty noticeably isolated themselves from their peers, and from almost everyone else as well. These sculptors remember "it wasn't a happy time in my life" (A-11). Others became student leaders (student government, the school newspaper, varsity sports) in traditional, wholesome ways. "I tended to be a popular guy" (A-15). A few remember their adolescence as "teenagerhood" (A-6), defined by rock and roll music, dates, and cars. Finally there were a few for whom family problems or discipline problems were predominant concerns.

One-third of the teenagers did very well in school—"First in my class" (A-2), according to one. One A student explained her good grades this way:

> I was just a fanatic student. I liked it, but also I think that I was intimidated by the whole system. You know, I didn't want to fail (A-19).

At the other end of the grading continuum a few of the sculptors reported being terrible students. For these college-bound youngsters, being a terrible student meant "grades which were probably around the 73 or 74 average" (A-7). The rest, the majority, reported being average compared with their college-bound peers. "I was like a B everything . . . B student, B athlete, B person" (A-10).

INCREASING INVOLVEMENT WITH ART

What these adolescents had in common was an increasing involvement with art. They did more artwork, and their efforts became more systematic. They were more public about their artistic interests. They were identified as having art ability by others their own age and by their families. And they began to identify themselves as people who were at least moderately good at artwork. Of course all of this took place gradually, over a period of about six years.

Many of the changes that took place during this period can be outlined with a brief sketch of one sculptor's experiences. A-7 entered seventh grade with a history of drawing and painting, on his own, for pleasure. He was apparently uninterested in thinking seriously about his artwork or about how it fit within the discipline of art. He explained his level of art appreciation then by giving this account of a class trip to an important art museum, one of his first museum visits:

> We all basically looked at the tits on the sculpture and the guys' balls and couldn't believe it. So that was my experience with seeing art, and that was pretty much what I was interested in looking at at that time (A-7).

During junior high school he "started to do watercolors," emphasizing that medium over all others. "We lived in a beautiful country area, and I would walk over to the waterfront and sit down and do watercolors." When asked what he did with his work, he noted that at first, "I just put them away. And then I began showing them to friends."

His work was well received by his friends, although not necessarily for aesthetic reasons. He could do something that they couldn't. Most important for A-7 was that "my friends said, 'Oh, you do something special.' I mean part of it was that I began to sense an identity that I had as a result of doing this."

As A-7's art interests were recognized, "I began to broaden the network of people I knew making art." When he was sixteen, through "a friend of a friend" he learned about a summer art program for high school students run by a college not too far away. He decided that he ought to attend that summer program, where all he would do was make art, "and see if this was what I really wanted to do. And see if I should pursue it, and maybe I would go to school doing this."

The summer of intensive artwork did not make a dramatic change in A-7's life at the time. But he did decide to take an art class in school the following year. When the time came to make decisions about college, A-7 chose to study art at a school that had been highly recommended by a fellow student at the summer art program.

The specific experiences of doing watercolors or learning from "a friend of a friend" about a summer art program are unique to A-7. But his continued artwork, his recognition as an artist, and so on, are common to most of the sculptors' histories.

RECOGNITION FOR MAKING ART

The youngsters' interest in making art went public, so to speak. Sometimes this meant that they began showing their work, which they had previously kept to themselves. More often, it meant simply that their friends became conscious of the amount of artwork they were doing, just as they became conscious of the different skills and interests of each of their friends.

As the youngsters' art interests became more widely known,

they were identified as "the class artist" (A-10) or "the artist of the family" (A-3). They were referred to as "Rembrandt II" (A-11) or "poet and artist" (A-4) in a school yearbook, for instance. The power of the special label seems enormous, even though it had very little to do with art as the sculptors know it today or even as knowledgeable outsiders know art.

With the label came both privileges and burdens. "I did scenery for the school" (A-11). "If there was ever a special project, if the teacher ever wanted something special, a poster for a football game, I was always picked" (A-8). "I did all of the posters for all of the games, right? And all the decorations for all the dances. . . . I won't call it art, but lettering and building props and things" (A-19).

FEELING SPECIAL FOR MAKING ART

"I had a special thing I could do" (A-11), we heard again and again. "Art was the one thing I could do and [my sister] couldn't" (A-4). "When I found I could draw really well, nobody could beat me in that, . . . I really pursued that" (A-14).

The parents of one of the sculptors gave their child private lessons expressly because they wanted him to be able to feel the power of being able to do something that his brother could not do.

> When [the sculptor] was in junior high, we were concerned [about] this attitude he expressed as never being as good as [his older brother] or always feeling like maybe he was in the shadow. . . . It was then that we thought that we've got to give him interests that will separate them. Give him something that [his brother] doesn't know how to do. And art seemed to be something that he was interested in. I found a man who taught drawing in his home on Saturday. He was an artist who had become a commercial artist. So I took [the younger boy] there [M of A-3).

Being special for one's interest in art did not preclude being capable in other ways as well. The sculptor whose parents found a private art teacher for him when he was in junior high remembered his high school years this way:

> When I was in art classes, I was always better than most everyone else. . . . In everything else [in school] I was also always among the best (A-3).

Another sculptor reported,

> I was always first in my class—a respectable, nice kid. So no one could bark at me if I spent four hours in the art class whenever I felt like it after school (A-2).

Several of the youngsters excelled in athletics. "Being good in sports was a way of being accepted. . . . Art was just another sidelight of my personality" (A-5). Two were unusually good young musicians. "I was the best in music, [and] I was the best in art" (A-8).

For the most part, though, the sculptors with several areas of expertise thought of art as different from sports, music, and the like. The other activities were "something everyone else did, and I got into it too" (A-14). Art was an area that was their own. Art was not matter-of-factly provided for them, it was something they found for themselves.

THINKING OF THEMSELVES AS ARTISTS
The youngsters were formally and informally introduced to others with similar interests. They broadened the network of people they knew making art. Finally, they began trying out the label of artist on themselves, checking again and again, in different ways, to see how it fit.

How good were the young artists? They were "the best" or among the best of their peers. "Nobody could do it better" (A-14), according to one. Another reported,

> There were a couple of other kids who could draw better than me, I thought. They went on to art school too, and ended up working

for Walt Disney and things like that. So I would admire their work and they would admire mine (A-5).

Those who built, carved, or welded were not necessarily good at drawing; those who painted or sketched were not necessarily proficient in construction.

The sculptors were recognized as good artists by their peers and sometimes by their high school teachers. Not one was noticed by a professional artist or art critic. But since their lives did not overlap with the world of professional artists, they didn't need that kind of recognition to think of themselves and feel good about themselves as artists. They never even noticed its absence.

PARENTAL INVOLVEMENT

The sculptors were evenly divided between those whose parents were noticeably helpful to their artistic development during this period and those whose parents provided little if any assistance. The parents who were supporting and encouraging their child's art activities did so in several different ways. Five families found special art instruction for their children during this period. They found museum classes, special high school programs, and weekend or evening classes taught by artists who were supplementing their incomes.

The sculptors remembered the classes primarily as a low-key introduction to the world of art. There, they tried out materials not available to them at home or in school, or drew from live models for the first time, or were given an "insider's" tour of a museum. They met others their own age and older who shared an ongoing interest in making art of one kind of another. Two recall being aware that their teachers were professional artists.

The fact that the parents did find art classes for their children seems to have been far more important than what took place during these classes. Art instruction was not easy to find. Very few of the children in a community or of a certain age were taking art classes. The parents had to make an effort to find the classes, and the youngsters knew that something out of the ordinary was being done for them, maybe even because *they* were out of the ordinary.

> My mother decided that I should have formal training with a professional artist and was willing to cart me that distance, which was more than an hour away through heavy traffic (A-8).

> [My mother] was willing to help me find something. And she really did make that effort. . . . As kind of meager as it sounds, I mean going to [certain] art classes, it proved to be important in getting me one step further (A-17).

Other parents went out of their way to provide their child with equipment or a setting especially helpful for the youngster's artistic development. For instance, one sculptor was given a small set of welding equipment for Christmas when he was sixteen, a set that only burned acetylene. His father taught him how to use the equipment safely, and then left the son pretty much on his own. "Then it was the following birthday that I got the oxygen to go along with it. . . . So that was the way it went" (A-19). Another father who was a carpenter of sorts converted the attic in the home into an art studio for the sculptor (A-14) we interviewed and his younger brother. There, in addition to painting and drawing during high school, the teenager learned how to stretch a canvas and how to build his own stretcher bars.

That the teenagers' work was displayed prominently was also seen as a symbol of support.

> We'd put [my drawings] up all around the house. [My parents] weren't concerned about only having the masters around the house—my work was up all over. I'd do a painting in high school and it would take the prime space in the family room (A-3).

More than one of the sculptors has come to regret, on occasion, that show of support.

I painted a lot of horses, a lot of landscapes, and a lot of flowers. Eck. . . . My mother still has it hanging on the walls. Going home is a major trauma. . . . Last year I went camping with . . . one of my mentors and favorite teachers and two graduate students from here. They met us for dinner . . . at my mother's house. Here was all this stuff on the walls. I was just humiliated [laughs]. . . . Everybody was too kind to say anything, you know. Probably their mothers are the same way (A-19).

ART IN THE HIGH SCHOOL

It was very difficult to get any information about art classes the sculptors may have taken as part of their junior and senior high school program. Fourteen of the twenty sculptors did have some sort of art instruction in school. Another studied architecture, not art. The remaining quarter of the group had no art instruction in school, or nothing they could remember. ("I don't even remember. I'm sure it wasn't much" [A-17].)

Three or four of the individuals who did have art instruction in school remember taking an art class almost every year, and one had more than one art class during her last two years of high school. The rest reported experiences like this: "I had one art class in junior high school which was not particularly important, and I had one industrial arts woodshop class. . . . I was an average shop student" (A-18). The sculptors had little of substance to say about these experiences. One who talked most easily about her classes summarized her experiences, and those of most in the group, this way: "You know, the kind of art that you're fed . . . in the public schools is pretty schmaltzy" (A-19).

Art was not considered by the schools to be an academic subject. The students typically thought art to be "the class you took to get credit and not do anything, . . . for flunkies" (A-12). "The art classes were filled with people who weren't going to college" (A-4). The sculptors did not remember anything particularly challenging or informative about the classes. They drew from still lifes and models, and did "projects." "Today, class, we're going to do moods" (A-8).

The biggest problem with the classes, the predominant reason for the sculptors' indifference to them, seems to be that the teachers treated art as a set of crafts, perhaps because they were not professional artists themselves. Art did not involve serious thought and discussion, nor did it seem to be an activity with a future. One sculptor explained the situation this way:

> In high school, art is such a confined subject. It's nothing you can really strive to be. And then I went to college and these were professional artists who were teaching. . . . That really made it come alive (A-3).

Another sculptor reported this predicament. His high school art teacher "sort of told me I was pretty good. I don't think she told me about going to art school or talked to me about that at all" (A-14). "The guidance counselor didn't tell you" either. The youngster knew he was very good at art. However, "I didn't know what I could do with it, where I could take it" (A-14).

PLANNING FOR COLLEGE
When the teenagers finished high school, there was still little evidence to suggest that they might someday achieve unusual artistic success. They had not been noticed and specially encouraged by professional artists, art critics, or even, for the most part, by local art teachers. No one in the know had suggested to them where and with whom to study for the best possible professional art education.

Seventy percent (N = 14) were headed for college with "the idea of being an art major" (A-9), but it was a very vague idea. (Only two of these went to schools that were exclusively for art education.) Two others intended more specifically to study architecture—"only because it had implications of making money" (A-14). There was, therefore, some commitment to the study of art. Only four were not even thinking about it, and one of these was not headed for college. The strength of the commitment, however, is better judged by noting that the adolescents did *not* choose the college they would attend on the basis of the quality of art education they might receive at those schools.[3]

Although the teenagers had a predilection for making art, they had little experience with the study of art and an equally limited idea of what such study might involve. By customary criteria they were not even well qualified for professional studies: Most had no portfolio to show an art school admissions committee, had few high school art classes on their high school transcript (and not always a grade of A for the few classes they did take) and had no letters of recommendation from art teachers or artists.

Their lack of credentials was almost always matched with a lack of direction for their lives. Their parents had not suggested a direction, so there was nothing for them to follow or even to rebel against. Although they enjoyed making art, they did not yet realize the possibilities inherent in the study and practice of art. The teenagers knew they were headed for college, but even that was a very hazy goal, as one can see in the way the choice of college was made.

"I wasn't very directed about it" (A-6). "I went to [school name] for not very specific reasons" (A-10). "My parents mostly chose it" (A-4). "That was really parental advice" (A-9). "Where I went to school did not seem to be one of the important decisions in my life" (A-8).

If the parents felt strongly about a particular school or type of school, the adolescents went along with those preferences. In one instance there was a "family" school; two or three parents suggested Ivy League schools or schools of that sort. The next most likely determining factors were proximity and cost: "My father just didn't want me to go away my first year" (A-

---

[3]It is not obvious how they would have done so, even if they had wanted to. Neither the parents nor the youngsters had yet acquired much knowledge about the art world or professional art education. Nor were there people readily available to whom they could turn for information.

1). "We were poor and it was [only] fifty dollars a semester and it was about half a mile away" (A-19). Artistic concerns influenced the choices only when a final decision had to be made between two schools that seemed very much the same. "[The chosen school] had a whole building for its art department, so it looked more impressive [than the second choice]" (A-4).

SUMMARY OF THE ADOLESCENT YEARS

When the sculptors left high school, there were still no clear signs of the successes they would realize. Neither they nor their parents would have predicted their later accomplishments. But their subsequent development is not entirely a mystery. A solid foundation had been laid for artistic development. Several features or characteristics of the adolescents' experiences seem especially important.

Although many young children draw, sketch, build, and so on, the sculptors continued doing artwork through their adolescence, when such activities often fall by the wayside. They enjoyed it. Some had adult models to follow—they saw parents, uncles, or godfathers making art for their own pleasure. The rest were never discouraged, never made to question the appropriateness of their activities.

Making art was a natural part of their lives. It was more than a school activity or a weekly after-school lesson, it was theirs to do after their obligations had been met. The adolescents didn't think about it; they made art matter-of-factly, whenever they felt like doing so and wherever they were. It was part of who they were and how they lived.

The sculptors were well rewarded for their art activity—perhaps more so during their adolescence than they had been earlier. Consider the following sorts of benefits that accrued to many of the adolescents:

- An identity for oneself
- A sense of competence, of ability and adequacy
- The chance to feel special in at least one way, different from and perhaps better than brothers and sisters or classmates

- Out-of-the-ordinary treatment in school and at home (e.g., being allowed to miss a class in order to direct the construction of scenery for a school play, or having one's work displayed prominently at home and hearing parents brag about one's talent)

Finally, the youngsters had not developed an equally strong attachment to anything else. There was nothing else competing for their wholehearted involvement. Some of the teenagers were quite good at other things—academics, sports, music—but for a variety of reasons, they didn't feel committed to those activities, nor even especially certain about their successes in them. Some reported that the other activities were not as meaningful as art because they were "something everyone else did" (A-14). Others favored an activity that was important to their parents over one emphasized in school. "[Music] came out of the schools. The art thing was encouraged at home, but as I say, not in the schools" (A-8).

Still others reported not feeling especially competent in other areas despite considerable evidence that might have suggested otherwise to a different teenager. One sculptor reported this experience, for instance: As a senior in high school he

> won the gold medal in the state competition for my event. . . . That's some success. I wasn't Olympic material, but I won the state. And [state] was a tough league, and I was always fairly proud of that achievement (A-18).

When asked how he knew he wasn't Olympic material, he gave the following explanation:

> You know these things. You start to know what the top is in anything that you're very involved in. . . . You're talking about a sport that took up four or five months of the year, every afternoon after school, for two and a half hours. And you played against other people who were going through that very strict kind of training. And you knew who was really good (A-18).

Another sculptor, who as a youngster was a tennis player, "had a state ranking when I was twelve. Which means nothing. I mean I got to go to the State [annual tournament] and got my ears torn off. I drew the top seed . . . he was great" (A-9). These are the most obvious examples of youngsters who might have created an identity for themselves from something other than art. They give a variety of explanations why they were not able to do so, none of which really seems to explain well enough. How it happens that a person feels very competent in one area and not very competent in another, although objective evidence would suggest the reverse, is a problem beyond the scope of this study. What matters here is that as high school graduates the one activity the youngsters were most attracted to and felt best about doing was making art.

Although the youngsters were without the official credentials often used to separate those who will study art from those who won't, they were well prepared to become artists nonetheless. They did have the combination of basic skills and motivation necessary for successful study. "It's not really how much formal training that I'd had. It's that I had always painted and sketched" (A-8). "I think that I probably did know what my strong cards were somehow" (A-17). They needed to study art, however. In fact they needed to study with certain kinds of teachers in a certain kind of environment.

Advanced Art Education: Becoming a Student of Art

All but one of the sculptors did study art in a degree-granting institution. Three-quarters of the artists have earned master's degrees in fine arts (MFAs).[4] They did not necessarily begin their formal art education immediately after high school, however, nor did they always earn their undergraduate degrees with a major in the fine arts.

---

[4]One of the sculptors does not have a degree in art.

The route was circuitous for some. For instance, "I started in the university to be an architect. . . . I transferred into psychology . . . and then into the art department" (A-5). Another individual worked for three years after high school, then went to college intending to study history. He earned a college degree in sociology before proceeding to art school, where he completed both a BFA and an MFA.

For others the route was as direct as graduating from high school in June and enrolling in art school (or entering the art department of a college or university) the following September.

> When I got there, I knew it was absolutely right for me. It was like a door opened. . . . I knew I was with people with whom I could identify. . . . I think it was just that the shoe fit and I was lucky to have found it (A-17).

Getting to just any kind of art school or art department was not enough. One of the several sculptors who transferred from one school to another noted that art classes at the first college "were more for people that were involved with education and would go out and teach. It wasn't for artists" (A-1). That kind of education wasn't for these students.

There was, apparently, a rather specific environment crucial at this point for the sculptors' development. The environment included teachers who were professional artists themselves, fellow students who also aspired to making good art, and some sort of network for information about the art world that existed beyond the students' immediate horizons. It was within this kind of setting that the students worked day and night, learning to be artists.

ARTISTS AS TEACHERS

If one had to select the most important part of the sculptors' professional art education, it would probably be the fact that they all had teachers who were, first and foremost, professional artists. "First stringers. They were all pros. . . . I've never had a teacher who was an educator first and a professional second" (A-15). The professional status of their teachers was pointed out by one sculptor after another.

Being surrounded by professional artists, the students realized that there was a future for them in art, there was something to strive for. One sculptor explained the importance of a particular teacher this way:

> He was an artist first, and he did teaching second. He was treated like an artist. . . . Somehow that appealed to me. That was the first time I had seen something that matched up with what I had in mind (A-12).

The teachers laid bare the life of an artist, and "they seemed to have a really good life between their teaching and their studio" (A-10). They also modeled the process of being an artist.

> The teachers there were such good teachers because they made their art there. And you saw the whole process. From beginning to make it, to crating it and shipping it, to the opening, and then reading the reviews. And you saw the whole thing (A-19).

> [Teacher] was an artist in his own right . . . [and] his studio was right adjacent to the studio where we worked as students. And he made things. And we saw his things coming and going. . . . Knowing that [teacher] was in there was a big thing for me (A-18).

The sculptors talked about the importance of teachers who are "absolutely committed to what they are doing . . . because you get it. The attitude and the commitment" (A-12). The professional teachers inspired and energized their students.

> You weren't just getting people who were coming in and doing their 6 hours or 9 hours or whatever they had to do. They were telling us what they believed in, and that was about art. And that was the exciting part. And they turned us all on . . . It's like being stagestruck (A-17).

About one-third of the sculptors had the opportunity for an apprenticeship of sorts with one of the professionals. For instance, one student spent two summers working with one of the "founders of contemporary sculpture."

> Someone asked me if I wanted to work for him, and I said, "Are you kidding? I'll work free." As it turned out, it was a very nice situation. . . . We had lunch every day, and that made for conversation and comradery instead of . . . a straight boss/worker situation. . . . It's the same relationship that a younger heart surgeon has with an elder heart surgeon. . . . It was an apprenticeship in a way. . . . I wasn't his protégé, I was his worker, but it's a good position to be in (A-15).

Some of the sculptors had little more than the short, formal contacts of studio classes with their artist-teachers. That was good enough. "I mean he was a very important person in the art world. And the fact that he was teaching at that school, it was the spirit of it or something" (A-7).

The professional artists set high standards for their students, because their own standards were high. "The demands were enormous. I mean I remember staying up until four or five in the morning, and loving it" (A-17). The atmosphere was rich in energy and ideas. "You grew up fast. Your teachers were professionals. We went to New York. We saw the shows. I knew what was going on" (A-8). One sculptor made the importance of studying with professional artists seem suddenly so obvious when he asked, "If you don't have contact with someone who is doing good work, how do you know what's possible?" (A-3).

We probably cannot overestimate how important the artist-teachers were to the process of exceptional development. They not only created a context for successful learning (inspiring, modeling, setting high standards), but they also provided individual assistance and encouragement in many different ways. Teachers told students about special summer programs (one at Skowhegan and another at Yale, for instance) and arranged for them to take part in these intensive workshops. These programs exposed the students to other professional artists and serious students, and to the different perspectives different artists bring to their work. Teachers helped some of the students get into important graduate school programs when the students had neither enough artwork nor good enough work to justify their admission. In a few instances teachers arranged for their students' work to be shown, and, they all hoped, to be reviewed by art critics.

Almost all of the artists singled out at least one teacher as having a powerful impact on their lives.[5] They talked of "key pivotal people in my life, in terms of mentors. . . . My definition is someone who is exemplary in some way, and who a person strives to be like" (A-17). "[One teacher] decided it in that sense for me. As soon as I was involved with that class, that's what I wanted to do" (A-18). "Knowing [teacher], I think that he is one of those people who couldn't not change your life" (A-8).

WORKING INTENSELY AND WITH ONE'S PEERS

The artist-teachers created an environment within which one could learn a great deal about making good art. The students helped each other make sense of the environment and use it to their best advantage.

> It was the other students who were, in a way, the most important teachers. Because they are more on your level. They are the ones there at three in the morning working too. And they are the ones you learn from. You know, you learn big things from your teachers but you learn the everyday things from other students (A-19).

"They were just as serious as I was," one sculptor noted about a small group of his fellow students. "We would talk a lot . . . we fed off each other. We perpetuated each other" (A-5).

---

[5] Two mentioned the same teacher. They worked with him in different years at different schools.

Two sculptors gave very similar accounts of a friendly competition between peers that is both instructive and energizing:

> [My friend] would call me up and say, "Come see my newest work." And I would think, "Boy, I've got to work harder, faster, because she just finishing something." It was very good (A-4).

> I think there's a lot of competition among artists, but hopefully it's a healthy kind of competition, which is really nice. . . . When somebody does something really good and everybody else turns around and says, "That's incredible." And then they rush home to make something better. That happens a lot and that's great (A-6).

A few of the sculptors remember becoming "the star" (A-2) in their art classes. The sculptors were more likely to report "I was not the student who won any of the awards of the school" (A-7). The same sculptor told the interviewer,

> The class I was in . . . there are a handful of people who could be within your group [for this research on outstanding artistic development]. They are among the top. . . . We all probably showed the potential in some way, but none of us were singled out at that time (A-7).

Another sculptor who was at the same school (although for different years) found, at the beginning, "there were some people remarkably talented, who would touch anything and it would turn out great. I was not one of those people. I didn't have . . . what they call facility" (A-10). But he and most of the other sculptors found that facility was not enough to make a great artist. "Your ideas play into it . . . and determination" (A-10). In his class of twenty "some people were in the studios until ten at night, some of them were out partying." He, like most of the other artists we talked with, was in the studio.

> I didn't really have any idea that I had any talent until I got to college. Now I know that essentially anybody has talent—it's a matter of drive and allowing yourself to think that way and get involved with certain ideas (A-1).

I became so hungry to know everything about it. I read every art magazine, every art book that I could. . . . I'd stay up until three or four in the morning doing drawings, and the next day go to school, and come back and continue working (A-5).

I stayed up night and day. It was no longer just a course. It was no longer just getting through. [I was] painting all night. Going through every book in the library. I mean really doing it (A-8).

More than anything it is perseverance and hard work (A-4).

The sculptors generously acknowledged the dedication and the talent of their fellow students. About one-third were both surprised and grateful to have studied with a group of students who "are among the top" (A-9) or "who would eventually make it in the art world" (A-17).[6] "It's interesting how these little groups gather" (A-8), reflected one artist as she recited the names of several fellow students who have gone on to unusual success in different kinds of art. Another sculptor reported,

A surprising portion of the graduate students . . . are still making art. . . . I'd say at least 75% are doing quite well and selling their work. And I bet 95% of them are still at least making art. Which is really unusual. The school was really special . . . at that point (A-19).

DEVELOPING PROFESSIONAL SKILLS AND ATTITUDES

The half-dozen years of observing and working with professional artists as well as learning from and competing with fellow students were referred to as "very intense" (A-2) years. The agenda for those years included learning the language, the history, the rituals, and the techniques of making good art. It also included, toward the end, learning how to get the good art one made into the marketplace.

---

[6]The sample for this study included sculptors who studied in the same schools or with the same teacher in different years, although it did not include sculptors who studied with one another.

There was an official comprehensive introduction into the language, history, rituals, and techniques for some of the sculptors.

> It was called the Foundation, the course we all take.... It provided you with a foundation for anything that you might do. And what that included was a history of art, a color course, a two-dimensional design course, a three-dimensional design course, maybe print-making—I'm not certain—but figure drawing. It was something that you could build on it whatever direction you moved in (A-17).

As a rule the sculptors have all done some work in each of those areas. They created their own "core" program, when it was not officially required, sampling different aspects of art as the need or interest arose.

A considerable portion of the sculptors' professional education seems to have involved doing "projects." The students were given tasks intended to teach them how to work with either specific materials or specific art concepts. "You were given a project and it had to be in metal . . ." (A-14).

> He said, "Well, I see that you have had experience in taking away material. But you've never done anything where you have to build up." He said, "That's more interesting in sculpture today." He said, "I want to give you something and I want you to work with it." . . . Four months later I had built this thing . . . (A-18).

> The first couple of years we had projects . . . [to] teach you to get your hands to do what your brain wanted them to do, or your eye. . . . It was exercises. . . . Then we [gradually were expected] to rely on our own ideas (A-10).

Work on these tasks was often done in the presence of other students, in large rooms (studios) provided for the students by their school. Professors would observe the students' work and comment on it from time to time, and be available to discuss problems the student was having as the problems arose.

There's no one standing over your shoulder showing you how to do certain things. . . . If they saw something good about something you were doing, a painting or a drawing, they would show you how to make it better. . . . We were taught certain skills and certain techniques pertaining to sculpture—carving or welding or whatever. And then you were allowed to explore personal ideas that you had (A-14).

After several years of formal schooling the students heard much less about skills and techniques and much more about "issues in art and how to relate to them" (A-14). Many became intensely involved with art history or art criticism for a while—not for the subject matter itself but for how it might help them make better art. "Students on a graduate level get caught up in what people who came before them think and say" (A-15).

Several of the artists were so intensely involved with what people before them had done that they found themselves copying other artists. Now, instead of trying to reproduce a comic strip as they had done when they were younger, they were trying to reproduce the work of Jackson Pollock and other important artists. "I wanted to make Giacometti things. I made some Henry Moore things" (A-9). Their copying was more sophisticated now. Simply reproducing an artwork was no longer enough. They were trying to understand "what's the essence of Giacometti, what's the essence of Rubens" (A-7). The copying was done "before you realize how to separate influences, or how to learn from influences in a richer and more subtle way" (A-9).

Some of the artists were not aware, while they were making the art, that they were imitating other artists. They "discovered," after the fact, that they had "gone through a Jackson Pollock stage . . . an early Picasso stage . . . [before I] sort of settled into my [own] stage" (A-20). Whether the imitating was conscious or not, it was a phase that many of the sculptors went through and then outgrew.

Through projects, classes, relations with teachers, the

"copying" of other artists and informal discussions the students slowly learned the language, the history, the rituals, and the techniques of making art. "I began to pick up on certain key ideas and concepts" (A-7). "My professional awareness was formed" (A-18).

Eventually the sculptors had to create work that was uniquely their own. They report that the ideas for their work come "probably from looking at other stuff" (A-9), but the problems the artists find, and the solutions they propose, are expected to be unique.

> In art you make up your own problems. And the art problems usually come from the immediate history. . . . If on the walls of Fifty-seventh Street they're hanging abstract expressionist paintings, the [art student] will usually pick up from that point and say, "Now where do I take Jackson Pollock from here? What do I do next?" (A-8).

Many of the sculptors credited the camaraderie and competition with their peers as an important part of learning how to find and solve their own problems. They reported that the intense and extended discussions with fellow students forced them to move beyond imitating artwork they saw in books or on the walls of galleries and museums.

> We would constantly tear each other's work apart. We were very good friends, but we would say terrible things about each other's work. They became my conscience. . . . It's very hard to get away with anything when you have three of your best friends asking why you did that. [You can't say], "I saw it in an art magazine" (A-5).

DECIDING TO BE A SCULPTOR

When the artists began their professional studies, they were intent on making art, seldom on making a particular form of art.[7] "I had no idea my interests would be sculpture" (A-15). At

---

[7]Two of the twenty artists have always focused their efforts almost entirely on sculpture.

that point, one could hardly expect them to know what their specific interests would be because they knew so little about what was possible.

Most of the artists studied painting, and were good painters, before they shifted to making sculpture. The study of painting before sculpture was seldom their own decision. It was decided for them by artists and art educators. "Education is very painting oriented" (A-3). "[Painting] is the one media that's cheap to do and easily understood and accessible. And that's the one thing they start you out with" (A-19). Furthermore, "to be taken seriously as an artist you had to be a painter. So I was a painter" (A-11).

It is said to be much easier to teach principles of art through painting than through sculpture. Students can typically make paintings faster than they can make sculpture. Thus, given an equal amount of time for formal education, students who paint can be given more "lessons" than students who sculpt. It is usually less expensive to paint than to sculpt, and the former almost always requires less working space than the latter.

Some of the artists painted for only a short time before they shifted to sculpture (or to pottery and then to sculpture). More than half were still painting when they went to graduate school. Only one continues to paint now—to earn the money that provides her with the time and materials for making sculpture.

The shift from painting to sculpture was a process of learning more and more about making art until one could decide what particular form of art seemed best suited for one's own strengths and interests.

Certain people are more interested in color. . . . Certain people are more interested in form. And certain people are more interested in space. These are all elements of art. And as you proceed, you discover what you're most interested in. Certain artists are more involved in black and white. . . . I'm not color. I am space. Black and white. Okay, and then you discover how you are going to do that (A-8).

Painting didn't have that magic. . . . The two-dimensional aspect of it made it not so exciting. I was not a particularly good colorist. It just wasn't the right thing for me, and sculpture was (A-10).

The decision to make sculpture rather than to paint was more often worked out than thought out.

I started making pictures that became more and more three-dimensional. That meant that they were painted reliefs. Reliefs that started coming off the wall, and I started painting them and kept painting them. And eventually they took on a three-dimensional presence of their own. They were no longer on the wall, they were objects (A-17).

It was like the surface wasn't enough. I wanted to see behind [the painting] and on the side (A-20).

With me it happened to be making a painting and then realizing that the stretcher bars on the canvas were what made up the painting. That meant that as soon as you got interested in the fact that there was a structure that made the painting, you could alter the structure. So the painting started to become more pieces of wood with canvas on them, and they became more three-dimensional objects. I was doing painting, and it wasn't quite doing what I wanted it to do, so I altered the painting, and the painting turned into sculpture (A-6).

The paintings got bigger and bigger. I got into seventy-foot paintings. I got to the point where you couldn't build stretchers. I mean, they were being built in sections. I was having engineers design them. . . . And it just got to be a problem. A technical problem. The canvas would sag. . . . And I realized that what I was doing was working with space. The paintings I was doing were spatial. . . . It was so big that it was changing as you—if you looked at it from here, it would be one thing. Well, this was all intentional. If you looked at it from the middle, it was going out of your field of vision. And I realized that what I was doing was making sculpture on canvas. The walking was really the essential thing about it. And at that point I began doing things out in the landscape (A-8).

Interestingly, the artists were divided on whether or not the physical nature of sculpture was important to them. Some reported that since they had always been interested in building, constructing, and generally working with their hands, it was natural that they would prefer sculpture over other forms of art.

> I think my interest had always been in more physical interests and relationships to things. Being more physically involved (A-12).

> I wanted to go into three-dimensional work because I can change it. . . . I could manipulate the object itself as opposed to working toward an end (A-5).

On the other hand, some reported that the process was of little importance to them, the product was everything. They were perfectly happy conceiving the work and leaving most of the physical construction to students or laborers they hired when they could afford to do so.

> I was always interested in the object. Its size, its shape, its gesture, versus my size and shape and gesture, and me the viewer, . . . are more important than the making. . . . I want the situation more than I want the activity. . . . The work that I've done the past five or six years is conceived, then the factory stamps it out of metal . . . (A-15).

> I don't have the attitude about work that physical work for its own sake is good. I came to making sculpture [for the results]. I made painting and I probably would have preferred to continue painting because it's easier. You don't have to work as hard (A-6).

PARENTAL INVOLVEMENT

Many of the sculptors' parents seem to have been surprised and uncomfortable when their college-age child began to study art exclusively.

They had no objections to it in terms of what it is as a moral act
. . . they're just concerned about making money, enough money to
get by. When I was younger, it was not a big problem, because it's
good for a kid to have an art interest. There's no reason to believe
he's going to be foolish enough to choose it as a way of life. . . .
[Later, my mother would] tell me about this lawyer friend of
theirs who was an artist in college. And architecture, they thought,
would be at least a little more reasonable. But I wasn't heavily
pressured at all (A-3).

Being happy and enjoying what one was doing was less on
the parents' minds now than that their children earn a decent
living.

My father [was] basically saying, "Alright, enough of this already.
Great, so you made the Dean's List. That's wonderful. You got into
Yale [for graduate work], that's just great. We're very proud of
you. *But*, the bottom line is, what are you going to do to support
yourself when it really comes time to do that? Come on, you've got
to start realizing that I'm not going to just pay the money continually." Right until the time when I was twenty-five years old and
my work was shown in the Guggenheim and I was chosen as one
of the ten artists throughout the whole country [for that show]
(A-7).

[My mother] would worry about me being an artist. . . . "How are
you going to make a living?" . . . "Can you take courses on architecture?" She was really obsessed with this architecture (A-10).

For the most part the parents did not work hard to dissuade
their child from pursuing a life as an artist, they just offered
some "practical advice."

Practical advice, like, well, it's probably not a good idea to be an
artist because you can't make any money, so maybe you should
figure out something else you can make money at and be an artist
as well (A-6).

At one point my father said, "Well, you know, I'd like you to take
some drafting courses. Because if you end up, you might find it to

your advantage to be an architect and do this on the side so you can make a living. Not a whole lot of sculptors make a living." . . . I didn't take them. And he never said anything about it (A-9).

A few parents do seem to have become very angry at their child's decision to work toward being a professional artist, and they made their displeasure clear to the aspiring artist for several years. The majority, however, took the decision in stride. They provided financial assistance (for school tuition, art supplies, studio space, and sometimes just so that the artist would be able to work full-time at making art) when it was possible for them to do so. The families without money to spare made space available for the student to work in, found alternative and inexpensive art materials, and, most important, provided continual emotional support.

The parents were not able to teach their children about making art. However they were both willing and able to learn from them. According to one mother, "I really learned a lot about it . . . and I could follow his talk about certain artists or this and that" (M of A-10). The sculptors were delighted with their parents' involvement and growth. "My mother is totally aficionado now. She joined the museum. . . . She keeps abreast of contemporary art now" (A-19). "[Mother] has actually gotten interested in it, in a more intellectual way. And she spends a lot of time going to museums now and looking at what's going on and reading about different works" (A-6).

SUMMARY OF ADVANCED ART EDUCATION
There are several noteworthy characteristics of the artists' later years of learning. First, they studied with one or more teachers who were established artists. These teachers modeled professional behavior. They introduced the sculptors to the people, the institutions, and the experiences central to the world of art. They pushed the students to think and act like professionals.

Second, there was almost always someone supporting and encouraging the sculptors' efforts and helping them move one step further than they were already. "Sometimes it was a teacher. A lot of times it was friends or other artists . . . different people at different times. . . . A lot of it was emotional support" (A-11). Some sculptors were especially grateful for the financial as well as the emotional support they got from their parents. Others spoke at length about practical support from teachers who arranged for their admission into graduate schools, first shows, reviews by art critics, and so on.

Third, the sculptors had the good fortune to study with other students who were also serious about making art. The students provided emotional and technical support for one another while they struggled with their teachers' high standards and demands. They also pushed one another to the limits of their respective abilities, and helped one another stretch those limits. The quality of the fellow students, as well as the quality of the teachers, created a rich atmosphere for learning to make good art.

Finally, the sculptors worked day and night—making art, studying art, arranging for showings, and so on. They were ambitious. "Ambitious to be a great artist, not [simply] to have a great reputation" (A-8). They were willing to make the persistent and consistent effort necessary to realize their ambitions.

From Art Student to Artist

MAKING A COMMITMENT

I didn't know I wanted to be an artist really until my senior year in college. . . . I realized that it was probably the only thing I could do with my life, realistically. It wasn't a choice that I made. I gave into it is what happened (A-19).

Choices had been made along the way of course—to take art classes, to spend more time making art than doing anything else, to major in art while in college. Typically, those decisions had been made without conscious awareness that they set a direction for one's life. Furthermore, those were decisions about being an art student, which is not at all the same as being an artist. When the sculptors did, finally, find a direction for their lives, they were often surprised by what seemed so obvious. "I suppose it almost felt like I fell back into what I had been doing all along" (A-2).

The decision to try to become an artist was "a progressive or sequential revelation. It's nothing like a blinding flash. It didn't happen at any one time" (A-18). The same sculptor reflected,

> It was clear that in high school if I had wanted to pursue something that would have been very social—if I had wanted to go into politics—I probably could have. In college, if I had wanted to go into the life sciences or gone into anthropology or archeology, I probably could have. And when it came up sculpture, I don't know. I suppose it was a kinship with *things*, and the business of making. . . . And then this bloodline of people (A-18).

At least half of the artists clearly could have done something other than make art. One surely would have been a fine musician. Several had the option of joining a family business. Others could have pursued those things that students with top grades from top universities go on to do with their lives. Few were aware of their options, however. Their lives had become steeped in making art.

> It was an accumulative experience. You meet more and more people who had bigger and better dreams and knew more and more about the art world, and it all rubbed off. It was always something up there, something to grasp at, something you didn't have yet but you knew smelled right. It looked tantalizing, and I just went after it (A-17).

When they found their direction, they "went after it" ferociously. "What I got at [school] was the absolute determination to be an artist, no matter what" (A-8). "I had a stake in it . . . and I had to pursue it. I had to push. I had nothing else to do. I didn't want to do anything else" (A-5). "It would have been absolutely unacceptable for it not to work out, just absolutely unacceptable" (A-4). Even when their early artwork was undistinguished, the sculptors themselves were noteworthy for their energy and the intensity with which they worked. "I just did everything one hundred percent" (A-12).

LEARNING TO LIVE IT

There's the book-learning aspect, there's the training-the-hand aspect . . . but the step beyond all that is learning to live it (A-8).

It is fortunate for the artists that they were intensely determined—it may even have been essential that they were so committed—because part of "learning to live it" means making art day after day, month after month, usually with very little feedback. When there is feedback, it is not always positive and encouraging.

"The thing about being an artist is that you just have to keep doing it" (A-6). "If you don't have the self-motivation and the self-discipline to continue doing it, no one cares" (A-11).

You have to have discipline and you have to have this total belief in what you're doing. The results are not absolute like in math. It's not always that way in art. Nor are the gratifications sure or constant. . . . People who make terrible, terrible stuff often make a lot of money, and there are great artists you've never seen or heard of. I think a lot of that kind of stuff [gratifications] comes from within (A-10).

The sculptors' ambitions kept them working day after day. So did the community of artists.

There's a large group of artists, and you get to know people who are doing some of the same activities you are. . . . You meet other members of your own peer group. And they become your educative process. And the interaction with them becomes your grounding. . . . We would boost each other along. . . . In the beginning it's one person helping another (A-6).

Being in [an art] community was incredibly important for me, because it was feedback (A-9).

Again and again I keep going back to the current scene. And I think the most important thing about being an artist is being *there*, and knowing the people, seeing what's going on (A-8).

Almost all of the artists faced a test of their commitment to living the life of an artist.

I actually had to struggle very hard for about seven or eight years after I was out of school. Partially it had to do with really floundering around for personal identity as well as artistic identity. It wasn't at all easy for me when I got out of school (A-17).

You just hang in there. And you just wait. And sooner or later something comes along. You make the most of whatever you get. That's all you can do. You just keep working and you just keeping hanging in there and you just keep waiting. And I guess for some people it takes longer than for others (A-8).

Those who felt reasonably successful often talked about being lucky. But they added that they prepared themselves to be lucky, and worked hard to take advantage of the chance opportunities that came their way.

I've had this uncanny luck at always being at the right place at the right time with the right people. Through no fault of my own. I mean it is totally odd how things have fallen into place for me. . . . I stumbled into things. . . . So I can't really say that it is because it's something that I alone have done. It's really fortunate. But some of the students that I was with that really didn't make it maybe weren't that excited about what they were doing and they weren't really willing to work hard. I mean it's just the old Protestant ethic (A-19).

I also had amazing luck. . . . There's a certain amount of being in the right place at the right time. There are an awful lot of good artists, and some will be discovered and some won't. . . . Once you're given your chance, you have to have the goods or it doesn't amount to anything, but I've always been under a lucky star (A-10).

Lucky star or not, the sculptors are well aware of how long and hard they have worked to earn a place of respect in the art world.

> I still get reviewed as a young artist. . . . I'm middle-aged [forty]. I've been showing in New York for, like, ten years, showing here and internationally. . . and I still get this thing of "young artist." I just think it's very funny (A-11).

Although they are known as "young artists" to the older, more established artists who have honored them with Guggenheim Fellowships and the like, many are no longer young men or women.

Some of the sculptors are reasonably well recognized now; others are still struggling. They all seem convinced that they are doing what they want to do, what makes them happy, and that it is worth continuing no matter what their level of public recognition.

"I am absolutely secure in the fact that I am doing what I should be doing" (A-8). "Nobody calls me in the morning and says, 'Hey, it's time to mix that concrete, kid.' . . . Nobody asks you to do it, nobody needs you to do it. You do it because you want to do it" (A-20).

> For me it's a question of interest. I mean if it keeps my attention and I'm interested in doing it, then it's really a fulfilling thing to do. And making art does that. I'm always fascinated with it. So that's why I do it (A-6).

> [My work] really means something to me. And I think I always have stuck with making art that I wanted to do. . . . I think the fact that I found a personal image that was satisfying is part of my reason for success. Because it really wasn't for anybody else. It was really wonderful when other people responded, but that was never really the issue. It was for myself. And it was sustaining (A-19).

All of the sculptors are practicing professional artists. They "tend to be a little obsessive about art . . . to think about it all the time" (A-2). They do what they enjoy, and they do it very well.

5

★ ★ ★ ★ ★ ★

The Development of Olympic Swimmers

Anthony G. Kalinowski

The initial pool of subjects contacted for the study of swimming talent consisted of twenty-four freestyle sprinters (male and female) who had been members of at least one of the 1968, 1972, or 1976 Olympic swim teams for the U.S.A. Success at the Olympic Games in no way affected the selection of the subjects for this study; some of the swimmers we talked to did extremely well in their events; others not nearly as well as they had hoped. Twelve of the initial set of possible subjects were men, twelve were women. All were between the ages of eighteen and thirty-four when contacted.

At the study's end, twenty-one of the twenty-four swimmers and one or both of their parents had been interviewed. The final sample consisted of ten male and eleven female Olympic freestyle sprinters.[1] The interviews with the swimmers followed an interview guide and typically lasted one and a half to two hours.

---

[1] All but six of the swimmers who took part in the study were retired from active competition.

Our Approach to the Data

In our attempt to bring order to the massive amounts of data collected on the swimmers, we have found it useful to divide that information along roughly chronological lines into the early, middle, and later years of career development. By delimiting the careers of our subjects in this way, we do not want to suggest that it is the passage of a certain *fixed* amount of time that marks off one phase of a career from the next. The duration of the early, middle, and later years varies from swimmer to swimmer, just as it does from one pianist to the next and one mathematician to the next. What does not vary are the tasks completed during each phase: Within each phase certain skills are learned, relationships formed—between the swimmer and his or her parents, coaches, and peers—and values acquired. It is the nature of the skills learned and relationships formed that distinguishes one phase from the next.

It is very important to note that the "tasks" to be completed in each phase of a career are not simply skills that have to be learned. When we refer to the tasks of the early, middle, and later years, we also mean to draw attention to the interpersonal relationships formed by the persons we studied, and the attitudes and values that emerged from these. More than ever it is clear to us that learning is fundamentally an interpersonal process. After having studied twenty-one Olympians we are certain that no one can become an Olympic-caliber swimmer without the direct support, instructional and otherwise, of many people. Thus the focal point in our discussions of talent is rarely the swimmer alone and more often the relationships between the swimmers and their parents, the swimmers and their coaches, and the swimmers' parents and the coaches.

The Early Years

We begin, appropriately enough, with the early years. From our reading of the data, these are the years of playful encounter with the sport of swimming, the years of discovering the excitement of organized competition and of being a part of a team. It is a long period of time inasmuch as it begins with the birth of the later-to-be Olympian and proceeds through first exposure to water, becoming comfortable in it, learning to swim, and finally recognizing swimming as a sport—maybe even *the* sport—to excel at. These are crucial years, even more crucial than those that follow, because it is during this period that our subjects became interested and caught up in the sport of swimming. In time that interest became self-motivating. Had there been no excitement during the early years, and no sense that the young swimmer was very successful, there would never have been a middle or later period.

THE CONTEXT OF A CAREER: THE DEVELOPMENT OF VALUES, ATTITUDES, AND HABITS

From birth until the child goes to school, the child's developing ties to his or her parents are the most important factor in the acquisition of values and attitudes conducive to a later ability to learn. Simply put, parents who get the message across to their children (either by their own example or by explicit instruction) that being smart is better than not, that reading or active learning is better than watching television or wasting time, and that taking responsibility for certain tasks and for one's self is important, produce children who are more able and eager to learn and consequently higher achievers. Parents who do not feel that learning is that important, or who for some reason are not able to get that message across to their children, tend to produce youngsters who have a harder time learning, presumably because they find it difficult to put in the effort required.[2] Though the educational research addressing the problem of the home environment's impact on achievement has focused largely on school (cognitive) achievement, the same conclusions are without a doubt relevant to swimming achievement. That is to say that parents who teach their children to be disciplined and responsible and to value success are more likely to produce high achievers than parents who do not pass along these skills and values.

According to the swimmers and their parents, if anyone had cared to take a look into their homes prior to the domination of swimming they would have left unimpressed. All of the families were intact and made up of a father, a mother, and an average of a little over two children. The latter were usually born three years apart. Extended family was distant, and there was infrequent contact with them. Seventy-five percent of the twenty-one pairs of parents had at least some college education, 30% had four or more years of college, and 12% had gone on to complete professional training in business, law, medicine, or dentistry. In all but four cases the father was the primary breadwinner in the family, the mother was the homemaker. In the four exceptions the mother shared the burden of working outside the home. The fathers usually held white-collar managerial or sales positions, the mothers who worked were teachers, nurses, or secretaries. Only four of the parents held professional positions.

The parents of our swimmers were for the most part people who had grown up during the Depression and entered young adulthood around the time of World War II. Several of the swimmers or their older siblings were born while their fathers were away at war. Like a lot of people who struggled through these trying years, the parents of our swimmers learned to believe in the values of hard work, self-sacrifice, and self-discipline.

---

[2]For a review of the literature on this topic, see Kalinowski and Sloane (1981) or Getzels (1968).

They just have this work ethic . . . this Protestant work ethic. . . .
Where you have to work and this is what you get—you have to
work to get it—you don't get it [for nothing]. . . . That's kind of
how I've been raised (S-9).

As far as we can tell, the message they passed on to their children was "you can do anything you set your mind to, if you
want to do it . . . [and] if you work at it (M of S-12).

The ideas that typify the work ethic held by the parents of
our subjects were well summarized by Bommo Chung (1964)
in his study of family values and school achievement:

Successful people work hard to become so. Success is a constant
goal. There is no resting on past glories. People must work . . . continually to convince themselves of their worth. Perfectionism is a
necessary means to a worthy end [p. 52].

The interesting thing is that while all of the parents seemed to
hold this ethic very strongly, only about a third of them
seemed to live it themselves. In particular, only about a third
of the parents seemed to be constantly driving toward greater
and greater success in their own work lives. The majority
seemed to have found a comfortable place for themselves in
the mainstream of the work force and stayed with it, not increasing their pace in order to move up to higher salaries or
rank and not slowing down and risking a pay cut or demotion.
To be sure, they worked hard at their jobs, and most used their
leisure time to work around the house, but the drive to advance in their work lives was missing. The following excerpt
from an interview is not an unusual description of the parental
goals and aspirations:

They have very narrow horizons, both of them. . . . They still do.
All they really want is what they see. And if they don't see it, then
they don't want it. . . . They had strictly middle-class standards. . . . They don't have ideas like I do—to go out and make

money. . . . They just want to make their payments, have a respectable life, and see their kids happy. . . . They don't really want much more than that—just a simple life (S-9).

Of course, several parents (and swimmers) noted that the Depression and the war had drastically altered their career plans (particularly their plans for higher education). Nevertheless, it seems to us that the discrepancy between the ethic proposed and the ethic lived by their parents created a tension that later found an outlet in the careers of our swimmers.

Later, when their children became deeply involved in swimming, most of the parents in our study found no sacrifice too great, no price too high to ensure their child's success. Indeed, several fathers arranged to have time off from work, and one even retired early, so that they could get their children to swimming practices, meets, and clinics. So far as we can tell, the rule they lived by was "I want to give mine the opportunity that I never had" (F of S-10).

With only one exception, S-13's mother, who wanted one of her children to become a musician, none of the parents we talked to said they started their families with great plans in mind for their children.

I didn't have any aspirations for them. . . . I didn't know. . . . I think I was too dumb to think like that. I had kids and I was too busy taking care of them to think about that. I never thought in terms of "my son the doctor," or "my daughter the attorney." All I thought of is that I want them to be happy and not hurt (M of S-1).

Too many parents say my child is going to be this or that, and I didn't do that because I think they all have to make up their mind what they're going to do—you can't tell them. You can [only] suggest (M of S-4).

Certainly none of the parents admitted to wanting to create an Olympic swimmer.

I don't remember thinking about possible careers for the children. I didn't think of raising the first woman president or anything like that, nor did I think about raising an athlete. I just wanted them to be kids I could be proud of . . . and that they could be proud of themselves. We were just average parents trying to raise kids (M of S-9).

Indeed, contrary to what we might expect, most of our swimmers did not come from homes in which swimming was presently, or had been, a part of either parent's routine. We estimate that slightly less than 30% of our sample had at least one parent with some background in competitive swimming. The quality and extent of these backgrounds ranged from a season or two at the YMCA to many years of Amateur Athletic Union (AAU) and pre-Olympic competition.

On the other hand, almost 75% of the swimmers had at least one parent with a definite, though usually passive, interest in athletics. Typically, this interest of the parents was carved out during their high school and college years and pushed into the background with increasing adult responsibilities. Still, these parents saw the value of sports and competition and encouraged their children to get involved in both. Some saw a link between physical fitness and positive thinking, others a tie between competitive sports and character and integrity.

It was important to have some kind of athletic thing. If you have an athletic child who is very energetic, you always look to some kind of sports. It helps to keep them in shape . . . it helps to condition them psychologically as well as physically (M of S-12).

In seeing the value of athletic competition the parents of our swimmers showed their pragmatism. As far as they were concerned, competition would bring out the best in their children. It would help them to find a focus for their energy, give them worthwhile goals, and teach them the value of hard work, discipline, and organization. As one mother put it, "If you are not competitive, you kind of get lost in the shuffle" (M of S-12). The emphasis was on physical activity, and sports in particular, because they were accessible and they were tangible. For some reason the parents of our swimmers seemed to find it easier to see hard work and discipline at the pool than in the classroom, in the library, or at the piano.

It was very important to these parents that their children not get lost in the shuffle. Right from the start they emphasized the necessity of having goals, of working hard, and of being disciplined. As one of our swimmers put it, "No one in our family has ever believed in the easy way out" (S-15). Others described their homes in the following ways:

> I think I had a very, very happy childhood. I feel I was brought up under fairly strict conditions, but if I had a child now, I would hope that I would rear that child the way I was reared. We were pretty much a highly disciplined family . . . approaching jobs with the idea, "Do the best you can do or don't do it at all. Do it until it's done well" (S-17).

> . . . from age six on I had my duties, I had my chores. I knew what they were and [that] they had to be done before I could go out and play. So from a very young age I was taught discipline. And I think that an athlete, any athlete, has to be a very disciplined person to stick with [the kind of] schedule I was on (S-19).

All of the swimmers in our sample had fairly ordinary responsibilities around their homes long before they got caught up by the demands of year-round, competitive swimming. These chores were expected to be completed on a regular schedule. The swimmers were also expected to perform their chores correctly.

> We always told them that there were right and wrong things and we always stressed that anything worth doing is worth doing well. No matter how many times you do something, you always try to do it as well or better than the time before (M of S-14).

But the primary way in which our swimmers learned to be perfectionists in these early years was through parental example.

I always have to do things the best I can. My dad is the same way. . . . It can't just be good enough to pass, it has to be right. I can remember my dad working around the house—I can't give you a specific example—but [it was always the case that] if something wasn't right, he'd just rip it up and redo it (S-5).

From their parents' example they began to see the importance of not wasting time. Self-sufficiency was strongly stressed.

My father's philosophy was, "Once you're eighteen, you'd better know what you're going to do because you're on your own." They were very liberal in their thinking, especially my father. They sort of said, "You go ahead and make your own decisions. Do what you want to do and we'll support you. If anything really goes wrong, we'll be there to help you" (S-8).

They taught us a lot of self-sufficiency. You won't see me calling home every weekend. They did not breed dependency, they bred independence—from peer group, from them (S-15).

Perhaps most importantly, in these very early years the swimmers also learned of their parents' personal commitment to them and their welfare. Though we do not have any hard evidence on it, we get the sense that more than most adults, the parents of our swimmers saw themselves as parents first and foremost, husbands and wives next. This is clearly true during the middle years, when swimming forced its way into every aspect of family life, and we believe it was also the case during the early years. It is the unconditional commitment to the child so apparent in the following excerpts from our talks with parents and in the tone of our discussions with the swimmers that leads us to make our claim:

I would have been happy if Jean had been good at other things [besides swimming]—and just to try to do something really well. Whatever it required of us, we would have been happy to do. If she had wanted to be a ballet dancer, we would have been just as [happy]—or ice skating, ice skating is even worse than swimming.

We would have encouraged anything and been willing to give (M of S-17).

I always had . . . my parents around. There wasn't a time I can remember that my folks went on a trip somewhere and I didn't go with them, which, looking back on it, was a good thing. I know my mother and father—they were with me (S-7).

Neither of the parents pushed me. . . . [They] really didn't know the "ins" of the sport. Take my mother, I could come home and have said, "Well, I swam [such and such] time today!" and she would say, "Great! Beautiful! I love you!" but she really didn't understand the time. She was just there to support me in anything I did (S-8).

So far as we can tell, this willingness to give encouragement and support on the part of the parents (and siblings) is one of the major distinctions between the families of these Olympic swimmers and other families. It was the basis upon which the importance of success and the method of achieving it—diligent hard work—could grow to be powerful personal guidelines for our swimmers.

INTRODUCTION TO SWIMMING

Despite their general lack of familiarity with competitive swimming, like most parents those we studied felt that their children should learn how to swim if only to be safe around water. Consequently, some time between one and seven years of age the Olympians in our study were exposed to the water for the first time and taught how to swim. The average age at first exposure was four and a half years, and almost all knew the basics of staying afloat and moving through the water by the time they turned six. Initial swimming instruction was brief (in all but a few cases lasting only a few weeks during the summer) and low key inasmuch as it stressed the basics of moving through the water and having fun while you were doing it.

More often than not, our swimmers' first instructors were high school or college students holding summer jobs. Occasionally there was a high school football coach who did the job. Rarer still was there a master teacher, someone who was clearly an excellent swimming coach—though there were one or two. A few of the parents actually taught their children these rudimentary skills themselves. But, in general, there was essentially no investment demanded of either parents or child other than that the child should show up for these brief lessons.

At the same time the return was small. In terms of skills, the emphasis was on learning to move using the freestyle. Smatterings of breaststroke and backstroke were also taught. Less than a handful of these future Olympians had first instructors who paid attention to the butterfly, turns, or the details of stroke quality. Like most people who learn to swim in city parks or club programs, our subjects had plenty of opportunity to develop bad swimming habits, which they would later have to work hard to break.

FIRST COMPETITIONS:
COUNTRY CLUB SWIMMING
The average swimmer in our sample spent the next two and a half years from the ages of four and a half to seven swimming just for fun during the summer. There were no practices during this period, and no competitions, except for occasional races between siblings, friends, and even parents.

> We'd have races—pretend races with her [mother]—my brother and I. And we'd either just tie her—in the beginning she'd clobber us—but as we got older—when I was about thirteen, I tied her. She kept her speed for quite a while (S-19).

Sometime around the age of seven, about half of our swimmers joined a country club swimming team or YMCA (winter) team or its equivalent. The remainder of the group skipped this step and went directly into AAU swimming. We will talk about them shortly. The stated reason for joining country club teams was to get more pool time and to have a more organized setting in which to interact with other children. The idea was simply to have a place to play with brothers, sisters, and friends during the summer. These were summer programs, programs that emphasized fun. "Practices were fun . . . we played a lot of games like fish and shark . . . you're having so much fun that you don't realize you're exhausted" (S-1). In two out of three cases the swimmers we studied moved into country club swimming with an entourage of siblings and/or friends. Practices were regularly scheduled, but they were short and infrequent, one to two hours three or four days a week. Most of the parents were simply spectators at this point in their child's career; they had no real investment in swimming itself.

Just about all of the swimmers who joined country club or YMCA teams were very successful. "She was beautiful . . . she just had a natural love for the water . . . she was immediately a good swimmer. Her stroke was good" (M of S-13).

> They put her on the varsity after one meet. She was just a darn good little swimmer. And then after she went into AAU she broke a lot of national records. . . . She was a winner from the start, which made it very easy for us to be enthusiastic (M of S-17).

Even at this very first stage of competitive swimming, many of the swimmers in our sample seem unusually good—not so unusual as to be considered prodigies, but very good in light of their recent starts. Of course, most were swimming in a "small pond." Some knew that.

> We [she and her siblings] set all kinds of records around here, but it was really a small pond too. . . . We thought it was kind of nice, but I think we realized what the competition was. . . . It was really neat, but at the same time we knew we weren't really that hot (S-21).

But whether they realized who their competition was or not, all found these early wins seductive, parents as well as swimmers, and thought it natural to go on to the next step in the sport. For them swimming had begun to seem less and less recreational and more and more sport.

At least in retrospect, some of the parents (and a few of the swimmers) think that it was at this point that the difference between the later-to-be Olympian and his or her siblings, particularly those that swam, began to show. Sometimes the differences noted were physical: "Everything came easy for [the swimmer] . . . [our other son] had to work harder at it . . . and when it came to a meet, he wouldn't win as often" (S-16). "My brother and I both were breaststrokers. He did the IM³ too, but he was never very limber and always had trouble with the butterfly" (S-19). More often mental characteristics and attitudes made them stand out. "She's always done what she wants to. . . . I mean [she has] strength of spirit—she never gave in. I don't care how discouraging things might have been" (M of S-13). Often described as more determined, more aggressive, more competitive than their siblings and peers, our swimmers tended to do well right from the start and thus to some appeared gifted.

THE NEXT STEP: AAU SWIMMING

Actually, for a little more than half of our twenty-one swimmers this was the first step, the start of competitive, year-round swimming. It usually took place between the ages of six and seven. For these youngsters there were no country club "fun times"; they went right into Amateur Athletic Union (AAU) age-group swimming.⁴ Their reasons for starting with an AAU team were the same as those of their peers who had joined country club teams. The AAU clubs were convenient, and there were siblings or friends already on the team.

---

³IM stands for individual medley, an event that combines freestyle, backstroke, breaststroke, and butterfly.

⁴Age-group competition is typically broken up into five categories: eight and under, ten and under, eleven to twelve, thirteen to fourteen, and senior swimmers.

A next-door neighbor had a son who was going [to swim with this AAU team], so we thought we'd give it a try—to see what it was like (F of S-2).

There's a joke in our family that they took me to swim meets . . . because everybody else in the family went. . . . They only put me in events just so that every once in a while my mother would know where I was, and if I wasn't there, she'd try to find me (S-6).

We moved to [our new hometown], and there was a brand-new [AAU] team starting [there]. My older sister had been on the swim team in [our old hometown], and for some reason—I don't know why, I didn't think about it twice, it was just natural that I would be on the swim team too, I would follow her . . . (S-9).

Since the AAU organizes all serious amateur swimming competition in the United States, all of our swimmers had to become involved in it sooner or later. The swimmers in our sample who had taken the intermediate step of joining a summer club team typically were nine or ten when they made the switch to year-round AAU swimming. The reasons for the move varied; some were still following their friends, others had been noticed by AAU club coaches.

He [AAU coach] got me out of the summer club championships. He spotted me swimming in the meet and asked me and my parents if I would be interested in swimming AAU. So that's how I started (S-17).

Well, it got to where—both my brother and I were doing well in our age groups, kind of at the top of our age groups, and . . . we didn't have much competition. And my coach just looked at me one day and said, "Why don't you go AAU? I think you'd do all right." . . . [It] had me scared for a little while. Then I went to a meet and found that it was no different (S-18).

AAU teams took swimming more seriously than most country club teams. Winning was very important to them. Such seriousness required greater investments of time, energy, and money from the swimmers and their parents, much more than typically invested in a summer club team. For the average swimmer, the move to an AAU team initially meant not only year-round swimming but twelve to sixteen hours per week of practice time (two to two and a half hours each afternoon six or seven days a week). Of course, there were a few swimmers who practiced less—perhaps only one and a half hours a day—when they first joined an AAU team, and there were some who practiced more, swimming two (and during the summer even three) workouts a day for as much as four hours of practice a day, six days a week. This was a two- to three-fold increase in practice time for those who had previously swum in summer clubs.

In sixteen out of twenty-one cases, the quality of the coach and the caliber of the team had little or nothing to do with the choice of the AAU team. Most often, the team chosen was the only local team, or the most convenient team. As just mentioned, in a few cases the swimmers were recruited by AAU coaches who thought they might do well on their clubs. And occasionally, slightly crasser motives, such as a coach needing a twelve-year-old to fill out a relay team, decided the quality of the swimmer's first real (i.e., year-round) coach. In 80% of the cases, the quality of instruction available from the coach and the quality of competition provided the swimmers were not major factors in the choice of coach or team. Convenience ruled.

> [The AAU club] was about five minutes away from where we lived. [My parents] said, "Tom, if it were another five minutes away, we probably wouldn't have let you do it." It was just too convenient to pass up. . . . If it were ten minutes farther away, or ten minutes more inconvenient, I wouldn't have done it, because they wouldn't have supported me (S-15).

Very few of the parents had actually gotten caught up in the early signs of promise shown by their child at this point; indeed, not all of the swimmers had shown signs of promise yet. Even fewer parents supervised the selection of coaches. Swimming was generally not yet a family affair; it was the child's affair. Most parents did not know enough about swimming to be able to tell the difference between a good coach with a good program and a not-so-good coach with a mediocre program. For them the benefits of swimming were simple:

> Mom was glad to have me out of the house. It was something I enjoyed, I developed a peer group, not to mention the fact that my shoulders were getting broader and my homework, my schoolwork, was getting better because I was more organized and disciplined.

> You can't work out four hours a day and . . . I mean, you learn to squeeze the rest of the day into it. You don't procrastinate in workouts, so you don't put off anything else either. You just do it on a regular organized basis (S-15).

> I think [my father] . . . was relieved that I was swimming. I think he felt like, "She won't get into trouble. It's a good healthy outlet for her and she's doing something constructive." He was just all for it. He thought it was great (S-19).

Despite the general lack of attention paid to the quality of the coaching, it turned out to be quite good. About two-thirds of our subjects' first AAU coaches had trained, or were training, at least one nationally ranked senior swimmer. Most of these coaches tried to present swimming as a science to their charges. The emphasis, particularly early in the season, was on strokework, turns, and pacing. The first half of the season was time for conditioning. A lot of distance was covered. Speed work filled the latter half. In all but two or three instances, boys and girls practiced side by side in the pool. This was particularly helpful to the girls, who would compete with the boys in the lane beside them.

Most of the swimmers were clearly identified as freestylers within the first year or two on an AAU team. However, several were known as predominantly breast- or back-strokers until the very end of their careers. Regardless of stroke preference, just about all of the swimmers practiced all four strokes.

Weight training as a ten-, eleven-, or twelve-year-old was rare among those in our sample who swam in the 1968 Olympic Games. It was common among those who swam in the 1972 and 1976 Games.

SUMMARY OF THE EARLY YEARS

The transition to AAU swimming marks a major change in the relationship between the swimmer and the sport of swimming. Though parents and swimmers alike report that the move to AAU swimming just seemed natural, in hindsight it seems to us that the willingness of the swimmer and his or her parents to make the much larger investment for AAU swimming reflects a change in their commitment to the sport. Prior to joining an AAU team our swimmers say they swam for fun; after joining the team they were swimmers first and foremost. Gradually schoolwork, leisure, and (nonswimming) friends receded into the background. Though these other activities remained important, they took second place to swimming in the swimmer's mind. For most of our subjects, the step up to AAU swimming was an admission of choice, the choice to excel in swimming. It therefore marks the end of the early years.

At this point a recap of the early years might be useful. We began by noting that the twenty-one swimmers who took part in our study came from families that were very child-oriented and held a strong work ethic. As far as we can tell, they encouraged ("demanded" might be putting it too strongly) their children to be disciplined and responsible and by their own example around the house showed how being disciplined and responsible paid off.

In this environment swimming came by chance. Though many of the parents were more inclined to athletics than anything else, such as academics, none of them foresaw the great success of their child in the sport. For them swimming was a way to keep the child busy and working toward some goal. It was also an opportunity to make new friends and be a part of a team.

Early success changed things. While none of our swimmers

broke national records in their first year, most did well enough that they wanted to become more involved in the sport, to swim more often, and to swim against better competition. As we will see in the next section, success continued and led to an even deeper commitment to the sport. However, in the middle years parents are also required to make a commitment to the sport. In the middle years swimming becomes a family affair.

The Middle Years

The middle years are the years in which the swimmer becomes engrossed in the details of the sport and works hard to master them. Among our subjects the transition into this period seems to be marked by the addition of a morning workout, that is, by jumping to two workouts a day. The attitude of the middle years is one of growing competence; with the recognition of swimming as a sport (in the early years) the swimmer is now faced with the task of carving out a place for himself or herself in the sport.[5] In short the task of the middle years is to define oneself as a swimmer. For the people we studied, we guess that this effort began sometime between the ages of seven and eight (for those who had skipped summer club swimming and gone directly to AAU swimming) and ten or eleven (for those who did spend a year or two swimming on summer club teams).

Becoming a swimmer, especially a successful swimmer, is much more than one person's doing. It is during the middle years that we see this most clearly. Serious swimming demands substantial investments of time, money, energy, and inconvenience from all of those in the swimmer's immediate family. If we were to be simplistic for a moment, we might say that yet another hurdle of the middle years is for the swimmer and his or her coach to convince family members that these in-

---

[5]That is, in terms of the attitude of the swimmer, his or her family, and that of his or her coaches.

vestments are worthwhile. Actually, we know that things are not that simple. During the middle years it is often the case that family members, that is, the parents, have to convince the swimmer and the coach to push harder and to make use of the resources they are willing to provide. It is this give and take between family and swimmer, family and coach, family and school (swimming does take time away from school), and swimmers and their peers (both swimming and nonswimming peers) that leads to the development of a network of supports that is requisite to the development of talent in swimming. Such a network provides the resources necessary to sustain increasing involvement in the sport and keep the swimmer on task.

In the middle years the work begins in earnest. There is a newfound seriousness about the activity and a growing commitment to the sport. Other interests and hobbies fall to the side and eventually disappear. Friendships that do not revolve around swimming begin to fade. New and better coaches are sought and found, and the amount of time invested in swimming makes a quantum leap forward. The emphasis is on precision, on learning to swim efficiently and quickly. Hard work is the norm; self-discipline and self-motivation pave the way. The importance of the middle years is as straightforward as that; without them there is not sport, there is only recreation.

THE BEGINNING: EARLY SUCCESS
AND ITS CONSEQUENCES

No phenomenon crystalized the transition into the middle years more clearly than our subjects' success as AAU swimmers. All but three of the swimmers were doing quite well in age-group competition within a year of joining a team; most were winners from the start. Typical reports from the parents were:

> He was a winner from day one. . . . Once he got over the stage fright, he was immediately one of the stars. He always won. He was like a fish (M of S-1).

And,

> She set quite a few of the local AAU records. She was always at the top of her age group (M of S-16).

From the swimmers we heard,

> Swimming was my biggest genius. As soon as I hit the water, I was good. I could get in the pool and beat anybody. . . . (S-2).

> I started winning in my age group real quickly. . . . I started winning and that's how I started having positive reinforcement . . . right from the start (S-11).

> I was real successful at the age-group meets (as an eight and under). I won a lot of first places (S-17).

FOR THE SWIMMER

Though these first successes (of approximately 90% of our subjects) were often just at local (sometimes regional) meets, they were frequent enough that they galvanized the child's commitment to the sport. They made it easier to wake up for morning workouts, to give up one's free time, and to work hard in practices. When there were occasional slumps in performance, these successes made it possible to endure and to continue with the work. Early success carved out a future for our swimmers.

> I liked the idea of winning, and I broke my first national age-group record as a ten-year-old. . . . When you taste the sweetness of success early, you say to yourself, as I did—I remember to this day coming home and telling my folks . . . that I [had] broken the national age-group record. My dad said, "You can do better." And I believed it. And I said, "Dad, you know, someday I'll go to the Olympic Games" (S-7).

> She loved it when she joined [the swimming club] and could see improvement and [in time] began to work her way up to beating some of the girls she had looked up to. From then on, until after the Olympics, she never spoke of quitting (M of S-5).

As is often the case, the success of our swimmers brought them newfound importance. Many became noteworthy members of their swimming teams, because when they did well, the teams did well.

> It was fun to do well. . . . I was recognized in the newspapers when I was in junior high school. . . . My friends admired me for it. You get a certain amount of respect from your teammates and from your competitors. Winning was a way of attracting attention (S-6).

In the middle years, belonging to a team and being a member of the community of swimmers became crucial to those we studied.

> When you're working out in a group . . . and you all really like each other, you're all striving for recognition from the coach and your teammates; that's what you're there for (S-8).

Someone had to be there to help one through each day of practice, and someone had to be there to take note of one's success.

> The people I swam with in those first years have been my friends ever since. . . . You spent too much of your time in the water, too many hours, too many days, too much pain, too much happiness with all those people . . . you have to build a common strong bond (S-9).

> If you had to do it by yourself, I don't think you could do it. . . . You're always with other people you know [are] hurting as much as you are . . . that [are] going through what you're going through. You're all doing it together. . . . Everyone knew it was going to be hard. And it was. But not everyone had the same bad feelings on the same days. Like maybe you'd go one day and say, "Oh, no way! I can't go through with it!" And someone else might have a good day and say, "No, it's okay. We can do it." A week later they might be having a bad day and you're having a good day. . . . It makes you more of a team. . . . That's probably what kept me in swimming. Even if I wasn't doing well or wasn't making Nationals, I think I'd probably still be in swimming just because of the people you see everyday (S-16).

FOR THE COACHES

Coaches also noted the successes of our swimmers. So far as we can tell, their responses varied depending on whether they noted just the success of the swimmers or the success and personal ingredients that went into it, such as the swimmer's determination, competitiveness, and desire to do well. Coaches who noted that it was the swimmer's determination, competitiveness, and desire to do well that led to their success were more typical in our study. Like their colleagues who focused only on the swimmer's success, and not on his or her person, these coaches demanded more work from their swimmers when they saw their early wins. Unlike their colleagues, however, they were not afraid to make their relationship to the swimmers a personal one. The nature of these relationships is described as follows:

> He's [my AUU coach] been very much a father figure, he's been my father all through the years. He takes me everywhere. We did everything together and we were really close. . . . I mean, I don't want you to think I'm bragging, but as the years went on, I was obviously his best by far (S-9).

> He [the coach] wasn't all that knowledgeable about the physiological aspects and all the technical aspects of swimming. He just knew it from . . . gut experience . . . and he was also a good friend (S-11).

> He [my second AAU coach] was like a father away from home. I think a lot of times a lot of girls and guys [on the team] would like to think, "Boy, this guy is on my back all the time. He's doing it on purpose. He doesn't like me." And he was really strict, but he used to swim himself, and that's the way he was brought up. . . . On the other hand, if you were in a bad mood when you left workout, he'd call you at home. And on weekends we'd get together after workouts and go out (S-13).

> We [my first AAU coach and I] got along great. He was kind of like my dad. I just really admired him a lot. . . . I was always around him. . . . You see him every day . . . a lot of times I'd talk to him

when my parents weren't around or something. . . . It was a really tight working relationship. He had to know everything (S-16).

He gave me a heck of a lot of personal attention, fine points on stroke, and starts and turns which helped me later. . . . He used to walk me up the block before every race and talk to me . . . tell me things to think about during the race. I think he thought of me as his little daughter (S-17).

From the coach's point of view, the personal ties to the swimmer had practical implications. As one of the coaches we talked to put it, "They have to know that you're their friend even though you might chew them out, otherwise you're not going to get to them." They wanted their swimmers to see a personal challenge in the sport, to give it their utmost. That required the personal commitment of the swimmer. The natural first step was a commitment to the coach.

The coach is god. You're just too dumb to know any better [in the first few years of serious competitive swimming]. He says what you should do and you do it. You're just a blind maniac and just pouring your guts out. You'll do anything. It's suicidal almost. . . . He commanded a lot of respect (S-8).

When Mr. —— came, it was really weird. It was like God was walking in the door and you're going to do what[ever] he says. I was terrified of this guy . . . it was just automatic respect for this man. There's no other coach like him. And I don't care who I had after him . . . I would always consider him my coach (S-13).

Those coaches who took note just of the swimmer's winning—and there were two or three of them—made less of a personal response to the swimmer. Theirs was a more mechanical approach. They focused on the team and more on short-run success. Unlike the more typical coaches we heard described, these men made little effort to get to know their swimmers, what they wanted, needed, and could stand. The first and only step they took was to increase the amount of work done by the swimmer. Sometimes that got out of hand:

> I went through a summer [as a fourteen-year-old] where I literally worked out in the pool three times a day, seven days a week. . . . The second summer after my arriving on the scene . . . my coach said, "We're going to go on a horrendous workout schedule, but I think it will make you better." Well . . . every person has a different approach to work both mentally and physically—you have to take those two in combination. You cannot throw a human being into a pool . . . and work them until they drop dead. . . . I was swimming nine or ten miles a day. . . . I was just plumb worn out, mentally and physically.

> [My coach] lost sight of the fact that . . . you're dealing with not only the physical attributes, but [also] the mental attributes. [He never asked] can this person withstand the mental strain of being torn down like this. . . . [After a while] I just couldn't tolerate it anymore. I just lost confidence in my coach (S-7).

Though none of the other swimmers received responses of this intensity from their coaches, swimmers who had coaches like S-7's were consistent in reporting their own disaffection with them. Like S-7, they realized that the coach had lost sight of them, of what they wanted and what they needed.

> He [our coach] was a nice guy but . . . there was something about him that made us think we could do better on our own. [So] we just kind of blocked him out a little, doing what he said but in our own way. . . . He'd get upset and stuff like that, but that was too bad. In meets and stuff I never would go up and ask him, "Hey, what do you think I should do here?" . . . I don't remember much about [him] encouraging me or boosting my ego a lot. The main thing I remember . . . is [him] just being there and giving us a workout. [My success] was all on my own, I think, or at least a lot of it was because. . . I could [have] cared less about what he thought (S-13).

Most felt that they were in a bind; they wanted to defer to the coach and do the work, but they were afraid it would not lead them anywhere. There were three paths out of their dilemma: Some had a parent step in and assume the role of a "nonofficial" coach that superseded the "official" coach.

> My dad was literally coaching me by that time. . . . He had picked up enough to keep me afloat (S-7).

> I think I learned everything I know about [swimming] from [my son's first AAU coach]. One of the [later coaches] said, "The only coach [my son] ever had is his father." Well, [his first AAU coach] was his real coach—in his formative years. . . . I just remembered all the instructions, how to hold your head, how to put your arms in the water, your kick, your breathing (F of S-2).

Others moved to another coach.

> We decided to change . . . we changed coaches to ———. He didn't necessarily have great champions, but he had the right attitude that . . . we were looking for, which was a little bit more personalized workouts. In other words, everyone didn't just do the same thing . . . and we liked that (S-11).

And some, like S-13 above, took over their own coaching: "My job as a swimmer was to learn how to coach myself" (S-15).

Regardless of the type of coach the swimmers worked with, the results of the extra work and attention they received were greater success and an identity that more and more revolved around swimming. In the middle years the environments of our subjects became circumscribed. Practices and meets filled more of their time. By the time the average swimmer in our group turned thirteen, the enormity of the demands that would be incurred by continuing to swim were recognized. The recognition forced several swimmers to stop and consciously decide whether it would be worth it to continue.

When I was fourteen, I made a decision (helped by my coach) that I would be swimming year-round. I'd go strictly with the swimming. All my friends were in other sports, and you know, you kind of lose something from that. . . . The flow of things was to stay with your friends. . . . Now I think [that] if you really want to excel in every case, you have to put all your marbles into one can (S-8).

I was just starting out [with this new AAU team], so I wasn't sure what the result was going to be. We had just made a move . . . and I was just making new friends and everything. . . . It was a lot of time that I had to give up, and I wasn't sure if I wanted to be with my friends or I wanted to continue swimming (S-21).

However, most of the subjects did not make an *explicit* choice to continue with the sport. More often than not they tended to continue in the routine they had become used to over two or three years of competitive swimming. Their success, of course, made it less likely that they would question their ways.

My dad stuck me in [swimming], and it was on my head to do it. . . . It just got to be something that I had to do—like brushing my teeth (S-5).

I had all these national age-group records right away, the reason being that we were swimming two workouts a day [right from the time I first joined the team]. . . . And I didn't ever really think about it . . . about my friends not doing it. I never really was that interested in having friends. . . . They always seemed so young to me. I was beyond that. . . . It was more fun to swim (S-9).

What other kids were doing was nothing. What were they doing? They were going out to Little League practice just trying to make a cut when I was the best in something else. Why give up something and . . . go to mediocrity? (S-11).

INSTRUCTION

In the middle years, instruction increasingly emphasized precision in stroke. The swimmers usually entered the middle years with good backgrounds in the four competitive strokes but lacked the ability to fine-tune. Most were also short on endurance and strategic skills. The instruction of the middle years worked toward these ends. Both the number of workouts per week and the intensity of these workouts increased dramatically during the middle years. In fact, this was the period in which the swimmers learned just how much work swimming could be.

All of our swimmers began practicing twice a day during the middle years. Some started slowly with only a few morning workouts a week, but within a year or so of joining an AAU team all but two of our subjects were swimming every morning. Morning workouts were typically "easy pulls" (i.e., using just arms) through a good bit of distance and long sets[6] of kicking or long-distance swims using freestyle. The workouts were usually preceded by thirty to forty-five minutes of weight training (regularly scheduled weight training was less common among those swimmers who competed in the 1968 Olympics). All told, morning practices lasted about two hours. In the first month or so of each new season, afternoon workouts also emphasized conditioning, and long distances were swum freestyle. As the season progressed, afternoon workouts were more and more devoted to speed, technique, and strategy. Interval training[7] was the rule because it taught the swimmer how to pace himself as well as developing cardiovascular endurance. Strokework was designed to promote power without sacrificing efficiency. The idea was to stop windmilling down the lane and to learn smoothness, to kick just as hard as was necessary to keep the body resting high in the water and minimize drag, but not so hard that you were too tired to finish.

The coach was interested in stroke technique, which very few coaches are because most coaches are trainers, not coaches. Train-

---

[6]A *set* is a series of distances measured in yards or meters swum in practice. The size of the unit and the length of the series can vary; e.g., one set might consist of eight 200-meter swims, another of three 1500-meter swims.
[7]Swimming sets on prespecified time intervals is called *interval* training.

ers make you do your laps—coaches make you do your legs and stress stroke technique.... At thirteen I started to get into the sport as a science. I started reading health books. I started watching stroke-technique films. I would watch films for an hour everyday and then go out and try to do it. [And] we did a lot of weight training (S-10).

He [the coach] worked just hours on my stroke and how I felt. I mean I looked like I was in slow motion, but it was really neat [because] I would take maybe fifteen or twenty strokes less than somebody else in a 50-meter pool doing freestyle, and many of the guys couldn't keep up with me. You know it was really neat! (S-12).

Afternoon workouts tended to run for about two and a half hours. Thus, two years into AAU swimming all but one or two of our subjects were swimming four hours (or more) a day, six and sometimes seven days a week. During the summer even more time was spent in practice.

Afternoon workouts were designed to be very competitive. Teammates were routinely paired off against each other to swim the same sets side by side. In all but two or three cases boys and girls swam the same workouts. Inevitably the swimmers paired off against each other and raced to see who would finish first. For our swimmers it was important to be the "hare" and lead the lane. Of course, they were not fast enough when they first joined the team, but within a year or so most were lead-off swimmers.

One swimmer mentioned other strategies she used to enable her to work harder during practices. Though other swimmers did not mention them specifically, we believe most of them developed similar strategies for keeping themselves highly involved in what by this time had become a difficult routine.

I remember thinking as I was swimming that I wanted to make sure that I got to a certain point in the pool before I caught up to the other person [behind me in the lane]. In other words when you're swimming circles you pass people swimming the other way, and I swam my hardest to meet them at the second black line instead of the fourth one. To be almost to the wall before I saw them. . . . And I'd try singing a song and [to] have the song finished by the time I was at a certain point in the pool, or to see how many times I could do something [like] blowing water or holding my breath [and trying to reach a certain point in the pool] (S-17).

STANDARDS
Goals changed too. It was no longer necessary to win every race you competed in every week. The focus instead turned to time, to how fast you could swim. Most of our swimmers worked together with their coach to set the standards for workouts and meet performances, during the middle years. A few claimed either not to have set goals or to have done it alone. When it occurred, the process always began with the swimmer setting his or her sights on winning or placing in a specific meet, e.g., placing in the Nationals, translating that into a time standard, and then working backward to short-term goals.

> [The coach] had a system of organizing the season so that the kids could be goal oriented. He would sit down before the season would start and say, "These are the meets we want to do well in, and I think these are the times you should be looking at." . . . It was kind of a negotiating thing. Then he would say, "These are the splits you're going to have to do in order to do that time. These are the times you're going to have to do at that meet, and these are the splits you're going to have to do at these earlier meets" (S-10).[8]

> And he'd write it all down on a piece of paper, and when he was all done, you had numbers all over this page that meant a lot to me and to him [but] nothing to anybody else. And he'd put it on my

---

[8]A *split* is the amount of time it takes a swimmer to cover some portion of a race, e.g., the amount of time it takes to cover each of the four 50-meter distances that make up a 200-meter race.

locker so that every time I went to workouts . . . it was staring me in the face. . . . it became kind of a security blanket for all of us—because he knew where you were (S-10).

[The coach] made us set little goal cards. Just a little 3-by-5 with all our strokes or whatever on it. . . .

I used to have goals of bettering a time, "I want to do a 30.3, my time now is 32.0." And my goals were always just to better my times that season. I never really placed an importance on winning, [on] being number one (S-18).

As important as the standards they negotiated with their coaches were, our swimmers made it very clear that their teammates provided even more compelling standards. During the middle years it became very important for the people we studied to prove themselves each and every day. The attitude they had developed over their several years of swimming was well expressed by one of the men in our sample: "I guess I had a big enough ego that I wanted to do well and couldn't stand to accept [second best]. I didn't like to get beat. I couldn't stand getting beat!" (S-6). Consequently, as one of our swimmers reported, "You could just feel the tension as you walked into afternoon workouts" (S-5).

I was a little hot ticket and there were a couple of guys on the team who would push me and I'd keep up with them. Initially one guy would push while the other would loaf, then the first guy would loaf and the second guy would push me. . . . They didn't realize what they were doing because I just took off. By the time I was twelve, I had seven national [age-group] records and thirteen national first places (S-2).

I swam with all the guys all of the time (from nine on) and that's where I learned to work hard. They were models and they really pushed me. . . . You get to that age where you have a goal in sight and you really get hungry for it and you've got these older guys to push you—[they were] someone to catch, someone to beat (S-8).

I never got beat in practice. I'd win every set, every day, day after day. . . . You're really just looking for someone to push you. . . . I always wanted to be very consistent (S-8).

When you're working out in a group, you've got maybe four or five swimmers to a lane and there's maybe six or eight lanes. . . . The coach might have two lanes doing butterfly and two lanes doing different strokes. And a lot of times you'll go off [start] together, and if you're doing repeat sets on a set interval, everybody's leaving at the same time. So of course you've got so and so next to you—usually the fastest person leads off the lane and then the next fastest—so that you won't be on anybody's tail. . . . So there was— I call it friendly competition. . . . [It makes] it easier to work out. . . . Sometimes you pace yourself, but other times you're fighting it out. It's nice to have someone there (S-18).

PARENTAL INVOLVEMENT

Though all of the parents initially saw swimming as a recreational activity for their children, within a year or two (for those whose success did not come so quickly) their child's consistent success in age-group swimming changed their orientation. From the child's point of view the report was,

> If I was going to be in it, I was going to do my best. There wouldn't be any messing around or stuff like that (S-14).

And from the parent's vantage point,

> Once in a while I would watch her and she would start playing around. And that made me mad because I was holding two kids and had to drive her there. . . . I told her, "You don't ever come down here again unless you want to work, because we're putting our effort into it. It's not just you, it's the whole family, and it costs money—that's all there is to it! And besides, you're wasting the coach's time" (M of S-20).

Swimming was still supposed to be fun, but most parents (not all) had acquired a new sense of their child's potential.

They also saw how clearly the development of that potential rested upon their willingness to increasingly invest their own time and money in the sport. Coaches encouraged these impressions. Without exception, at least one, but usually both of the parents made these investments. They volunteered to work at swim meets, sold raffle tickets to raise funds for the team, and scheduled and cooked as many as three dinners a night—one for father, one for the swimmer's siblings, and one for the swimmer. All but two or three spent a good portion of each day driving their children (and sometimes their teammates) to and from practices and/or meets. After one or two years of serious AAU swimming, the families in our group had made the swimming success of the one child a clear-cut family issue. From the parents we heard,

> Swimming was our way of life. All our vacations and extra money went into swimming weekends—that was our recreation—swimming, swimming, swimming (M of S-1).

> All I can say is that it [swimming] became a way of life. . . . My husband made himself available to anything [our son] wanted (M of S-7).

> Dinner-table conversations were usually about their sports—and we didn't do enough talking about politics, I'm afraid . . . because we were just so darn wrapped up in swimming, I guess. . . . We didn't do as much as we should have about more cultural things (M of S-17).

And from the swimmers,

> It was an obsession most definitely, the sport of swimming in the family. But there was a justification for it, because I was the best in the country. . . . When I got involved in swimming, everything . . . revolved around this family being involved in the sport (S-11).

> At one time we had everybody [i.e., each of the children] swimming. It was really wild, because Mom and Dad were racing around trying to get us to certain places and we were all swimming in different pools. My brother and I were out of town just

about all the time because we were swimming with the [AAU club] (S-13).

It's almost a way of life when you get involved. I'm sure it's like other sports or activities, but we got involved with it, and then it was weekends and meets—and my mom and dad would come to the swim meets and take us here and there. They would enjoy the companionship of the other parents, and we would enjoy the other kids, so it was a good family activity. I guess that's how it started out at least (S-18).

In terms of money, we estimate that the average set of parents invested anywhere from $1,000 to $2,000 each year for the first four or five years of regular year-round swimming. In terms of time, the investment was enormous. It was not uncommon for a mother or father to wake up at 5:30 A.M. every day to get his or her child to practice, wait almost two hours while the child swam, then on schooldays rush him or her off to school and on weekends run home to make breakfast. The same schedule would be repeated each afternoon, this time starting from school and going to practice. Less than half of our subjects reported that they carpooled. Weekends offered no relief because there were usually scheduled practices, and if not, there were meets. Though more and more swimming teams now travel by bus to meets, that was less frequent when our subjects were swimming. Typically one or both of their parents spent many of their weekends at meets.

Some parents played more than supportive roles in their child's swimming careers: These parents were directly involved in their child's progress, sometimes on a day-to-day basis. There were two types of direct parental involvement apparent in the middle years: The first and more common type was the setting of goals and standards for the child; the second type was actually coaching the child. Each of these is important because they illustrate just how caught up some of the parents were in their child's swimming.

There was great variability in the type of standards parents set and in the way they were set. At one extreme there was the father who simply gave his thirteen-year-old daughter a watch with "Montreal 1976" (i.e., the Montreal Olympic Games) engraved on the back for Christmas, and the mother who pointed out Olympic swimmers to her ten-year-old daughter, a serious age-group swimmer, and said, "You can do that too, if you want to" (S-14). In the middle was the mother who reported,

> We always tried to keep our kids from being too energetic at a young age because we didn't want them to burn out. And really serious swimming and national swimming was where the emphasis was in our house. Working hard to go to the Nationals was really the goal that everyone tried to make. . . . (M of S-12).

And that father who "always tried to instill that thought of winning. They say it's playing the game, but don't let them kid you" (F of S-2). Toward the other end of the spectrum were parents such as the following:

> [As the children got older], my husband always kept a book on each one of them and what their times were, so that when they wanted to make goals and project what we thought was a realistic goal, he did all those things. . . . The coaches did all the coaching, but my husband would say, "What time do you think you're going to be able to do today?" That kind of thing (M of S-12).

> [My dad] kept a chart . . . with the different events that were on the swimming program across the top and the different meets I went to down the side and he entered my respective times in each box. And if it was my personal best time for the week, he'd circle it . . . my job was to beat the last circled time (S-15).

Two or three parents were assistant coaches for the teams their children swam on, but they made a point not to get involved with the actual coaching of their own child. There were also three parents who actually coached their child during the middle years. None of these fathers who took up coaching their sons did so "officially." There was no way to get pool time with that kind of arrangement. Instead each was "the coach behind the coach" (M of S-7). And the person who "kept an eye on your stroke [so you wouldn't] fall into bad habits" (S-2). The parents of S-12 were the most active, offering their sons

> a set of brush-up lessons at the beginning of each year [in March or April before they went to the swim team]. [Because] it was important to give them the best, and if they were going to do it, they might as well do it right. So they would have lessons on starts and turns (M of S-12).

These would be taught by one of the coaches at the club.

TALENT

There are many reasons for these profound investments made by the swimmers and their parents. We can identify three at a glance: the parents' keenness on "giving ours the opportunities we never had," the child's enjoyment of swimming and swimming friends, and the child's early success. In the middle years a fourth factor emerges to rationalize (or justify) the expenditure of time and money on one child's swimming career, namely, the child has *talent*.

One of the more startling discoveries of our study has been that it takes a while to recognize swimming talent. Indeed, it usually takes being successful at a regional level, and more often, at a national level (in AAU swimming) before the child is identified as talented. Since these levels of competition are first faced during the middle years, we have come to see the discovery of talent as a phenomenon of the middle years.

One child, for example, started competitive swimming at the age of seven and broke a national age-group record at ten. But it was only when he turned eleven, his mother recalled, that

> The coach of the [YMCA in the neighboring town] who had seen [our son] in several meets, came to us . . . and said, "You know, what you people don't realize [is that] you have a kid here who is a star" (M of S-7).

Similarly, another mother recalled that her daughter's coach really never saw her potential even after five years of working together on a daily basis. He thought

> . . . she was good. [But] he didn't know how good because he had another [apparently more promising] girl at the time. . . . He recognized that she was better than average but perhaps not the caliber she was (M of S-5).

She made the Olympic team, whereas the other girl did not. S-1 was told "he had it" when he was fifteen and ranked as one of the best freestylers in the country, though he had already broken a national age-group record as a twelve-year-old and had done well in competition against senior swimmers for almost two years.

It was the same for almost all of the swimmers we talked to.

> I got clobbered between the ages of eleven and thirteen. . . . They didn't say I had talent until I started to get real good [and made the Senior Nationals at sixteen]; then they started to say I had talent. . . . By then I had worked my ass off! (S-4).

> I did pretty well [when I first started swimming]. I think I was—I know I was blessed with some natural ability. My brother was pretty athletic also [but] he didn't progress as far in swimming . . . I know I have some natural ability. . . . Because people told me. [But] I worked my buns off too (S-18).

> The only reason I got to go to swim practice was because of my sister. You see my sister started out swimming—she just went right to the top, she got all first places in her age group and everything. And then my mother took me to swim practice with her because she was taking [my sister]. She [mother] admitted that openly, "The only reason you got to go [to swimming practice] was because your sister was going." When I started to show some promise and my sister went away to college, she [mother] allowed me to continue. But really, in the beginning it was all my sister (S-19).

Over and over again the swimmers we studied described their talent as *"a feel for the water."* According to the coaches we talked to, a feel for the water is an ability to know instantaneously (i.e., without reflection) the body's alignment in the water at any particular moment and to correct or make adjustments to misalignment quickly, efficiently, and completely. It is the ability to know what one's limbs are doing at any moment and the ability to control them in the smallest detail. According to Howard Firby (1975), this "feel" also has a psychological component, a calm receptivity. Firby also notes that experts disagree as to whether a feel for the water is an innate characteristic or something learned in the course of good instruction. He holds the latter view.

For some of the swimmers we studied, having a good feel for the water meant,

> Everything really came easy to me. I never had a tough time with anything in swimming. . . . I was just more comfortable with it (S-13).

> I can pick up things easier where a lot of people have a hard time. . . . It just comes natural to me (S-16).

For others a good feel for the water was something like the following:

> Timing and feel . . . I caught on faster and I was always fairly good at correcting my stroke (S-6).

> I remember being very aware of what I was doing in the water. I just remember finding it very enjoyable to analyze my stroke completely, to catch, and feel, and know exactly what I was doing underwater (S-17).

> I have a smooth stroke. . . . I've been told that it looks effortless. Now to me swimming isn't effortless. I used to work at it really hard. But I have a slow stroke over the water and then a firm pull that a lot of people don't get. . . . I've been told that it looks so easy! (S-18).

A few of the parents described the same ability.

[She had] an ability to put strokes together, almost flawless in her freestyle. . . . She was able to take control of herself and her strokes (M of S-3).

[My son] knew how the strokes would go. He could tell when he was doing it right and when he was doing it wrong. He probably had the best understanding of the actual swimming—how to make the stroke change the way he wanted [it] to (M of S-12).

Several parents also commented on their child's *unusually good coordination*, like the mother of S-16:

She was well coordinated . . . wasn't clumsy . . . was always good at running . . . agile. Whatever [she] tried, [she] had early success with it. I mean no matter what it was . . . [she] did [it] well (M of S-16).

The swimmers noted it too. Many parents reported that their children had seemed well coordinated long before they started to swim. "[My younger son] was well coordinated from [the time] he was a little fellow [whereas, his older brother] grew fast and clumsy. [The younger boy] was a slow grower, so he didn't go through the clumsy stage" (M of S-10). One or two of the swimmers qualified their parents' reports by pointing out that their coordination was peculiar to the water. "I was pretty gangly and uncoordinated. I might have killed myself on land" (S-5).

When pressed to point to the differences between the future Olympian and his or her siblings or peers, few parents turned to "a feel for the water." Instead what they talked about is the incredible *independence, determination, and competitiveness* of the swimmer that went the farthest. The mother of S-5 described her daughter as "a fierce competitor," unlike her older sister, who also swam. The mother of S-12 described her son as someone "who wanted to improve himself. He always wanted to be the best. He's a very competitive boy." Others said the following:

> [My son is] not very big, he's always been very thin. In grade school he played football—he was a tiger—but he was so small. . . . He was always very sharp and alert . . . he was my best student in school. . . . He was the most outstanding [of all my children] in schoolwork. And when he made up his mind to do something, he did it. Like when he played football, he was the smallest one on the team, but he was a little tiger. The coach still talks about [him] (S-4).

> She was different—everybody knew it [from the time] she was two years old. Just quicksilver and very independent, always wanting to do things for herself. Very bright—I don't know if she was particularly brighter than the others—but [she was] more determined to do things (M of S-9).

> She always set her own goals, even as a young child . . . when she decided that she wanted to do something, it was almost impossible to get her to see that she couldn't do it (M of S-14).

> She's always done what she wants to. With some children you could reason—sure I spent time trying to do that [with her], but I don't know if I ever made an impression. . . . I think I mean strength of spirit—she never gave in, I don't care how discouraging things might have been (M of S-13).

> All children in all families are different—[even though] they're brought up the same way. . . . [The older girl] was very outgoing, had it easy growing up, always had dates, [was] popular with her peers. Whereas [the swimmer] was much more shy and sensitive. If she was given an assignment of 1,000 words [in school], she'd write 2,000. She was always striving to do her best. She overdid it at times, we thought (M of S-17).

The swimmers seconded these remarks, and a few acknowledged motives such as the following for their single-mindedness and competitiveness during the middle years:

But one thing I can tell you—I hate losing. And that stems back to my father's feeling, "You know, if you're a loser, they don't pay much attention to you. But if you're a winner, people start listening!" (S-7).

SUMMARY OF THE MIDDLE YEARS

The main task of the middle years is to become a swimmer, a very good swimmer. From our study we have learned that this task can be broken down into three components: the acquisition of expert swimming skills, the establishment of a network of interpersonal supports, and the progression toward a complete psychological commitment to the sport. The completion of each of these component tasks requires enormous expenditures of time, money, and effort.

No one directly connected with the swimmer, e.g., immediate family, friends, schoolteachers, and coaches, escapes from making his or her contribution to the cause. Parents contribute time and money and do not impose demands that the swimmer work around the house and hold a summer job. Because of the expenses of swimming, brothers and sisters often receive a smaller share of the family's resources than they might have had otherwise. Many seem to get less time and attention from one and sometimes both of their parents. Almost all suffer from constant comparison with their talented brother or sister. Because serious swimming demands a great deal of time, friends at school find fewer opportunities to socialize with the swimmer. Many compound the problem by avoiding the "celebrity" because they fear that they are not good enough, not important enough. The swimmers, of course, pay on all these accounts.

In spite of these costs the careers of our swimmers progressed and became more and more successful. So far as we can tell, there were two reasons for this: The first was that parents, siblings, and friends seldom took time to question the costs they were paying; the second that ever larger successes of the swimmers convinced them that no cost was too great. To put it simply, everyone got caught up in the careers of these swimmers, caught up in careers that were snowballing in success. The mother of S-9 described this process well:

> If I had known what we were getting into, I would have said, "Why don't you cut out paper dolls instead?" I had no idea what we were getting into. When the [oldest daughter] came to us and said she wanted to join the swim team [because] all her little friends were on it—we said okay. It [only] cost a quarter or something, so it sounded okay.... Then [the later-to-be Olympic swimmer] decided she wanted to [swim] ... and by then it was getting to be kind of fun—they were winning a few things. Then we moved to [another city], and all of a sudden it was big business. It was too late. I suppose if we had gone into it with our eyes open, we would have done the same thing. But I had no idea of what we were getting into—at all! (M of S-9).

The Later Years

The later years are distinguished from the previous phases of learning to be a swimmer mainly by the extreme intensity of the swimmer's commitment to the sport, the enormous demands of practice, and the exceptional quality of the swimmer's coach and teammates. In the later years swimming and the lessons learned from it become more fully integrated into the swimmer's self. There is a realization of how talented one really is and knowledge of what needs to be done to bring that potential to fruition. Intensely hard work, sacrifice (both personal and familial), and trial by competition become routine during the later years. More than ever, success is the norm. Confidence swells in oneself, as well as in one's coach, parents, and teammates, and there is growing excitement about one's possibilities in the sport. To realize those possibilities, each day of the later years becomes filled with swimming, swimming, and more swimming.

What we see in the later years is the swimmer gaining some perspective on his or her place in the sport and learning what it means to be a swimmer. There were two parts to this lesson:

the first, learning what swimming has done, and is doing, for me; the second, learning what I am doing for it. Answers to these two questions did not come easily. Such insight progresses in fits and starts. Our swimmers did not move into the later years of their careers and quickly come to understand these lessons. For most, this task of understanding was only begun during the later years.

THE TRANSITION INTO
THE LATER YEARS

In swimming, as in other fields we have studied, it seems to be the case that the transition to the later years is often marked by a move to a master teacher, an accomplished professional with a well-documented ability for bringing out the best in students. About two and a half years after joining their first AAU team, fourteen of the twenty-one (66%) swimmers we studied moved to another coach and/or to a more advanced competitive team. We have come to call these coaches finishing coaches because they were the swimmer's coach when he or she qualified for the Olympic team.

Three factors tended to distinguish these coaches from those who had previously worked with the swimmers: First, they worked with a number of championship swimmers at any one time. Consequently there was a pervasive and very powerful emphasis on meeting the highest and most stringent standards in one's events. Because competition against one's peers was designed into the daily routine, our swimmers found that working with these coaches meant struggling to be the best every day. Second, these coaches were not afraid to aim for international success when they found a swimmer they thought might make it. And third, the finishing coaches were quite expert at their jobs. They had a great deal of experience and approached the sport of swimming as a science. At the same time, and perhaps most important, they were flexible; they wouldn't follow the book if it seemed wide of the mark on any particular day and they could trust their swimmers to know what was best for them.

Fifteen of the twenty-one swimmers we studied made the Olympic team while under the supervision of a coach who had already produced at least one other Olympian. Having coached swimmers through top international competitions, these finishing coaches knew the kind of preparation and training that was necessary to do well in them and were very aware of the pressures these meets could put on their swimmers.

> I would always tell people when they asked me what the difference was [between my first and my second—and last—coach] that he [the finishing coach] had the capacity to put that psychological— he knows how to coach physically—but he also knows how to coach psychologically. He can get anybody, as far as I'm concerned, up for a race. He can talk them into doing anything—at least he could with me (S-19).

> He just made you do things that you probably thought you could never do . . . as far as being an example too. . . . He always seemed to know just what you were doing as far as swimming events, where you should be, what you could do, talking to you. . . . I guess you could call it psyching you up (S-21).

Thus the deliberate move to a new coach after several years of AAU swimming marked a change in the swimmer's perspective. It was a move into the big league.

> . . . my parents and I decided to go to [the better club], which was a bigger team and . . . had bigger things in mind. . . . We felt I had gotten to the point where I had reached what I could reach on the team I was on. I had to break into a bigger team to do bigger things (S-16).

> Everybody [in the family] agreed—we were to go to California because there was nowhere else to go. She needed the coach, she needed the competition . . . that's where all the best swimmers were coming from. I told her—here you're a big fish in a little pond—there you'll be a little fish in a big pond. . . . But she wanted to go for it; she told us go (M of S-20).

Of course, every one of our subjects did not make the transition into the later years by making a calculated move to a better coach and a better team. Of the seven swimmers who did not make a planned change, five (two males and three females) already had very good coaches and had no need to move until they entered college, and two (one male and one female) moved to finishing coaches just by accident. In the latter two cases, the girl moved to a finishing coach by chance when her first AAU coach left her club and was replaced by a better coach, and the boy switched to a finishing coach when his family moved out of state and he began swimming at the pool most convenient to his new home.

We believe that each of these swimmers began to pass into the later years once they began to compete with some regularity in the AAU Senior National (indoor and outdoor) competitions. By then it should have been clear that they were top-rank swimmers with the potential to go further. As one swimmer said, by the time he entered high school and had qualified for and competed in the Senior Nationals,

> I knew what I had to do, and I guess I had a big enough ego that I wanted to do well and couldn't stand to accept second best. I didn't like to get beat. I couldn't stand getting beat! (S-6).

Certainly by the time any swimmer in our study began to place in the Senior Nationals—usually in the third or fourth such meet—they truly had made the transition into the later years.

> Workouts were always the same until I placed in the Nationals in 19—. That put me on the Pan American team. And I made that, and I think I got a taste of what it was like to be good—a great swimmer—and to be able to make trips and go places [and] display your skills in front of people. That was almost the spark, you know. . . . It kept me working for the next Nationals. So I think I might have been more dedicated after that as far as really knowing what it was like to be good, to be on top continually (S-16).

INSTRUCTION AND THE RELATIONSHIP
WITH THE COACH

Although good coaches are always looking for more effective methods of training their swimmers, it was seldom the case that new instructional materials or techniques were introduced in the later years. The few changes that were introduced in the later years were usually brought in to try to break the monotony of what had long since become a daily ritual, or to keep the swimmers from reaching their peak condition prematurely. An example of one such change (that only affected one or two of our swimmers) intended to have both effects was the introduction of water polo as a conditioning exercise in the first months of each new season. According to one of the coaches who uses this technique,

> . . . basically we overdo it. We get people in shape by December for a meet that doesn't happen until April. . . . Water polo . . . is another way to get into shape [after the summer lay-off]. For most of the kids it's also fun. . . . [and] some people are more successful at water polo and [so] their self-image comes up (Coach-1).

Though there were few changes in instructional methods per se, there were differences between the kind of work done in the later years and that done before. Without exception practices were more intensive and painful than they had even been before. There was less rest between the elements of each set (sometimes called "repeats") and between sets. At the same time more distance was covered in each workout. During the school years, our swimmers were practicing four to five hours a day, six or seven days a week with meets on weekends. In the summer, practices lasted six hours a day. The amount of distance covered in practice varied from swimmer to swimmer and depended on how far into the season one was. For the swimmers in our sample who competed in the 1968 Olympic Games it was unusual to cover more than 12,000 yards on a stress day. For those who competed in the 1972 or

1976 Games the total distance swum in a day might be as much as 22,000 yards. Most of our subjects used all four strokes to cover that distance. All but a handful of the older swimmers in our study lifted weights regularly during the later years, and several went on strict diets so as not to be slowed down by excess body weight.

Goals were more explicit in the later years than ever before. In most instances these goals were concerned with time rather than winning. While many of the swimmers we studied said they had their hopes set on making the Olympic team two or three years prior to the Games, none of them ever formulated a plan of training and competition that was specifically aimed at Olympic Trials two or three years distant. Long-term goals never went beyond any one season. Most often they focused on the Senior Nationals competitions. This, of course, is in marked contrast to the training programs of their counterparts in the State Socialist countries, which typically cover the four years of the Olympic cycle (Balyi, 1980).

For most of the swimmers, the move into the later years meant a different kind of relationship with their coach. With the long history of working under several different coaches, competing under a variety of circumstances, and still succeeding, the swimmers had become much more self-directed.[9] By the time they began placing in Senior Nationals competitions, most had come to realize that they could swim against anybody; they had done all of the drills a thousand times, had gone through several national championships, and felt they knew what they needed to bring out their best. They therefore sought a more collaborative relationship with their final coaches—not directly of course, and not all at once. But slowly they began asking for more of a say in what they were supposed to do in practice and in meets. In most cases they got it. As might be expected, the more authority the swimmers had over themselves, the more they saw that their coaches re-

---

[9]On the average it took the swimmers eight years to begin to place in Senior Nationals competitions.

spected their feedback, the more devoted they became to the sport—their sport.

The degree to which the relationship between the coach and the swimmer became collaborative depended on a number of factors, such as how old the swimmers were, how mature and responsible they were, how hard they worked, and how well they had been doing. It also depended on how flexible the coach was. So far as we can tell, none of the swimmers was considered (by himself or herself or by the coach) truly the coach's equal, particularly before they had competed in their first Olympic Games. After competing in the Olympic Games several swimmers did demand much more of an equal say about their training. In most of these cases this caused such strain in the relationship that the swimmer eventually either found another coach or stopped swimming altogether.

The collaboration between coaches and swimmers was nowhere more clearly illustrated than in their approach to the question of tapering, i.e., cutting back the amount of practice time before a big meet. The following lengthy excerpt from an interview with one of our swimmers points out the difficulties that occasionally came up in the later years when the coach and the swimmers really did not share the responsibility for the swimmer's training. It is presented because it illustrates well the kind of flexibility the best coaches have to have, the kind of trust they have to put in their swimmers, and the kind of self-confidence a world champion swimmer has to have. The story begins with S-16 describing how after three or four years of being one of the top women swimmers in the country she hit a slump.

> Things weren't clicking. I wasn't winning. . . . We [my coach and I] both knew it was happening, but it was like "Well, next time we'll get it." And then when the next time came around . . . the same thing happened. I think that's when I started losing confidence, the confidence that I had in myself. And my mom . . . saw it . . . that I wasn't as aggressive, you know, and I wasn't going out to win and be the one; that I was kind of settling for what I was doing.

Explaining that she thought her problems stemmed from her coach working her too hard and not tapering her soon enough, S-16 went on:

> I think I did lose [confidence in my coach]. . . . And I think he might have known that too. [But] for the [spring] Nationals I tapered myself . . . I felt I knew myself better. I mean I gave him a lot of credit but . . . I went a lot on my own feeling. . . . I think that when I tapered myself, it might have hurt him a lot. But it wasn't because I didn't believe in him. It was because I wanted to believe in myself. I wanted to be in charge of what I was doing because if I failed, then I knew it was my fault, that I was messing up. . . . It was a risk on both our parts [for her to taper herself]; for him, because I think it was hard for him to just sit back and let me do it. He wanted to be in control of everything, yet I wanted to, too. With combined efforts we did okay (S-16).

TEAMMATES

In the early years teammates were important because they kept our swimmers excited about the sport and wanting to be a part of it. In the middle years they helped our swimmers get through the ever-increasing amount of painful work that was practice. In the later years while continuing to be enthusiastic and supportive, teammates played a much more important role in the careers of our swimmers. Being championship swimmers themselves, they provided such rigorous standards in daily practice that our subjects could not escape doing the kind of work that would enable them to become the best in the world.[10]

The importance of this role cannot be overestimated. So far as we can tell, over 90% of the swimmers we studied benefited crucially from competing on a day-to-day basis (in practice) with their teammates. The simple fact of the matter is that no one but these (better) teammates could breathe life into the

---

[10]It should be remembered that in all but a few cases the teammates of the later years were not the same teammates our swimmers had in the previous phases of their careers.

world-class standards our swimmers had to meet; no one else could make them so immediate, so tangible, so compelling. While coaches and parents might have been able to pass along enthusiasm and perseverance to the swimmers in the earlier phases of their careers, they could not provide the same kind of impetus to work hard as a strong competitor in the next lane of the pool could.

One of the women in our sample described particularly well the powerful influence of her teammates. She began by noting how problematic being the only serious swimmer on her first AAU team was for her.

> I would do fantastic, just phenomenal times in workouts [swimming against the clock] . . . and did fantastic in [local and regional] meets . . . but when I got to Nationals, I just did not have the psychological concentration you need to keep your mind on your race. . . . I guess I didn't think I was as good as [the other people in the race] because . . . [even though] time-wise I was as good [or better] . . . when I swam against them, I did not perform . . . well (S-19).

Because she repeatedly failed to do well in national competitions, despite swimming record times in workouts, she eventually moved to a new team and her finishing coach. Within a short time she began doing very well in Senior Nationals and qualified for the Olympic swimming team.

> It was just the fact that I was swimming with senior swimmers— national swimmers—my own age. Frankly, it was they who pushed me along in the freestyle. . . . Working out with them everyday, [I] proved to myself that I could keep up with them, beat them. [That] gave me the confidence that I needed . . . that was my first big breakthrough (S-19).

There are two points of particular interest in S-19's description of her own experiences. The first tells us how competition among teammates, which we have previously mentioned started during the middle years, was different in the later years. According to S-19, with the move to the new AAU team she began to swim with and against "senior swimmers—national swimmers—my own age." The key difference then was the quality of the swimming done by the teammates. In the later years most of the people in our sample swam on teams that had a number of national competitors.

The second point made by S-19 concerns one of the mechanisms triggered by intrasquad competition, which is increased self-confidence. Intrasquad competition pushed the swimmers not only physically but also psychologically. In standing up against real competitors day in and day out our swimmers learned to manage their prerace anxiety about losing, to pace themselves, and to concentrate under a pressure more real than any clock on the wall could ever provide. They also experienced the satisfaction of really winning. And with each success their confidence grew. For swimmers like S-19, leaving workouts exhausted from having successfully withstood the challenge of one's teammates everyday was more important than anything else.

PARENTS

At first glance it appears that the parents of the swimmers became mere spectators in the later years. Actually they were spectators more than ever before, but that is hardly all they were. Though most parents had less direct influence on their child's swimming, their commitment to their child's participation in the sport of swimming was as great, and sometimes greater than ever, in the later years. For example, while most of our swimmers became old enough to drive themselves to practices and meets during the later years, at least half of them had already spent a year or two working at the pace of the later years before they turned sixteen or seventeen. Their parents had to continue to chauffeur them to and from practices, meets, and school until they could drive themselves.

All of the parents continued to prepare the extra meals required by later afternoon and evening practices and to take time off from work or reschedule vacations in order to attend big swim meets. All continued to pay a fair amount of money for club dues, entry fees, swimsuits, and travel and lodging. This could be quite a lot of money, as much as $9,000 a year, according to one mother. These expenses continued until the swimmers placed in the top three of their particular events at the Nationals. After this they were usually subsidized by their team, a corporate grant, or the AAU (for international trips).

During the later years six or seven families in our sample were forced into even greater investments than those just described. For these families the desire to see how far their child could go in the sport required moving across the country to find a better coach or sending their child off alone to a better coach in a different part of the country. For at least two of the families that moved cross-country, the search for a better swimming program had the unhappy effect of separating the father from the rest of the family temporarily. Because the work both of these fathers did was not within commuting distance from a home near the pool, they moved out to live in rented rooms (during the week) near their place of work. Both would rejoin their families on weekends.

Thus, during the later years most parents played behind-the-scenes roles. They kept things moving by infusing more and more of their time, money, and energy into their child's career. Up front they looked like spectators who attended every meet to cheer their child on. In reality, without them much of the effort would have come to a halt. Though these young swimmers were incredibly fast and their coaches incredibly expert, their participation in the Olympic Games could never have been realized without parents who were willing to give everything it would take.

THE OLYMPICS
The ultimate goal of the commitments made by the swimmers and their families was to make the Olympic swimming team and win an Olympic gold medal. As one mother put it, "It was

bigger than anything else to make that Olympic team. It was the ultimate. She just thought of nothing else" (M of S-13). We can estimate that it took our swimmers about two years to go from first-placing in the Senior National competitions to swimming in the Olympic Games. Thus for the average swimmer in our sample it took roughly ten years of year-round competitive swimming to reach the pinnacle of a career. The range was from six to fourteen years of competitive experience.

For all but six of the swimmers we studied there was only one Olympic competition, and it effectively ended their competitive careers. Though many of our subjects continued to swim after they had competed in the Olympics, few ever again worked as hard or swam as fast. Among those who continued to swim, there were three types: those who had to swim for scholarship reasons, those who swam for fun, and those who swam to prove something to themselves. Of course, any one swimmer could have continued for all three reasons, but for most, one reason predominated. The latter group is a particularly interesting group. It is by no means the smallest of the three. From those with a need to prove something to themselves we heard the following:

> I don't think I ever reached my peak at all! Not even close! And I don't think I reached my goal of what I wanted—I wanted an individual gold medal. [But] I didn't do well in the individual event, . . . I'm happy with what I got, but, I always thought that I would never really want to go back to the Olympics because I'd won a gold medal [on a relay team]. I'd hate to [go back and not do well, not win a gold medal for an individual event]; I'd like to end on a good note.

> I guess that's why I kept swimming for about three years after [the Games]—to see what I could do. I didn't want to leave. Everyone else was still swimming (S-13).

We might describe S-13 and the other swimmers like her as "hangers-on." The essence of hanging on is the ambivalence beautifully expressed in the preceding quote. Having grown up believing they were special, most of our swimmers didn't know what to make of their failure to win a gold medal in their individual events. Their problem was that the Olympic Games only come once every four years. That was too long for one more try. They were tired. Thus they were left questioning whether they were really as good as they thought (and were told) they were and with no way to know.

Of course the nature of the sport is such that for a variety of reasons it ends—there is nowhere for a successful swimmer to go after the Olympics. Thus, even those who did well at the Games went through a lot of turmoil after their careers ended. There was a lot of the same questioning and a lot of the same doubts about their worth.

> It makes you happy at that point in time. It makes you feel like you're the greatest thing on earth. [Having] the adulation of many . . . where millions and millions of people know you or know who you are . . . but it's like literally being alone in a crowd of friends. And that's a difficult thing. Believe me it's difficult.

> I have . . . gold medals from the Olympic Games. They sit on my wall, they don't talk to me, they don't help me in any way. . . . They are historic remnants (S-7).

For most of our swimmers the year or two after the Olympics were a time of reorientation. It was a time to get reinvolved with nonswimming peers and school, to find new goals and new challenges. To us it seemed that they had learned some very important lessons: how to set realistic goals, how to persevere and work diligently, how to pace oneself, and how to be responsible for whatever success or failure came their way. Perhaps most important, they learned the limits of what they could do, not only with their bodies but with their whole selves, if they were willing to put forth the effort. When we spoke with them, most seemed to be at ease with themselves. Several were well on their way to what appeared to be very successful second careers.

SUMMARY OF THE LATER YEARS

The perspective one obtains of oneself in the later years of swimming is very different from that obtained in other fields inasmuch as the later years of swimming very quickly turn into the last years of swimming. Part of learning what it means to be a swimmer is learning that one does not stay a swimmer (i.e., a nationally ranked swimmer) for long. The anxiety which arises with the recognition that greatness is "now or never" made it easier for the swimmers, their families, and their coaches to meet the ever-increasing demands of the sport.

There is no question that swimming in the later years was exceptionally demanding. The stakes were higher, the practices harder and longer, and the competition was fiercer. The task of the later years was to find one's limits, to push the boundaries of one's skill as far as possible until either body, spirit, or opportunity was lost. What makes the swimmers we studied so exceptional in addition to their supportive families, their master teachers, and their highly talented teammates was their willingness to pay the price to be great.

Future studies of talent development would do well to look more closely at the nature of the price paid by great individuals and their families and to try to uncover the mechanisms that make it possible to pay.

REFERENCES

Balyi, I. "Talent Development in Sport: The Case of the State Socialist Countries." Unpublished paper, The University of Ottawa, Canada, 1980.

Chung, B. M. "The Relationships of Role Expectations and Value Orientations to the Achievement of Higher Mental Processes." (Ph.D. diss., University of Chicago, 1964).

Firby, Howard. *Howard Firby on Swimming.* London: Pelham Books, 1975.

Getzels, J. "The School and the Acquisition of Values." In *From Youth to Constructive Adult Life,* edited by R. W. Tyler, Berkeley: McCutchan, 1968.

Kalinowski, A., and Sloane, K. "The Home Environment and School Achievement." *Studies in Educational Evaluation* 7 (1981): 85–96.

6
★ ★ ★ ★ ★ ★

One Olympic Swimmer: A Case Study

Anthony G. Kalinowski

To bring the previous discussion of the developing swimming talent to life, the story of one of the swimmers who participated in our study will now be presented. Though we have collected similar information on twenty-one other swimmers and their families, we have decided to present the case of Peter Smith.* Only one case is presented, because we believe that Peter is representative of all of the Olympians we studied. He is, as far as we can tell, the typical swimmer.

We present the case of Peter Smith in the hope that by getting acquainted with him and seeing the changes that he and his family went through over the course of his career, the reader will get a clearer understanding of the work and commitment required from all concerned in the development of extreme talent. Perhaps more important we would like to give the reader a sense of the environment in which that work and commitment evolved; to see that no one person can claim the entire responsibility for the great success that the swimmers enjoyed.

When we call Peter Smith typical we are saying several

---

*The name of this swimmer has been changed.

things about him. First, that his involvement in, and commitment to the sport of swimming evolved gradually and carefully—but not so carefully that it seemed prepackaged when we looked at it. Neither of Peter's parents saw an Olympic swimmer in their infant son. While they did wish for a successful son, our interviews with both Peter and his mother lead us to conclude that at the beginning, the success could have come in a number of different ways.

Second, despite the physical capabilities he was born with, it took Peter several years (six by our estimate) to appear gifted. This is the predominant, though not exclusive, pattern found in our data on swimmers. Most of them are said to be "natural" or "gifted" after they had already devoted a great deal of time and hard work to the field.

Finally, Peter's involvement in swimming seems to fall into three or perhaps four distinguishable phases in terms of the quality of his relationships with his parents as well as with his coaches. These paralleled changes in his own expectations of himself.

PREFACE

At the time of our interview with him, Peter was in his thirties. He had graduated from college several years earlier and in the meantime had become quite a successful businessman. He was articulate and seemed forthright in his discussion of himself. He had no apparent difficulty remembering the details of events that took place as far back as twenty years ago. An interview with his mother corroborated much of his story. Where there are significant discrepancies between Peter's and his mother's viewpoints, it will be noted in the text that follows. Like all of our interviews with the parents, the interview with Mrs. Smith was not conducted by the same person who interviewed Peter. And while much of the material brought up in our talk with Peter often served as the basis for questions presented to his mother, there was never any time when his report was shared with her or vice versa on subsequent discussions with Peter.

FAMILY BACKGROUND

Peter was the second of two boys born three years apart to George and Mary Smith. His parents were both born and raised in small midwestern towns. Each received a college education from a nearby state school during the last years of the Depression; Mr. Smith had his tuition paid by an athletic scholarship, Mrs. Smith worked her own way through. After college Mr. Smith took a job in a bank and began taking night-school courses toward an advanced degree. Though he received his degree several years later, he had decided by that time that the cost of moving into a professional position would be too high and so stayed with the firm that he had been working for all along.

Mr. Smith met his wife-to-be on a business trip. Mary was teaching elementary school at the time and had taken a summer position as a camp counselor. Shortly after they were married, World War II began, and George Smith went overseas. Peter was born after his father's return.

Two themes dominated the interaction between Peter; his older brother, Tom; and their parents. The first of these concerned the value of success and the path of hard work leading to it. The second had to do with Mr. and Mrs. Smith's hope that their boys would be honest and fair-minded people. Though Mrs. Smith occasionally refers to times when the boys as youngsters found these two sets of values to be in opposition to one another, there are no references to these problems once they became teenagers.

George and Mary Smith wanted their children to have every opportunity to become successful individuals in the field of their choice. They tried to be supportive of what they thought were constructive efforts by their boys and were patient and accepting in the event of failure. They were not afraid to be directive and even a little pushy when they felt their children were in danger of losing out on something they thought was important or when they were failing to live up to their responsibilities. However, according to Mary they tried to wait for each of the boys to pick their own direction.

From Peter's point of view both parents were strict and disciplined, but also quite caring.

They weren't oppressive—a lot of parents are oppressive in their support. They call them Little League parents, or swimming parents, or . . . whatever you want to call them. My parents were very encouraging [and] smart enough to know not to overencourage me or not to be oppressive, because a lot of people will rebel and just back away.

Both Mary and her son Peter remember that George Smith was particularly invested in his sons' athletic activities. Believing that he had grown up under circumstances that did not allow his own true athletic ability to shine, she recalls, George frequently rationalized his enthusiastic response to the boys' efforts by saying, "I want to give mine the opportunity that I never had." Knowing her husband as she did, Mary remembers responding to these declarations with a laugh and, "You're going to give him the opportunity whether he wants it or not."

At the same time Peter recalls that his father thought athletic success was not enough.

My dad felt that although it was important to do well in athletics, it was important to do well in school too. I think he had seen a lot of outstanding athletes that were just bums—[people who] once their sports were over didn't have anything to do. He really wanted to encourage us to do well in school; do well because it was schooling that would keep us in [good] stead the rest of our lives. He used to say, "You can't live on your athletic achievements the rest of your life. The people you pass on the way up, you'll see on the way down."

Thus, school and sports were the two areas in which Peter and his older brother seemed to have the best chances to succeed. These were the areas their parents knew best. Both parents had strong athletic backgrounds and continuing interests in sports. Mr. Smith had been an outstanding football player in high school and college and played golf regularly when the boys were growing up. Mrs. Smith had been an excellent swimmer, basketball player, and tennis player as a young girl and continued to play tennis and occasionally teach swimming (for extra income) after she had her sons. Though they tried to expose their boys to other activities, such as tap dancing and music lessons, the boys never really found anything in these to hold their interest. Looking back, Mary was explicit in saying that the strong investment she and her husband had in athletics (and school) probably swept whatever opportunities the boys might have had in fields such as music and art to the side.

> My oldest son has become quite an artist. What a shame—here we were concentrating on sports all the time when his real love was art! . . . He took it up on his own [later in life] and he's quite good—he could care less about watching any athletic events. I'm sure he only played football and entered any of these things to please his dad. . . . When I look and see his interest in art now, I think neither one of us realized it because we didn't have it ourselves. . . .

And from a more positive side,

> Peter's father is very athletic and has a lot of natural talent. I was a hard worker and had a lot of quickness and determination, but he's a natural athlete. [He was] quite an outstanding football player in both high school and college. Peter gets his natural ability from his father, and from me he gets his love of sports, a [sense of] determination, and quickness. . . . We both love sports, and our boys grew up liking sports because we did.

But while it was Peter's mother who brought him to his first swimming lessons and saw herself as most active in guiding him from one step to the next in his swimming career, it was his father who brought to life the importance of being a good athlete. From Peter's point of view it was Dad who set the direction and Mom who kept the ball rolling.

I'd say my mom was supportive of everything my father did; my father encouraged us in athletics and encouraged us in school, and my mom was extremely supportive all the way through.

By the time Peter was six, George was bringing both of his boys to the local high school football games on a regular basis. At seven, he and his older brother were running pass patterns for hours on end with their dad as quarterback. In the winter it was basketball, and in spring it was baseball, with George taking time to throw pitches to the boys so that they could improve their batting.

Both boys did well in the sports they played. They both did well in school too, but Mary notes that Peter stood out because of his good work habits and determination to do well.

He was a very conscientious child ... an organized child ... [really] a very easy child. ... He was competitive all his life. We first noticed it when he wanted to be the best student in his class. He was not happy unless he made the best grade in the class.

Even in his first years of grade school Peter worked hard to do well in school. And though he never said a word about it to anyone, he was annoyed if somebody got a better grade than he did. While this conscientiousness and determination stood Peter in good stead as he grew older and more demands were placed on his time, it was in marked contrast to his brother's behavior. Tom was not very neat or orderly. And if he was determined, it was to find another way to put off doing his homework.

SUMMARY: THE FOUNDATION FOR SUCCESS

Several aspects of Peter's family background are worth paying special attention to inasmuch as they seem to be important and perhaps even necessary ingredients in the development of great swimming talent. First, we get a sense that after the boys were born, both George and Mary Smith thought of themselves as parents first, husband and wife second. The children came first and were to have every advantage and opportunity the parents could provide, whether or not it was convenient or affordable.

Second, both parents were hoping that their boys would move up in social class. According to Peter, his father was more concerned that the boys eventually acquire positions that held great status and prestige rather than those that paid a great deal of money. No doubt, a position that yielded both money and prestige would have been better, but status was most important. Even as an eleven-year-old, Peter remembers his father talking about how important it would be for him to someday attend an Ivy League college and go to medical school. Peter reports that his brother was similarly "programmed" to attend an Ivy League school and become an attorney.

Third, neither parent felt competent or comfortable enough to guide their children in activities other than those having to do with school or athletics. Both parents knew well the kind of work habits and discipline required in athletics and schooling and made a point of acquainting their boys with them. Implicit in the Smiths' actions toward their children is the belief that sports could provide recreation, good habits, and a solid, fair character. Both parents went out of their way to keep close tabs on the boys' schoolwork, and at least one parent always had time to help with difficult homework and the like. As mentioned previously, the same close eye was kept on the boys' sporting activities.

INTRODUCTION TO SWIMMING

According to Mrs. Smith, Peter was first introduced to the water and to swimming when she taught him the basics in the summer of his sixth year. Though she was not explicit about it, all indications are that her efforts were a mix of play and lessons on floating, swimming, and water safety. The boys' first formal instruction began in the winter of that same year, when she took them to a community center that had a swimming program.

Peter did not remember, or failed to mention, his mother's instruction. As he recalls, he and his brother learned to swim at a club where his mother played bridge. He did remember that his mother stayed through their lessons. By chance, the swimming program at the club was very good. The coach at this club had in fact produced several Olympians and was very well known. Peter emphasized, however, that neither of his parents knew of the coach's status at the time they started there. The program was simply more convenient for them than others.

Though Peter could not remember very much about his first formal swimming instruction, he did remember that while it taught him how to swim well, it did not teach him all four strokes. He also recalls that he had a very good instructor who, though known as a taskmaster by the older children, was very patient and not very demanding with youngsters like himself who were new to the club. He also noted that whatever superior physical qualities were attributed to him as he grew older and more successful, they were not apparent back then. "I wasn't a good pupil, I was just a normal kid in terms of learning ability. My strokes were terrible until I was thirteen. . . . I didn't show a lot of promise."

Peter really did not begin to swim on a regular basis until he was nine when his family moved across the country to the East Coast. By chance, his new home was convenient to a large lake that was a favorite swimming spot for local townsfolk. The lake became the place where Peter and his brother played every day during the summer. The swimming was simply for fun. It was not the only sport the boys were involved in. Both played baseball, football, and basketball and were quite good in these. Under their mother's tutelage both were also learning to play tennis and golf.

Sometime shortly after their move to the coast, an incident occurred on a visit to his mother's grandparents that seems to have been critical in getting Peter started in competition. During that visit both Tom and Peter were invited by their mother's brother, himself a swimming coach, to watch some workouts. According to Mary Smith,

> Peter would watch what the other kids were doing and wanted to do the same thing. The other boy [Tom] wanted to play. . . . And so my brother asked me—he said Pete had the best kick of any boy he'd ever seen—if he could take him down with his team to put him in a little meet. I said, "Sure." At that time Pete was better at backstroke, [but he] just entered him in freestyle, and he came in third in his heat.

A cousin diving in the same meet came in second overall and won a medal. Mary remembers, "Peter didn't get a medal, [and] we bragged on Kenny until finally Peter said, 'I've heard all I want to hear about that medal.' So I brought him home, and he really wanted a medal just because his cousin got one."

Peter agrees that because he had done well, but not well enough to win a medal, he was eager to have another try. The opportunity came at the end of his first summer in his new hometown, when his mother asked if he and Tom would like to compete in a novice meet at the lake—kids who lived on one side of the lake against those who lived on the other. Tom wasn't interested, but Peter said he was "hot to swim in this one." His mom says he won every event he was in. His success was noticed by the parents of other swimmers on the lake, and shortly thereafter Mrs. Smith was contacted by the coach of a local club, who asked if Peter would be interested in practicing with his (AAU) swim team. He was.

Thus at nine and a half Peter began to train as a swimmer— "Formal training three times a week . . . for maybe forty-five minutes [at a time]." While the training was not very rigorous and "not scientific at all" in hindsight, it did emphasize stroke work and probably laid the start of a good foundation in the sport. It was important because it exposed Peter to a coach "who had a tremendous love for kids and taught them to love swimming. . . . Every kid who swam with [him] loved the sport. So I was very lucky." Within six months he and his mom report he was doing well on the team.

After a year of swimming, Peter's first AAU club disbanded, and he was forced to find another club. The next club he joined was the one where, according to his mother, "the better swimmers were." It was also twelve miles from home. Practice time jumped from three to five days a week for three-quarters of an hour per session. According to Peter, though this second coach spent some time working on stroke and pacing techniques, the emphasis now was on training hard. His mother recalled things differently and reported that the new coach was a freestyle specialist who did emphasize hard work but also underlined the importance of technique and efficiency in the water. According to Mary, this [second AAU] coach paid particular attention to Peter's handstroke in the freestyle.

Mary also notes that this second coach had previously worked with a number of Olympic swimmers and therefore had a special appeal to both the swimmers and those parents involved in their children's efforts. He was, she goes on to say,

> A very fine man. He . . . really taught those kids discipline. If they weren't on time for swimming, they didn't swim; if they didn't pay attention to him, he'd kick them out of the water for the day. They learned to listen. He was the strictest coach Peter ever had, but a very likeable person, a very fair person.

The discipline and training paid off. Peter did well as a ten-year-old in age-group competition. "And I don't know why . . . I was small for my age, I wasn't strong, [and] I didn't have good stroke coordination. At eleven I was terrible again, [and] at twelve I was just mediocre."

Despite Peter's ups and downs in swimming, the Smith family was becoming more and more invested in the sport. With the club twelve miles from home, double workouts (from the time Peter turned eleven until he left home at fifteen and a half) meant that Mrs. Smith traveled forty-eight miles for her two round trips a day. The twelve-mile one-way trip was just far enough to make return trips impractical while Peter was swimming, so Mary stayed for Peter's practices. Since the coaches closed the practices to parents, Mrs. Smith ended up with four or five hours a day to catch up on her reading.

Why did she do it? How could she bring herself to commit so much of her time, energy, and money (though we have not discussed it, the cost of this career was substantial) to her younger son's swimming?

We sort of backed into this gradually. I didn't know what I was getting myself into. We only went twice [Peter says three times] to swim [at the first club]. And then he was getting pretty good by the time he was ten and the coach at [that club] had left and the better swimmers were over at the [second club], so we joined [that] and let him swim. . . . He would swim about forty-five minutes a day five days a week, and that wasn't too bad. He had a coach who had had Olympic swimmers, and he would start talking to the kids about [how] if they were really good someday, they could be on the Olympic team, and so that interested Peter.

Then he started having team practice two times a day. We'd have to get up in the morning before school and then take him after school, so then we'd started to really get into it.

Funny how you get into these things before you know how much work it's going to entail.

While there is no doubt that Peter's swimming turned into something far bigger than the Smiths ever expected, our conversation with Mrs. Smith indicates that neither parent was much of a spectator. Being the parent who was at home most often and also the one who knew the most about swimming, Mary Smith was able to keep a close watch on her son's progress in the sport. Though not intrusive, she was always available to guide, support, and encourage Peter at every step of the way. Having taken Peter to and from practices almost every day, Mary was quite familiar with all of his coaches, their methods, and their relationship to her son. While she says she always deferred to these men on issues of training in a face-to-face discussion, her discussion with us leads us to believe that in the long run she knew how to get around them when she thought they weren't doing things quite right. For example, while watching Peter work out soon after moving to his second AAU club, Mrs. Smith noticed that the best of the older children could do flip turns, which Peter had not yet learned. Rather than bother the coach, who did not seem concerned, she arranged for Peter to be taught by some of these older swimmers.

> Peter learned to do a tumble at the end of the pool long before other kids [his age] learned it because I saw the kids [who] were making progress doing it, and I got one of the girls who could do it to teach Peter flip turns long before the other boys could do it. . . . The coach was not teaching all of them flip turns at the club, [but] Peter learned to do flip turns right from the beginning.

Rather than let things fall where they may, when things were not in line with her hopes for her son, Mrs. Smith intervened in such a way as to ensure that his lack of training was corrected. Apparently, the coach did not notice her efforts and had no cause for hard feelings. That is not always the case.

We suspect that in the event that the coach's philosophy or practices were clearly out of line with what parents like Mrs. Smith wanted, he would either be fired or these parents would move their children to other clubs. In fact this is exactly what led to the dismissal of one of Peter's coaches. For most of the parents of the talented swimmers studied in this project it was the coaches who were out of line, not their children.

As anyone knows who has participated in a sport such as swimming or had a child who did, the family routine is quickly affected by the twin demands of school and sport. We cite the following excerpt from our interview with Peter at length to show how the Smiths adapted:

> We never all sat down to dinner. I would come home from school, and my swimming workout was from 6 to 9 [P.M.], so I would have

to eat at 4 o'clock. As soon as I got home from high school, I would have to eat dinner, and that meant my mom would fix a meal for me and then I would study from 4 to 5:30, or whenever, and then I would go off to work out. . . .

I guess maybe my dad was the next to come home. Sometimes he and my mom would eat then, or they [might] wait for my brother to come home. . . .

But very often my mother was fixing three dinners: one for me, one for my brother, and one for my dad. So there was never, you know, [a time when] we all sat down to dinner. . . .

When I got home from workout, dinner would be done for the rest of the family. My brother would be studying in the kitchen—my homework was probably done, or if I had some extra homework, I would go into my bedroom and do it.

Both mother and son agree that the primary motivation for continuing to swim over these early years was the fun of being on a team, traveling, meeting other people, and, occasionally, winning. Mary commented on this twice:

It was more of a fun thing at [the first two clubs]; the swimmers weren't that good. We used to go to the meets with the little kids, and you never got so excited in your life when he [Peter] was in the Olympics as you were when he was nine, ten, and eleven years old.

He [Peter] got to be real good friends with the others [on the team], and he enjoyed it. . . . He got to go on trips, and the parents would go on the trips when they were younger. We all went together, and we'd all stay at the same hotels. The kids would have fun, and we did too.

When Peter was thirteen, his second AAU coach was fired and replaced by a man who maintained his predecessor's emphasis on hard work but also underlined the importance of technique and efficiency in the water. This third coach was a stroke specialist who approached swimming as a science. For the first time, stress was placed on learning to be a better swimmer by watching films and reading books on technique.

This coach had each of his swimmers involved in weight-training programs several years before most coaches advocated it. He also kept his swimmers on strict diets. According to Peter, this was the coach who "started me on my way."

Peter had been traveling to regional age-group championships since he had turned eleven, but it wasn't until he turned thirteen and was working with his fourth coach that he began to make the finals. As soon as he started making the finals, he also started winning. Within two years he went from nowhere in his age group to the top. From thirteen on, Peter consistently won most of the events in the meets he entered. Given his successes, he decided at thirteen years of age (with or without assistance is not clear) to compete against senior swimmers. Age-group swimming took a back seat.

Peter says that it was rough for the first year, but by fourteen he was beating even his college-age competitors. In fact he was beating everyone in his home state and doing quite well in regionals. It was at this point that his parents, particularly his mother, began seriously to ask themselves whether or not their son had the ability to make the Olympic team. Once they had decided that Peter was talented enough to make the Olympic team, they then asked themselves what more they might do to help him do that. Their answer: find him a better coach, one who definitely knew how to develop Olympic talent (because he had done it many times before) and who could challenge Peter with better competition and high goals.

SUMMARY: THE EARLY AND MIDDLE YEARS
So far we have seen Peter move from what might be called an introduction to swimming, where the emphasis was on having fun, to a second phase, where the stress was on carefully learning stroke and pace techniques in addition to building up cardiovascular endurance. Peter himself notes that by the time he turned twelve, swimming had gone beyond being fun to being a challenge, a way in which he could prove and improve himself. In chapter 11 (by L. Sosniak) we refer to the progression

from getting acquainted and having fun to hard work and careful study as the transition from romance to precision. These are the first two phases of a natural learning cycle made up of three phases. The third phase of the cycle is one of generalization, the time when the task being learned becomes a part of oneself. We believe that at fourteen when it was clear to Peter and his parents that he could go quite far in swimming, the stage was set for the step from precision to generalization to take place.

It seems clear that the motivating forces both inside and outside of the individual facing a task such as swimming must change as he or she moves from one phase to the next. We believe that in the beginning just belonging to a team, which is a kind of grown-up thing to do, was just about all it took to keep Peter going. While being on the team demanded hard work and responsibility, at the same time it provided him with friends, trips, fancy swimsuits, and warmups and, on occasion, the praise of others and a medal or trophy for winning.

But, in fact, even in the early days being on a team was not always enough. Even as competitive, determined, and skilled as he was, Peter could not sustain his investment in swimming without the very strong, indeed, commanding support of his parents. Peter explains,

> At eleven I wanted to bag it because I was doing very badly. I'd go to swimming meets and not make the finals; I was getting hassled by my parents because they'd say, "Hey, we don't care if you win, but at least try hard, we've driven these 200 miles and spent a lot of money for the motel. . . ." And I wasn't trying. I didn't like it anymore. All my friends were beating me.

Coming after pretty good success as a ten-year-old, Peter's failure as an eleven-year-old was hard to take. For a while he toyed with the idea of taking up football, as his older brother had—"Swimming was always a sissy sport for the kids around here anyway." But his parents intervened.

My dad at that point did something that was very important. . . .
He said, "If you want to quit, that's fine. But I don't want you to
quit simply because you're losing. If you're losing and you want to
quit, you're just going to be a loser all the rest of your life. So I'm
going to continue to drive you to workouts and force you to swim
and once you turn twelve and [are] at the top of your age group,
you'll start to do well. If you want to quit then, that's fine."

Peter's mother also reported sometimes reminding her son
that it was important not to quit when he was behind. She
added, "We never had to force him to swim [though]. I would
never, never have said, 'You've got to swim, you've got to.' . . .
It was always his decision."

The point in all of this is that Peter's parents were very active in helping him maintain his investment. They expressed
their values clearly and deliberately. They made it perfectly
clear that while having a change of heart was all right, running away from failure was not. Moreover, they seemed to be
saying to Peter, "If you are patient and continue to work hard,
there will be no stopping you."

Peter did begin to do well again as a twelve-year-old. Upon
turning thirteen and starting to compete against senior swimmers, he had another bit of a slump, but things had changed
by then. More and more it was him against some absolute
standard or quality. He was no longer the Peter Smith who
swam in the afternoon for fun. He was Peter Smith the swimmer. Everything else had to fit around that or be cut out.

THE LAST STEP

When at age fourteen he was confronted by his parents' suggestion that he leave home and move inland a few hundred
miles to work with one of the best coaches in the country, Peter
at first refused. His reasoning went as follows:

When I was a small kid, I wasn't very well accepted. I was the runt
of the class. And as I got older, I still wasn't accepted . . . because
I was in a sport that none of my buddies were in. . . . I was considered a sissy. But when I started doing very well in that sport, and

particularly my freshman year in high school—getting my varsity letter and winning two state titles—all of a sudden I was respected in my class and socially accepted. I kind of liked that. It had never happened before. And my parents' suggestion that I leave . . . boy, I fought it. I didn't want to. I was happy in my life-style, happy in school.

So he didn't go. But over the course of the next year and a half his mother kept in contact with the coach she thought her son needed, exploring further how arrangements might be made to accommodate her son. Her husband, she says, was also pushing for it.

When Peter was fifteen and a half, his parents convinced him that if he was going to be serious about trying to make the Olympic team, he was going to have to switch coaches. He was doing extremely well in his state at the time. His eventual agreement to go was not a full-fledged commitment, because he still hadn't convinced himself that he was willing to pay this kind of price to have a real chance at making the Olympic team. He left home with the idea that he would only be staying with his new coach for a couple of months. "I was adamant that I was just going there to give it a shot, and if I didn't have tremendous success right away, I'd come back and just be a good swimmer."

Workouts were much harder with his new coach. The distance he swam each day increased, and the resting time between sets decreased. Not really knowing anyone in his new home, he said it was easy to put all of his energy into just school and swimming. When there wasn't anyone to talk to and his schoolwork was finished, he would drop to the floor and do situps and pushups. Soon this was routine—pushups and situps each morning and evening in addition to workouts.

Within three months of his move Peter was doing well enough in senior competition to qualify for his first AAU Senior Nationals. When he placed in all his events that very first time, any thoughts he had had of going back home were put aside.

For the next year and a half Peter continued to work hard under his new coach. As the next Olympiad approached, upon his own request, Peter increased to three workouts a day. This included two hours before school, one hour at lunch, and two and a half hours in the evening. In the summer before the trials, Peter's life was filled with only eating, drinking, sleeping, and swimming.

Where his mother had guided him before because she knew the most about swimming, his coach was now in charge. Peter never questioned him. He now refers to this coach as a second father. Mr. and Mrs. Smith kept in close contact with their son by telephone calls and writing. They made a point to get to all of his bigger and more important meets. Still, he only saw them occasionally during the year and went home only for Thanksgiving and Christmas.

> Slowly but surely I kind of grew away from my friends back at home, though I still felt close to my parents. . . . But I had to do a lot of growing up. I mean at that point [fifteen and a half] I was on my own since [the family I was living with] didn't feel very close to me. You know, I was walking to workout, or taking the bus, or hitchhiking or doing what I had to do—which I resented. And I was having to have a bank account, cash checks, and stuff like that, things that a fifteen-year-old [didn't ordinarily have to do] . . . in essence I became a freshman in college at fifteen because I was on my own.

He didn't have any trouble making the Olympic team and doing well in the Games.

7

★ ★ ★ ★ ★ ★

Learning to Be a
World-Class Tennis Player

Judith A. Monsaas

Over the last two decades, tennis has become a very popular sport in this country. Of the thousands of children who take up tennis each year, most play it primarily for fun and sport. Of those who take it more seriously and become involved in organized competition, very few make it to the highest levels of accomplishment. This chapter will describe the process of talent development, from early childhood to adulthood, of those tennis players who made it to the highest levels of achievement in the field. More specifically, we will describe what the parents, coaches, and other significant individuals did, as well as what the tennis players themselves did to become among the top tennis players in the world.

Tennis was chosen as a second athletic field because there appeared to be some interesting similarities between tennis and swimming. Both were individual sports and had clear-cut criteria for identifying the top players in the fields. In choosing the athletic fields, team sports were excluded because it was felt that it would be difficult to separate the efforts of the individual from the efforts of the team. Thus the development of team sports was left for future researchers. In all the talent fields we confined our study to individuals who were below the age of forty. The purpose of this age limit was to increase the likelihood that their parents and coaches would also be available for interviews.

THE CRITERIA FOR
SELECTING TENNIS PLAYERS

The criteria that we ultimately arrived at for selecting tennis players were individuals who were born and raised in the United States and who had been ranked in the top ten in the *world* sometime between 1968 and 1979. The year 1968 was chosen as a starting point for two reasons. First, persons reaching the top ten in the world in 1968 or later met our age requirement, that is, all players who met our criterion were under forty at the outset of the interviews of tennis players. Second, 1968 was the year that open tennis began. Both amateurs and professionals were able to play in the same tournaments and were ranked according to the same criteria. The only distinction that remained was the requirement that amateurs not be allowed to collect prize money.

There are four organizations that rank the top ten players in the world. Probably the most prestigious rankings are the rankings of the Association of Tennis Professionals (ATP), the men players professional organization that ranks only men players, and the Women's Tennis Association (WTA), the women players organization that ranks only women players. Both ranking systems are computerized systems that objectively rank players on the basis of the previous fifty-two weeks of play. Unfortunately the ATP has only been ranking players since 1971 and the WTA since 1975. Thus it was necessary to find additional ranking systems that went back further.

Two tennis magazines, *Tennis* and *World Tennis*, rank the top ten men players and the top ten women players in the world. *Tennis* magazine has been ranking players since 1972 and *World Tennis* magazine since 1953. Both magazines have a panel of tennis experts and members of their editorial staffs who sit down with the players' records for the previous year and arrive at a consensus. Informants from each of the magazines indicated that the criteria they used were roughly the same as those used by the ATP and the WTA, that is, tournament play, prize money, and beating a highly ranked player.

Several advisors were consulted to assist us in refining our criteria and to assure us that our criteria did get only the very top players in our sample and not miss any clearly top players. Our advisors were top officials in the local tennis community as well as members of the editorial staffs of the tennis magazines and representatives of the ATP and WTA. They agreed that 1968 was the best year to begin our sample selection and supported the use of these four rankings as our criterion. They also confirmed our view that these rankings do reflect the consensus of the tennis community.

THE SAMPLE

Twenty-six U.S. tennis players were ranked in the top ten in the world between 1968 and 1979. Of the twenty-six players, we were unable to reach three, and five indicated that they were unwilling to participate, usually citing a busy tournament schedule as their reason. The final sample we interviewed included eighteen tennis players, ten men and eight women. A comparison of our final sample with our original sample of twenty-six shows no important differences. The average ranking, average number of years in the top ten, socioeconomic background, and region of the country were roughly the same for both groups. The only difference was in age, with the final sample of eighteen being slightly older (average age of thirty-one years) than the original sample (twenty-nine years).

The players in our sample came from middle- to upper-middle-class families. The fathers of half (nine) of the tennis players were businessmen, three were tennis pros, three were professionals (e.g., doctors, lawyers), and the remaining three were blue-collar or service workers. The mothers, with one exception, were housewives while the tennis players were growing up, although most had worked before their children were born.[1] The parents of the tennis players tended to be more educated than the average population. Twelve (65%) of the fathers had graduated from college, and six of these had at least one advanced degree. Twelve of the mothers also had attended college, and five of these had graduated.

With only two exceptions, tennis players had both parents present while they were growing up; the families had an average of three children including the tennis player. Thus most of the tennis players came from families that, at least on the surface, were typical of the families in the fifties and early sixties; that is, both parents were present, the fathers worked, and the mothers stayed home to "take care of the family" (T-10).

This chapter will attempt to describe what happened in the development of these children both in the home and on the tennis courts to help them reach the highest levels of achievement. The development of tennis talent is divided into three sections: the early, the middle, and the later years. There are a number of reasons for such a division. It makes the analysis and explanation of the findings more manageable. It is consistent with the treatment in the other talent fields. And, most important, it appears to reflect the changing emphases in terms of family relationships, coaching, the individual's and families' commitment to the talent field, and the dramatically increased time investment by the tennis player. In the early years, tennis was mainly a fun activity, while in the middle years a more serious commitment was made to tennis in terms of time and a narrowing of other opportunities. In the later years, the tennis players devoted full time to tennis and the

---

[1]A few of the mothers did do occasional part-time work, such as helping out at the tennis courts (especially the wives of the tennis pros) and selling Avon cosmetics to make extra money. But they generally considered being a housewife and taking care of the home their primary responsibility. The one mother who worked did so in a tennis-related job and did much of her work in her home.

professional tennis tour, and this required, at least temporarily, closing off other career options.

The Early Years

THE FAMILY

An interesting, but not surprising, characteristic of our sample was the large proportion of families in which one or both parents played tennis regularly. In about 80% of the families, at least one parent (usually the father) could be considered an avid tennis player.[2] That is, he played tennis whenever he had the free time, he took the sport very seriously, and was very competitive when he played.[3]

> My dad just had . . . very much of a drive to compete and to excel in sports (T-2).

> [My husband has] been an excellent player for years. [He] started out I would guess around the age of ten or twelve, on his own joined a little local men's tennis club. . . . Played a lot of junior tournaments and has played tournaments all his life. He's still playing tournaments (M of T-7).

About half of the mothers played tennis, although they were typically referred to as "club players" by their children and not considered to be as serious about tennis as the fathers. For example, one mother took up tennis because "[I]t was the way,

---

[2]In two of the remaining four families, athletics was very important, but the parents didn't get involved in tennis until the tennis player became involved through a local park district. The other two players began tennis in a park district program and were noticed by a local pro who took them under his wing and, in effect, made them part of his family.

[3]The fathers of two-thirds of the players had played some tournament tennis either while in college or after college, and about one-third of the fathers continued to play in tournaments when the tennis player was growing up.

starting early on, to find Dad on weekends" (T-8). Another player described his mother's tennis:

> [She played] social tennis, just for fun. She liked to get out there and hit the ball. She plays in a lot of the women's foursomes. . . . She's not overly athletic, but she's pretty competitive (T-4).

One characteristic that emerges in almost all of our families, whether the family played tennis or not, is what is viewed by our tennis players as a special family closeness. The parents spent a great deal of time with their children, and many activities were done as a family unit. This, in itself, might not be so unique, but it appeared to set the stage for the relatively easy assimilation of the important family values of hard work and doing well. Further, it made the careful monitoring of the child's development in tennis and other areas a natural progression of family relationships.

In many of the families, a great deal of family recreational time was spent at the tennis or country club[4] from the time the child, and his or her siblings of course, were very young. Family time was devoted to several other activities in addition to tennis. The parents would spend time golfing, playing tennis, and just socializing, while the children would play, swim, and sometimes play tennis. Nevertheless, in some of these families much of the family time was devoted to tennis.

> [W]e've been a very close family because we were always together. After school, we all went to the tennis courts. I mean all of us. . . . And I think in a situation like that you maybe tend to be a little bit closer than the family that's kind of going all separate ways (T-2).

> My family always did a lot of stuff together. We belonged to a country club and we used to all go to the country club. That's

---

[4]Some families were members of tennis clubs, while other families belonged to country clubs. Whether the club was a tennis or a country club, they typically had activities and facilities other than just tennis available, such as swimming pools and running tracks. We will refer to both of these as "the club" throughout this chapter.

where a lot of our time was spent, I guess after we were very young. . . . Most of my time was spent out at the club playing tennis. And the other kids would do that, play tennis, plus be at the swimming pool. We spent a lot of time out there doing that, and we'd take vacations together (T-10).

We spent so many hours on the tennis courts. . . . Since they were toddlers, they all had a racket in their hand—it was a natural interest for them to play tennis. . . . We were very close with the kids, they never went to camp or anything like that, we were always involved in their playing tennis and their going to tournaments and their doing what they wanted to do—it was just a way of life for us (M of T-10).

Sometimes I'd drop her off [at tennis practice], and we'd pick her up. Some days when she was playing tournament tennis I would stay with her all day long, most generally if it was out of this area. The same thing for [sibling]. . . . We were busy with the children. We had a good close relationship with them. I would say in all probability we spent more time with our children than the average parent (M of T-9).

Even those families that did not play tennis or belong to a club spent a great deal of time as a family. These families found other activities to do as a family and took vacations together. (When the children got older, the vacations often revolved around tennis tournaments.) Following are a few examples of how these families spent their time together:

We'd go to the movies together if we had any money. We never had enough money to go out to eat, so we started to . . . go to the hamburger joints on Friday. That was a big deal. We would go . . . to the mountains maybe, or to the desert, just to look around (T-9).

We used to go skiing quite a bit (T-5).

[As a family] we did a little bit of everything. . . . [W]e boated and fished. Basically, though, my younger days revolved around tennis (T-13).

In addition to the special family closeness, a second important characteristic of these families was the intensity with which they held to the traditional values of hard work and doing well. The parents held these values for themselves and for their children. Both the tennis players and their parents repeatedly emphasized the fact that in their families, the pervasive message was "anything worth doing is worth doing well." While this value is not unique in itself, what appears to be unusual is the intensity with which it was held and the fact that the parents spent a great deal of time with their children and thus were able to ensure that this ethic or value was upheld on a daily basis.

The parents of the tennis players transmitted the value and importance of hard work by example rather than by any direct pressure. Several of the tennis players described their fathers as hard workers. They worked very hard at everything they did, and the notion of finishing what you start was important to them. They worked very hard at their job, their sports (typically tennis), and their family. As we shall see later, when the tennis players reached the middle years and had made a commitment to tennis, the parents spent many hours encouraging and promoting their child's tennis. Many of them also spent long hours on the practice courts with their child and chauffeuring their child to tennis lessons and tournaments. The mothers were also described as being hardworking, but "softer" (T-3), less intense, and less competitive than the fathers.

[My husband] worked on a farm as a little boy. He's always worked all his life. He thinks that you should work and he enjoys working. When we lived in ———, he gave tennis lessons and he [was] very ambitious because he enjoyed it. He would catch businessmen before they went to work. . . . to take lessons early in the morning. And then he'd catch other businessmen who'd come in the evening. He was giving twenty-two lessons a day at one time. He's very, very healthy, but at the time he developed a little high blood pressure. He was doing too much (M of T-4).

The notion of following through had also been important to me. In my family it translated into—finish what you start. I had to finish all the food on my plate. . . . When I wanted to learn to swim, I had to take lessons. When I asked my father if I could play in the junior high school band, his first question was, "Are you going to stick with it?" (T-14).

Most parents want their children to do well in school, in sports, in piano, and in any other activity in which they become involved. The parents of the tennis players were not different in this respect. The difference between these parents and other parents is the fact that not doing well or doing less than one's best was just not acceptable.[5] Further, the way in which this value was manifested in these families also appears to have influenced the tennis players' development. In more than half of the families, "doing well" was equated with winning or being best. In these families, doing well was not enough, you had to be better than others in the activities that you pursued. Of course tennis was the obvious activity to pursue in these families where the parents were active tennis players. Following are some quotes that exemplify the value of doing well and being best in many of the tennis players' families:

There's a whole thing about levels of excellence. . . . Unless you do something really well, then why brag about it. I mean rankings [for example]. Why care if you're number six or seven, if you're not number one it doesn't matter. It's okay to be six or seven, but unless you're number one, it doesn't matter (T-8).

I think our family always felt that if you're going to do something, you might as well do it well . . . it was expected of you to do well, and that was it (T-4).

I guess [my father] never really said directly to me that "I want you to become good at whatever you do." But there must have been that sort of influence (T-5).

---

[5] The influence of this value on some of the siblings who were not as able or motivated or competitive is an interesting story, but will not be discussed here.

> My father's always been very competitive. . . . When he sets his mind to doing something, he gets it done. It's at the expense of a lot of things and it's at the expense of a lot of people . . . a lot of times. If people can't perform around this family, they don't hang around too long. People get burned out pretty easily. For the most part it's a high-accomplishment family. . . . It's always been geared that way. It's just the way the family was oriented (T-10).

It must be noted that there were circumstances where losing was not frowned upon. Those circumstances tended to be situations in which one was competing with someone who was an older and more experienced player. If the child did his or her best and played as hard as he or she could, losing, while not quite acceptable, was seen as an incentive to work harder and do better next time.

While all players indicated that their parents wanted them to do well in both school and athletics, the actual pressure to do well in most of these families was in athletics. That is, the family's resources of time and money were devoted to providing for opportunities for the child to pursue athletics, especially tennis. Of course these parents wanted their children to do well in school and to attend college. Nevertheless little of the family time and resources were devoted to ensuring that this took place. As one player said, school "was secondary to tennis" (T-2).

> A lot of times we had to tell little stories when there were tournaments because the school didn't approve of them missing. . . . But tennis always seemed to come first (M of T-17).

Family time was so heavily invested in taking children to practice, tournaments, and so on, that little time was found or made to make sure the child did his or her homework. It will be seen in later sections that in two-thirds of these families, tennis influenced many school-related decisions, including the choice of a college.

In about one-third of the families, the pressure was clearly to do well in both school and athletics. The parents in these families saw to it that homework was done, that the children went to good schools and got good grades in addition to ensuring that the child had a good tennis coach and practiced hard.

> [Doing well in school] was very important to them. And my mother helped me study quite a bit. Almost every night . . . she would quiz me on whatever lesson I was supposed to learn. . . . All of it [was] memorization-type stuff. But that's what they teach you in grade school. And so as a result, you pick it up—I was learning quite well because of what she did (T-3).

INTRODUCTION TO TENNIS

The age at which the youngsters started playing tennis varied greatly. Some began playing tennis any time between age three and eleven. The average player began at six and a half with all but three beginning before age nine. The three players who started later were very athletic and played other sports regularly before taking up tennis.

As already mentioned, most of the players in our sample began playing tennis because their families played tennis and spent time at a tennis club or country club. Often the time of these children was split between playing tennis, swimming, and performing other activities with their family or other children at the club. However, a few of them focused strictly on tennis from the start. For most of the individuals it was "natural" that they get involved in tennis because that was what their parents did and virtually all members of these families played some tennis.

Seventy-five percent of the tennis players began playing tennis in essentially this way. They just began spending time at "the club" with their families. In most cases they started out playing with their parents or siblings, although some of them had friends their own age with whom they played regularly.

In our family, the time together was the tennis together. It was the kind of thing that was part of our household from when we were very young (T-8).

My dad . . . used to play a lot of tennis. We belonged to this club actually, about ten minutes away from our home. And when I was about four, they put in a swimming pool. . . . So starting about May, on the weekends, my dad would just go down there and play all the time. Sometimes my mom would come down and sit around because there were a lot of people. . . . And so on the weekends . . . my younger brothers and I would go down there and they'd hang out by the pool, and I'd play tennis. My dad would play tennis (T-7).

They [parents] wanted me to get an interest. My mom liked tennis. My dad played tennis. So I guess it was natural. . . . It was always a self-motivated thing except for [the] first few years. I think they just did the simple thing: They gave me a racket, the backboard was there and they'd hit with me five or ten minutes after they'd play. And that was about it (T-6).

Those youngsters (25%) who were not introduced to tennis by their family were usually introduced through a friend, given a racket as a gift, or, in one case, found a discarded racket. They were usually involved in local park district activities, and tennis was one of the several activities in which they became involved. That is, they began taking tennis lessons (usually free) with the same age group of children with whom they played softball, swam, and so on. Chance seemed to have played a larger role in the introduction of these few players to tennis than it did in the others, that is, they happened to be involved in athletics at a park district at a time when tennis lessons were available. This is in contrast to the other players, whose parents were active, and avid, tennis players. Nevertheless, these "park district players" for the most part came from families where athletics and sports were very important activities and they were encouraged to pursue athletic activities by their parents.

In all cases, when the individual began playing tennis, it was simply seen as a good recreational activity. Despite the number of fathers who played competitive tennis, none of the families initially had in mind the development of a world-class tennis player. It also appears that none of the young tennis players had this dream. In fact at the time (1967) that even the youngest member of our sample began playing tennis, world-class tennis was very different than it is today. There was very little money involved, and as one tennis player said, "To play tennis for a living was to be a tennis bum" (T-8). It was only after the individuals in our sample had been playing tennis for several years that making a living playing tennis and tennis as a career, other than as a club pro, became a real possibility.

Once the players began playing tennis, a few of them became fascinated with the game and focused on tennis very soon. However the majority of the players played other sports as well as tennis, at least through the early years. The boys were more likely to play several sports than the girls. For three of the eight girls, tennis was the only sport they played. The other girls played basketball (N = 3), softball (N = 1), swam (N = 1), and played golf (N = 1). Only one boy (out of the ten) played no sports other than tennis. The other nine were involved in organized baseball (N = 5), basketball (N = 5), football (N = 3), track (N = 2), soccer (N = 1), and ice-skating (N = 1). Baseball seems to have been the typical sport in the early years where it is common for boys to be on Little League teams, while basketball was played mostly in junior high school and in a few cases in high school. It was not uncommon for boys to play football and/or basketball in the fall and winter and then tennis and baseball in the summer. It should be noted that in these early years only a few of the tennis players played tennis in the winter.

THE FIRST TENNIS LESSONS
Just as it was "natural" for most of the individuals to play tennis, once they began playing tennis and showing some inter-

est, it was logical for them to take lessons. The average age at the first lessons was eight years. In about half of the cases, lessons were begun sometime after the child had been playing tennis. In the other half, either lessons were started at the same time the child began playing tennis or lessons were the introduction to tennis.

In the families that belonged to a club, lessons were initiated by the parents, who typically believed that all of their children should take at least a few tennis lessons. Tennis was what you did in the family. Since the family spent a great deal of leisure time at tennis clubs or country clubs, it was relatively simple for them to get involved in a few age-group lessons.

For some of these children, someone noted that they were interested in tennis and played fairly well for their age level.

> I think I took my first clinic when I was five. I think my mom probably put me in the clinic because she had been hitting with me and she knew I could . . . hit well (T-6).

Another player had been doing well without tennis lessons until his game started to falter at about age eleven.

> [Then] it got to where it looked like I was kind of floundering. I wasn't improving. . . . I was always much better than everybody my age around the place. Then a few guys started to catch up to me. . . . [Friends of his father] said, "This guy showed five years ago that he had some potential to be a . . . good player. . . . It's kind of obligatory to find someone to teach him how to play well" (T-7).

While these first lessons were usually initiated by parents who often noted some interest or talent in the child, little effort was made, at this stage, to find a special coach for the child. The first coach was either a parent, a local club pro, or a park district tennis instructor. This first coach was usually a good tennis player, but not great,[6] and had never been a professional tennis player or player on a national level, and sometimes did not teach particularly good strokes. One player's first teacher "was just the pro that was in town. He taught my sister also" (T-3). Another first coach was similar. He "was the pro at our country club. And I was quite young at the time, and so my dad thought, '. . . let's just start you out with this guy' " (T-10).

While these were not exceptional coaches, they tended to be very good with young children. They were regarded by the tennis players as extremely nice people who sometimes took on the role of a father figure.[7] Often the child hung around the courts when the coach was giving lessons to others, visited the pro's home, and became friendly with his family. According to one tennis player, he and his coach developed "a very close relationship. In fact we talked quite a bit about different [nontennis] things I was doing" (T-3). One park district coach "was fantastic because he just gave of himself" (T-9). The player became close to him and his wife and visited their home. Yet because of the large group lessons, the teaching situation "was really bad in a way, knowing what I know now. . . . [For example] we never got to rally much. So what we would do is drop the ball and hit it" (T-9).

What this first coach provided was motivation for the child to become interested in tennis and to spend time practicing tennis. One way the coach did this was by taking a special interest in the tennis player in our sample, usually because he perceived the player as being motivated and willing to work hard, rather than because of any special physical abilities.

---

[6]There were a few exceptions to this rule. The father-coaches were excellent coaches. In a few other cases, the player happened to live in an area and go to a club that had an outstanding coach.

[7]This first coach was always a man, and almost all other coaches were men, so the masculine *he* will be used to refer to the coaches throughout the chapter.

This special attention in turn provided additional motivation for the child to work hard and practice.

The majority of the time, in these early years, was spent in drillwork or practice. The instructor provided reinforcement in several ways to make this work more interesting and to motivate the child to practice hard. The tennis players received a great deal of praise and positive feedback when they mastered a stroke or even for getting the ball in the court initially. Children were frequently rewarded with Cokes, candy, and sometimes money, for successfully hitting targets set up on the other side of the net. One tennis player's first coach

> . . . used to always have incentives. Like we'd have a ball machine that would hit balls [to us]. And we'd have fifty tennis cans on the court on the other side. If we hit a tennis can on the fly, we'd get a dime. If we hit one on the bounce, we'd get a nickel. And he'd always say that if we got one inside the can, he'd take us out to dinner, which is almost impossible. . . . But we still tried (T-6).

In addition to demonstrations and drills, these first coaches put some emphasis on competition. This increased greatly over the years, but even at the earliest levels some time would be set aside for the children to play sets and matches among themselves so that the tennis player would feel at ease in the competitive situation from the start. One tennis player described the clinics he was in in the early years:

> There might be as many as twelve, fifteen people. They'd divide us up into two teams, and we'd play against each other, alternating around. . . . As a result, he always was putting [us] into a competitive situation. But he was [arranging] it where, when we'd hit the ball, he'd be correcting us to make us hit it properly. So you wouldn't just be doing something to get it over. He'd make us change and do the stroke properly (T-3).

Six of the tennis players first learned to play tennis from their father. Three of these fathers were established tennis pros.

I was six, and Dad had a group-lesson-type thing for the children at ———, a beginner-type group. And I started in that (T-2).

[He] was my only coach. He's my father. I [would] just go over and play with him, or get a lesson after his day was over (T-4).

The other players' fathers were good tennis players who felt they could teach the basics as well as the local pro.

He said, "Look. You know I love you, and either I do it or I pay a pro to do it. There are certain things I know and you might as well learn them from me" (T-13).

[My father] started me out. He's not a great player, but he knows a lot about the game, so he's always been able to sit down and take a look at [my game] (T-10).

The major difference between those players who learned to play tennis from their fathers and those who learned tennis from another coach was that "lessons" with the father were almost always one on one and they tended to be more frequent. There was also little distinction between "lessons" and "practice." In fact, these children tended to practice a great deal with their fathers, so they were, in effect, getting "lessons" whenever they practiced.

INTRODUCTION TO COMPETITION

About three-fourths of the tennis players in our sample began to enter local competitions one to three years after beginning to take lessons. The rest of the players entered their first tournament before they began to take lessons or at about the same time they began to take lessons. Many of these competitions were interclub or city tournaments. Occasionally the first tournament was at the regional or state level. The players in our sample reported entering their first tournament sometime between seven and thirteen. The average age was eight and a half.

In most cases a parent or teacher initiated this by simply

mentioning the tournament and asking the child if he or she wished to enter it. In a few cases it was a tournament in which the parent was playing.

> I was nine [when] I played in my first tournament. . . . My parents just said, "There's a twelve-and-under tournament. You want to play?" I said, "Sure" (T-7).

> My first tournament . . . I was ten years old and I'd just gone because my sister and father were playing in it. It's a state-level tournament. And so they entered me in the twelve-and-under (T-3).

Although most of the players thought that it was a parent who recommended that they enter their first competition, it was such a logical thing to do if one was a reasonably good player in his or her age group that they had difficulty remembering exactly how they were entered.

> I think when you're good at something, it's just the obvious thing in a sport. . . . I mean you can only hit on the backboard and practice with people so long. You've got to go there and test [yourself against] other people. Probably my parents found out about the tournament and mailed my entry in. . . . And so that was how it started at a very low, low level. And it just progressed through the years (T-6).

> I can remember a lot of the tournaments I played in when I was real young, but I don't remember the first time. . . . I'm sure it was my dad's idea. He said, "Why don't you do this?" And I said, "Sure." But I don't remember (T-4).

Although most of the players didn't remember exactly how they got to their first tournament, they did remember how well they did in it. They usually lost in an early round. They were upset by this loss, but it didn't discourage them because typically they were playing someone two or three years older than themselves and/or someone who had been playing tournaments for some time and was highly seeded in this tournament. Thus they were able to justify the loss and find consolation in having won a few points or a game against this player.

> This guy I was playing was much, much bigger than I was, and he was the number one seed in the tournament. . . . He killed me. He beat me six–love, six–love. But I did get one point [laughs] and I was so ecstatic. . . . And so I didn't start off immediately just doing very, very well. There were just little things that I would pick up on that I liked (T-3).

> The first tournament I lost [6–1, 6–1] to some guy. And the next year I played in one tournament and [lost] love, love. [Why did you go back?] You play some guy that's three years older and you lose, it's no big deal. I liked it. I wanted to see how I could do. I wanted to compete (T-7).

Most of the players started off losing in early rounds of the tournaments. But this was seen as an incentive to work harder and do better next time.

> I started playing in a novice tournament a few weeks after I had started playing. . . . There were four people in the tournament. And [a friend] beat me love, and love in the finals. [My coach] said, "That's okay." And I said, "That's not okay." And the next time we played . . . I lost to her in three sets and that was only within like three months. So it was that kind of improvement (T-9).

Within a year of tournament play, most of these players were doing well in local and area tournaments. And they then began to travel to state, regional, and, in a few exceptional cases, national tournaments. By the end of the early years, about age twelve, most of our players were winning, or at least making it to the finals or semifinals of the local and state tournaments. Toward the end of the early years, a few were playing in the nationals and doing well. They were generally viewed as being the top local players in their age group and were beginning to get some notice on a local level, at least by other tennis players and families.

At this stage, tournament play was not yet a great financial burden because families were not traveling great distances. But already the time investment for parents who were driving their children to tournaments and lessons was becoming great. Lessons and travel did require some financial investment because this was a time when the parents themselves were still young, it was early in their careers, and they had other children. So sometimes it was a sacrifice financially to provide for the child's tennis.[8]

The real investment for these parents was time. Some of the parents spent a great deal of time practicing with their children. (This was especially true of the fathers who were coaches, but also true of several other fathers.) It took a great deal of time to drive these tennis players (and often their siblings) to tournaments, lessons, and practice. Several of the players referred to their mothers as the family chauffeur because they spent so much time driving their children to tournaments and lessons.

> My mom used to drive me around to all different tournaments, and my sister used to play some. Just like we made one trip up to ——— . . . to play, and she took us there. And she was the patient mother waiting for us while we had our games, I guess (T-4).

> [My mother] supported the kids in taking us around to tournaments and doing . . . a lot of schlepping back and forth with kids (T-10).

> [My mother] traveled with me on the tour when I was a kid all the time. So she was my, you know, I got her a cap and called her my driver (T-13).

TIME, MOTIVATION, REWARDS
In the early years, there was a great deal of variation in the amount of time the players spent on tennis. Some players played only a few hours per week at first, whereas others be-

---

[8]It was and is fairly common for tennis-equipment companies to give free rackets, shoes, and so on to the top youngsters in an area. Therefore most of these families did not have to invest a great deal of money in equipment.

gan immediately putting in fifteen to twenty hours per week and more. During the winter, practice time varied even more. While the players from the South and West could practice year-round, in the winter, those from northern cities did not have easy access to indoor courts and so played only a few hours per week at most. Even those players in the southern climates played less in the winter because of school and conflict with other sports, especially basketball. Table 1 shows the contrast in tennis-playing time between the summer and winter months for the players in our sample.

TABLE 1
Average Number of Hours per Week Playing Tennis during the Early Years

	Number of Tennis Players	
HOURS PER WEEK	SUMMER	WINTER
0	0	2
1–10	3	11
10–15	6	1
15–20	3	4
20–25	1	0
25+	5	0
Average	16.8 hrs/wk	7.6 hrs/wk

Most of these players did not begin tennis with the idea of becoming great players. It was during the early years that they gradually began to increase their practice time until, by the end of the early years, most players were putting in at least ten to fifteen hours per week in the summer and a few hours per week in the winter.[9]

Probably [ages] six, seven, eight, I played Saturday and Sunday. Then maybe nine, ten, and eleven, I started playing maybe three [or] four days a week, maybe five days a week. And then in the summer, when I started being about eleven or twelve, I probably played about every day (T-3).

---

[9]Table 1 represents the averages over the entire early years.

In contrast, another player became interested in tennis right away and began immediately practicing

> ... as many [hours per week] as I could get. . . . The only trouble ... during the winter, the sun went down, and I used to get so ticked. I hated the winter because that meant I had two hours less to practice after I got out of school (T-9).

At this level, for most of the players, tennis had not yet become all-consuming. They mostly played because it was fun, they enjoyed it, and they got attention for playing tennis and doing well. For most players who had a parent or sibling who played, it was what one did in these families and it was logical that they would spend at least some time taking lessons and playing. One player practiced because she knew that was what her parents wanted.

> I think, in a way, to start out with, I know that it pleased Dad. And I think that a girl wants to please her father, maybe more than a boy does. And I think I enjoyed, I enjoyed it. But even above that I knew that it pleased, so I worked especially hard (T-2).

> I was just infatuated with the game right off. I'm sure a lot of that had to do with my parents, who were so into tennis (T-7).

Others began investing more and more time because they began doing well, and this in turn motivated them to put in time. For some this doing well was just at local club play, that is, they began beating children their own age and a few years older. Others began doing well in tournaments and knew that if they worked harder, they could do even better. Some also remarked that at this stage they were very competitive and hated to lose. One player talked about what motivated her to put in several hours a day in the summer playing tennis:

> When you start at age three, as I did, you don't even think about it. . . . It's just something that gets your fancy. It's more, maybe, a

curiosity. Finally, I think I just wanted to see how good I could get. I knew I was good. I was very competitive from the start (T-6).

Another player put in long hours practicing from a very young age because

I just knew I hated to lose when I was a little kid. I couldn't stand to lose, I used to work as hard as I could not to lose (T-10).

SUMMARY OF THE EARLY YEARS
A number of generalizations can be made about these tennis players and their families during the early years:

• The families of the tennis players in our sample were very involved in athletics. Further, tennis was an important part of family life for about three-fourths of the tennis players from a very young age. In these families at least one parent was actively involved in tennis, and a great deal of the family time was spent at tennis or country clubs. One important conclusion is that tennis players who reached the highest levels of achievement typically came from families that value tennis highly or families that value athletics.

• Most of the tennis players grew up in families that spent a great deal of time together. Pervasive throughout all of these families was the value of doing well in anything you try. In several families doing well was equated with winning, although an exception would be made if one were competing against an older, more experienced competitor. Under these circumstances, losing was seen as an opportunity to analyze one's weaknesses and improve one's game. The families valued doing well both in school and in tennis, but the emphasis in most families was to do well in sports in general and tennis in particular.

• The child got involved in some age-group tennis lessons at the family club or the local park district. Some players started lessons because there just happened to be age-group lessons available, and they took them. Others were doing fairly well in tennis, so someone (usually a parent) decided that they should have lessons. The first tennis instructor was typically selected because of his location (nearby) rather than his expertise as a tennis instructor. These first instructors did have some important qualities: They were good with children, they took special interest in our tennis players, and they spent a great deal of extra time working with them. While the first coaches were frequently lacking the important technical skills of a good coach (e.g., stroke production, strategy), they had interpersonal skills that were very important at this level, that is, they were able to get the child interested and excited about tennis.

• Tournaments played an important role in the early years in that they gave the tennis players a chance to test their skills against better players. It is noteworthy that most players lost in an early round in their first tournaments. They were not discouraged by this loss because they were frequently playing against an older, more experienced player. These losses motivated them to work harder so that in the future they would lose by a smaller margin and eventually win.

• Over the early years, the tennis players began to increase the amount of time they spent practicing. Most of the players began playing and practicing a few hours per week. Gradually the time increased, until they were putting in several hours per week in the summer and at least a few hours per week in the winter. Variation in time depended on the area of the country in which the players lived, availability of courts, and, to some extent, the age at which the player started. Several reasons were given for spending a great deal of time at tennis: It was fun, it pleased parents, and they were doing well at it. Further, since they were competitive and hated to lose, they spent much time working hard to improve their game. By the end of the early years the tennis players were beginning to get some recognition locally, and to some extent this led them to work harder to live up to the expectations. This also gave them a "sense of glory" or a sense that they were special.

The Middle Years

The middle years of tennis development were roughly from ages twelve or thirteen through the end of high school. Although the transition from the early years to the middle years was gradual, there are several characteristics that distinguish these two periods. If one phrase could be used to epitomize the middle years, it would clearly be "the development of commitment." Most of our sample of tennis players began playing tennis because their families or friends played. They stayed with it because they enjoyed it and because they were doing well at it.

During the early years, most of the tennis players had begun playing at local club tournaments and then went on to city and state tournaments.[10] A few had even played in national tournaments. Toward the end of these early years, they were surpassing their age mates and doing well in the state and regional junior competitions. As one mother put it, "We went from a little city tournament, which was fun, to maybe a district, to a state, and then you just moved on up the line" (M of T-12).

At some point along the way these tennis players realized that tennis was no longer "just a game." It was serious business. Sometimes the tennis players floundered a bit, that is, didn't do as well as they had been doing, and determined, with the help of parents and coaches, that a more serious commitment was needed. Other players continued doing well but realized that to beat the older, more experienced competitors in

---

[10]The junior tournaments are organized by sex and age group, such as Boys 18 and under, 16 and under, 14 and under, 12 and under; Girls 18 and under, and so on. The major tournaments are sanctioned (or approved) by the U.S. Tennis Association. The tournaments are arranged in a hierarchical order, and a player must do well on one level to compete at the next level. The tournament levels include the following: club, city, state, regional, and national.

the tournaments, they would need to commit themselves more fully to tennis. In our interviews, the players would begin with statements like "When I really got into it . . ." (T-5) or "When I started taking tennis seriously . . ." (T-12) and would then talk about how they increased their goals and the amount of time they spent practicing.They also added that they now focused on tennis exclusively. Frequently, the transition was more gradual. The tennis players became aware that they were now working harder than they had in the past at tennis, practicing more, and, as one player described it, "eating, sleeping, and breathing tennis" (T-2).

There appear to have been three major changes that characterized the transition from the early years to the middle years. First, the tennis players' self-images changed. They began to view themselves as tennis players, not just people who played tennis. The coaches, parents, peers, and members of the tennis community gradually began to view them as tennis players. Articles and pictures in the newspapers described the players' wins (and losses). Important people in tennis noticed them. They were viewed by others as being "talented" tennis players and they began to view themselves as such. But as they began playing tournaments in older age brackets and began participating in regional and national tennis tournaments, the competition became greater. It was now time for them to work seriously to "develop their potential."

Secondly, the players also realized that they needed a new type of coaching and sometimes a new coach.We have seen in the early years that the first coaches had been good at getting them interested in and excited about tennis. The tennis players felt that now they needed someone to teach them precision and technique as well as some strategy; they also needed to tailor their tennis game to emphasize their own personal strengths and compensate for any weaknesses they might have.

This emphasis on developing precision and strategy led to the third change: a greatly increased time investment. In short, in the middle years we see the tennis players working harder and practicing longer hours, often with a new coach or a new coaching method. This increased time investment and commitment was accompanied by increased recognition and in some cases acclaim from significant persons in the field of tennis.

SPECIAL ATTRIBUTES OF THE TENNIS PLAYERS

The tennis players in our sample had a great deal of difficulty describing any special physical characteristics of theirs that may have contributed to their success in tennis. The parents and the coaches were no better at describing special physical characteristics than were the players themselves. One explanation may be that the tennis players, unlike athletes in some other fields, come in all shapes, sizes, and body types. Some tennis players were tall and others were short. Some were husky and others thin. (All of course were in good physical condition regardless of body type.) In fact several tennis players stated that they chose tennis over other sports for the very reason that they didn't have the physical requirements (e.g., a 6-foot 2-inch player who felt he was too short to play pro basketball) to succeed in some of the other sports they played. Nevertheless, a few players were able to assist us a bit in defining some physical qualities they felt they had.

About one-fourth of the tennis players indicated that they had some specific physical characteristics that contributed to their success in tennis.[11] The skills mentioned included quick reflexes (N = 3), hand-eye coordination (N = 2), and left-handedness (N = 1).

> One thing about tennis is that you're always reacting to a given situation and dealing with it. . . . I love that reacting. I've always had quick reflexes, so I ended up being a volleyer (T-9).

---

[11]Over half of the tennis players were reported as having exceptional athletic ability by themselves, their parents, and their coaches. But they were unable to describe what they meant by athletic ability. When questioned about this, they typically reported that they knew that they had exceptional talent because they did well in almost every sport they played, and most of them did well in tennis at a very young age.

[My coach] thought that I had a lot of potential. . . . [because] I was left-handed. And at that time not many left-handed tennis players were around, and so you'd have sort of an advantage. He felt that he would work on a lot of things that were advantages to left-handers, such as the serve where the ball spins differently than the right-hander. . . . Then he spent time working on different angles of passing shots and things like this. All things that were just an advantage because I was left-handed (T-3).

From the examples just given it is clear that some of the tennis players had physical attributes that worked to their advantage with the help of their coach. We also have examples of players who were noted as having had specific physical drawbacks or who were not viewed as being particularly athletic. The parents and coaches worked hard with these players to overcome these disadvantages or worked to strengthen a particular aspect of the game in order to compensate for a specific weakness.

[My son] accomplished an awful lot, his size is against him. He doesn't have the big serve that the other pros have, [but] he always had a lot of guts. He was willing to stay out there and get the points. . . . We felt that his serve would never be powerful because of his size, but we felt that what he accomplished was amazing (M of T-10).

[I had] an "I'll show you" attitude. Everyone said, "You can't make it." And I said, "Well, we'll see." It made me work harder. . . . [And] drove me to be as good as I possibly could (T-10).

I don't think [anyone noticed any special talent]. . . . First of all, when you're between six and eleven, it's very difficult to know how talented a kid is going to be because they can change. Everybody knew that I was a pretty good young player, but they wrote it up to the fact that it was a tennis family. . . . I don't think anyone said, "It looks like he has some special talent,"—not before the age of thirteen or fourteen (T-12).

The few players with specific weaknesses (e.g., T-10, just quoted) often developed a baseline game (which is a slower game) in order to compensate for not being very fast or for being short. The players also compensated for physical drawbacks or for lack of any extraordinary physical qualities by working "twice as hard" as their peers to do well in tennis.

Almost all players reported that they had personal qualities that they considered as important if not more important than their physical characteristics. One of these qualities was *determination* or *willingness to work hard*. The players remarked that what people noted about them was the fact that they never gave up. They would do whatever they had to do to reach a goal or win a match. If that meant spending many hours on the practice court or playing a five-hour tournament match in 100° + weather, that's what they would do. This determination is related to the second quality noted by the tennis players: They were *extremely competitive*. Winning was all-important to them. Almost all the tennis players we talked to reported that they would work hard and practice long hours because they *hated to lose*. Following are some examples of these important personal qualities:

[My daughter] is not the greatest athlete, but Chris E. isn't either. . . . They make up for it in different ways. . . . [My daughter] is a fighter. She doesn't give up and she can get way down in a match and come back. It's more than just natural talent to win a tennis match (M of T-2).

I was a fighter. I'd never give up. That's one thing, I was an excellent competitor. I couldn't stand to lose. If they had to drag me off the court, I'd stay out there and do whatever I had to do to win the match. If that meant staying out there five hours, I'd stay out there on the court for five hours to win the match. . . . I was really determined. Plus I practiced twice as hard as anybody else. I used to just go out and play for hours and hours and hours. And I used to feel that I had to do that to make up for some of the lack of physical size. . . . So my competitiveness and my willingness to work hard have always been the two biggest things that have gotten me as far as I have, I think (T-10).

I was competitive. . . . I know [my coaches] liked my tempera-
ment. I didn't get upset too fast. . . . and they say that I worked
hard (T-5).

People noticed that I worked hard. That I practiced hard. That
probably even intimidated a few of them. . . . [Also] I was a highly
competitive person (T-12).

THE COACH AND COACHING

By the middle years these tennis players had been playing for
an average of four to five years and taking lessons for three to
four years. They had learned the basic strokes of the game
(e.g., forehand, backhand, serve) and had, over time, developed an extraordinary enthusiasm for the game. As they began
to travel to regional and national tournaments and play
against older and better players, the competition became
greater.

It became apparent to the players and their parents that
they needed a different type of instruction and sometimes a
new instructor if they were to continue doing well in the game.
The coaches of their early years didn't have to be particularly
good players or teach particularly good strokes, as we have already seen. Their role was to get the child interested and motivated. The middle years, with its tougher competition,
required improved strokes, technical skills, and attention to
strategy. As one player put it, in addition to knowing *how* to
hit the ball, he had to learn "how to pick apart the opponents'
weaknesses, and *where* to hit the ball, [and] *when* to hit the
ball" (T-5).

The instruction became very organized at this level, with
repeated drills that the tennis players worked on with their
coaches and practiced to perfection on their own time. As already mentioned, for the tennis players to reach the world-
class level, it was critical that they have good strokes and that
the strokes be so automatic that the players could concentrate
on strategy during a match rather than on the strokes. Vic Bra-
den, a noted tennis coach, refers to this as getting "the muscles

to memorize the strokes." One mother described her daughter's strokes thus:

> She looks pretty much picture-book. Everything looks the same when [my daughter] hits the ball. You can see that she had hit thousands and thousands of balls the right way. Her strokes show it (M of T-2).

In order to teach this precision, specific teaching strategies were adopted by the coach: repetition and individualization. As T-2's mother reported, she hit "thousands and thousands" of balls. This is not atypical. Clearly, to develop the level of precision needed to make it to the top in the world, the players needed extensive repetition and drillwork. Players would spend hours (during and after lessons) practicing hitting the ball in exactly the same way until they got it perfect and it became automatic.

The tennis players also changed from group lessons that were once or twice a week to almost-daily individual or small-group lessons. This change was necessary because the tennis players needed more individual attention to perfect their game. And, especially, they needed a coach to work with them on their own personal strengths and weaknesses. Many of the lessons focused primarily on drillwork. Each session would include a large amount of practice on the strokes already learned as well as the new strokes being introduced. One player described a lesson:

> Say my forehand was not right, we'd spend forty minutes on the forehand every day. And ten minutes on the volley, ten minutes on the backhand. We always spent a lot of time on the serve because I always had problems with the serve. . . . We'd work on strokes maybe an hour a day, then I'd play sets after work on the strokes. But we'd go through the whole repertoire and work on each stroke every day (T-4).

Extra time might also be devoted to a particular potential strength, as in the case of a left-hander spending a great deal of time perfecting the serve. The instruction and practice were tailored to promote the individual's strengths, keep other parts of the game in top form, and to correct the individual's weaknesses.

Although the primary focus of the lessons during the middle years was to perfect the players' technical skills, more and more time was being devoted to strategy or teaching the players how to think during a match and how to modify their game to beat a particular opponent. There were a number of ways in which the coaches helped the players with strategy. Often the coaches would play with the players and stop frequently to analyze a specific play. Other times the coaches would set up matches between two players. They would observe the players and stop the game occasionally to discuss their playing. Occasionally the coaches would go to tournaments with the players, watch future opponents, and discuss how they should play a specific opponent in a later match.

> [My coach] would watch me play this boy . . . and then say if I lost, he would point out why I lost. If it were a stroke deficiency, we'd work on that stroke. If it were tactics, he would show me and explain what I should have done (T-2).

> I would play with [my coach], and we would play some sets out. And we would play a point and we would analyze the point. . . . He would say, "Why did you do this?" . . . and "If you see a guy in a certain position on the court, then you should watch out for this shot" (T-5).

The transition to the middle years with the different coaching requirements was often difficult for both the individual and the coach. In fact, one-third of the players decided that they needed a new coach to work with them in the middle years. Numerous reasons were given for changing coaches. In a few instances the coach moved away (or died).

> [My coach] left town when I was fifteen. . . . And right before he left, he and I were talking and . . . he said that there was only one

reason that he felt bad about leaving town and that was because
he felt I was going to be one of the top players in the country [and]
that by leaving, he was losing his coaching of me. And so he felt
bad about that (T-3).

[My first coach] was a really great guy. He became kind of like a
father image to me . . . . He taught me basically my very first
ground strokes. And then when I was fifteen, he committed sui-
cide. [It] really crushed me (T-11).

In other cases the parents made the decision that their child
needed a new coach because they were either not progressing
or had progressed so rapidly that they had surpassed their
early teacher.

I know my dad played at this place where [a different coach]
taught. . . . He was supposedly a better teacher than [my first
teacher] and therefore I went to him for some lessons. . . . Those
were private lessons. . . . [The new coach] seemed to get more involved in precise techniques of hitting the ball the same way every
time (T-5).

[My first coach] didn't do a whole lot for me. . . . [I took lessons
from him] for two years . . . and I still wasn't improving, and so my
parents said, . . . "We'd better find someone better." And then I
went to this guy [name]. . . . He was further away but he had a reputation . . . for being a good coach (T-7).

Switching coaches often created unpleasant conflict between the parents and the coach because the early coach was
reluctant to give up a very promising junior player. A coach's
reputation is usually based on the number of highly ranked
players with whom he is working. Also the coaches felt hurt
because they had invested a great deal of time in the player,
often without pay, and had treated the child as part of their
family. Nevertheless, in retrospect, these players all recognized that they could not have progressed much further with
the early coach and thus needed someone new.

Something I found out later was that Mom wanted [a new coach].... It's funny, I can't really put a pinpoint on what changed, except that I know it was the right decision. I don't think I could have gone a lot farther with [my first coach], it was sort of a messy deal (T-6).

The remaining two-thirds of the players stayed with their first coach. Some of these players stayed with their first coach because he was clearly an excellent coach. Some of the first coaches were among the top coaches in the country. The three players whose fathers were coaches are included in this category. These coaches were exceptional in that they were able to make the transition from the emphasis on fun and motivation of the early years to the emphasis on structure and precision required in the middle years.

Some of the players who remained with their initial coach went to special summer programs or had additional specialist coaches to work on specific aspects of their game. Although these first coaches were described as having a good understanding of the game and what was needed to succeed in the game, they were not necessarily able to teach every aspect of the game. One player whose father was his major coach had this to say:

[I] would work with a couple of pros in the [area].... [One of them] was number one in the world for a couple of years. She would work with me on my game a bit. And the other guy ... we started to work on volleys and serves and different aspects of the game.... My father would basically make those decisions. He would sit down and say, "I hear there's a really good guy over there and you really need to work on ——" (T-10).

Another player worked with a former champion on weekends for one summer.

[When told a former champion would work with her] I lit up like a light. I said, "Let me talk to [my coach]," because I didn't want to hurt [his] feelings. [The coach] said, "You've got to take it. She's a champion.". . . . [T]hat's a good coach, he let me go because he knew I'd get something from her (T-9).

Two other players went away for an entire school year during high school to work with a special coach.

That was [my coach's] decision. . . . He just said to my father. . . "[Your son] is very good, but if [he is] going to remain very good, [he has] to go to such and such a place where [he] can play twelve months a year" (T-14).

INCREASED COMMITMENT

Possibly the most important change made in the middle years is the increased commitment in terms of time and effort. As previously mentioned, the tennis players found that the demands of the instruction at this level required a great deal of practice time. Up to this point, the tennis players who lived in the North generally had been playing only during the summer. They now needed to arrange practice time during the winter. And even those players who had been playing for a few hours per week in the winter now made an effort to increase their winter playing time. As one player put it,

I knew if I didn't play x number of hours or time during the week, that somebody on the West Coast or Florida who had more open availability was doing it at their leisure (T-13).

Arranging for indoor court time during the winter in the 1960s and early 1970s was considerably more difficult than it is today. There were fewer indoor courts, and those few indoor courts had shorter hours. Often the tennis players had to make special arrangements to practice.

The first time I ever played indoors was when I was about thirteen. . . . My dad thought I shouldn't just quit the game for [the winter] months. . . . [He] decided it would be good for me to play just once a week so I wouldn't totally forget. So when I was thirteen, fourteen, and fifteen, I played once a week. And then when I was sixteen, a new indoor club opened right in my town, so my dad organized . . . an early-bird session. . . . So we each had a key and we'd go down there . . . from 6:00 . . . to 8:00. Two hours maybe. Then I'd go to school. And I did that about four times a week (T-7).

I didn't play a whole lot of tennis in the winter until I was fourteen. Then I may [have played] maybe three . . . four times a week. . . . Winters were always tough, between school and the weather (T-6).

The tennis players from the South had less difficulty practicing year-around, although they practiced fewer hours per week during the fall, winter, and spring because of school. Nevertheless these southern players also increased their year-round practice time.

I guess I had the attitude that if practicing twenty minutes a day was going to make me the fiftieth-ranked player in the U.S., then four hours a day would probably make me number one (T-12).

During the summertime, from the time when I was eight years old through the time I was seventeen years old . . . I was out on the court seven or eight hours every single day. . . . Just practicing and playing tournaments. . . . In the wintertime when I was thirteen or so . . . I would practice for three hours after school every day. And on the weekends all the time, just all day long (T-10).

In the summer, all of the tennis players were putting in at least two hours per day on the tennis courts, and many of them spent all day at the courts. There was more variation in the number of hours spent practicing during the winter. Table 2 shows the amount of time the tennis players spent practicing during the middle years. Of course this is an average, and the number of hours changed over time, typically increasing over the middle years.

The tennis players found that the dramatic increase in the amount of tennis practice made it almost impossible for them to invest the time needed to be good in other sports also. Thus, they gradually began giving up the other sports in which they

TABLE 2
Average Number of Hours per Week Playing Tennis
during the Middle Years

	Number of Tennis Players	
HOURS PER WEEK	SUMMER	WINTER
less than 10	0	2
10–15	2	8
15–20	5	8
20–25	6	0
25+	5	0
Average	21.4 hrs/wk	13.9 hrs/wk

had been involved. In some cases this was suggested by their coach. In other cases, the tennis players themselves realized that they were not able to invest the necessary amount of time in two or more sports and they had to make a choice. Of course, all of our players chose tennis over the other sports. Several reasons were given for the choice of tennis. Most of them had to do with the fact that these players were doing better in tennis than in the other sports and/or that they didn't feel they had the physical or mental makeup for high levels of success in the other sports. A few also commented that they preferred an individual sport over a team sport.

> [I was] better at tennis. . . . I knew I'd be a good professional in tennis. Whereas in basketball . . . I wasn't physical enough. Those guys, they're big. They're physical. . . . They were bigger. I was maybe smarter. But I didn't have the raw physical assets (T-4).

> I played football through most of high school. But there are physical attributes that go [with being] a football player. I mean I'm not that big a guy. You don't have to be a giant to play tennis. But there are other things you have to be. You have to be quick but you don't have to be quite the same as a football player. . . . Maybe [I chose tennis] because I'm an individual player rather than a team player (T-3).

> I played basketball, baseball, and a little football. . . . I played baseball regularly, and that was probably my first love . . . besides tennis. And it was a problem because it's played at the same time of year. . . . And I couldn't do both after a while. I did do both for

a couple of years, [but] I just didn't have the time for it. [I chose tennis], I guess, [because of] the uniqueness of the sport maybe. And I had done well in it. . . . And while I liked playing team sports, I guess maybe the individual aspect did something for me (T-1).

A second problem that the tennis players confronted at this level was the difficulty in finding other good tennis players with whom to practice. Most of the players had far surpassed the other children and teenagers in their area. In order to continue improving, they needed competitors who posed a challenge, that is, competitors who were at least at their own level of play or better. About one-fourth of the players were fortunate to have been in the same area as another top junior player with whom they practiced. Others played with top adult players, and some of the girls practiced with boys. Many players took advantage of a combination of the above, for example, playing with other top-ranked juniors and adults. Some of the players discussed how they solved the problem of getting good players to practice with:

[My father] was always setting up games with the men because I could beat all the kids. So when I was eleven years old, I had to start playing with the best men players around. I [started] playing with the best men players at our club. And . . . then [as I got older], he'd set up games for me with the best men players in [the area] (T-10).

. . . being able to play against better players like my [older] brother and, when I was nine, ten years old playing with the local men players. That kind of competition. . . . [Although] they weren't great players, they were good or better than I was. . . . The key is being smart and being able to play with better players (T-1).

[I practiced with] other men around the area. Usually men. . . . When I was young, before . . . twelve or so, I played with other kids my age or a couple of years older, usually a couple of years older because I was usually better than most of the kids my age. But at the club there were a lot of good [men] players (T-7).

PARENTAL INVOLVEMENT

At this stage, the parents found that they, too, had to increase their commitment to their child's tennis. In the early years, the child's tennis time had, for the most part, coincided with the parents' tennis. That is, the parents had to do little more than take the children along when they played tennis. During the middle years the child's tennis became central in the family life. The new coaches they found were not nearby, and the tennis players typically had to be driven to their tennis lessons. They also frequently had to be chauffeured to the tennis courts where they practiced, at least until they were old enough to drive themselves. Further, they were beginning to play in regional and national tournaments, which often required a significant investment of both time and money. In all, the parents were spending more time and more money on their children's tennis. In fact, they frequently found that their daily lives revolved around their child's tennis instruction, practice, and tournaments.

For the majority of the families the increased frequency of lessons and court time plus travel and equipment involved at least some financial sacrifice. In most of the families the financial burden was not excessive because the local tennis associations provided some help.

It was always yes it was a hardship and no it wasn't. "We're spending more money on you than we are on the other kids. But don't worry, it's not a problem." It was kind of "Be appreciative. Don't just think money grows on trees." . . . I heard that statement a few times. . . . But . . . there was never a feeling that someone else would have to sacrifice because I was getting a tennis lesson (T-7).

Well, it wasn't so expensive in those days to start out with. But the tennis patrons association in [city] helped with a number of those trips [to national tournaments]. . . . They just offered to kind of sponsor me. We never stayed in very luxurious places either. . . . We always took a hot plate and cooked our own food. Never ate out. So it didn't cost . . . an exorbitant amount of money (T-2).

However, some of the families did have great difficulty in finding money for their child's tennis. Sacrifices were made, other relatives helped out, and the local tennis associations raised funds to send the tennis players to national tournaments and to hire coaches for the children.

> My mother started working. My dad took on another job. . . . So we had three jobs. They had, not we. I felt like it was we because they were getting tired all the time. . . . They were always trying to provide opportunities for [sibling] and me. They'd be trying to get [sibling] to a [sports event] and me to a tennis tournament. . . . Just to keep tires on the car, keep tennis shoes on my feet and those kinds of things were just tough on them (T-9).

> My clothes were made by my grandmother. All my tennis equipment was given to me free by the companies. So we had travel expenses. I had some friends of my grandmother who gave . . . $400 or $500 over a couple of summers. And my grandparents gave me money. My dad and mom gave me a minimum, because they couldn't afford it (T-11).

While there was variation in the amount of financial investment, *all* of the families found that they were investing a great deal of time in their child's tennis. Mothers drove the tennis player to practice daily. Families drove to tournaments on weekends. Family vacations were spent going to tennis tournaments or tennis camps. After school and on weekends time was spent at the tennis courts. In short, we found all families making great time investments in their child's tennis. For example, one family had moved across the state to a place where there was no tennis available, "so we brought [our son] back to the east coast every weekend to get his practice" (M of T-17).

> . . . during the summer we all went to the club and spent the day. Of course when we went to school, I'd go to school, and then immediately they'd pick me up and we'd go to the tennis courts. And that was six days a week (T-2).

[We went] to tennis tournaments as a family. . . . We [had] a vacation place . . . in [state name]. And we used to go there and we'd play tennis (T-3).

Obviously when I couldn't drive [to daily lessons], my mom would take me. Often when I'd have my lessons from [my coach], she'd take me and drop me off. . . . And sometimes she'd stay through the lessons. I didn't like that, because I guess I wanted to be on my own a bit. They'd come to my tournaments, all my junior tournaments just about. My mom traveled with me to all my national tournaments (T-6).

We always went with the children. . . . We didn't have any other interests . . . but tennis. It was our hobby and our lives and our business and pleasure and everything. Tennis was everything, and it grew to where tennis was the main thing in our lives, and everything circled around it (M of T-12).

The previous examples, while exemplifying the amount of time the families spent on their child's tennis, also indicate the extent to which tennis became central in the family's life. As the mother of T-12 states above, "It grew to where tennis was the main thing in our lives." Tennis was the subject of dinnertable conversations. If families had previously taken ski vacations or gone fishing or boating in the past, they now went only to tennis tournaments. Mothers cooked special meals so that the "tennis players" in the family could eat a late supper. There was very little that the families did that was not tennis-related at this stage. Further, these tennis-related activities were primarily directed at providing opportunities for practice and competitive play for the tennis player in our sample rather than providing opportunities for the entire family to play tennis as we have seen in the early years. In one extreme example, tennis was in part responsible for one family's decision to move from a Middle Atlantic state to Florida:

We finally decided to move [to Florida. My father] had his business down here, and it would be good for the kids' tennis, and he enjoyed it, and everyone else would enjoy it. . . . It was great for my tennis because I could play all year round (T-10).

In about half of the families, one parent, usually the father, took on the day-to-day supervision of practice as well as some of the coaching of the child. Tennis had become central in their daily lives. In a few other families, the father had a major supporting role in that he worked with the tennis player on particular aspects of the game, especially on the basics. These fathers also supervised daily practices and arranged for the tennis player to work with other coaches on specific parts of the game. The families where a parent took on a major coaching or supervisory role exemplify an extreme amount of parental involvement in the child's tennis.

Ultimately we did [go to a local pro] only because my dad didn't have enough time and didn't feel that he could have enough time to go out and teach me what I would call the mechanics of thought processes, [that is] why do you hit a ball here and why to hit a ball there. He taught me all my strokes and really grounded me in the game, and then we had a pro who was at the country club who knew the game well [and] knew the court strategy well . . . (T-13).

[As I got older], I'd play a lot with my dad. Every afternoon my dad would come home from work, and we'd go out and just spend two hours just hitting balls. And trying to see if we could hit thousands of balls without missing (T-10).

SUMMARY OF THE MIDDLE YEARS

The middle years were clearly a time of commitment for our tennis players. They were investing a great deal of time and effort in tennis but reaping the rewards of this increased effort. They were getting ranked nationally and receiving a great deal of notice in the tennis community. The following generalizations can be made about the middle years:

• In some sports, particular physical qualities are necessary for the individual athlete to reach a high level of talent development. However, the tennis players we interviewed didn't fit into any special body type or size. In fact, one of the reasons some of the tennis players gave for choosing tennis rather than another sport was that their size or shape didn't work against them as it might have in another sport. With the help of a good coach in the middle years they felt they were able to modify their tennis game to capitalize on what they considered physical assets (e.g., quick reflexes) and compensate for physical drawbacks (e.g., short stature). In other words, it appears that specific physical attributes may have influenced the type of game these tennis players developed but had less influence on their level of success in the game.

Many of the players felt that certain personal qualities had a greater effect on their success than their physical attributes. Most players attributed their success to the fact that they were willing to put in many hours practicing tennis. In addition to being willing to work extremely hard, the players felt that they were successful because they were so competitive. Statements like "I hated to lose" and "Winning was all-important to me" cropped up repeatedly in the interviews. This desire to avoid losing increased the players' motivation to put in long hours on the practice court because they knew that that was what they had to do to win.

• During the middle years the coaching and sometimes the coaches changed because the players needed to refine previously learned skills and develop new skills to win against the better competition at this level. In the early years the emphasis had been on motivating the child by making tennis interesting and fun. In the middle years, the players had to develop precise technical skills as well as make their strokes so automatic that they didn't have to think about them. In this way they could "free their minds" to concentrate on strategy during a match. Because the coach and player worked closely to tailor these technical skills in order to capitalize on the individuals' strengths and compensate for their weaknesses, the lessons were more frequent than they had been (usually daily) and were on a one-to-one basis.

The change in emphasis during the lessons in the middle years was sometimes accompanied by a change in coaches because it appears that some of the coaches who were good with young children couldn't teach the more precise skills of the middle years. Even those players who stayed with their first coaches found that they needed to arrange for special instruction with other coaches on particular aspects of their game.

• All the players needed to increase their practice time to develop the precise strokes that their coaches were emphasizing. Players in the North (or their parents) made a special effort to arrange court time in the winter for practice. During the summer, players in both the North and the South often spent all day on the courts. This increased commitment to tennis necessitated giving up other activities and sports so that the players could devote more of their time to tennis. In fact, their daily lives were beginning to center completely on tennis instruction, practice, and competition.

• The families' activities also began to revolve around their child's tennis. The parents spent a great deal of time driving their child to lessons, practice, and tournaments. Time was also spent finding good coaches and practice partners for their child. Family vacations revolved around tennis. Family conversations were about the upcoming tournament or news in the world of tennis. In short, during the middle years much of the family activities were devoted to tennis and especially the tennis of the players in our sample.

The Later Years

The transition from the middle to the later years is characterized by the decision to play tennis full time. During the middle years the tennis players had spent a great deal of time perfecting their tennis. It was now time for them to test their game in the world of adult professional tennis. This year-round full-time investment would involve giving up competing activities such as jobs, other careers, and further schooling—at least for the present. The age at which the decision to devote full time to tennis was made varied greatly. One player accelerated her progress through high school to join the tour year round in her teens, whereas at the other extreme one player went to graduate school and received a master's degree before joining the tour full time. The majority of our sample made the decision sometime during college and chose either to leave college early or to complete college (sometimes at an accelerated rate) and then join the tour.

COLLEGE: A TRANSITION
FOR MOST PLAYERS

All our players were doing exceptionally well in tennis by the end of the middle years. The records show that about three-quarters of them had won at least one national junior tournament and the rest had been ranked very highly as juniors. They clearly viewed themselves and were viewed by others as being among the top junior tennis players in the country.

During high school a decision had to be made as to what to do after high school. About 80% of the tennis players chose to go to college, and because this was a significant transition for most of the players, much of this section will be devoted to college tennis.

Some of the players attended college because it was what the family expected. These tended to be the players whose parents valued doing well in both athletics and school. The parents had gone to college, and their children would do so too. For these players, tennis was a consideration in the decision of which college to attend but not the decision to go to college. For the other players, tennis was the major reason for attending college. College tennis was seen as an interim place to improve one's tennis before joining the adult tour. For these players, the decision to go to college as well as the decision of which college to attend was made strictly for tennis reasons.

Of the eighteen players in the sample, fourteen attended

college.[12] For almost all of the college attendees the quality of the tennis coach and the tennis team were important considerations in determining which college to attend. About half of these players wanted a college that had *both* a good academic reputation and a good tennis team.

> I wanted a school that was academically very strong . . . but also athletically very strong . . . . That made me shy away from the Ivy League schools because I don't feel that they match up [athletically] the way the other schools do (T-3).

> First of all, there was a good job of recruiting by the coach. I thought it was a good tennis program, but also I thought it was a good school. I didn't want to go to a lousy school just because it had good tennis (T-7).

For the rest of the players who attended college, tennis was the only consideration in the choice of college.

> . . . I wanted to go to a college where I could play on hard courts because I knew for my game to make the next step, I had to learn to play on faster courts (T-10).

> I chose to go to —— because [another tennis player] who I knew and who I had a chance of playing doubles with was there. . . . I [thought] if I go there, if he and I play well, then we could be a doubles team and I could get accepted more quickly because [he] . . . was a more accepted personage on the tour (T-13).

> [I chose ——] for several reasons. One, because of the reputation for tennis. Two, I liked the smallness of the school. . . . There were some other top junior players that were going to be freshmen the same year that I was. So it looked like we were going to have a good team (T-1).

---

[12]The men were somewhat more likely to go to college than the women. Only one of the men (10%) did not attend college, whereas three of the women (38%) did not attend college. One explanation for this different rate of college attendance was that a number of colleges had very good men's tennis teams, whereas only a few had women's tennis teams at all.

In the end, the college choices were made on the basis of the reputation of the tennis team and coach as well as the players' impressions of their personal compatibility with the coach. (And as we have just seen, some players took into account the academic reputation of the college as well.) Almost all of the tennis players were recruited very heavily by the tennis colleges because their junior tournament records were so good. They were very aware of the reputations of the various college tennis teams and college coaches.

> I had [tennis] scholarship offers to seventy to eighty schools. . . . And the coach from ———— just called me every single day. . . . Finally, I just decided that's where I wanted to go to school (T-10).

The parents also played an important role in helping their son or daughter select the right college. Parents often visited the school with the tennis players and talked to the coaches. They also discussed the various college choices, with their son or daughter helping them weigh the pros and cons of each college. Finally, once the decision was made, they were very supportive of the decision.

> I discussed [my college choice] quite a bit with [my parents], because I was getting letters from all over the country . . . and you kind of get barraged and you really don't know exactly [what to do]. And it came down to basically [two schools]. . . . And so it was kind of, we decided it would be better all around just to go to ————. And it was a joint decision (T-3).

The situation was very different for the women in our sample. Of the five who went to college, only two chose the college for its tennis. The others were often resentful of the fact that the opportunities for women in college tennis were so poor and especially of the difficulty women had in getting tennis scholarships and playing on college tennis teams.

> It wasn't an era where there were women's tennis teams. . . . I just arranged some games. I would try to play every day or two. I never

really played much with the men's tennis team—none of that was available. I never pushed it in a way that California kids would (T-8).

There were not [tennis] scholarships available [for women]. . . . They didn't have women's coaches then. The men's tennis coaches wanted me to go to their school. [So she went to a local university and practiced with the men's teams] (T-9).

Once in college and on the tennis team, the tennis players in our sample worked very hard to be the best. For most of our tennis players who went to college, tennis was clearly the priority once they got there. As freshmen, they set the goal of becoming the number-one player on the team. They began to work even longer hours than they had in the middle years and to work even harder. Team practice sessions in college tended to run three hours a day, and most of our players practiced extra hours after the team practice ended.

For the players who wanted to do well both in tennis and in academic subjects, there was very little time for activities other than playing tennis, training, attending classes, and studying.

I worked on my game really hard. I remember going out and just playing with the guys on the team for hours after class. And then going and running and working on weights. . . . My game improved unbelievably. . . . And I worked really hard in school. I can remember I'd get up and go to classes and go to practice four or five hours and do my weights, then go to the library for six or seven hours. I was doing that every day. I never had a date at school until April of my freshman year (T-10).

I was number one on the team from the first day I was there, and so the coach spent a lot of extra time with me. . . . Plus I would come out early. Practice started at three o'clock and I would be there at two o'clock. That was my [decision] (T-3).

For most of the tennis players, doing well in academic subjects was not a major aim. Preparing for professional tennis was the most important goal.

I did okay for a couple of years [in college]. I made the dean's list for a couple of times, and then I said, "Why am I working so hard, I mean, who cares?" I'm not going to try to get a Ph.D. or anything—I mean, you know, it wasn't a big deal (T-13).

I did mediocre in [my coursework]. I would think of my priorities in terms of tennis, social, and then academics. I was putting in the whole afternoon on tennis, whether I was practicing or not. I was there every afternoon from [about] one to six getting to know the [team], talking to the coach . . . [and] practicing (T-15).

Sometime during college the tennis players decided to join the professional tour. Most of them had made the number-one spot on the college team and had done exceptionally well in tennis. They had achieved the tennis goals they had set for themselves in college (e.g., to play on a new surface, win a college singles title). They had improved their game greatly, but college tennis had become less challenging. About half the tennis players decided to leave college without graduating. They decided that they were now ready to play tennis professionally.

My third year in school I was the number-one player in college. I was 26 [wins] and 0 [losses] . . . and I was better than everybody. . . . It seemed like a total waste of time to go back to school and to play just to get my degree, which I probably wasn't going to use anyway because I was just going to become a pro. My rationale was, "Hey, I can go back and get my degree when I'm fifty. Why do I have to do it now and be totally bored and just waste a year?" (T-7).

That freshman year when I was in [college], that next summer I was ranked number ten in the U.S. in men's . . . and I kind of suffered through one more year of [college] there without . . . any real competition and then turned pro in my sophomore year. . . . I went to [college] for three years, but I didn't finish (T-10).

The other half of the players decided to complete college before joining the tour. A number of reasons were given for completing college. For some players, timing was important, that is, they graduated from college before or just in time for open tennis. At least one person gave up a tennis scholarship for his senior year to finish in two quarters and join the tour early.

> Tennis . . . kind of worked out nicely with my whole college career, because when I graduated from college, I was named to the Davis Cup team . . . and tennis became open. . . . And so I could choose to play professional . . . do the same thing I was doing all summer before, in fact, all year round (T-5).

> Even when I graduated from college, there was no pro tour, so even at that time I wasn't taking tennis seriously. . . . And so it was exactly two years [after] I graduated college . . . that I joined the tour (T-11).

> I turned pro after my junior year. I paid for school instead of taking my scholarship. But I did go for my fourth year [and graduated] (T-3).

THE COACHES

As we have just seen, the major coach for most of our players was the college coach. For most of our players, more time was spent with this coach than with any previous coach simply because tennis practice was several hours per day during fall, winter, and spring. (Summer months were typically spent on tour.) Despite this amount of time, most of the players reported that this coach helped them very little on strokework. It was assumed that if they were on one of the top college tennis teams, they already had developed good strokes.

In the later years we find the coaches working primarily on strategy with the tennis players. Our players reported that for an individual to reach the highest levels, he or she must know not only how to hit the ball but when and where to hit the ball. Strategy is also needed to analyze an opponent's game and play to his or her weaknesses. Several players discussed how their college coaches modified their game:

> It was just a new philosophy. Rather than hitting every ball as hard as I could, to try and play the percentages a little bit more. I improved. Just not be quite the gambler. Just use a little common sense (T-7).

I'm known for having quite a good serve. And when I went to [x university], I had a good serve. [My coach] said that was fine. And we continued to work on my serve to keep it strong. . . . I had a tendency to always try to serve very hard, and so, as a result, the shots that back up the serve were not that good. And so any day that I wasn't serving very well was going to be a very difficult day. [The coach] made me spend time in practice . . . [serving] at half speed . . . so that other guys would give me a lot of [practice] for my other shots, which improved my game (T-3).

Competition in college and on the adult tour is much more difficult than that at the junior tournaments. Further, to win a set on the men's tour, the player must win three out of five games, as opposed to the two out of three on the junior tour. Thus one thing that the college coach spent time on was conditioning for endurance. Long hours were spent on running, calisthenics, weight training, and two-on-one drills.

[W]e'd do what they call two-on-one drills, which is where two people are at the net with a bucket of balls and one guy's at the baseline. And the two people at the net are just running the guy everywhere. And when he misses, they just grab another [ball] out of the bucket, so you don't get any time to rest, to go pick up balls or anything. So you go through a whole bucket (T-3).

[My coach] was in the Air Force. And he had these Air Force calisthenics and these things he had learned. During the winter, before our season had actually started, we went through these drills. . . . So we would do these drills and we'd just get exhausted (T-5).

The four tennis players who did not attend college and the three women who did not go to a tennis college went through a similar emphasis with their final coach.[13] They also needed

---

[13]The exceptions to this rule are the three players whose fathers were professional coaches. As mentioned previously, these coaches were exceptional in that they were able to adapt their teaching to the needs of the player at the different stages.

someone to work with them on strategy and conditioning. They felt that they needed a coach who had actually experienced the rigors of the pro tour and/or who had worked with other players who had made it to the top in the world. There are only a handful of coaches who have worked, at one time or another, with several of the top players in the world and who had also been top players themselves.

These remaining few players went to one of these top coaches to get the same finishing touches on their games, the strategy, and the endurance conditioning, that the other players were getting from their college coaches.

> I'd never really worked on my game properly. Like in the cardiovascular work as well as the technical work. A lesson with [my coach] was a killer. . . . [We would do] two-on-one drills. . . . It's a killer. . . . Eventually after doing this for a few days and a few months you are in the best shape of your life, and it doesn't matter how long your matches go, you can go forever. . . . And then we would go into technique and learn the game strategywise (T-9).

Weight training was relatively new for most of the players in our sample, although today it is fairly routine. In a few cases, the coaches set up special weight-training programs to increase the player's overall strength or correct a specific weakness.

> [My coach] and I talked about [weight training]. We seemed to feel my upper body strength wasn't enough and I needed more strength in my arms and more strength in my wrists and so we went to the trainer . . . in charge of the football teams . . . and asked him to figure out a program for me to work on. And he just put me on a program (T-10).

> [I started weight training] for my shoulder. . . . I just went fanatical over it, I just did the weights and I just did everything . . . and I made the darn [shoulder] stronger. . . . It's funny . . . I think my mom was a little bit concerned. . . . I don't know whether she was afraid her little girl . . . was going to start looking like some hulk or something. But it doesn't work like that for women (T-6).

Almost all of the finishing coaches (including the college coaches) appeared to have one characteristic in common: They were described by the players as rigid disciplinarians. Most of them were coaches of the top college tennis teams or had coached some of the top players in the world and thus had excellent reputations. Because of this, they had the players' respect, and their authority was accepted by the players. Practices were highly organized, and the tennis players were expected to attend daily and work hard during practice. This does not appear to have been a hardship for our tennis players because they were used to working hard and were highly motivated to do well.

[My coach] was another one of these rigid types, which was kind of good for me. He's a discipline fanatic. We used to do the same thing every day. All the drills were the same. The same regimen. He was totally organized all the time. And he was big on hard work. . . . Everyone respected him (T-7).

He was a disciplinarian. And, I guess more than anything else believes in building on somebody's strengths. . . . [H]e said . . . you're going to be with me for four years here. . . . [When you leave here] you're going to be bigger, you're going to grow some more, you're going to be stronger, you're going to mentally mature. He drummed all that into you . . . and sure you believed it. Hell, yes, you believed it. Here is *the* tennis coach from [x university], mighty [university] talking to you, winner of [many] previous NCAA titles. . . . More than any other tennis coach ever (T-14).

After joining the pro tour and reaching the top ten, many of our tennis players obtained further coaching. Because this is beyond the scope of this chapter, it will only be mentioned briefly. After reaching the top ten in the world, the tennis players often find that they still need a coach to help discipline their practice time and to help them fine-tune certain parts of their game. Also it takes a great deal of hard work to remain at the top, so our players sometimes sought a new coach to work with them when their game started to fall off or they needed more hard work to reach an additional goal, such as reaching number one in the world.

> I worked with different coaches at different times, but nobody that was a full-time coach. . . . [His current coach] worked a great deal on disciplining my practices. . . . [S]o he zeroed in to where I work on specific areas, even more than I used to which I did a great deal before, but he zeroed in on really detailed things (T-3).

> I needed a coach pretty much full time. I knew [his current coach] couldn't do it. So I went to [a different coach]. I called him up and said, "Listen, my goal in the next two years is to become top five in the world. Here's what I need to do. I need a coach who's going to travel with me fifteen, sixteen weeks of the year. I need somebody that's available all the time when I need them. . . . Are you available?" I became top five for the first time in [year] (T-10).

Who were these coaches that the college players worked with after leaving college? They were typically the same coaches that the noncollege tennis players had worked with. That is, they were those coaches who had coached the other top players in the world and had often been top players themselves. Some of these coaches had tennis camps where the top players went for a few weeks several times a year to brush up on certain aspects of their game. Other coaches traveled with the players several weeks out of the year.

As we have seen all along, the tennis players often went to different coaches for different aspects of their game, or they changed coaches because the previous coach no longer met their current needs. In short, we see almost all of the players, even after they have reached the top ten in the world, finding further assistance to overcome the weaknesses that have arisen in their games and to help them reach further goals, such as reaching the top five, or becoming number one in the world, or to help them win a certain major tournament, such as Wimbledon.

PARENTAL INVOLVEMENT

In most families the later years signaled a physical break from the family.[14] Almost all of the players moved away from home, whether to go to college or to join the tour full time. The families' financial support for most of the players was minimal because the college players were on tennis scholarships and the others were at least getting expense money from the tournaments.

The parents still went to most of the tournaments within driving distance as well as important national tournaments. Nevertheless there were fewer tournaments nearby as the tennis players began playing in more national and international tournaments. Throughout the early and middle years, the parents had traveled to most of the junior tournaments. Some of the parents missed traveling to tournaments and felt a bit left out in these later years.

> [My parents] would come to . . . all my junior tournaments just about. My mom traveled with me to all my national tournaments. But then when I started playing pro [my coach] started coming to all the tournaments. . . . [S]he may have felt left out a bit. She loved the junior tournaments. She just loved to watch tennis (T-6).

Nevertheless most players' parents made the transition to a less active role in their child's tennis more easily.

Despite the fact that the parents were providing less support in terms of time and money, most parents were still providing "moral support" in that they followed their child's tennis progress closely both in the newspaper and through frequent calls and letters.

---

[14]The two exceptions to this are the two tennis players whose fathers are coaches. Their fathers traveled to most tournaments with them until they were in their late twenties.

[My parents] would phone all the time. Every day I'd play a match. And we'd phone three or four . . . times a week just during regular times. . . . I would phone in great elation when I won and in tears when I lost and they were very sweet about it (T-8).

SUMMARY OF THE LATER YEARS

The significant event in the later years was the decision to devote full time to tennis. After high school, the players followed one of two paths to professional tennis.

Most of the players went to college and played college tennis before joining the pro tour. College tennis served to add the finishing touches to the tennis players' games; the college coach worked with the players to fine-tune their strokes, improve their strategy, and build their endurance for the rigors of the adult tour. Sometime during college most players began to surpass most of their contemporary college competitors and decided to play tennis professionally. Some players waited until they finished school, whereas others left college early to join the tour.

A second group of tennis players went directly from high school to the pro tour. The women in our sample were more likely to take this path because there were very few opportunities for women in college tennis until recently. But these players also worked with special coaches to develop the same skills (strategy, endurance) that the majority of the players were developing in college tennis. In short, the tennis players, whether in college or not, were working with a new coach refining old skills and developing game strategies and endurance in the later years.

Most parents had moved into the background and were playing a less direct role in their child's tennis career. They were still providing moral support, but because the players were usually away from home, they were providing much less support in the way of time and money than they had in the past.

Looking Back

Although many of the tennis players described the hard work, the long hours of practice, the loneliness of life on the road, and the difficulty of maintaining friendships when one is rarely in one place for very long, few players seem to have any regrets. Remembering friends that they grew up with, they had little feeling that they really missed out on very much.

> I loved tennis. To me it was productive. I must always be doing something productive. That's the way I feel. And to sit in a Steak and Shake in a car with four or five sixteen-year-olds . . . that didn't interest me a bit. I never felt I missed that. I felt that I wanted to do something different. I was going to be something (T-11).

> I can remember in high school thinking what it would be like to have a normal life or normal relationships with people. I mean even when I had a serious girl friend in high school, I always thought I would have to leave her for five months. . . . But I always knew that if I wanted to be the best, and that's what I wanted to be at something, I knew there were certain things [I had to give up]. When you look at it in life, there are sacrifices. But they're not really sacrifices. They're just something you choose to do. . . . Looking back on it now, I don't really feel like I missed out on anything. There's a couple of ways that you can do things, and I just happened to do it this way. . . . If I could think of going back and doing it again, I would never do it differently. I like the way I turned out, so I can't think of anything I would do to change it (T-10).

In discussing what they've gained from tennis, all players mentioned that it has been financially lucrative. Even those who played in the late sixties and early seventies—before the days of big prize money—made good money and tended to invest it wisely. Those who are still playing are typically extremely wealthy. The players also mentioned that they had had a wonderful opportunity to travel and see the world. But the money and opportunity for travel are mentioned by the players only in passing. What clearly appears to give them most satisfaction is the fact that they know that they did something special and were the best in the world at something.

> I know I've gone after and can do something if I set my sights on it. . . . And having been one of the best at something is a nice feeling. And I don't have to tell people about it, it's just that which I did (T-8).

> [Tennis] provided a sense of self-expression for me. . . . It's a sense of self-satisfaction, something you can't buy. I mean you can't buy a backhand down the line. It's an effort involved, a time investment. An emotional investment (T-9).

One mother very adequately summarized the development of her child's tennis, and we will end with one long quote to summarize the development of tennis talent:

> [A]s far as planning for them to be tennis champions, that wasn't it at all. It just sort of evolved. We took one step at a time. . . . When they won the city, then you thought, "Well, let's go to the State to see what might happen." It was just sort of a thing that developed as we went along. We were all in it together. We always went with the children. We were never parents who said let them go with a group of people or go on their own. That was never the case. [My husband] and I have been the kind who never wanted to leave them with baby-sitters. People who didn't know too much about us. We have been very, very close as a family. We didn't have any other interests much but tennis. . . . Tennis was everything, and as it grew, it got where tennis was the main thing in our lives. And everything else circled around it. It wasn't like most people [where] a job and a social life and school came first, then if you could work, tennis is—fine. It just wasn't that way. Tennis was first, we worked everything else around it.

> And the children—it wasn't that [my husband] forced it on them— he didn't. They just sort of picked it up. And then he got real interested in them. They were good for each other. But I've seen a lot of tennis parents. In fact, especially now from what I've seen there's

a lot of money and a lot of these parents are so eager for their kid to play that they almost lose sight of reality. It wasn't that way with us. In fact I'm glad that we came along when we did, because it was sheer love of the game. There was no money involved. [We] just loved the game and wanted to see how good you could get and you just got better and better. And the better you got the more fun you had (M of T-10).

8

The Development of Exceptional Research Mathematicians

William C. Gustin

The research mathematicians whose development will be described in this chapter are a select group of relatively young people, raised in the United States, who have reached the highest levels of accomplishment and respect in their field.[1] The criteria used to identify this group were suggested by mathematicians and mathematics educators themselves.

The mathematicians included in our sample have received Sloan Foundation Fellowships for their work. The informants we talked with recommended this highly competitive award as the most objective measure of excellence available for mathematicians under the age of forty. According to the foundation, the fellowships are given to "those who show the most outstanding promise of making fundamental contributions to new knowledge."

To ensure both objectivity and exclusivity, we used two other methods to arrive at our sample. We used the Science Citation Index to identify those Sloan fellowship recipients who

---

[1]The mathematicians had to be under the age of forty at the time of data collection to be included in this study. The final sample ranged in age from twenty-nine to thirty-eight, with a mean age of thirty-five.

had been cited often by colleagues—a well-established procedure for identifying unusual accomplishment. Finally, we asked mathematics professors at six American universities with graduate math departments reputed to be among the best in the country to judge the capability and productivity of the young mathematicians and to offer the names of others who might be equal or superior to those on our list. Our analysis of the professors' responses led us to omit four people from the original list and include three others who also met either the Science Citation Index criterion or the Sloan Fellowship criterion.

Twenty-three people met the standards set to be included in this study of the development of talent. Twenty (87%) agreed to talk with us about their experiences. (Two were abroad, and the third was not interested in taking part in this study.) Subsequently we were able to interview the parents of seventeen of the mathematicians for supplementary and corroborative information.

There is only one female in the group of accomplished mathematicians. In order to avoid making her conspicuous, all references to the mathematicians will be masculine. Some readers might also be interested to know that 70% are the oldest children in their families. Four are so labeled because they are only children; ten more are the firstborn in homes with two or more siblings. The following pages describe the process of becoming an exceptional research mathematician, beginning with information about the homes into which the children were born.

The Early Years

WHAT IS OF VALUE?

The parents of the twenty mathematicians included in this study were well educated. Fourteen (70%) of the fathers had advanced degrees: Five earned Ph.D.'s, three M.D.'s, two law degrees, and four master's degrees. Three of the remaining six attended college, whereas the other three did not go beyond high school. Eleven (55%) of the mothers earned at least one college degree, four more had some college experience; and all but one of the remaining five graduated from high school. Reaching such levels of educational attainment was especially noteworthy because those parents who went to college generally did so during the Depression, often going to night school or extending their education over several years because of the necessity to work. Even so, several managed to distinguish themselves. One father was a Rhodes Scholar, and several of the parents graduated with honors.

Education and achievement, especially intellectual achievement, were mentioned by most of the mathematicians as the characteristic values of their parents.

> My father is a man who is from the Enlightenment. One thinks, one reads, one speculates . . . (M-7).

> I think my father has a terribly serious commitment to serious intellectual activity—as being the entire purpose of life, so to speak. . . . His entire existence is devoted to the life of the mind (M-12).

One set of parents had less formal education than many of the others, but even they

> . . . were education oriented. . . . They always particularly insisted on using good grammar, which is not all that common where I was raised. It's not just that they spent any time correcting us, it was just noticeable. I remember vividly—it was incredible (M-4).

The father of one of the mathematicians was himself an academic who

> . . . certainly valued education. . . . I just always had that impression. . . . My parents always regarded themselves as intelligent and expected that their children would be the same (M-10).

Another set of parents valued

> ... education, science, intelligence, and art. I guess somehow I had the impression that we were scientific. I remember as a child having said that people are either scientists or artists. My parents had to point out that the majority of people weren't either (M-11).

The fathers of half of the mathematicians were involved in research or teaching in areas including physical science, medicine, and engineering. Another 30% of the fathers were in business or accounting. The mothers of three-quarters of the mathematicians were housewives, and most were active in a wide range of outside interests.

The parents of the mathematicians believed it would be wrong to direct the interests of their children. They report trying to treat them as "normal."

> I think it's a waste to try to make a child into something you want rather than providing them with the things they are interested in and letting them become what they want to (M of M-4).

> I have strong feelings against pressuring children and tailoring them to fit parental expectations (M of M-21).

> We tried to protect him and make him normal ... the idea was to see if I could have a bright child who was well adjusted, getting along with people, having friends, having a lot of interests—not being singleminded (M of M-17).

A few of the parents would impart practical advice, such as "Be your own person," "Be well rounded," "Get the most out of your abilities," "Be organized,"

> ... so there were recurring themes. They were also warm and loving. They were very conscientious parents. Well, I would say they were oriented toward achievement, especially academic achievement. . . . You know, I think it was sort of a typical thing where I was an only child and relatively late in life for them and they decided I was bright and it was wonderful for them (M-5).

In spite of their efforts to avoid pressuring or directing their children, the values, beliefs, and expectations of parents had a strong impact on the mathematicians, not only in the early years of their development but in the later years as well.

The parents of the mathematicians were attuned to watch for signs of intellectual ability from their children—not mathematical ability specifically, but intellectual ability in general. The verbal behavior of their children was significant to these parents. Some of the mathematicians began talking early, and some not until quite late.

> [He] talked early—by twenty months old he could recite nursery rhymes (M of M-4).

> . . . he talked so early. By nine months he knew two or three words, and by twelve months he knew about thirty. He talked like a kid much older than he was (F of M-2).

> He didn't speak for such a long time that I thought, "What's wrong with this kid?" (M of M-19).

> If he hadn't looked so bright, I might have been worried. He was really quite slow. He didn't say his first sentence until he was twenty-four months old (M of M-21).

Such a wide range of observations makes it difficult to be conclusive about the significance of whether a child begins talking early or late. Nevertheless, the verbal behavior of their children was very significant to the parents of the mathematicians.

The value of intellectual and academic achievement was transmitted to the mathematicians. They learned to value what their parents valued, even though their parents were reluctant to direct their interests. Working hard, doing well, and being precise are a few examples of what the mathematicians learned. Often they were unaware of or at least unable to explain how they had learned what they did.

For some reason, I don't know why, I felt it important that I do well. My parents never really explicitly said that, but I was somehow encouraged to try to work hard (M-2).

There was sometimes an unspoken type of pressure to achieve—whatever that meant—academically, I guess, but it came out to me as congratulations for doing well. At each stage that just seemed like a great thing to do (M-17).

The parents of the mathematicians valued intellectual achievement and often devoted their own free time to intellectual ability.

My parents were reading all the time. My father went to his study every night and worked on reading journals (M-7).

The model of behavior to which the mathematicians were exposed was intellectual. Their fathers were devoted to their work. They were models of persistence, careful attention to detail, and the importance of the development of the mind.

Another example both of a parent as an intellectual model and that indeed values are transmitted from parent to child was recalled by one of the mothers:

My husband spent a lot of time working in his study, reading and writing. . . . He spent almost his whole life in his study . . . when ———— was about four, he started using my typewriter. When he was about six, he told me he was going to write a book. So he typed a book, it was pages and pages of no words, just pretend words with spaces. . . . He was trying to imitate his dad (M of M-19).

Yet another mother explained that her son never talked baby talk. She always spoke to him as if he were a "thinking individual."

He was always a thinker. In nursery school the teacher asked them what church they attended. He explained that they didn't go to church because they didn't believe in God. She took him over to a tree and asked, "Where does this tree come from?" He said it came from a seed. And she said, "Where does the seed come from?" He said, "I wish my father were here, he could explain to you all about evolution" (M of M-23).

One mother recalls reading to her boys "constantly." She thinks "that must have been a tremendous influence on them" (M of M-11). Most of the mothers emphasized the importance of reading in the home.

> We did a lot of reading aloud to our children. In fact, my husband and I still read aloud (M of M-3).

The parents made no effort to teach their children how to read before they learned in school. "I didn't approve of it," one mother explained.

> I think that the teaching of reading has to be done in the classroom. I didn't want to teach him and then have him get into a classroom and have a teacher who wanted him to learn to read another way (M of M-10).

And so, believing that "children understand more than they are capable of reading," she continued to read "rather difficult" books to him until he was in third grade.

Even though their parents made no effort to teach them, perhaps three of the twenty learned to read before they started school. One, for example, became impatient with his dependence on his parents and taught himself to read when he was four.

> He would take a newspaper or book and write down words on a blackboard and ask me what they were. I can't take credit for getting him to do things, I didn't know whether or not it would be good for him. I just let him go on his own. I would read a story to him a couple of times and he would "read" it back to me (M of M-4).

At the age of four, this child had a blackboard and had learned to write letters, words, and numbers on that board.

CURIOSITY

The most consistently mentioned early characteristic of the young mathematicians was their curiosity. Their parents recall,

> He asked a lot of questions . . . he had intellectual talent. . . . I remember he wanted to know how everything worked, he wanted to know about everything (F of M-2).

> The thing I remember most—there were workmen in the home often. He followed them around all the time. I thought he would drive them crazy. He asked them question after question (M of M-3).

> As an infant he looked like he was thinking. . . . He would look at things like he was wondering what they were, what to do with them. . . . He asked questions at a very young age—constantly asked questions. He just couldn't wait to learn (M of M-4).

There are similar examples from almost all of the parents. Of course, most children go through an inquisitive period, asking, "What is that?" or "Why?" What appears to make the parents of the mathematicians unique is the nature of their response to their children's questions. They responded to the questions seriously, often encouraging even more questions.

> My desire for my kids was that they enjoy learning. I showed them things, answered their questions, encouraged them to ask questions (F of M-2).

> I listened to my child . . . I talked with him . . . I answered his questions, I read to him (M of M-21).

One set of parents had an interest in photography. The mother explained that her son

> . . . absorbed knowledge like a sponge. As a young child he asked many questions. His father generally answered them in some de-

tail. He wouldn't talk down to him. By the time he was a year old he had a vocabulary of at least one hundred words and could hold conversations. His first word was *Kodachrome* (M of M-11).

The mathematicians themselves recalled being inquisitive.

I've always had this urge to figure out anything that I didn't know (M-6).

I was always interested in how things worked. I would take toys apart and look at the gears and I was fascinated with valves and gauges and dials (M-3).

They also recalled how parents and others responded to their curiosity:

Every curiosity that I had toward something intellectual was encouraged, even marginally intellectual things. I guess I was spoiled, but I didn't think of myself as spoiled at the time. In fact, materialistic things were not encouraged. But any interest in radio or photography or something like that was encouraged (M-13).

I saw my father as somebody from whom I could get scientific information; he was a source of all kinds of interesting knowledge (M-11).

I was interested in stars and stuff like that. I can remember asking my brother, very early—he had a friend and they were always looking at the stars at three o'clock in the morning—"What does E equals m, c, two mean?" He said, "How stupid, that's squared!" At that point I resolved that I was never going to be stupid again (M-16).

Very few of the mathematicians recall being interested in numbers when they were young. When there was an interest, it seemed not to be more significant than any other.

My father was not particularly adept at numerical subjects. When I asked, he would try to explain. . . . I think that I played around with adding up the first ten numbers and got lots of sums, and then someone asked, "Why don't you add the first and last and so on," that sort of thing. And so I did play around with it, but it wasn't special to me (M-7).

The wide range of home environments notwithstanding, intellectual and academic achievement were valued highly in the mathematicians' homes. Models of cognitive and intellectual behavior were available. And the first signs of curiosity—questioning, wondering, wanting to know—were encouraged and nurtured.

I definitely have the feeling that this is tied up with motivational factors, things that are part of the larger experience of life. I can't imagine someone coming totally out of cultural context with no support from the family, and then somehow through some cleverly designed educational program turning into a mathematician. It simply seems completely impossible. One sets up values from early on. Not only things that are desirable or not, but things that you feel capable or not capable of doing. You do this by copying the people around you. If there's one thing that stands out to me, it's that the whole business in some peculiar way really boils down to people. If you are in contact with the people who had the right sort of approach and the right type of ideas, then you will wind up at least having the opportunity of doing certain sorts of things, and otherwise you won't (M-12).

EARLY LEARNING

Almost all of the parents noted that as young children the mathematicians were content to play alone. They were able to focus on fairly complex tasks for extended periods of time.

He would spend hours building a tower of blocks, precariously balanced. There would be a wail of exasperation and anguish when it finally collapsed. And then he would start redoing it (F of M-11).

When he was young, he would sit in the playpen with a toy mailbox with slots. He took blocks and "mailed" them into the slots. He would sit for very long periods. He evidently had good powers of concentration. Instead of demanding a whole lot of attention, he would play with toys which engaged him for a long time (M of M-17).

The parents of the mathematicians did not intend to impose their own interests on their children. And while the parents may not have influenced the specific interests of their children, they played a very significant role in determining the manner in which those interests were pursued. It has already been suggested that the way they responded to the questions and questioning behavior of their children was influential. They also initiated early learning experiences for the future mathematicians.

> We played a lot of games together. I taught him how to play cards. In the evenings there would be card games or board games. He was good enough that he wasn't too boring to play with (F of M-2).

> ———— played with blocks a great deal. The other children didn't do that to the extent that he did. He could look at things in different ways, build different things. We played games like dominoes, throwing dice and adding the numbers (M of M-3).

> When it came to trains, we didn't buy an electric train. We bought trains that had little wooden tracks that you put together and little wooden trains, because if you had those, the children had to put the tracks together themselves. You could make figure-eight's or ovals or any kind of pattern you liked. You just took them apart and put them together. They could do it all themselves (M of M-17).

Another mother also recalls teaching her son "a lot of little card games." She expressed a point of view common to all the parents:

> I didn't have any ambitions for him except that he be successful in whatever he chose to do. I didn't intend to influence him. We just did our best to train him to think for himself so he could be on his own. You do that by example. And, of course, reading to him, play-

ing card games, influenced his ability to learn additional things. We tried to introduce him to as many different things as we could (M of M-10).

Most of the mathematicians couldn't remember their earliest learning experiences. One did recall that

[My mother] gave me this big cardboard device with a big dial in the middle and lots of pictures of things and numerical problems and stuff written on it. You'd pick one and dial it up and you could open this flap on the side and see if you got the right answer. I played with that a lot. When I was in the second grade, she showed me how to do long division, which she was doing once because she was figuring out the grocery bill or something and I was wondering what these fantastic figures were that were so much more interesting than the addition we did in class. And she gave me a bunch of her old books at that time too, an old *Book of Knowledge.* And she gave me her high school chemistry book, which I found absolutely magical at the time (M-4).

There was no effort on the part of the parents to emphasize mathematics, neither was there any effort to avoid it. Some of the early learning experiences certainly did deal with numbers and arithmetic.

I remember when he had an omelet, his father would say, "This is half, this is a quarter, this is an eighth. . ." to this little kid when he fed him (M of M-17).

That particular mathematician recalled,

When we were very young, both my brother and I liked to play games. My father was especially good at playing games with us and keeping it fun. I remember him telling me some really exciting things, which would turn out to be some kind of math, and I would play with the ideas. My father was a sensitive teacher, and I'm sure he did all kinds of subtle things that didn't seem like teaching (M-17).

FAMILY DISCUSSIONS

Most of the parents believed they shouldn't teach their children reading or arithmetic before they learned them in school. They avoided doing what they believed was the responsibility of the school.

> We had been told it would interfere with later school learning. Instead, ———— and his father had discussions about astronomy, chemistry, and physics. When ———— started first grade, he couldn't read, but he could do chemical equations (M of M-11).

The parents supported the interests and activities of their children and did what they could to assuage their curiosity without jeopardizing what they would be learning in school. Family discussions were mentioned by half (ten out of twenty) of the mathematicians as an important part of the early years of their development. Meals were a popular time for this kind of activity.

> We played word games aimed at expanding the children's vocabularies. We would go around the table, each giving a definition or the word to match a definition (M of M-3).

> Topics would fill our lunches and dinners. . . . We used to have breakfast, lunch, and supper together. I'd ask, "Look, if I add up these numbers, I get this. Why?" My father would say something and I would say, "But what if?" That's what it would be like. You see, my father wasn't trying to push me (M-7).

Often these discussions involved only the mathematicians and their fathers. Because of the reluctance of the parents to interfere with the "normal" development of their children, the discussions were seldom structured. That is, they tended to be initiated by the child, not the parent, and occurred randomly. Furthermore, the parents seem to have been somewhat selective with the type of subjects they were willing to discuss. The topics were generally scientific.

When the mathematicians were very young, the parents were able to answer most of their questions, but soon the questions became too specific. Rather than discourage the questioning, the parents taught their children how to find answers on their own.

> I remember I used to play with numbers. I wasn't very good at adding columns of figures. I wasn't interested. But I do remember making the usual try at Fibonaci numbers ... and, I think by chance, found certain properties and showed my father, and he told me, "Yeah," and pulled out a book about Fibonaci numbers, and so I did that (M-7).

> He would find out different things. Do what you call research. We would send for all kinds of pamphlets. After he was interested in fire trucks and trains, he would be interested in planes, and so we would find out about them—the types. I probably got him started. As he got a little older, he would do it on his own (M of M-16).

> I have a sense that [my mother] encouraged my curiosity. . . . I was very interested in astronomy, stars, planets, and space stuff. And to answer my questions she would read me the astronomy articles [from the encyclopedia]. So [I certainly learned] all the standard intellectual values: that you find out things by reading, if you want to find something out, you try to look it up in an encyclopedia, and if its's not there, you go to the library (M-21).

The mathematicians began to value the process of inquiry. They didn't want to be told what an answer was, they wanted to figure it out.

> I know that in first grade, when they started teaching us arithmetic, I was annoyed at the fact that they would teach us each thing, whatever, that five and six were eleven, instead of having us figure it out. . . . I simply was interested in figuring those things out (M-11).

> I would get some crazy idea and [my teacher] would say, "Let's go and do some research." . . . My father and the good teachers would definitely not tell me the answer (M-17).

Several of the fathers (perhaps seven of the twenty) had sufficient background to have taught their children mathematics at least to the level of calculus. However, only two, both engineers, seem to have actually "taught" their sons mathematical subjects, and even then the material was elementary.

My father tried to interest me in mathematics at a relatively early age. I showed an interest in it and enjoyed it. Of course I was also interested in other things, I learned some things the other kids didn't know. It wasn't my whole life, certainly. It was just something I seemed to be more interested in than most kids. But most kids didn't seem too interested in anything at all. When I was six or seven, he taught me a little algebra, how to solve simple little equations. At various times when I was growing up he might teach me something else. It wasn't something we did every day, it was sporadic. Periodically, he would tell me about something else (M-5).

SPECIALNESS

The mathematicians are modest about their accomplishments and abilities. Functioning as they now do at the limits of man's knowledge would seem to require a strong belief in their extraordinary capabilities. The recognition they receive from a few colleagues is an important aspect of their current success and motivation, but the initial formation of their self-concept was strongly affected by their parents. Although it was the intent of the parents that their children develop normally, these parents believed that even as children the mathematicians were "special."

I thought he was brilliant when he was little, because he learned so fast and understood so much (F of M-4).

We, of course, felt he was an unusual child, but we didn't try to make a lot of it (M of M-4).

——— was given an IQ test. Of course, he went beyond the possibilities of the test. His father and I are also in the highest percentile, so we weren't very impressed. And we didn't feel there was anything we could do about it. We wanted him to have the same kind of education that everyone else had (M of M-10)

We never wondered about his having a good brain. We knew it, he knew it, everybody else knew it. What did get special attention was when he demonstrated original thinking. That was not a matter of high IQ but rather of applying his intelligence, of course I mean in an academic way (F of M-11).

And the mathematicians were aware that they were believed to be exceptional.

My parents certainly did think I was bright. I mean, I guess they wanted to think so. When I was in nursery school, I did well on an IQ test. From then on they were convinced I was a genius (M-5).

I know that my father always felt that we were brighter than the other kids. Well, evidently there was some truth to it, and I believed it then too. It's nice to believe it. He was always convinced we were brilliant (M-6).

My mother was pleased when I did well, although it was taken somewhat for granted. . . . There was a sort of foregone conclusion that I was obviously brilliant and that I would do well. There wasn't any question (M-12).

I don't ever remember being punished for not being first, but there was an unwritten expectation that one would do well (M-13).

READING AND INDIVIDUAL PROJECTS

Once they learned to read, three-quarters (fifteen out of twenty) of the mathematicians were enthusiastic readers.

———— always liked books. He asked for books ahead of toys. . . . He got his first library card at seven and could walk to the library. He did that often (M of M-4).

I just read constantly . . . I read a series of books about a farm. I remember finding it very fanciful that all the animals talked. Then I remember reading a little later with enormous preoccupation. I think I read all the Tom Swift, Hardy Boys, Nancy Drew, every kind of book like that you could get your hands on (M-7).

I was quite a voracious reader, I don't remember from what time, but I think through most of school. But I was completely indiscriminate. I would just grab something—it could be [the label on] a ketchup bottle—whatever was closest (M-9).

I would spend all of my time reading. It bothered my mother; she thought I should be outside playing with the kids (M-19).

In these early years the reading was primarily of general subjects, although about half mentioned reading scientific books, science fiction, or books about planets, atoms, or famous scientists.

Much of the reading was done for enjoyment, but there was a gradual shift toward reading with a purpose. As their curiosity about the world grew and their parents were no longer able to answer questions, they searched for the answers in books. One of the mathematicians was given a *Handbook of Chemistry and Physics* by his father.

He read it the way other children would read novels. He had been busy inventing algebra. I said to him, "You know, there are these books," and his eyes absolutely popped. He went to the library and found four or five advanced algebra textbooks, which the librarian let him have only after she called us to see if it was all right (M of M-11).

As the mathematicians did more reading on their own, they became less dependent on their parents. Their parents were willing to allow them, even to encourage them, to develop their own interests.

We were never palsy-walsy. We were not twelve years old when he was twelve years old. We went on with our life. We realized what a special person he was, but we had our own lives too. I think it was good for him, because it wasn't as though we were making his life as ours (M of M-11).

About half of the mathematicians recalled having an interest in scientific or mechanical projects or building models before the age of twelve.

When I was seven, I certainly wanted to be a scientist. I certainly meant to get a scientist's degree. When I was eleven, I wanted to be a nuclear physicist. And when I was twelve, I wanted to be an astro-physicist. Science was in the air then. I had a little laboratory in one of the houses we lived in. I had a chemistry set and a microscope, and my friends would come, and we would go back into the laboratory and play (M-4).

This may not seem related to mathematical development, but in my mind it is: I began building model airplanes of balsa wood when I was very young. By five, I was already building them by myself. My parents would buy me kits you would have to cut out and measure. By the time I was ten, I was making my own. I was designing them myself. I used to see in my mind what they would look like and how all the struts would go in and turn the designs over in my head. Soon I began building with absolute preoccupation. At first my father worked with me, but he didn't have the same standards. He would help, and they would get finished, but somehow I wanted to do it all myself. I became absorbed with making sure everything was perfect, straight, aligned, and in the right proportion. Once I had the picture in my mind, what I built had to match it. I did fly them, but that part didn't fascinate me as much (M-7).

Another of the mathematicians recalled a similar attraction to model building:

I think I spent a lot of time by myself as a youngster. The first dollar I ever saved I spent on a model airplane. I sanded it, glued it, put it all together and painted it. I just fell in love with the whole process. The planes got bigger and better. I was interested in the way that they looked. I never wanted to fly them. I liked them as art objects. I liked them to look as close to the real thing as possible. . . . (M-15).

The parents felt their role was to supply the materials their children needed.

> We bought him chemistry sets, crystal radio sets, etc., despite the fact that a lot of people didn't feel he should have those things. But he was interested, and I thought that a child should be given the tools to work with what he is interested in (M of M-4).

> When he was seven, ——— approached his father with the idea of doing ham radio work. He got his license at the age of nine. We actually moved to provide him more space for his hobbies. He took over the entire basement. He built transmitters and receivers, experimented with his chemistry set, and set up a darkroom. . . . He was always interested in how appliances worked. I sent him to repair shops to learn how these things were put together (M of M-13).

One of the model builders gave a sense of the time that was devoted to reading and working on projects:

> In the summers I would get up as soon as the sun came up. I would work on model airplanes until I got tired of that and then I would read. I was always by myself. I didn't play with other kids that much. The grammar school that I went to didn't give any homework, so until the end of sixth grade, school was not so much of an intrusion. I used to go down to the basement the moment I came home from school and spend the evening. I also read. I mean, I spent a lot of time with this (M-7).

This example is perhaps a little extreme. However, in all but three or four cases, the mathematicians were devoting remarkable amounts of time to reading or working on projects—on their own.

SCHOOLING

Academic achievement, doing well in school, was valued by the parents of the mathematicians. Eleven of the twenty mathematicians were sent to nursery school. However, they attach little if any significance to the experience. Two had forgotten it completely, and the fact that they went was revealed by their parents. Others had more specific recollections:

> . . . that's where I picked up my dislike for school (M-19).

> I went for a year or two, something like that. I mean, it wasn't really a school. You could go there and climb around on some jungle-gym apparatus. They concentrated on a lot of skills like learning to play with other children and eating without getting food on your face (M-5).

One mother explained that her children attended nursery school because it was "nearby and convenient." She felt that they "needed to get away. It was important to let loose, to get away from Mother before school" (M of M-6).

It might be assumed that any group excelling in cognitive development would have had special schooling. However, nineteen of the mathematicians attended public elementary schools (the other one attended a university lab school).

Another assumption about individuals who have reached the limits of learning in a cognitive field might be that their formal schooling would have been positive. In general the mathematicians were not at all enthusiastic about their elementary school experiences. Six had difficulty learning to read. In one case the problem was caused by a need for glasses, while the other five gave the impression that the difficulties may have been more complex.

> Strangely enough, I had some sort of problem learning to read. I don't know, maybe it was the environment, maybe it was—I don't know what. But the same thing with telling time. Everybody learned how to tell time immediately, and it took me longer. It may have been several things. I might not have been able to see properly. I mean, if they're telling you how to tell time and they're holding the clock in the front of the room and you sit in the back of the class, then maybe you couldn't see. . . . It also may be that I was in an environment where I had to somehow conform and do

what they wanted me to do. Unfortunately, I was just very independent and wanted to do what I wanted to do (M-7).

I learned to read in school with a fair amount of difficulty. I think one of the precipitating reasons for getting me out of the private school was that it was a progressive school and they didn't actually find out if you knew anything or not. So somehow by the end of the year my mother realized that I hadn't learned to read yet. In fact, I was sort of scared of it. . . . [I]n the second grade I happened to have a very warm and sympathetic teacher, and whatever anxiety I had built up about reading, she overcame (M-21).

At least eight of the mathematicians had difficulty relating to other students.

I definitely had the feeling of being apart, I've always sort of had that feeling (M-12).

I don't feel that I was good in anything but science and math. I don't think I was any good in social matters at all, and I definitely felt inferior in that respect (M-6).

I was pretty unhappy during a lot of school . . . maybe some of the disadvantages along the way were in my favor, because I learned to persist and to think for myself (M-20).

I think one of the most . . . molding things that happened to me when I was in grade school was that I was something of a social outcast. Outside of a very small collection of friends, two I think, I was really an outcast. So I found my ego in doing things and succeeding, and I suppose in part being at least good in school. That was one thing that sort of carried me along, at least I did well in school (M-15).

Most of the mathematicians felt that their elementary school experience was quite ordinary and considered themselves essentially similar to other students.

There's nothing I could point to as being significant at the elementary school level. As far as the curriculum . . . it just wasn't an influence . . . I never took it that seriously. It's very hard to recall anything that contributed to intellectual development . . . certainly nothing that ever had any influence on my mathematical development (M-5).

It's very hard to describe this exactly, but I read, I think, more than the others, and I spent time by myself. School really was just—it really didn't have so much to do with my life in some sense, or my ambitions or my hopes. It was something I did. When I was in grammar school, I was just like any other kid, there was no question (M-7).

In general the mathematicians were very good students in elementary school. Thirteen of the twenty (65%) seem to have been outstanding in all subjects. Three excelled only when they were interested (usually science or math), and four others recall being quite average.

[I have] pleasant memories of being with other exceptional children, [but] . . . I was still among the two or three best in the class (M-11).

. . . that was just the way it was, I guess. . . . There was never any question in my mind that I was clearly superior to anyone else that I have ever gone to school with. I don't know that I took any tremendous pleasure in it, it never seemed to lead to any great reward. . . . (M-10).

I think I was very average in many ways in elementary school. In reading and spelling and things which didn't relate to science, I think I was quite backward. I think in science I was already much more interested and ahead of the class, but in basic skills and even in basic arithmetic I was very slow to learn (M-3).

. . . my first-grade teacher wanted to keep me back, my parents resisted that, luckily . . . I hated arithmetic because it was boring. . . . I didn't take to drill. . . . I did poorly in social studies, compiling reports. I daydreamed a lot. I wouldn't think about what I was supposed to be thinking about in school (M-20).

Arithmetic seems to have held no special significance for them. For most it was easier than their other subjects. They frequently knew about a topic before it was presented in school.

I remember by the time I was in first grade I could count, and the teacher was very annoyed because he was trying to teach us to count and I already knew how (M-2).

I remember in the third grade I had a friend and he and I had somehow figured out, the week before we were taught it, how to multiply and divide fractions. And I remember in the fifth grade learning from the encyclopedia this . . . algorithm for doing square roots. And maybe there was only one other kid in the class who knew that. But I didn't have any sense of myself as exceptional or wishing there were other people who could understand what I was thinking about. There were just a few times I remember catching on to things before other people, but I was happy just doing what I was supposed to do (M-21).

In elementary school I had absolutely no interest in studying different things. I used to bring my algebra book to school and put it under my desk and read it when the other kids would subtract numbers. I understood arithmetic faster than the other kids. . . . Everything that they were learning, I already knew. In practice I would forget to carry and things like that, and so when you look at my grades in arithmetic, they weren't necessarily all A-pluses, but it didn't mean anything. Even at nine or ten, math for me did not mean arithmetic (M-22).

Success in research mathematics requires skills that are qualitatively different from those learned in arithmetic. Hence the indication from so many of these mathematicians that elementary school arithmetic had no effect on their training. However, schooling involves more than just arithmetic. Many aspects of this period certainly did affect their development; perhaps the most significant were those that established more firmly the independent nature of the mathematicians.

I never really learned any mathematics in school. I've learned everything I know on my own, except some arithmetic. Once I started studying on my own, I never learned any mathematics in school. I've had some inspiring teachers, but they've always been intelligent enough to see that I'm very independent and that the best thing that they could do for me was to give me the books and let me work on my own (M-16).

It was noted earlier that nineteen of the twenty mathematicians attended public elementary schools. The average elementary school teacher is not trained in methods for identifying or instructing students with exceptional abilities. As a result, whatever special abilities the mathematicians may have had during this period generally went unnoticed or were ignored. In the few instances when their talent was noted, they preferred to be allowed to pursue their own interests. The "best" teachers were seen as the ones who would supply books or materials so that the mathematicians could work on their own.

I can remember at least one experience in second grade. I was writing out numbers and I said, "Look, I counted up to a billion, I skipped some numbers, but I know what the in-between ones are." My teacher said, "Gee, that's great. Now, is that a billion or is that a hundred thousand? Let's go and do some research and find out what it is. Maybe you're right." And then I went and found out that she was right, but it was my own project, and she was very encouraging even when I was wrong. The good teachers would definitely just wait and let me do what I wanted to do and not tell me the answer or not tell me what to do next and not try to drill me or get me to go quicker or anything like that. It was that they let me do what I wanted to do at my own rate (M-17).

Elementary school was a situation where I had to do what the teacher said. Well, I figured it wasn't the right way for me to learn. Elementary school teachers don't know much about mathematics and they don't have much interest in it, and it just doesn't work out. My parents made an effort not to teach me anything before I was supposed to learn it in school, because that was the propaganda. It wasn't that I knew anything before the others, it was that I didn't take to drill. I daydreamed a lot, I wouldn't think about what I was supposed to. My [own] children like to sit for hours doing a single thing, they don't like to be forced to stop what they're doing and start something else. I suspect that that was part of my problem, too (M-20).

SUMMARY OF THE EARLY YEARS

Future mathematicians—by the end of elementary school—are as yet unaware of what a real research mathematician does. What, then, is the significance of these early years? Perhaps the most effective interpretation of what emerges from the stories of these mathematicians is a process of becoming: becoming a person with certain skills and characteristics that only much later would be found to be consonant with being a research mathematician.

The parents valued academic achievement and were models of intellectual behavior. They were typically more highly educated than the average parent, and most had professional occupations. They believed it was important for their children to develop their own interests, but expected them to do well in school. Most of the mathematicians were aware, even in elementary school, that eventually they would be going to college.

The parents encouraged the intellectual behavior of their children. From the earliest years reading was an important family activity. Perhaps the most significant aspect of these early years was the way the parents responded to their children's questions. Questions were treated seriously, and when the parents didn't know the answers, they taught their children how and where to find them. These parents believed that their children were special and shared with them the excitement of discovery.

Research mathematics tends to be a very intense solitary activity. Even as young children many of the mathematicians were content to play alone for long periods of time. As they grew older, reading, model building, and other independent projects occupied much of their time. Most were very good students in general, but attached little significance to their elementary school experience. They felt that their "best" teachers were the ones who let them work on their own.

The Middle Years

The second phase of the development of the mathematicians began at about the time they started junior high and continued through their graduation from high school. Perhaps these middle years may be characterized most accurately as transitional; much of the activity and many of the interests pursued during this period were an extension of earlier development as well as an anticipation of what was to come later.

PARENTS AND OTHERS

The experiences of the mathematicians range widely during these middle years, and no consistent picture of family life emerges. One of the mathematicians mentioned watching television "a lot" and another of being "addicted to TV," while a few didn't even have a television in the home. There is a sense of structure in what they do say about daily routines. Most families sat down to meals together. Parents insisted on homework being done before the children were free to watch television or work on something else. The adjective most frequently used to describe their youth was "normal."

The mathematicians continued to be influenced greatly by the values and priorities of their parents. While the parents did not monitor the daily work of their children, they were interested in their progress. At report card time at least one set of parents would

> . . . be ecstatic, and that would make me feel good. And if I sometimes got a bad grade, they treated it sort of lightly. There was never a negative feeling. The positive reinforcement was so built in that I'm sure it had a strong influence on my whole development (M-17).

The involvement of the parents during these years may be classified into four categories roughly equal in size. One group of parents restricted their involvement mainly to moral support. A second group made sure their children had materials for their model building and experimentation. A third group, fathers mainly, worked together with their sons on projects or had discussions with them about math and science topics. Finally, the parents of five of the mathematicians were directly involved in arranging special opportunities for them—summer programs or early admission to college.

Several of the mathematicians (about 25%) were also influenced by other relatives or friends of the family.

> I think my grandfather did influence me a great deal in the direction of mathematics. There is no doubt that he's the greatest hero I've ever had, and it was clear to me that he regarded pure mathematics as the highest calling. We discussed mathematics some, partly his philosophy but also little problems, too. I think he picked out my mathematical ability at a very early age, and when I really turned to mathematics, I think he was very pleased. I wasn't aware of it at the time. He was a very wise, perceptive person. I think he would have overwhelmed me if he'd really expressed his pleasure (M-3).

> The two biggest influences in my life, academically, were an uncle who encouraged me to do work in science and physics, and another uncle who was an attorney, a judge actually. The one who's a judge is very, very smart and he just constantly inspired me. In fact, he graduated from college when he was sixteen, that sort of thing. I wanted to emulate—I think if you were looking for a role model, he was probably the one (M-13).

The early interest of about half of the mathematicians in models and erector sets evolved into a fascination with chemistry sets, rockets, or electronics. In a few cases the fathers participated for a while, but in most cases the mathematicians worked on their own.

My father is a chemist. . . . We sort of improvised a small chemistry set. It had pretty much what we needed. At one time I wanted to make a barometer, and you have to have the glass blown just right, and so he got a friend to blow the glass. Later, I wanted to build a solar furnace and needed a lens and parabolic reflectors. We went to the junkyard and got headlights, and he got someone at the lab to cut the fronts out (M-2).

I had chemistry sets, and electronics was an interest . . . I used to try to make fireworks and rockets. I used to make little bombs and set them off in the backyard. That was not encouraged. It was rockets that I was really interested in, I was trying to get something to fly in the air (M-6).

His mother also recalled the experiments:

Most parents wouldn't allow their children to handle chemicals, but I did. He was one child I could trust with being careful. I signed a paper giving permission for him to buy chemicals at the store. He used to experiment in the basement. He spent lots of time at it when he was about fourteen. He and a friend built a rocket using a steel tube they purchased with their own money (M of M-6).

Materialistic things like cars were not encouraged, but my interest in ham radio was encouraged. It turned out that I built essentially all of the equipment, some from Heathkits, some from designs out of *Popular Electronics*. I had in fact an uncle who was an electrical engineer who lived around the corner. He was not a ham, but he helped with the designs I took from magazines. There was some rather difficult mechancial work that had to be done, building chassis and things like that (M-13).

Again, a mother's perspective:

He took over the entire basement, built transmitters and receivers, fixed radios, put together electronic kits, experimented with his chemistry set, and set up a darkroom (M of M-13).

Often, doing scientific things becomes an end in itself. Research scientists become expert at "doing" science. The mathematicians were certainly attracted to science and enjoyed doing scientific things.

> He would set his alarm and get up in the middle of the night, get dressed, and go out to see the stars (M of M-19).

What they enjoyed most was a process: wondering, questioning, wanting to know, wanting to figure something out.

> I liked the idea of understanding. You look up at the stars, you want to know what's going on (M-7).

> One of my big pleasures was to master something or other, whatever it was. I'd have little projects from time to time, learn to do this and that. And so I've always enjoyed the feeling of accomplishment that you get from learning to do something that is difficult (M-12).

> I've always had this urge to figure out anything that I didn't know (M-6).

INDEPENDENT LEARNING IN SCIENCE AND MATHEMATICS

Mathematics is called the language of science. Almost all of the mathematicians were attracted specifically to the physical, as opposed to the biological sciences. Gradually they realized that mathematics was at least equally as interesting as science.

> I was very interested in science when I was young. A friend of my parents was a favorite of mine because of his interest in ham radio. I was a novice radio ham in high school, but I didn't have enough support around me then. It wasn't something my parents could help me with, I didn't have the people to learn from or the finances to buy proper equipment, and so that sort of withered. But it really withered in the sense that at that time my interests turned to mathematics (M-3).

There was a formula for determining the trajectory of a rocket and the range. It is a trigonometric formula with the sine $2x$, and I wanted to let x be equal to 75 degrees. So that means that you have to compute the sine of 150 degrees. Well, the tables only go up to 90 degrees, and I didn't know how to compute. So I had to look at my brother's trigonometry book and I decided then that the mathematics was more interesting than the physics (M-16).

After reading enough books for children I thought, "Alright, I'll read a real book." So, well, I don't know if you would call it a real book, but I read a high school chemistry text. I was also interested in how rockets worked and things like that. I wanted to learn the real thing. And the next thing I tried was a physics text. I was completely snowed. I didn't understand why, but I couldn't understand anything. My father said, "Oh, it has math in it," and he got me an algebra book. I started reading that. I read it quickly and said, "Could I see the next book?" (M-22).

I bought a little plastic slide rule in a drugstore, because I was intrigued by all the little marks on it. I was in junior high. Of course I figured out how to use all of the scales. I had to learn some trigonometry at the time, because there were some trigonometric scales. I had to know what those were. Somehow I date that as the start of my interest in mathematics. First it was just the marking and the idea that it could mechanically do something that required a mental process (M-6).

Sixteen of the twenty mathematicians did independent work in mathematics while they were in high school. The specific type of work they did varied considerably. In one case,

I would typically learn what was in each of my courses before it was underway. I would sort of learn a fair amount about the next term or the next year's stuff on my own by reading ahead . . . I enjoyed being on top of the stuff (M-17).

Another more extreme example is the case of a mathematician who was doing research while still in junior high:

. . . there is one piece of nontrivial, semitrivial mathematics that I did before I entered college. When I was in junior high, I wrote an article that was published in a mathematics magazine. I was very naive, and yet it is something that has come up again (M-11).

At least seven of the mathematicians read books that their fathers or brothers or sisters had used in college.

I was getting books from the library and setting myself little problems and trying to solve them. By late high school I was stealing my sister's calculus books and teaching myself. I was trying to do her college work. At one point she took an algebra course and didn't know from beans what was going on, so I did her final exam. It's very funny. She passed. I literally didn't know what I was doing, but, you know, you can make guesses (M-9).

Once I got to high school I spent enormous amounts of time just by myself doing mathematics or analyzing board games—working out strategies and trying to analyze how to play a game. . . . And I read. I taught myself some calculus, using texts that my sister had from college (M-3).

One of the mathematicians, who didn't have access to the books he wanted, took the initiative to write a letter to the chairman of the math department at a nearby private university.

He invited me to come to visit him. I talked with him, and he wrote a letter for me when I was a sophomore [in high school] giving me permission to use the math library. That permission, that letter, was probably the most influential, the most decisive thing that ever happened to me. That was like opening up infinity to me (M-16).

Scientific magazines were available in the homes of about half of the mathematicians.

My parents subscribed to *Scientific American*. I would pick it up from time to time. I liked the games. I think I wanted to do them more than the others. I tended to win, and so it was sometimes hard to find people to play (M-20).

The exact significance of the independent study is difficult to assess. The mathematicians rarely considered it extraordinary. The content—what they actually studied—seems to have been much less significant than the fact that they were learning to learn on their own. They enjoyed learning and they worked by themselves. Very few mention ever working together with other students. Five of the twenty seem to have enjoyed discussing math and science with other students, but their homework and the independent work they did seems almost always to have been done alone. Mathematics was well suited for their efforts because it was something they could pursue without supervision.

No one really checked my work, no one. I knew if it was right. I knew because there were answers in the back of the books and things like that. You don't have to have someone check your work. You know if you are doing it right. I suppose I made some mistakes, three or four a year maybe. But you know if you are right, it makes sense (M-16).

I remember that it was perhaps about ninth grade that I did some things on my own. I would go to the library and check out books on college algebra and spend evenings trying to learn, to memorize all the formulas in the book. It was entirely on my own (M-6).

I remember when I was in high school. I would work in the fields driving the tractor, which can be very boring. I would work things out in my head. I mean, derive various formulas and things like that. . . . I got a lot of satisfaction out of understanding these things. I would get a lot out of being able to derive it from scratch. And that's the sort of thing I would do (M-18).

Learning, wanting to know, was indeed an important aspect of these intermediate years.

As far as high school was concerned, I think that I was doing about the same assignments that the other students were. I was probably doing it easier, but I don't think I was doing things that were qualitatively different. Then I had the sense that I wished that I could have done a lot more. That was part of the reason that I started reading my sister's books (M-9).

Perhaps the most significant aspect of their formal secondary school experience was that it did not disturb the tendency of the mathematicians to be independent learners. Nothing that went on in school was more interesting than what they were learning on their own. In a few cases they knew more mathematics than their teachers. The most frequent tactic, used by the high school teachers especially, was to let them work on their own. The mathematicians recall,

> I guess I never expected that teachers did much good. I sort of figured out that I wouldn't get any help. By the time I was thirteen, I was trying to teach myself calculus, and nobody who taught at my school knew calculus (M-4).

> By the time I was in high school I used to sit in the back of the class and just read or write. Some of the teachers caught on that I was interested in mathematics but didn't make a point of it. They were nice to me, and I came to class. You see, I didn't want to be one of these little Wunderkinds that were really not Wunderkinds at all. I mean, most whiz kids don't amount to anything at all. I didn't want that (M-7).

> I decided, I guess it was in the ninth grade, that I would read mathematics. I finished all of the books on my own. In the eighth grade they put me in the ninth-grade class. In the ninth grade I didn't take any math. I was doing some reading on my own, geometry, algebra, and trigonometry. By tenth grade I had finished the calculus. When I started the tenth grade, they put me in the twelfth-grade algebra class, but I was so obnoxious that they took me out (M-13).

> My seventh-grade teacher picked up right away that I knew a lot of math and told me that there would be no point in my coming to his class, so I spent the hour in the library reading some books he gave me. Most of my teachers had a very bureaucratic attitude toward teaching. I mean, you covered this and then this and then

this. My twelfth-grade teacher was different. He knew that if I was ahead, way ahead, there was no point in having me cover what I already knew, so again, I didn't go to his class. I spent time in the library. He just said, "Do whatever you want to do" (M-19).

Some of the high school teachers just gave me their college books. I had a pretty good choice of college books without knowing too much about it. I read most of the classics. . . . Those high school teachers really helped me a lot by giving me those books and telling me, "You don't have to do the work, just sit in the back of the room over there and do your own stuff" (M-6).

SCHOOLING

The college preparatory mathematics curriculum is essentially standard throughout the United States. Typically, algebra is taught in the ninth grade followed by geometry, advanced algebra, and advanced math (trigonometry, analytic geometry, and functions). Eighteen of the mathematicians followed the traditional sequence through advanced algebra. Seven were involved in special programs in which the three years of junior high were condensed into two. Consequently they were accelerated in math by one year. Nine took at least a semester of calculus their senior year, which was a fairly innovative opportunity at the time.

Typically, mathematics and science "came easily" to the mathematicians, and they were assigned to honors classes when available. All of the mathematicians were considered exceptional math and science students (although two received only average grades).

I was a good student. I was considered one of the brightest kids. I wasn't interested in French, I wasn't interested in current events like other kids were. I was one of the very best kids in math and science. And in other areas there were other kids who were the very best students (M-5).

I was, in fact, super fast in mathematics. The challenge on the college boards was to see how fast one could go and still get 800. Basically I would go ten times as fast as the limit of the test. In other words, if it was an hour section, it would take me about five or six minutes (M-13).

I really liked geometry. In geometry I was clearly the best in the class. I really worked hard. There were other kids I had to compete with. The teacher was asking me all the questions; he was paying a lot of attention to me (M-2).

Twelve of the mathematicians (60%) were also considered superior students in all of their courses.

I had for a very long time been treated as the smartest kid in the class (M-22).

I did well on everything. I didn't care really for history or foreign language, but I did reasonably well in them. I did like English a lot, and there was something that appealed to me a little more about science and mathematics than some of the other areas. . . . There was never any question in my mind that I was clearly superior to anyone else that I had ever gone to school with. I don't know that I took any tremendous pleasure in it, it never seemed to lead to any great reward . . . (M-10).

I don't think there was much of a sense of competition among the other kids in the class, they just sort of accepted the fact that I was the best in the class. . . . I guess I tried not to talk about anything which was very academic with most of them . . . and it worked out okay (M-18).

He was outstanding academically. . . . He did well in all subjects [and was valedictorian of his junior and senior high school] (M of M-17).

As noted earlier, nineteen of the twenty mathematicians attended public schools. Their parents wanted them to have a good but normal education.

We wanted him to have the same kind of education that everyone in the country had. We wanted him to make the most of it, but we didn't want to push him, particularly. It was up to him to push himself. So long as he kept up his grades in school and did what he was supposed to, well, that was sufficient (M of M-10).

The mathematicians were divided evenly regarding the quality of their formal secondary school experience: Half had negative recollections, whereas half were generally positive.

You see, many bright kids consider high school to be almost a total waste of time. A lot of people take the point of view that people who really have the stuff, who are really going to make a contribution, will survive in the face of all adversity (M-5).

I had very good teachers for many, not all, but many of my elementary school years. And for that matter, fantastic teachers in junior high and high school. At each stage doing well in school just seemed like a great thing to do. Going to school was a very positive experience, I really relished going to school (M-17).

Difficulties or disappointments with school were generally attributed to poorly trained teachers or methods of instruction with which they were not comfortable.

I had mixed feelings because there were some things that I was proud of knowing or proud of being able to do, but then my grades weren't very good. It was pretty frustrating during those years. I blamed it on the educational system. I thought it was the methods the teachers were using, not the teachers themselves. There were a lot of assignments that I didn't find interesting. I didn't like the switching from class to class. I decided it would be much better to be able to concentrate on one subject for several hours at a time. I don't know if I identified learning with grades, but I thought I could have learned a lot more (M-20).

. . . already in junior high I went crazy. My seventh-grade class was just a disaster. We had the new math and we had a teacher who wasn't used to teaching it and who didn't have the vaguest idea of what it was about. She would ask me a question. I would give an answer which I knew to be right and she would mark it wrong and give me a wrong answer. Other kids would copy that wrong answer. . . . I guess it didn't occur to me that anything could be done about it. I assumed that you would go through school and you would have some teachers that you wouldn't like. That was part of life. My parents were sympathetic, but I think they also felt that you can't expect to go through school and like all of your teachers (M-22).

About the eighth grade I began losing interest in school, and then I started doing quite—well, in many ways quite poorly, actually. I just lost interest. . . . In tenth grade you had a fellow teaching geometry, but you couldn't interrupt him because he would forget his proofs. It just became to me worse and worse. After tenth grade I began to do math on my own, and it was very interesting that I could do perfectly well when I wasn't there, but when I was in school, it was impossible. Tenth, eleventh, and twelfth grade really have nothing to do with my education. If we had to do it in school, I didn't want anything to do with it (M-7).

Most of the mathematicians were unable to recall any extraordinary high school teachers. They viewed their experience as quite traditional, indeed ordinary.

They taught it, I learned it. And they taught it well enough that I could learn what they had to teach and that was that (M-15).

Plane geometry is in some sense the only pure mathematics that anyone has in high school. I wasn't particularly good at it. I wasn't bad at it, but I wasn't crazy about it. For instance, I certainly know people who when they were in high school they had this thing where they discovered all the theorems. I mean, I never discovered anything. I was in the course, I got good grades (M-21).

What seemed to impress the mathematicians was when teachers "knew their subjects" or were "interested" in what they were teaching, when they actually became involved and were able to transmit the excitement of the learning process. One especially influential teacher was a member of

. . . a group of people preparing a program in modern mathematics. It was developed by starting with a few axioms, and then,

rather than memorizing by rote, we would derive the basic algebraic rules. And then there was the question of proving various
theorems. You have rules, and from these things you deduce other
things and build up a bigger and bigger body of consequences. I
really enjoyed this sort of intellectual exercise. I think it stimulated my thinking. It's interesting that I wasn't unique in that
either. The whole class responded to the environment. They enjoyed the challenge of proving this is equal to that. They enjoyed
the constructions and using the rules and making the desired deductions. Some of these were twenty- to thirty-step proofs. Even
though most of the kids in the class clearly were not going to be
mathematicians, they understood the appeal and the nature of
mathematics. . . . I went to that first year of high school thinking I
wanted to be an electrical engineer, but at the end of the year I
wanted to be a mathematician. I was really seduced by it. I really
enjoyed the intellectual exercise of my courses. That high school
produced, within a three- or four-year period, three very successful mathematicians (M-3).

My geometry teacher had quite a positive effect. She liked geometry and she realized that it involved thinking. This teacher actually understood what she was saying and she would try and get
the class to understand. I think she was a very traditional teacher.
Her approach was completely traditional, but the point was that
she obviously enjoyed the subject and she knew what she was talking about. . . . I was exposed to very little of what you would call
gimmicks or techniques or cleverly designed tools or any of that
kind of thing. . . . If you want a positive experience, you need to
have an interpersonal type of relationship with someone who suc-
ceeds in creating a positive experience. My view is that although
the materials certainly have some significance—it's better to have
a good book than a bad book and it's better to have this method
than that method—that sort of has a second-order effect, really, it
doesn't tell the tale. A good educational experience has to do almost entirely with interpersonal effects. . . . The point is that you
tune in to the person. The main function of teachers is to make
things interesting, to produce positive motivation, to serve as an
example, do something that you can copy to a certain extent
(M-12).

Teachers in public schools are usually not able to devote much time to individualized instruction. Consequently, very few of the mathematicians were singled out for any special work.

> No. I fell asleep in mathematics. In those days there was heterogeneous grouping, everybody was in the same classroom, doing the same thing, and you would go at the same rate as the slowest person in the class (M-13).

Over half of the mathematicians believe their teachers recognized them as good students, regardless of the fact that little was done for them.

> I had the same teacher for geometry, physics, and calculus. He was very good. He seemed to be very interested, but I never had any private conversations with him. I certainly felt that he knew more of what he was teaching than the others did. I thought that he expected me to do well—not from anything explicit, but just the way he acted in class (M-2).

> What I remember most vividly is a junior high teacher who was the first person who decided in no uncertain terms that I was a genius. . . . There was another teacher in high school who used to joke whenever I coughed that geniuses always died of tuberculosis. She was a very funny woman. I just treated that as one of her jokes. But she was very encouraging, and I enjoyed her attention. It was a very good thing for me (M-9).

SPECIAL EXPERIENCES

Several of the mathematicians were members of their high school math team (6), or participated in statewide contests (3), science fairs (2), or the Westinghouse Talent Search (2). Five attended summer programs sponsored by the National Science Foundation, and two were selected for a Saturday program at a local university.

These extracurricular experiences were significant to the mathematicians for a number of reasons. The content of these experiences was different from what they were taught in class. It was more challenging and interesting to them. They had the opportunity to explore topics with which they were fascinated and develop their own techniques for solving problems. Math became special through these experiences, as did the mathematicians. That is, by excelling in contests and fairs the mathematicians discovered the excitement of doing something well and being recognized for it.

My mathematical ability was essentially discovered during the last half of the ninth grade. I think that's significant, I hadn't done very well in the beginning of the year. I remember one of these contests came up and the instructor gave the whole class an exam to see who would go to the regional meeting. Evidently I won. I was first. I think he must have been very startled. I don't think he believed it, because when he gave an exam to the two tied-for-third people, he made me take it too. I don't know if I was first on that one, but I was surprised, too, I don't know why. The problems, of course, were different from the usual homework assignments and the coursework. There was something different about them that I was able to do. I worked very hard for that exam and won a silver medal or something. So that was it from then on. That was my first recognition. It was important—that those exams had such an effect on me (M-6).

I was involved with the math team. There was a fairly substantial amount of activity. In the beginning of high school I spent a lot of time going through old English algebra texts, and that was fantastic training for the math team. And one did have to go into training for it. I remember learning all of what is now considered to be freshman [college] calculus in about two weeks or so, just sitting down and doing it. I would be working on many, many problems, just taking piles of old exams home with me and working them out. . . . One of the principal motivations for fine-tuning the ability in mathematics was competition. The fact was that I was much better than anyone around me at the mathematics and I could compete reasonably well with anyone. The only sport skill that I had was running, and I was not nearly as good at that as I was at the math (M-13).

The first year I made it to the National Science Fair was when I was a junior in high school. I guess the judges didn't like my project too much. But the next year one of the judges sat down and started looking at what I wrote, and I guess he knew something about it. He said, "Some of these theorems are not known!" So he sent some of the other judges over to take a look at it again. That was very nice, I really enjoyed that. I was a first-place winner. In some sense that was the epitome of my high school career (M-16).

Four of the mathematicians skipped their senior year in high school (one skipped tenth, eleventh, and twelfth grades) to start college early (one other transferred to a prestigious private school), which was a fairly rare occurrence and required the initiative of parents or teachers.

By his junior year in high school he had taken all of the math courses offered in the school. They felt he needed something more. The school didn't offer any higher math courses. He had already taught himself calculus. So the guidance counselor and the math teacher encouraged us to send him to an expensive private school. We had to make some sacrifices. Of course I was perfectly willing to do that so he could have the advantages we wanted him to have (M of M-4).

When he was a junior in high school, a friend told me about a special program for high school students interested in mathematics. So I called and I talked with the professor in charge and told him of ——— 's background. At the end of the program he told ——— he ought to skip his last year of high school and enroll in college. We thought about it very carefully . . . scholastically, he didn't need the classes, but you worry about the social implications. We decided it was a good opportunity (M of M-11).

Another especially significant aspect of the extracurricular experiences was the opportunity for the mathematicians to meet, compete with, and share a special interest with other exceptional students.

I guess I would like to stress the role of peers in education. Especially in high school. You learn mostly from your peers and not from your teachers. It was great to be around a very bright group of kids who, I guess, learned from me, but I learned from them also. We challenged each other—and a good question is as valuable as a good answer (M-13).

Well, it was a strange social life. The other kids and I were just interested in different things. I wasn't at all athletic. I was a small, weak kid. The other kids weren't interested in science, and I also think I was just a rash, obnoxious kid. I didn't have any friends at all until I got to junior high school. There I met other kids who were interested in some science, who were at least academic instead of athletic. And that made all the difference in the world (M-22).

BEING DIFFERENT

Being different can be a major trauma of adolescence. Half of the mathematicians seem to have survived relatively unscathed. In short, they appear to have made a fairly normal social adjustment; there were classmates or friends in the neighborhood with whom they shared common interests and values. However, even though they did have friends, very few seemed "social" in the sense of belonging to several clubs or being involved in extracurricular activities. Very few mentioned playing an instrument in the band, and fewer still were ever involved in athletics. They characterized themselves as typically "good" students, perhaps better than most (especially in math and science).

Several of the mathematicians were acutely aware of the more negative aspects of adolescence. A few withdrew to pursue their own interests; they describe themselves as loners. Again, a fascinating range of experiences was recalled by these individuals.

Well, I was always sort of singled out by the rest of the people in the class. I was somehow always described as the brain and all that sort of thing. And everybody related to me in a slightly strange way. I guess as time went on, it became more specifically related to math. But I wasn't all that comfortable with it. It set me apart from everybody and made me feel awkward and in fact uncomfortable. I think I preferred to have the ability and do the stuff and not to be singled out. I think I had enough self-confidence that it didn't make me feel that I had to live up to anything, but I didn't cope too well with the social results. It definitely made me feel very different (M-12).

I went to camp each summer through high school. It was, for the most part, very unpleasant. I was picked on horribly and didn't know how to relate to other kids. It got better, both because I learned to be more tolerant of people who were different from me and because they were growing up and not being so sadistic. The block where I grew up had almost no other kids. At camp I was really tormented. I suppose that I was somewhat arrogant in my intellectuality and my contempt for their attitudes. I didn't see myself that way, but I'm pretty sure that I was. I knew that I valued intellectual things and that they didn't and that they valued sports and success in fighting, which I, well, sports I wasn't opposed to but fighting I was (M-11).

In high school I was so much more advanced than the other students were in class that they were scared of me. Rather than ostracize me, it was that they felt that even with extra work they couldn't catch up. I don't think that they felt competition from it, because they just said, "Well, he does that" (M-13).

One of the mathematicians became so disenchanted with high school that he stopped working and was nearly failing all of his courses. Purely by chance he met a friend of the family at a party. The friend was a graduate student in mathematics, who sensed his frustration and encouraged him to sit in on a few college classes and get an impression of what real mathematics was like. He did and was so captivated that he began auditing college math courses while he was still in high school. He recalled,

> I was marked as being unusual. I mean, I could do things that the others couldn't do. I read much more than the others, and the way I thought about the world was . . . in some way different. I would have ideas about things that they didn't have. When I was in the

tenth grade, I memorized one hundred and fifty pages of James Joyce's *Ulysses*. . . . I did it for various reasons, but it did serve to make me different. I didn't like so much going to school and I wanted to learn. I remember thinking, "If I read this book all of the way through and look up all of the words, then I will have learned something." So I would educate myself. I was very isolated and had to have something to do. I felt very lonely and this was the only way I knew to make myself worthy or something. It's very hard to say. It's very complicated. . . . I liked mathematics at the age of fifteen, because in some sense it seemed to me that the world was falling apart, and mathematics seemed to have some integrity. Everything else seemed fraudulent. The teachers in the public school, the people in the community, everybody was posing as something. And in mathematics the one thing that you cannot be is a poser. You can't fake it. . . . Then I started auditing math courses at the university, and suddenly, my life changed. I mean, here, now I was good at this. At this point, it changed completely. Here I was, sixteen years old, and I was taking graduate courses in mathematics and doing well, if not better, than anyone in the class (M-7).

SUMMARY OF THE MIDDLE YEARS

As the mathematicians began their transition into the second phase of their development, they had already learned to value intellectual achievement. These intermediate years were an opportunity to rehearse skills and enhance characteristics that had been initiated earlier.

The initial curiosity of the mathematicians about the world in general was gradually focused on scientific, mechanical, and mathematical interests. The parents of the mathematicians encouraged and supported their interests through discussions, by supplying books and other materials for their projects, and by arranging for their involvement in special programs.

The values and priorities of their parents continued to have a strong influence on the mathematicians. They were successful in school. Through their participation in honors classes, math teams, and fairs, their reputation and identity gradually became associated with their intellectual ability and especially their skill in mathematics.

They were attracted to mathematics; it suited their independent style of learning. Their most effective teachers were enthusiastic and knowledgeable and respected their desire to work on their own.

The Later Years

The development of exceptional talent as a mathematician has two major facets. There is the longitudinal process of becoming mathematical, which is recounted in the first two sections of this chapter, and then there is the actual training in the work of mathematics, which is presented here as a third and final phase. During this third phase the mathematicians learn to do "real" mathematics, to do research, and they make a commitment to mathematics as a career. Finally asked to comment about his years in college, one of the mathematicians said, "Now we're getting to the people who really had an effect on my mathematical life" (M-7).

THE COLLEGE YEARS

Given the value that their parents placed on education and academic achievement, the mathematicians assumed they would be going to college.

> My parents felt very strongly that I should go to college. They simply had a very strong "religious" belief in college as the key to a better life. It was a major theme. They encouraged me to go to college. It was clear that they respected people who did. They respected colleges, in some sense almost reverenced that sort of thing (M-15).

> I was expected to go to college. I don't even remember a time when I didn't think I would go to college. That was a given, part of the environment completely (M-7).

College was the step after high school. I never imagined not going to college (M-11).

I don't think I ever thought of doing anything other than going to college, especially from sixth to eighth grade or so. I wanted to be an electrical engineer, and that meant a college degree. And when I changed to mathematics, it didn't change the idea of going to college, except that I wanted a graduate degree as well (M-3).

As undergraduates the mathematicians attended one of eighteen different colleges. Although half of those colleges had math departments that were rated among the top ten in the nation, there seemed to be no consistent theme in the way the mathematicians chose which college to attend—indeed, there was an interesting variety of rationales for their choice:

My brother also went there. It may have been that my father went to a state school and figured they were all the same. And it was cheap (M-2).

I didn't know anything about colleges then. I knew that Einstein used to hang around Princeton, and it sounded like a good place (M-4).

My choice was a reaction against high school. The college sent out a lot of literature that sounded very good. They emphasized independent study, no grades, and so forth—that's why I was interested. I didn't want to go anyplace that seemed like a continuation of high school (M-20).

We lived near the state university, so it was natural for me to go there. And it was inexpensive and, in addition, it was adequate. I believe it was adequate in every way. I don't think there was any real thought of my going anywhere else. I was very naive about these things. I just wanted to learn all they had (M-6).

The parents of the mathematicians wanted them to feel free to choose whatever career they wanted. Even though eighteen of the twenty had worked independently on math, few—less than half—thought of mathematics as a career as they finished high school. They had done well in science and math, and although thirteen started college as math majors, seven started in programs other than mathematics—chemistry (N = 3), science, engineering, physics, and biology. But even those who enrolled in other majors also anticipated continuing in mathematics. Consequently, they took math courses as freshmen. Soon mathematics became increasingly central in their lives.

> I went to college with the intention of becoming a chemistry major. I also had a very good math professor. He was a good lecturer. He had a little seminar for people who wanted to learn a little extra on the side, and I joined that. He was willing to talk with me. I saw him often. [My choice of math as a major] may have been [a result of] the two professors I had, the chemistry professor was very distant (M-2).

Perhaps because of their earlier experiences, the mathematicians did well in their first math courses and came to the attention of their teachers. As a result, at least fifteen enrolled in honors sections, graduate courses, or were selected for special programs as early as their sophomore year. Several of the mathematicians recalled that period of emergence:

> It just happened, I was better at it than anything else I tried—and I enjoyed it (M-6).

> The teacher that I had for freshman calculus was picked out to start an experimental program in mathematics in which essentially all of undergraduate mathematics was going to be shoved down our throats in something like three semesters. And then we would start doing graduate work. I was one of five or six students picked out to do this, on the basis of how well I had done in the first semester, presumably on the basis of being able to understand theoretical material. He had personally picked us out. Most of us went on to become professional mathematicians (M-9).

> Actually the idea of physics appealed to me more, but I didn't do particularly well and I did do well in math, so my sophomore year when I declared a major it was math. Also I enjoyed it more, probably because I was doing better. I was doing well by the time

I was a sophomore and was to a certain extent taking graduate courses. The best undergraduates at that time were quicker and better than the graduate students. This became apparent in class. We could solve the problems that they couldn't solve and were just better at these things (M-10).

I started taking graduate courses during my sophomore year. I did very well in a modern algebra course, which was a graduate course. There were three undergraduates in that course who could essentially do nothing wrong (M-19).

I got started in mathematics basically because of one man. He and two of his colleagues had decided that the standard math sequence was just terrible. You could not only teach real mathematics to anyone, you should. So with wonderful reformist zeal they convinced the administration that everyone was going to be in this new course. They were going to teach real mathematics. You were told that you were going to do these good things. And so I took the course and I thought it was terrific. The deal was that people who got at least a B in the first term would be allowed to go on and take the second term. So that was the big event. . . . It was obvious to me, and I think to everybody, that I was at least as good as anyone else here. There were a few of us who were sort of known as the people who were really good at mathematics (M-21).

I got to know the faculty quite well. My undergraduate adviser was especially encouraging. I took calculus, which I found to be rather boring. Based on that class I started in the honors program. They presented things at a much more rapid pace. There were just four or five people in the class, and the faculty enjoyed teaching. They certainly took a lot of interest in me (M-18).

What seems to emerge from these quotes is the disarmingly matter-of-fact way in which the mathematicians view their introduction to "real mathematics." The fact of the matter is that each of them must have been quite impressive in their first courses—at least enough to have drawn the attention of their instructors. Perhaps the independent work they did in high school gave them an advantage over their classmates. In any case, once they began taking graduate courses or honors sections, the nature of their mathematical experiences intensified: Class sizes were smaller (often only three or four in a class), they were exposed to more interesting and more challenging material, and they were, some for the first time, able to share the experience with other capable students. Another very significant aspect of this period is their introduction to exceptional mathematicians.

> In college, for the first time, you got to see some real mathematicians, some real famous big shots (M-5).

College teachers affected the development of the mathematicians in at least two ways: first and more tangibly as instructors, second and more illusively as role models. As instructors, teachers impart facts and skills, the basic techniques and knowledge necessary to succeed in a field. As role models, teachers demonstrate a way of being, a sense of enthusiasm and "style."

> Sure, there were particular professors who were inspiring in various ways, in a sense of some charismatic personal style. Some introduced me to areas of mathematics I found new and exciting, opened up a whole new world. Some you could admire because of their obvious brilliance. So certainly there were a few that I remember as role models—that kind of thing, you know: "I want to be like them." In each case they were showmen to some extent. Their style of doing mathematics was appealing. They made it come alive. The kind of mathematics they were doing seemed extremely interesting, the ideas and concepts. One was aware that these were well-known people. You'd walk into an office, and somehow there would be a little electricity in the air. It was exciting when for the first time you began to learn what mathematics was about (M-5).

> Most of my formal instruction was abysmal, with one exception. That was my calculus teacher. Somehow or another, when he explained things, it was beautifully clear. And I guess he made me understand what mathematics could be. Sort of what the spirit

was. He made it obvious to me, the simple beauty and methods of mathematics. In other words, he made clear to me that mathematics is not complicated, that when you understand it right, it never is complicated. And that's the way to approach things. He did not show me how people who do research think, but he did show me that there were some basic principles in calculus and what they were, and he made it really clear to me, not right away, I think my first exam I got a D, but not long after that I began to catch on (M-15).

I learned a lot of mathematical facts. I certainly learned things from my college teachers and I also think that it is important that I remember looking up to them, hoping that when I was a grown man, I could be like that. I think both things were important (M-21).

Facts and procedures may be taught and the enthusiasm of an exceptional teacher may be contagious, but can one be taught how to do research mathematics?

... what is a teacher? You see, mathematicians don't think of themselves as teachers. That should be clear. They lecture. Sometimes they like to and sometimes they don't. But that's not what you [as a teacher] think of. You think of yourself as doing mathematics [while students observe] (M-7).

Success in mathematics is not simply a matter of how many facts or procedures one knows, but rather how one applies those facts and procedures to the selection and solution of particular problems. The same mathematician continued,

... there was one teacher, I was completely in awe of him. I liked his style. It just appealed to me, it was just right. You can tell. I think the way you learn mathematics is in some sense you imitate. You don't know. You do it. So I was around him and I would imitate. He'd approach a problem a certain way. And that's what really it's about. How you go about it. And this is the most important thing of all: taste. It's something enormously important in mathematics. There are very smart people who do very hard things, extremely hard things. But these things are uninteresting. They don't have the taste to really pick the gems. He had good taste (M-7).

For many of the mathematicians, college was the first opportunity to be with other students who had similar interests and abilities. Advanced classes are generally quite small and attract only the most capable students. Whereas they had previously learned much of the mathematics they knew on their own, in college they enjoyed competing with and learning from peers. They still studied and worked on their own, however.

> Contact with peers was very important, being part of a peer group with people who were interested. It was just of continuing importance. . . . So in college the idea of being able to sit at the feet of great men, so to speak, was very important. You could really learn a lot of mathematics from these teachers. They were inspiring as an ongoing influence, but also, having one or two good friends of your own age, interested in this sort of thing, who you could learn from, compete with, have interchange with. It was something, certainly, that was always very important (M-5).

> One thing that was significant was that a half-dozen or so really serious math students formed a very tight-knit group. We would trade information and swap problems and discuss mathematics a lot, particularly as freshmen and sophomores. It wasn't a study group. We didn't get together for the purpose of studying. We just did a lot of things together during the course of eating lunch or anything. We would be constantly involved in this exchange of mathematical ideas (M-4).

It was during their college years that the mathematicians associated their own skills and characteristics with the doing of mathematics. For them mathematics was fun. They did well at it, devoted more time to it than to other subjects, and began thinking in terms of mathematics as a career.

One of the mathematicians revealed a sequence of events leading to his ultimate commitment to mathematics:

> First of all, I was fascinated by it. It's just beautiful. I liked it. I liked the order, here was something unquestioned. It had worth, you couldn't argue about it. Everything else you could. There was just endless debate about this or that. But here there was no two ways about it. I remember thinking this stuff has worth. And that was it (M-7).

Then came the motivation that sustained his involvement in the field:

> You have to have the sensation that you want to know. You have to have that. You have to just get a charge out of knowing this thing. You just want to know why it works. You do it because you want to be recognized, no crap about it. That's one of the reasons. You do it because it's fun. You have a good time. But you cannot make yourself work hard enough to do a really hard problem unless you want to know why it works. You just have to be fascinated by it. You just want to know (M-7).

And finally the commitment and its consequences:

> I can tell you quite frankly when I first decided I'd stop playing and really work at mathematics. I was about second or third year in college. I'd been playing at it. I'd learned. I'd read and all this, but that's play, it's passive. And then I did absolutely nothing else [but mathematics] for many, many, many years. It's impossible. I don't know anybody who does first-class mathematics who doesn't work all of the time. Your world becomes very small (M-7).

Although most of the mathematicians were extremely successful in their college coursework and they all chose to go on to graduate school in mathematics, many still had doubts.

> I was aware of things as an undergraduate: Do I want to spend my life this way? And at this point you have virtually no indication, I

mean if it occurs to you to ask, "How good will I really be at this? What can I expect if I become a mathematician? Can I expect to be a great mathematician? Can I expect to be a professor at some university in Podunk?" At that point you've done no original research. It's well known that there are people who are very bright who never do anything original. You just don't know. If it occurs to you to think about it, you can't answer at all, you know, if this is going to be a successful, satisfying life. But already at this point I felt a tremendous vested interest in the fact that I had done this, been successful up to that point, and been reinforced all this time. And I didn't know particularly what else I wanted to do anyway. Well, I was confident enough to proceed. There was reason to go on studying mathematics. Whenever I asked myself what else I might do or want to do, I could never think of anything else I wanted to do more (M-5).

SUMMARY OF THE LATER YEARS

The mathematicians were raised in environments where education and academic achievement were highly valued. Consequently, from a very early age, they assumed they would be going to college. They attended a variety of different colleges, but all had quite positive experiences—especially in mathematics. They did so well in their initial courses that they were encouraged to take honor sections and graduate courses. For the first time they would observe "real" mathematics done by "real" mathematicians. They met other students who valued learning as highly as they did and they began to think in terms of mathematics as a career.

GRADUATE SCHOOL

Just as previously they had "assumed" they would be going to college, graduate school became a logical next step for the mathematicians.

I really was mostly following my nose that this was the next thing to do and I was probably going to be a mathematician (M-17).

Again, as college students they had been successful in mathematics courses—usually more successful than in other courses. All enjoyed mathematics, certainly enough to continue in the field even though many had yet to discover what research mathematics actually was and that it would indeed be something at which they would succeed.

> At the beginning of my third year of college I realized that I wanted to go on to graduate school, after all. For some reason, I didn't think much, never have thought much, about what would happen next. Never. By that time it was mathematics. It was clearly what I was best at, and I liked it. So I applied to graduate schools. I guess by that time it was clear to everyone else that I was going to be a mathematician. But it wasn't clear to me. I didn't think, "Well, I'll be a mathematician and I'll do such and such." I just went to graduate school. I wanted to get a degree. But I never thought for a minute what I would do with it, because in some sense I still didn't know what mathematics was (M-6).

Unlike their somewhat haphazard choice of colleges, the mathematicians seem to have chosen graduate schools on the basis of some sense of the quality of the institution. The twenty mathematicians attended one of only eleven different schools, and eighteen of the twenty received Ph.D.'s from departments ranked in the top ten in the nation.

> I think most people working in mathematics have, at some point, close contact with a leading center of mathematics. In fact, I can't think of any example where a person has done great work without having such contacts (M-19).

Several of the mathematicians were able to recall specific reasons for their selection of a particular graduate school: Four went to study with individual professors, three chose departments with strong reputations in a specific field, and three mentioned the prestige of a department in general. Since all but one of the remaining mathematicians selected one of the six top departments in the country, it seems safe to assume that the reputation of the department was again a strong factor in their choice.

> I had decided I would like to work with a professor who was then at [my college], and it emerged in the middle of the year that he was moving to Princeton. So I applied to be a graduate student at Princeton and I was accepted (M-21).

> Someone in the previous class had gone to Stanford and I still had some contact with him and he liked Stanford a lot. . . . I got an N.S.F. scholarship, so I would have support wherever I went, so I chose Stanford. . . . It was partly prestige, going to a prestigious school. I thought it would be a big challenge to do something like that. I thought that the students there would be really great and I would have this tremendous chance to learn all this mathematics (M-18).

> Well, again, it was a question of prestige, which translated into something practical. Namely, they were known to be very selective there. There was known to be a lot of close contact between professors and students. . . . It was particularly strong in what I thought I was interested in at the time, [and it] seemed to have a lot going for it (M-5).

Each of the mathematicians was involved in a rather rarefied graduate experience. Top-ranked departments attract and accept only the finest students and indeed are ranked highly because of the quality of their programs and faculty.

> One thing for mathematicians is to look at the kind of environment they had during their education. One thing that meant a lot to me was that when I came here as a graduate student, 80% of the other students were just superb and they ate and slept mathematics. It was a very intense experience. It was much more intense than anything I was used to before. I really worked hard and I saw, for example, you would read about so and so's theorem and be impressed, and the next day you would see so and so munching cookies at tea (M-22).

There is considerable difference between learning to understand and repeat what other mathematicians have already done and learning how to do what mathematicians actually do. Graduate-level courses are an opportunity to see a mathematician at work. Graduate teachers do very little instruction. They continue as role models and in some cases approach becoming collaborators with their better students.

> I took ———— 's graduate course, which was, of course, on his own work up to and including what he was working on at that instant. And, in fact, in the very first lecture of that course he gave a very general survey and talked about some differential equation that was going to arise in the course and how one could conjecture that it was equal to some standard differential equation that occurred in some other context. He had been able to check in some very special case that this was true and thought it would be very interesting to do it in general. That became my thesis topic (M-21).

> . . . to have a good educational experience, it has to do almost entirely with interpersonal effects, one way or another. . . . The point is that you tune in to the person. . . . Basically the main function of teachers is to create a good environment. . . . They become more curious. You can sort of see a kind of attitude or way of looking at something that you can copy yourself, which somehow makes it clear to you what's happening (M-12).

> I think I first got involved in this course of [A's], and he, well, I just did very well in the course, you know. I did all of the work and he was quite impressed by that, I think. He gave me A-pluses in the course. He thought I was a great student. So . . . I started working with him. . . . He gave me some things to read, and that turned out very well. Within a few months we were getting some results. . . . My interaction with [A] made [B] aware of me. And [B] took a very strong interest in me (M-18).

Most of the mathematicians had taken honors or graduate courses from the time they were sophomores in college. Coursework, however, is not the same as research. Doing well in coursework is not a guarantee that one will do well in research. Several of the mathematicians still had doubts about the success they might have even after they finished their Ph.D.'s.

> But it wasn't until I was working on my thesis that I was really doing what you have to do to do research. I felt prepared to do whatever was next. I would look forward to the immediate goals, doing well in courses and passing my exams. But luckily I had an adviser who helped me a lot, partly just by leaving me alone and partly by serving as a model (M-17).

> In math there are no guarantees of success. [To earn a Ph.D.] in mathematics, you have to do something qualitatively different from anything you have done before. You don't know if you can do it. So the original goal is to write a thesis and become a Ph.D., and you feel great. But you also feel you have to keep a secret of the fact that you don't really know anything (M-5).

> The principal time of insecurity regarding my ability to do original mathematical work was right after I received my Ph.D., and the question then was, is one able to continue doing original work on one's own and not in the presence of the thesis adviser (M-13).

> I really had grave doubts about my ability to do creative mathematics. There's no way of knowing until you do it. You just can't tell until you get there. It turned out somewhat to my surprise, that I was able to do research, and to my even greater astonishment that I was pretty good at it (M-15).

The mathematicians included in this study were selected on the basis of their performance, their contribution to the field. Once they "discovered" mathematics, they began working very hard and devoting extraordinary amounts of time to the field.

> You have to immerse yourself in something. Think about it constantly. You work and work and get these ideas floating around and you have to reach a certain threshold and then some of the problems solve themselves. Some of them come to you two years later, but you have to concentrate, to focus (M-16).

To do mathematics you have to work a lot. . . . Mathematics is not a job, if you take it as a job, you don't get anywhere. . . . Now, I typically come here early in the morning and work all day, then leave here late at night and work all night. I mean, all these people are like that (M-7).

. . . it does take tremendous focus (M-9).

You can work for weeks and be absolutely nowhere. But it's necessary, the time is not wasted, because if you hadn't done the work and gotten nowhere, then you wouldn't get the idea that may solve the problem. It's half hard work and it's half play, but mostly it's just engrossing. You have to get to the end of this so you can sleep again. In some sense solutions are unpredictable. The only thing that you can predict is that you won't find solutions if you don't work (M-6).

It's more a question of how much time is not spent (M-19).

The way to do original work is just to be working on problems. The question is whether you work or you don't work. The people who "dry up" and don't accomplish anything really just aren't working on problems (M-13).

Despite the hard work and long hours, several of the mathematicians had a sense that chance and luck—being in the right place at the right time—were also an important element in their eventual success.

My initial success in research was partly due to the fact that in roughly the area that I was interested in a very important development had just taken place, and it opened up the field completely. I was very fortunate to appear on the scene at a time when there were a lot of new ideas to explore. I hate to think what would happen if I had to start now, things are much more resistant now (M-3).

The thing I want to emphasize is the incredible role that luck plays in this . . . having the right professor at the right time, being around when some new mathematical problem is coming into popularity, being exposed to interesting questions. I'm completely convinced that there are lots of mathematicians who are in any measurable way much smarter than I am, higher IQ's, they can learn more, they can learn faster, answer questions more quickly. I'm a much better mathematician in the sense that I've done better mathematics, and this is very largely a question of luck. Being in the right place at the right time. You have to be pretty good at mathematics, but if you are pretty good at mathematics but around people who are interested in uninteresting mathematics, you'll be pretty good at uninteresting mathematics (M-21).

Each of the mathematicians has devoted at least ten years to intensive—nearly obsessive—effort in mathematics. This period typically begins with graduate school (although for a few it began in college).

When I went to graduate school, I decided, "Okay, this is it. I'm going to spend a few years of my life really deeply learning something." And at the end of four years I knew a lot of mathematics and I started to do research. I got involved in my profession and continued to learn and learn. And at the end of a decade of that there's just no comparison. You need that kind of time. Nobody really does good mathematics of a certain kind without having put in a lot of time (M-15).

Motivation became increasingly central. In some instances, mathematics is the one thing they do well.

Certainly one thing I would mention is satisfaction and a sense of worth. In spite of what my parents would have had me believe, that I could do anything I set my mind to, I came to the conclusion that that was false. At this point in my life there isn't any particular evidence that I could do anything else particularly well. The point is that there is one area, and one area alone, that I know that I can perhaps in a relatively narrow way be doing something that's on the frontier of present knowledge. Here's one area where I've invested so many years and I've had a certain amount of success, enough to make me feel that I'm not wasting my time. That's a lot of motivation to continue (M-5).

Others find comfort in the definite sense of "right or wrong."

I think the original attraction was the simplicity of it. I remember in earlier education a lot of confusion about why things were the way there were alleged to be. And somehow the revelation of mathematics in college was that there are some initial axioms and everything follows from these axioms. There is a definite sense of being right or wrong. I have friends, mathematicians, who started out in physics and switched to mathematics for this reason. In physics they could never understand what the rules of the game were. In mathematics it was completely clear (M-21).

Most are enthralled with the excitement of a new result, a solution to a difficult and elusive problem.

The main thing is working on math itself. I know for the best two or three things that I have ever done there is a feeling of awe that's just incomparable. I feel privileged to have added a couple of things to the field. I love the subject, there is nothing I enjoy more than finding the solution to a problem after a lot of work. And even though it's occasionally very painful to fail, after working on some problem for a year or two, there is still in the back of your mind that thrill of the chase (M-22).

And finally,

I'm certainly seduced by mathematics. I couldn't help myself being a mathematician (M-3).

THE MATHEMATICIANS TODAY

The realm of a research mathematician includes extraordinarily abstract quantitative, spatial, and symbolic concepts and a largely deductive but often illusive process known as proof. The way in which they think, what it is they actually do, is essentially unknown except to other mathematicians.

I'll quote you . . . a very well-known mathematician. . . now in his seventies. . . . "Mathematics is done for the grudging admiration of a few friends" (M-7).

Typically, neither parents, wives, nor friends understand the work of the mathematicians.

> I'm writing a book right now, and . . . the stuff takes five years to write. There's only a handful of people in the country who really understand what I'm doing. . . . [M]y mother and father are very proud of me . . . [but] have absolutely no appreciation of the actual mathematics that I do, none whatsoever. I never discuss any mathematics with them (M-16).

A recent volume by Davis and Hersh (1980) entitled *The Mathematical Experience* contains a rare attempt by research mathematicians to present the meaning and purpose of mathematics. They endeavor to construct a portrait of an "ideal" mathematician, a most typical, "mathematicianlike mathematician":

> The ideal mathematician's work is intelligible only to a small group of specialists, numbering a few dozen or at most a few hundred. . . . He studies objects whose existence is unsuspected by all except a handful of his fellows. Indeed, if one who is not an initiate asks him what he studies, he is incapable of showing or telling what it is. . . . Mathematicians know they are studying an objective reality. To an outsider, they seem to be engaged in an esoteric communion with themselves and a small clique of friends. . . . If . . . a person accepts our discipline, and goes through two or three years of graduate study in mathematics, he absorbs our way of thinking. . . . But we must pause to realize that, outside of our coterie, much of what we do is incomprehensible (pp. 34–44).

This description was echoed by all of the mathematicians interviewed for this study. These people are driven by a desire to extend our knowledge of what is true. Their success is typically the result of massive amounts of hard work. They are attracted to and motivated by the order and beauty they see in mathematics. The personal characteristics that allow them to work "on the frontier of present knowledge" (M-5), at the limit of man's present cognitive ability, were developed over many years. While essential technical knowledge is learned relatively late, these individuals began "becoming" mathematicians while still very young. Learning how to learn was more important than what they learned. They learned a way of learning and developed certain characteristics and only then discovered a specific field in which to apply their talents. In a sense, they developed their talent and only then became mathematicians.

REFERENCE

Davis, P., and Hersh, R. *The Mathematical Experience.* Boston: Birkhauser, 1980.

9

One Mathematician: "Hal Foster"

William C. Gustin

The development of exceptional talent in mathematics is presented in chapter 8 as a composite, bits and pieces of the development of the entire sample of mathematicians. The emphasis is on the common themes which emerged from histories which are in many respects quite unique. The following case study should provide greater insight into the development of mathematical talent in general and also reveal some of the fascination to be found in the story of one very unique individual.

The common themes of the earlier chapter are certainly evident in the development of "Hal Foster."* Also in evidence are many aspects which belie the notion of a typical mathematician. Hal's story incorporates all of the essential ingredients for the development of his talent but also reveals the impact of a particular sequence of events and opportunities.

Medicine "was chosen" for Hal's father. After graduating from a midwestern medical school during the Depression, he found only one opening in his speciality, and stayed with that same job throughout his entire career. Hal's father was active

_____
*The name of the mathematician has been changed.

in professional organizations, a delegate to the American Medical Association, and president of the national society of his speciality. Hal recalls that

> He had very definite views on what it meant in the community to be a medical doctor, what the medical profession stood for, and so on. He worked very hard as a civic leader, in musical societies and the Rotary, and also within the medical profession.

Hal's mother "came from a sort of first-generation academic family." Her father had been a professor and her mother a college graduate. She majored in zoology and minored in math in college.

Hal's parents were very active musically. They courted while playing string quartets. Hal's father took voice lessons until quite recently. Both parents started playing recorders in the early 1950s.

> In addition, my father continued to play violin some. He had an unusual ability—he could pick up the violin after months of never touching it and play it quite well. A violin is an instance where you have to keep practicing. Of course being a doctor, his motor skills were quite advanced.

Hal doubts whether his father could ever have been a businessman, but commented that his mother "was very astute and very shrewd in setting up the estate and investments and looking after things."

Hal is the second of four children and the only boy. One sister is six years older, another a year younger, and the third six years younger. Only the oldest sister finished college, graduating with a degree in English. The middle sister studied music, and the youngest has recently started a program in physical therapy. The children all played musical instruments or sang. There was always music playing during dinner, even when they were very young.

They were 78 rpm records and had to be turned over every two minutes. My father was up and down from the dinner table. He played music which had an immediate appeal to young children—rhythmic things like Offenbach and Strauss waltzes.

Hal's mother recalled that breakfast was an important time when the whole family ate together.

We sat down together. Their father would use the time to expose the children to music. We didn't go into discussions about noticing this or that. . . . The children all went to concerts when they were old enough. We taught them to sing rounds and play recorders, but we never promoted music as a profession—we enjoyed it so much as a hobby.

Hal described his father as "rather a learned sort of person," a "distant figure in the home." He had a very definite image of a father as lofty and very eminent.

He loved words and had a great respect for people who expressed themselves very precisely, always having exactly the right word. All of us kids always scored very high on vocabulary tests . . . we'd been around so many of these words so much that it had that influence.

Hal believes that the children all felt closer to their mother. She supported their father. Any disagreements they had were sorted out between themselves and not in the presence of the children.

They had quite different personalities. He had a very fixed image of what was expected of him, what he should do, and so on, which didn't really adapt well with time. He had an image of the physician's place in the community, which is quite an old-fashioned attitude now. And he is extremely conservative politically. . . . My mother is quite conservative in the thrifty, businessman, New England sort of sense of values, but very much more a realist.

The Fosters lived in the country, so the children "were isolated." Hal's mother "had no way of judging [his] ability."

> He seemed bright. He was much quieter than many boys. He was competitive, though, but didn't have much in the way of competition in the family. His sister was so much older than he. They didn't do a lot together.

The family played games together when the children were young. There was some emphasis on math-related games in the family—throwing dice and adding the numbers.

> We also played games with flash cards—words on the front and definitions on the back—aimed at expanding the children's vocabulary. We went around the table, each child giving the definition or giving the word to the definition.

Both parents did a lot of reading aloud to the children, even more than playing games. The children liked to learn their favorite stories by heart. Hal's mother noted that he "seemed to need my undivided attention." When he was about four, she discovered a drawing he had made of a combustion engine. She had no idea who explained it to him and speculates that he was apparently learning to read on his own.

> I didn't try to teach him to read. He developed eye problems at age four and wore a patch over one eye for about two years. Because of that, I didn't push close work—reading and so on. He couldn't seem to start to read, but he'd take the *World Book* supplement and go through it. One day he was looking at a picture and I started to explain it to him and he told me about it—apparently he could read, but the learning process I never was aware of—I don't know how or when he learned to read.

Hal's impression was that his parents were aware of certain mathematical tendencies, possibly even by the time he was five years old. He seemed to exhibit "a real sort of abstract conceptual thinking" in the visualization of shapes, for example, or putting blocks into a box. Hal played with blocks a great deal. "With blocks he could look at things in different ways—build different things. We tried to keep materials around—paper, crayons, blocks, etc."

My mother has a drawing that I made when I was five or six of a perpetual motion machine. It involved a tank of water at the top and a pipe coming out of it running a turbine. The turbine was connected to a generator, and the electricity was used to run an electric motor, which powered a pump to fill the tank with water. My mother had quite a time trying to explain to me about the conservation of energy. But I think it was a very ingenious thing to think of at that early stage.

Hal was always interested in how things worked. He would take toys apart and look at the gears. He was fascinated with valves and gauges and dials and interested in radio and electronics from even a preschool age. One of his mother's most vivid memories is of the way Hal used to follow workmen around the house, where there was often plumbing and remodeling work to be done.

I thought he would drive them crazy. . . . He asked them question after question after question. . . . He was so incessant. His questions weren't repetitive, they were sequential. The workmen never seemed to mind, and he never touched the equipment. We trained our kids not to meddle with things—they learned that very, very early.

The afternoon schedule varied, since there was a spread in the ages of the children and they had different activities after school. The family lived seven miles from town. Consequently, Hal and his sisters typically played by themselves; they played games, practiced music, played in the yard, and read books and magazines, which were "all over the house." There was *Scientific American*, *National Geographic*, *Natural History*—perhaps fifteen different magazines in all. He also had an erector set, one of the larger models, with which he built all kinds of mechanical things, and an electric train, with which he played "endlessly."

By the time he started school, Hal's eye problem was clearing up, but he still had some trouble learning to read.

> The reading problem was very strange in that he tried so hard to know what was going on without reading. I don't know if it was that he didn't want to bother with all the little words or that the books were too dull.

Hal is left-handed, and when he first learned to write, it would frequently be in mirror image.

> I really didn't learn to read properly until I was about in fifth grade. I wanted to be an inventor. I thought I would just have a secretary read things to me. I didn't need to learn to read.

The Fosters felt strongly that each of their children should be free to choose whatever kind of career they found interesting. Their intent was to provide the best kind of education for them, so that they would be able to continue in whatever they decided to do. At first they had thought the children would go to the local school, a small country school.

> Now, that would not be adequate, because they wouldn't be able to enter college—they wouldn't fulfill requirements. So we transferred them to a school in town. . . . That was the purpose, if they wanted to go to college they could. . . . We felt that we should at least give them the opportunity so they could do what they wanted.

Hal talked to his mother about what he was doing in school, and she helped him with some compositions and projects. He was not an outstanding student.

> I don't think we ever pushed the children to get straight A's. We thought they should do whatever their abilities were and learn to

handle them and set their own goals instead of setting their goals for them.

He did not work as hard on subjects in which he wasn't interested. Hal recalled encouragement from his parents to the extent that they insisted he complete his homework. In his opinion, "They were not permissive in any way. They kept me on a short leash."

Hal believes the quality of his instruction throughout was generally quite high, but that he was "very average" in many ways in elementary school. In reading, spelling, and things which didn't relate to science he claims to have been "quite backward." He was interested in science and always ahead of the class, but "in the basic skills and even basic arithmetic I was very slow to learn."

When Hal was in the sixth grade and his older sister was taking physics, her instructor showed the class a demonstration (a self-priming siphon). Hal's sister drew a sketch, and Hal figured out what had happened. She told her instructor, and he was very impressed and wanted Hal to study with him independently. Hal's teacher wouldn't let him, because he felt Hal was deficient in other areas.

Through the eighth grade Hal recalls just having had the "regular workbooks," which he did as he was told. He did them quite easily and found them interesting.

> My mother told me that my seventh-grade math teacher had complained that I was working ahead in my notebook. I think my mother must have been appalled at the time, [but] finds it amusing now to think that working ahead wouldn't be encouraged.

Hal had school friends but thinks that he probably didn't develop in the same way socially as he would have if he had lived in town. His sense of a typical situation was that neighborhood children would play together after school—"and I have no experience with that really." Occasionally he would get to stay in town and go to someone's house, "but that wasn't a routine." On Saturday a friend might come out to play in the woods around the house, but he didn't have

> . . . the sort of constant social situation of the kids in town. And I think in some sense it probably stunted my social development. It wasn't really until I got to college that I felt on equal footing.

Hal spent a month every summer with his maternal grandfather, who was "an academic, a biostatistician. . . . His Ph.D., in fact, was in mathematics." They would build things, have discussions, and go for walks. When Hal was twelve, he wanted to build a table with a drawer. His grandfather had him draw out a blueprint in detail first—before they built the table. And he would talk to them. Hal's mother recalled one day in particular when he gathered all the grandchildren into his study to talk about math. She wanted to go, and he said she could if she didn't say anything—she realized then that she wasn't wanted.

> He was an excellent teacher. He enjoyed seeing how people handled ideas that he threw out to them.

Hal described his grandfather as "quite an outdoorsman." He took the grandchildren fishing and mountain climbing. He had grown up in northern New Hampshire in the White Mountains. He had a retirement farm, mostly woodland, but it included a mountain. "That is," Hal commented, "the place which is nearest to my heart."

> I think my grandfather did influence me a great deal in the direction of mathematics. There's no doubt that he's the greatest hero I've ever had, and it was clear to me that he regarded pure mathematics as the highest calling.

Hal's grandfather impressed him quite clearly with the importance of mathematics as a language and a tool of science. They discussed mathematics, partly philosophical matters, but also "little problems."

I think he picked out my mathematical ability when I was very young, and when I turned to mathematics, I think he was very pleased. I wasn't aware of it. . . . He was a very wise, perceptive person. I think he would have overwhelmed me if he'd really expressed his pleasure.

These summer visits to his grandfather's lasted from the time Hal was five until he finished college. Hal's mother commented that his grandfather was the one "who could really appreciate" Hal's ability. He remarked to her once when Hal was in high school that he thought Hal had an unusual mind. He appreciated Hal's way of thinking and handling numbers and mathematical ideas. He didn't push Hal's interest, however. The only time Hal's grandfather took a stand was when he felt the school where the children went didn't do enough in the way of drill and that Hal had not learned his multiplication tables. He requested that he be allowed to send Hal to school in the summer.

> He didn't do that for any of the other children, perhaps because he felt they were getting more traditional training, but I think, too— none of the others had the strong interest in mathematics.

The school to which his grandfather sent him was a private academy and one of "the foremost secondary schools in the country, a very high-quality place." He attended the academy for an eight-week summer term after his sophomore year in high school. He remembers working "terribly hard, harder than I'd ever worked on anything before." Halfway through the term he had two B's and one C, which was still considered honor roll. In the end he slipped to two B's and a D,

> but I was never so proud of a D in my whole life—that was in English. And considering that was the first experience I ever had of an English course in which I had to write compositions, in which I really had to pay attention to grammar and so on, I was completely unprepared.

Hal's mother was not at all complimentary about the D. She "was sort of silent about it." Hal recalled being satisfied with himself, thinking he'd done well. And "it was probably the last B I ever got in mathematics." His memory of the math course was not of new material, but "a lot more practice in just routine calculation." Hal wasn't told at the time that it was his grandfather's idea that he go to the summer session and that he had paid the tuition. Hal's mother explained, "My father didn't believe in encouraging a child to think that he was exceptional. Hal is exceptional in mathematics, he wasn't exceptional in a lot of other areas."

About the time Hal was in the seventh or eighth grade, a family friend made a small radio for him. He was very interested in science in general when he was young, and this friend of his parents, who was a radio ham, was a favorite of his. Amateur radio was one of his main interests, and he became a novice ham in high school,

> . . . but I didn't have enough support around me then. It wasn't something my parents could help me with, because they didn't have the technical knowledge. I didn't have people to learn from or the finances to buy proper equipment, and so that sort of withered—but it really withered in the sense that at that time my interests turned to mathematics.

A very significant point in the development of Hal's interest in math came during his ninth-grade year. His math teacher was a member of a group of people preparing a program in modern mathematics. Hal had started the year of algebra thinking he would want mathematics because it was the language of science and he wanted to be an electrical engineer. "But by the end of the year I really wanted to be a mathematician. I was really seduced by it."

The algebra course was designed to have students start with a few axioms and then derive the basic algebraic rules, thereby gaining a greater understanding of the axioms themselves as well as "the appeal and the nature of mathematics in general. Proving theorems became "like a little game." From certain rules "you deduce things and build up a bigger and bigger body of consequences." Hal enjoyed the "intellectual exercise," claiming that the approach used in the course stimulated his thinking. He responded to the "intellectual challenge."

The same approach was used in the geometry course—starting with a few basic rules and deducing consequences from them. Hal recalls that the whole class responded with enthusiasm. They enjoyed the construction, using the rules, and making the desired deductions.

> Some of these were twenty- to thirty-step proofs, and even though the students in the class clearly were not going to be mathematicians, they understood the appeal of the nature of mathematics. . . . I knew then what the nature of mathematical research was, which is quite unusual—I mean, I meet academics, distinguished academics, who really have no idea what mathematical research is all about.

Of this same time period, Hal's mother recalled how he took anything he was told could not be proven as a personal challenge. As he grew older, he seemed to become busier with his own thoughts and ideas, which was especially noticeable when the family sat around the table discussing something. Hal would be engrossed in his own thoughts and all of a sudden, after the discussion was over, he would surface and say, "Oh, what was that?" He preferred to let people argue and discuss and then "cream off the top."

> He was inclined to be busy with his own thoughts, and I think a lot of the time he was developing and solving mathematical problems.

Hal's mother also recalled that his teacher did not give him an A for the first term in algebra. When she talked to the teacher, he claimed that Hal was not working as hard as he might. But then the teacher gave Hal extra material, and eventually Hal created math problems to be used in the book that was developed for the course.

The program was effective for most of the students; in fact, three went on to become successful mathematicians. Each year, the classes were taught by a different teacher; the first was a very dynamic and energetic person, very much involved with the project as a co-author.

Hal did not feel pressured or encouraged by the teachers. He wasn't trying to win approval from his teacher by doing well in the course. Rather, "I think it was really just the intellectual challenge of the subject that I responded to."

Other than the involvement with the development of the modern math program at the high school, Hal was not involved in other organized math activities.

> Once I got to high school, I spent enormous amounts of time just by myself doing mathematics and playing games, analyzing games—working out strategies and trying to analyze how to play a game. Board games. . . . And I read, I taught myself some calculus, mostly differential calculus. I was using texts that my sister had had from college.

Hal's initial interest had been in science, but that interest shifted to mathematics during high school. He seems not to have been an exceptional student in any courses other than science and math. He liked math well enough to do work on his own. In fact, as he progressed through high school, he was spending more and more time involved in his own interests, especially in science and mathematics.

Hal's father and grandfather were powerful role models. Going to college was a foregone conclusion.

> I don't think I ever thought of doing anything other than going to college. Especially from eighth grade or so. I had wanted to be an electrical engineer, and that meant a college degree. When I changed to mathematics, it didn't change the idea of going to college, except that I wanted a graduate degree as well.

Hal's parents had always made it clear that his way would be paid through college. "There was never any question about that." His mother explained that they had considered sending him to a small private college, but realized that there was no graduate program, "and I said no. He needed to have more stimulation from people way beyond him."

Hal's grades overall in high schoool "were not terribly good." He always got A's in mathematics and physical science, but in other areas he had not been sufficiently motivated. He went to the state university, having applied to two private schools and hearing nothing from one and being put on a waiting list for the other. He took an entrance exam at the university and qualified for the honors program in math.

Hal had developed an interest in a particular branch of mathematics, even in high school. He found that the chairman of the math department at the university was in that field. Hal "came to his attention as a sophomore." This chairman was giving a problem-solving class to graduate students, which Hal took as a second-term sophomore. The course involved solving as many problems as they were able.

> I worked very hard on that course. I think I must have spent twenty or twenty-five hours a week on that course alone.

When he went to the university, Hal suddenly realized, "You know, if I didn't do well here, they'd kick me out." He started working very hard in all areas—not just in math:

> And to my surprise and pleasure started getting very good grades too. I thought, "This is sort of neat." I kept it up and graduated with 4.95 out of 5.

Hal described his undergraduate experience in mathematics as "a very rigorous honors program" with twenty or thirty students. His impression was that the syllabus was very well thought out and the teaching "superb." There was a variety of more difficult problems one could attack in addition to the routine problems. He did "quite a lot" of extra things, solving problems of his own invention, starred problems in textbooks, or problems out of the *American Mathematical Monthly.*

He generally did well in courses and "especially well in mathematics." His undergraduate advisor suggested that he go to Cambridge, which "was acknowledged as the center of my speciality in the Western world." He applied for a fellowship and a scholarship and won them both. (He accepted the Marshall scholarship.) A professor agreed to take him on as a student.

> [I] started to do research, exactly the sort of thing that was right for me, in the sense that I was ready to do research. I was much more mature in the research sense [than most students]. So I did research.

Hal also had a National Science Foundation grant for two years. He "wasn't in any rush." He viewed the dissertation as "a sort of pain in the neck" to write out. His preference was to do the research rather than to write it up.

Hal attributes some of his initial success in research when he started graduate school to the fact that a very important development had just taken place in his speciality. It opened up the field completely.

> A lot of new ideas were around, and a lot of progress was made in those years. I was fortunate to appear on the scene at a time when there were a lot of ideas to explore. I hate to think what would happen if I had started now . . . things are much more resistant now.

Hal considers himself very fortunate because from an early age he not only knew what he wanted to do, but was good at it. Often the two things don't go together.

> I had tremendous opportunities in the early exposure to modern mathematics and in winning the graduate fellowship. Those

things are very chancy. And starting graduate school at a time when research was just taking off in my area—so, I had a large number of good fortunes.

Hal mentioned having two particular goals. One is the introduction of a graduate-level text for which he feels there is a great need. The second is his attempt to make himself expert in a number of the branches of his field—to the extent that he could do significant research in any of those branches. He has done some very difficult things and some things that have "moved the subject forward in a way that might not have been foreseen." There are some unsolved problems of an even greater level of difficulty, "and I would like at least once in a while to knock off one of these problems."

> Littlewood has a comment, "You shouldn't be afraid to work on a very hard problem because although you may not solve it, you'll prove something else along the way." And I've had that experience time and time again.

Hal believes that his mind may work in a different way from other people's. For him, motivation is everything. If he is interested in something, he can "really absorb a tremendous amount of information in a very short period of time." If it's a task which is set for him and in which he really isn't interested, "it's dreadfully difficult to obtain just a passing knowledge."

His memory "is a funny thing." He remembers some things, but thinks that he carries fewer memories "sort of readily accessible in my mind than most people." He carries only a restricted amount of information on ready recall.

> My mother always thought that I was in somewhat of a fog. I would be sitting there and apparently listening and later show that I was miles away. That was always a vexation. I have a great ability to sit and think mathematics—just be mentally absent in a meeting or a lecture. I can think about mathematics during a concert—just sit there and not really be listening to the music.

Hal also believes that he has some curious conversational habits, which may reflect something about the way in which his mind works. Often while talking about one thing he may suddenly switch to something that seems to be unrelated.

It'a a matter of associating A to B, B to C, C to D, and then starting to talk about D without verbalizing the way that I connected it. These jumps can be very distracting to people.

Hal suspects that he makes these associations faster than one would speak in conversation and it doesn't seem relevant to carry through all the thoughts.

I think this matter of association is critical to the mathematics. I have an ability to isolate the critical mathematical element of something and then associate it with something somewhere else and bring the two together.

A final comment from Hal's mother:

We never felt inclined to push him ahead, which I think some parents might have done. It was better to let him do what he was interested in. We had the stuff around, we made it available. We were able to send him to the college of his choice. So I think he's done well and I'm pleased, but I don't think I get any extra credit.

And from Hal:

I'm certainly seduced by mathematics. I couldn't help myself being a mathematician. I'm fortunate I can actually earn a living at the same time, because it's a great love. Mathematics is something that really fascinates me—it's almost addictive.

10

★ ★ ★ ★ ★ ★

Becoming an Outstanding Research Neurologist

Lauren A. Sosniak

The research neurologists whose development will be described in this chapter were invited to take part in the Development of Talent Research Project because they met three criteria attesting to their unusually high achievement. First, they have been given generous and continuing (five-year) support for their research from the National Institute of Health. This support came in the form of either a Teacher-Investigator Development Award or a Research Career Development Award. The two are considered by expert informants in the field to be the most prestigious awards for young neurological researchers. Second, their work has been cited frequently in the professional journals most respected by their peers. Third, they are known and well regarded by a sample of chairmen of neurology departments at leading universities across the country.

Twenty-four people under the age of forty with M.D. degrees met those three criteria. Twenty of the twenty-four (83%) agreed to talk with us about their development. The individual interviews were conducted at a time and place convenient for each research neurologist.

At the end of each interview we asked for permission to contact the research neurologist's parents and request their participation in this study. Interviews were conducted with parents of fifteen of the physician-scientists. In one instance a neurologist did not give permission, in another both parents were deceased, and in three cases we were unable to interview parents because they were ill or unwilling to take part. The interviews with parents, intended to supplement and complement what the talented individual told us, were conducted over the telephone by another member of the Development of Talent staff.

A Context for the Neurologists' Histories

Nineteen of the twenty research neurologists are male. (Because of this, in order to avoid making the one female conspicuous in the description of the typical pattern of development, all of the subjects will be referred to in the masculine throughout this chapter.) They are typically the oldest child in their family (thirteen out of twenty, or 65%) or else the oldest male child (three more, for a total of 80%). At the time of our interview, they ranged in age from thirty-one to thirty-nine ($\overline{X}$ = 35.5). They had received their honor from the National Institute of Health between one and five years earlier.

Seven of the twenty (35%) were raised in the New York metropolitan area. Four others (20%) were raised in or around Chicago. The remaining nine grew up in separate cities or towns across the country.

ACTIVE, ACADEMICALLY ORIENTED FAMILIES

The research neurologists were typically born into active and academically oriented families. Their parents tend to characterize themselves as "very busy people" (M of N-1). This perception was held by their children as well. "My parents were always very busy, extremely busy" (N-20). "[My father] was— one adjective might be—busy. He was just always doing something" (N-3).

Busy, as it was expanded upon during the interviews, meant more than simply "active" or "occupied." It signified being (a) interested in a wide variety of subject matters; (b) involved in the community; and (c) fully engaged in work the parents considered meaningful. Comments like these were heard again and again from the neurologists' parents: "[I am] interested in . . . lots of things . . . an eclectic type" (M of N-3); "I did community things. . . ." (F of N-8). And from their children: "[Mother was] head of committees" (N-19).

Most of the fathers' activities revolved around their work.

My dad was always off working (N-1).

[My husband] had always been more active than any of his . . . colleagues (M of N-2).

My father is one of these kind of people who considers work and success the premium virtue of life, and so he really hasn't had time to develop what most people call hobbies (N-4).

[My dad] worked harder than most people in his institution . . . more hours than the people under him (N-8).

A few of the fathers added a variety of hobbies to their busy schedules. These included reading "avidly," for work and pleasure; fishing or camping; engaging in or watching sports; or tinkering and building in a basement workshop.

Two of the research neurologists' fathers were physicians themselves, and one was a dentist. Two were pharmacists. Three others did physical-science research for companies. (Thus eight, or 40%, were involved in medicine or medically related or scientific professions.) The other twelve fathers worked in a wide variety of occupations, especially working for or running small businesses. All were able to provide their families with middle-class or upper-middle-class life-styles, although about half worked for many years to move up from the lower middle class. "Most people really aren't all that ambitious, and all you have to do is be out just a little bit in front

of everybody else so you get noticed and . . . make progress,"
one father reported. "I did make progress . . . [and] we became
financially secure enough that I could retire and have no problems" (F of N-8).

The neurologists' mothers were typically reported to be
"very active." Eleven of the twenty mothers worked outside
the home regularly, some taking a few years away from work
to stay home with preschool children. And although they were
working mothers, "as was typical of that time . . . I did not
drop any of my own responsibilities when I went to work. The
house was mine, the washing was mine . . ." (M of N-1). In addition, these women engaged in many of the same activities as
the mothers who were predominantly "housewives": working
for the PTA and as volunteers in other social and community
organizations, teaching Sunday school, taking classes at local
colleges, reading numerous books and magazines, and taking
their children to and from assorted lessons and on various "ex-
peditions." One neurologist spoke for many when he commented about his mother: "She was not a stay-at-home lady"
(N-3).

The mothers' active schedules seem sometimes to have
been a compromise between their throwing themselves eagerly into a specific life's career and being "good mothers"
who were home and available for their children. One neurologist whose mother didn't work "until after we'd all grown
up" reported,

> There is a degree of frustration with her . . . that she didn't feel that
> she had carried her career as far as she [might have] or hadn't ex-
> celled academically as far as she felt she could (N-10).

Another neurologist spoke for many of the children and mothers when he noted,

> My mother was always busy with something and hasn't distin-
> guished herself per se, partly . . . because she's in that generation

where she's torn between self-fulfillment and being a good mother (N-4).

Mothers who did not work at paying jobs while their children were growing up were quick to tell us, "I always felt that (being with the children) was my primary job" (M of N-2). Those who did work while their children were young did so only as long as they could arrange their work schedules to coincide with their children's activities.

I always tried to be home when they came home from school. I had a very strong conviction that that was important (M of N-7).

There was one thing that was understood between my husband and I. Our kids were not . . . latchkey kids. That was absolutely of utmost importance. When they came home from school, I would be there (M of N-6).

Six of the mothers were schoolteachers, and two eventually became principals. Yet even though these mothers' working hours coincided with their school-age children's schedules, they still had reservations about whether they were being good enough mothers.

I did have very uneasy feelings about it, and went all out to see that I was home on time . . . and that I spent hours with them, and that I did not procrastinate or stay out after school so that when they were [home], I was there. That's how I always made myself feel better. It was a job that coincided with theirs. And I did stay in a straight teaching job until they were old enough. . . . I did know and still know how important it is to spend time with your children. . . . I believe it with all my heart (M of N-1).

At least half the parents were involved in community activities; the most frequently mentioned and apparently most important became the PTA or the local school board. "We always went to PTA meetings and school nights and all that. . . . We always took quite an active interest" (M of N-7). "One thing that contributed to [son's success in school] was the close ties [my wife] had with the teachers because she was the organizer of the PTA" (F of N-9). The same father was also involved as president of the PTA for a while. According to another mother, "I worked in the PTA and rose to the position of president of the high school PTA—the first woman president. It was a lot of fun, and the children enjoyed having me work with the schools" (M of N-2). The father of still another research neurologist served on the school board for seventeen years.

The PTA and local school board seem to have served two important functions for the parents. First, these organizations provided the parents with additional opportunities to be busy and involved. Second, and perhaps more important, these organizations gave the parents opportunities to monitor and have some impact on the quality of their children's education. A dominant concern of these parents seems to have been that their children get a "good education."

Many of the research neurologists' parents were well educated themselves. All but three fathers had some college education, and thirteen of the twenty (65%) had done some graduate work. All but three of the mothers also went to college, and one-third had done some graduate work, typically in the field of education. The most schooled of the neurologists' parents seem to have been passing their own parents' values of education on to their children. For instance, one mother reported on her own upbringing this way:

> Our father just drilled that into us, that we weren't a family with a lot of money, but one thing that would make us secure was an education. We just grew up knowing that we were going to get an education because that's the way it went (M of N-1).

The father of another researcher noted,

> Most of the men in [my] family had gone on to college, and that was one of the priorities—making it possible for them to go if they wanted to (F of N-9).

He added later, "We expected [our children] to go [to college] because we had gone ourselves." One mother explicitly made the connection between her parents' values and her own:

> Even as a child, I was always taught to respect my teacher. My parents, although they were minimally educated in Europe, they had a great deal of respect for education, and it's been handed down to me and my children. We always stress education. . . . It was very important how [the children] did in school (M of N-2).

Even in those homes where the parents were not very schooled themselves, the parents had strong academic ambitions for the children.

> There was a strong emphasis on educational achievement, academic performance. . . . Not much oriented toward specific careers, there was very little [of that], as I recall . . . just more an emphasis on academic achievement (N-20).

In almost all the homes academic achievement was viewed by the parents and presented to the children as the means to a secure future.

> My husband and I were both very ambitious for our children intellectually and educationally. We would have felt very badly if one of them said he or she didn't want to go to college—even though you can succeed in this world without going to college. For us, college education was an absolute must. . . . We were happy [when most of the children went on to graduate school] that we didn't have to push, they had that same drive themselves, after a while. It was a matter of livelihood, future, marriage . . . (M of N-2).

> We wanted them to be educated to their capacity and to do whatever it was that they would have wanted to do. . . . We wanted to see them have something better than we had (M of N-6).

A secure future meant not only financial security but also autonomy over one's work. Independence could be achieved by becoming a "professional." "We always told our children, 'You have a profession, you never have to worry, you always have work' " (M of N-2).

The neurologists were well aware how important their academic achievement and secure, independent futures were to their parents:

> There is no question that the primary, the thing that was at the top of the list of importance for my parents, was academic excellence, academic achievement . . . for both my parents. Although more so verbally expressed by my mother than my father. . . . I have a very clear recollection all through my childhood, that the one thing that was constantly being stressed . . . was academic progress (N-16).

> I think from the time I was born, my mother and especially my father wanted me to become a professional person. . . . My parents always assumed that I was going to college and that I was going to become a professional person (N-19).

> My parents, particularly my father, always wanted me to go to an Ivy League school. . . . I think that it meant that it would be easier for me to be successful later on. I think that that's it more than anything (N-3).

> I think they wanted me to grow up to have some kind of independent profession. . . . In a general sense they valued the concept of an independent profession as opposed to an organizational person in business or finance or something like that (N-13).

Typically, the parents' early dreams and aspirations for their children beyond those for a good education, independence, and financial security, were vague at best.

> Our thoughts were that we wanted to develop their own qualities to their utmost, whatever they happened to be (M of N-3).

> Whatever it is, they must love to do it (M of N-2).

> I always think everybody should do what they want to do and I knew that whatever they wanted to do, we would try our best to see that they could do it (M of N-1).

> I avoided trying to tell [my son] what kind of career he should have. I knew he was smart and I wanted him to go as far as he wanted to go (F of N-8).

Several parents were only able to recollect which vocations they hoped their children would *not* enter. One mother commented, "It was purely financial reasons that I really wanted them to get into something besides teaching [which was a family career]. I didn't make suggestions as to what" (M of N-1). Another mother recounted, "My husband never would have wanted them to go into the [family] business, because he himself was forced into this business" (M of N-6). She and her husband wanted their children "to do whatever it was that they would have wanted to do."

Being intelligent, well educated, and busy with work one loves to do was far more important to the parents than any specific career aspirations for their children. Six of the twenty families (30%) did hope that their children might someday become doctors.[1] The fathers in two of these homes were doctors themselves and enjoyed their work enormously. However, in two families becoming a doctor was expressly *not* the thing to do. The parents of one of the research neurologists were disappointed when their high school child reported interest in being a doctor because they thought of the profession of physician as a rather dull one, and of physicians in general as not all that intelligent. Another mother did not want her son to be a doctor for a different reason:

> I didn't want [my son] to be a physician because I wanted him to be a family man and I thought that when you're a physician that you wouldn't be around your family so much—that you'd be more involved with your patients (M of N-13).

---

[1]Although all of the research neurologists we interviewed do have M.D. degrees, most are, first and foremost, scientists. Their medical training was typically thought to be a way to broaden their scientific work. This will be discussed much later.

The Early Years—to Age Eight

The research neurologists were reported to be busy young children, "into everything" (M of N-2). They were busy with "boys' things: trains, things that moved, ... things that did something special. ... And many things were just taken apart for curiosity's sake" (M of N-2). Other "boys" things included "cowboy and Indian games in our neighborhood, and we would chase each other around, shooting imaginary pistols" (N-1). Two parents reported that their children's earliest aspirations were to be firemen.

The most frequently mentioned comment about the preschoolers was that they enjoyed being read to.

> He loved to have you read to him. I would set him on my lap and read. We had a lot of books for kids. I discovered that after I'd read a book to him a time or two, that I could stop in the middle of a sentence or in the middle of a paragraph and he'd go right along and finish it. He could remember it (F of N-8).

> I enrolled them for membership in the public library even before they could read. They could select books that they liked, and either I or my husband would read to them (M of N-2).

> I read him what I considered to be interesting children's stories that weren't too banal or stupid (M of N-3).

There were a large number of books and magazines available in at least two-thirds of the homes. According to one father, "I remember [the child] taking the *Time* magazine and looking at the pictures even when he was in the playpen" (F of N-9). One mother explained how matter-of-fact it was that her child could read when he began kindergarten.

> His father taught him. ... [Father] would come home and would lie down and have a book or a newspaper, and [son] would scoot up there with him and ask, "What's this word? What's that word?" And before you knew it, he was reading (M of N-6).

Several of the research neurologists recall being taught to read before they entered school—usually by a mother or grandmother who was or had been an elementary school teacher. However, one of the more unexpected findings from the interviews was that in six of the twenty cases the young child had some problems with reading at first.[2] "I was considered initially something of a dullard, in the slow reading group in first grade" (N-8). "I couldn't read well when I was in second, third, and fourth grades" (N-4).

> I have a dyslexic problem. . . . It just sort of developed over the first few years, so that by second grade it was becoming clear. . . . I couldn't read signs . . . I couldn't understand the words (N-10).

> [My child] never was a great reader . . . a slow reader . . . and didn't really like it all that much (M of N-7).

In all but two instances, the children seem to have made almost spontaneous recoveries from their reading problems. They were "off and running" by fourth grade. Or, as another noted, "officially caught up by the beginning of fifth grade. In fact, on the city-wide exam I was better than grade [level]. I don't know what accounts for it" (N-4).

Of interest to this researcher is that the difficulties didn't seem to have interfered with the parents' or children's own perceptions of the children's intelligence. One neurologist spoke of it as a "specific problem preventing me from letting my true brilliance express itself," or as a problem that "presented a front that made me look more incompetent than I was" (N-10). The father of another accounted for the fact that his son was "up and down" in elementary school "because in elementary school you have just one teacher, you know, and how you do depends entirely on that teacher" (F of N-8). Another neurologist noted, "I always thought it was a joke. . . . I was a lousy reader and knew it. . . . So I just tried to listen

---

[2]Two continue to have reading difficulties to this day.

more carefully" (N-7). This neurologist's mother accounted for the difficulty this way:

> [My child] sort of verged on ambidextrous. I know that there is a theory that people who are ambidextrous don't learn as well by sight. It might have been something like that because I can't see any other reason for this (M of N-7).

The research neurologists remember how quickly and easily they learned that their academic achievement was important to their parents:

> Mainly by how much attention they paid to what I did, and praise. . . . There was a lot of bragging and support for school papers on which a teacher had put stars or smiling faces (N-1).

> School was very important. We were not allowed to miss a day, sick or not. We had to have not only a fever but a high fever. . . . It was very important (N-2).

> As an indication of how interested they were in making sure that we had things around for us, there was fairly early on a *World Book Encyclopedia* or something like that and a dictionary so that things we'd need in school were available as a small library (N-2).

One mother asserted, "It undoubtedly came through to our children that we valued education and intellectual achievement very highly" (M of N-7). Another mother explained, "I was involved while they were going to school. I was extremely interested in their progress and also being a part of their schooling" (M of N-2).

The neurologists also learned that they were expected to do well, in all their schoolwork, as a matter of course. "[My mother] was pleased with good results, but also expected them" (N-11). After second or third grade,

> I didn't consider the alternative of bringing home less than good grades, and I have the impression that they really didn't either. And although they congratulated me on my grades, there was no element of surprise (N-5).

> I wouldn't want to imply that [a strong emphasis on educational achievement] was a very important *daily* sort of thing. It was more that it was expected that one was going to do well (N-20).

> Bad grades would clearly trigger more response than good grades would, [as these] were more or less expected (N-17).

If the children brought home a less than perfect grade, their parents were likely to ask why, or "they would have some explanation why, like I didn't eat a good breakfast" (N-1).

> I think they felt that I had a lot of potential. They always told me that they knew that I was smart. They told me, "You're smart. Go be smart. Do whatever you want, but be smart. Don't be stupid or cause too much trouble" (N-7).

The Early Years— Ages Eight Through Thirteen

As would probably be true for many of us, the research neurologists had difficulty remembering anything more than general behaviors and perceptions about their first seven or eight years of life. Their parents, too, were unable to say much about the children's earliest years. But all were able to talk at length and in detail about the time beginning when the children were about eight or nine years old. This may be because beginning at about the age of eight the children's lives became more structured. They suddenly had homework to do, for example, and they began engaging in a variety of clearly identifiable activities, organized or otherwise, separate from their parents.

PLAYING WITH SCIENCE AT HOME
The research neurologists' first detailed memories are remarkably consistent. For most, these are of playing with science kits and toy microscopes, or otherwise becoming interested in "science."

As long as I can remember, I had a microscope. One of my earliest toys was one of the small Japanese microscopes, eight or nine inches tall. When I worked part-time [in high school], I bought myself a real microscope with genuine objectives, [which] I used in the beginning of my medical school training. . . . The other [first microscope] was essentially a toy, although I used it for a long time and was able to do a number of experiments. . . . That was a present from my aunt, probably when I was eight or nine years old (N-4).

I always wanted a Gilbert microscope set or Gilbert chemistry set or an erector set or things like that. As long as I can remember, I wanted to be a scientist. We were kind of spoiled as far as getting those things. [That is, he got all of the sets he wanted] (N-1).

My parents would buy [chemistry sets and microscopes] for me. If something was educational, you know, we'd always get it. Nothing for pleasure. I mean, if we really wanted something that would make us happy, no. But if it was educational, fine you could have it. Educational was usually synonymous with boring. I liked the science stuff (N-2).

Fourth grade was also about the time that the neurologists remember beginning projects or experiments independent of kits. One physician-scientist recollected a rather elaborate scheme, concocted with an older brother, to watch a downstairs television while upstairs in the brother's room. This involved manipulating mirrors and a sound device. "We actually didn't watch it very much, but it was so much fun putting the whole thing together" (N-7). Another remembers his first independent project: mapping out the solar system. "The ultimate thing was that it was displayed at the state fair . . . it was a big event" (N-8). At about the same time, this same neurologist remembers,

Reading, for example . . . about basic optics and thinking about it but never actually building a telescope. . . . I got out the plans at least, and figured out where things would have to be . . . took the directions and measurements out of books—absolutely nothing that was creative (N-8).

Another neurologist, who had been fishing with his father for several years, recalls,

> At first it was something that I did with my father for fun. And then [about eight or nine] it became more of a thing I approached with a kind of scientific zeal. I was interested in the way [fish] lived, what part of the lake they lived in, what they liked to eat. Because it related so much to my interest, I thought I wanted to be a marine biologist (N-5).

One or two of the youngsters were more interested in the "building" than the science.

> Virtually all the stuff that I did in [my father's] workshop was not of an inventive nature, it was merely construction. Building things . . . from a pattern. . . . I did spend a lot of time in the shop by myself, and in the evenings my father would be down there. Often we would work together. Or he'd be doing something and have me help out (N-10).

The experiments and projects built upon one another. "[A friend and I] would do a lot of basement chemistry kind of experiments. All the standard experiments that would come with the chemistry set, and then we'd think of a few others" (N-18). One neurologist was given his first microscope and telescope while in fourth grade, a chemistry set in fifth grade, and a better microscope in sixth or seventh grade. "I had a full, regular lab in my room in a sense" (N-9). Another reported that by fifth or sixth grade "I had sort of decided that I wanted to be a scientist, and around . . . seventh grade I decided that what I should be was in chemistry" (N-8).

The research neurologists were quick to point out that either they had no idea what a scientist was or did, or else they had only a very childish vision. A scientist was, perhaps, someone sitting around looking through a telescope. "I just sort of liked the idea . . ." (N-8). Another had a vision of a "mad scientist like Frankenstein. . . . In my elementary school years I just thought it was neat. I thought labs looked interesting, a lot of bubbly things, lots of glassware. It was more a romantic idea" (N-1).

Science, however, was not the only activity the research neurologists recall pursuing out of school at nine or eleven. "It was the sort of thing that I would do if I was by myself and was looking for something to fool around with" (N-16), but it was only one of a wide variety of interests. The youngsters, like their parents, were becoming very busy people.

OTHER OUT-OF-SCHOOL ACTIVITIES
Reading was high on almost all of the research neurologists' lists of frequent, pleasurable activities.

> It was one of the great things to do when we were kids. . . . We really read a lot (N-8).

> Both my brother and I were the four-book-a-week types of kids in terms of getting books out of the library. Just chewing up everything. So we did an awful lot of reading (N-16).

> I bought a fair number of books, and [the family] used to go to the library every Friday and bring back some books (N-18).

There is no apparent pattern to the choice of subject matter, except that all report the reading was for pleasure.

Sixteen of the twenty youngsters (80%) also had some music instruction. They studied the accordion, clarinet, cello, piano, trumpet, or violin. Most began playing an instrument while in third, fourth, or fifth grade, and typically "gave it up" by the time they were in seventh or eighth grade. While a few of the research neurologists enjoyed playing an instrument, most "never liked it." As one mother noted, "He learned to read [music] and play it, but it wasn't inspired, he wasn't interested, so it became ridiculous after a while. . . ." (M of N-3). Typically, the time the elementary school children spent at musical activities would eventually give way to organized and informal sports beginning in junior high school.

More than half of the research neurologists reported having

religious instruction as youngsters. One-third reported taking part in (and enjoying) Cub Scouts and Boy Scouts. Some were "collectors" (stamps, rocks, license plates, and so on). Most were Little Leaguers. The research neurologists were, typically, "busy" children: involved in some activities of their own choosing, some that their parents thought were "good," and some that most of the children in their neighborhood were engaged in. "You would never find him moping around. He always had something to be interested in" (M of N-6).

SCHOOLING

As the children advanced through elementary school, homework became one more regular activity.

> I would get my homework, go to it, and do it well. I can never recall being told to do the homework . . . it was an expectation. One did one's homework, one's schoolwork, first (N-11).

> The primary emphasis for intellectual development came from my mother, and my father to a lesser degree, the emphasis being on doing our homework, our schoolwork . . . and if there were extra-credit work, to do the extra-credit work. There wasn't a particular time you had to have your homework done. . . (N-9).

> What I'd do, I'd come home, watch TV . . . and I'd sit down and do my homework. . . . There were some kind of rules in our house . . . you couldn't watch in the evening until it got done (N-7).

> I think it was pretty important to get the work [homework] done. I can't remember if we had any certain time to watch TV or to play, but I knew that getting the work done was important (N-6).

The exceptions—"I never really did a lot of homework. . . . I don't think I ever really learned to study" (N-18)—were rare. If there was homework assigned, which sometimes didn't happen until junior high school, the youngsters automatically took care of it.

Few of the neurologists' parents sat down and worked with their children on homework. Typically, "If I wanted help, they [parents] would give it to me" (N-7). The parents report, "He did not have to be driven to study" (F of N-9). Most of the parents' support for doing homework seems to have come in the form of psychological expectation, practical guidelines for ensuring that time was available to do the work, and excusing the children from chores, if necessary, to make sure that there was time to do the work that was so important to the parents.

> It seemed like my dad was always mowing the lawn so we could do our homework, and so it got harder to mow the lawn. And so, everything was provided for us with the idea that we could do better in school (N-1).

How well did the research neurologists do in school during these years and how intelligent did they perceive themselves to be? With one or two exceptions, the youngsters were clearly good, although not exceptional, students. They did "better than grade [level]" (N-4). "I knew I was doing well relative to the other children. . . . But I certainly wasn't at the top" (N-1). "I did well, but I don't know . . . if that was top of the class" (N-15). "I was quite studious, although I wasn't a brilliant student through eighth grade" (N-20). From a father, "I don't know that he was outstanding" (F of N-8).

The research neurologists knew they were good students. "I got a lot of stars on my paper, smiling faces and things" (N-1). "I would be the one pointed out to get projectors and stuff" (N-11). But typically they were not extraordinary. As one father noted,

> [My wife] kept in touch with the teachers, and if any weaknesses showed up, she was able to work those out with the teacher. I don't remember if there were any weaknesses, but there must have been some (F of N-9).

A few of the research neurologists recall being noticed by teachers for their achievement. They report that they didn't quite know what to make of this attention; they expected and assumed that they would do well in school and didn't see their achievement as anything special. "[Teachers] all told my mother how bright I was. I didn't believe them [laughs]. That's what I'd always heard" (N-2). As the mother of another researcher explained, "We always got interesting feedback [from the teacher] about how bright he was and the things he was doing. . . . Of course, at home we knew he was doing more than most other students" (M of N-3).

By junior high school, if the school they attended had honors classes, as most did, the youngsters would be placed in these classes. "I was never aware . . . too much about when we were chosen for honors. It was all just something that was done to us" (N-1).

Typically, the research neurologists recall thinking of their achievement in school in a matter-of-fact way. They expected it as much as their parents did.

> It would seem like my little sister and myself would excel in those kind of dominant-hemisphere sorts of things [academics] without too much effort. . . . I always did well in school. . . . Everything sort of came about rather naturally (N-13).

There was little memorable about elementary school achievement or school experiences to either the researchers or their parents.

The dominant theme conveyed by the research neurologists was of being "your basic elementary school kid" (N-11).

> I was a bright kid, typical of any of the kids in the neighborhood. I don't think [anyone] would have singled me out in any particularly unusual good or bad sense. . . . I mean, I can think of some children in the neighborhood that were super athletes, or they were super bright, or strange, withdrawn, bully, or that kind of thing. I don't think I would have fit in any of those categories. I think if the neighbors did describe me it would be in a general positive sense. Good child, rather than a bad child (N-13)

Parents' Involvement with Their Children

Parents provided models, standards, and expectations for their children. There was little question about the importance the parents placed on doing well in school. "I was pretty well motivated that school is very important and you had to do well in school" (N-19). Being seriously and wholeheartedly engaged in whatever activities one was spending time on was equally important. "It was always my thought, and my husband's, 'Don't get involved in something you really don't like' " (M of N-6). Parents typically provided a wealth of material for the youngsters to work with: books, kits, materials, encyclopedias, and the like.

We found no common pattern, however, to the kind or amount of activities that parents and children engaged in together. Some of the children spent many hours with parents, others spent time with their parents in a limited number of ways, and still others spoke of isolation or estrangement from their families in their day-to-day activities. The range is from very "close-knit" families, in which parents tried to get involved with whatever activities their children were interested in, to families in which parents were very seldom actively involved with their children's activities.

In the latter instance, some of the research neurologists recall spending little time with their parents. "I don't have a strong memory of a lot of interactions with my parents about anything" (N-3). Some recall that their parents were so busy with work—mothers didn't come home "until it was dark," and fathers "rarely ate dinner with the family—that the only times parents and children spent together were Sunday "brunches," Sunday evenings, or "each summer we took a trip for a week or two . . . they were very much fun" (N-6). One mother, speaking uncomfortably about her husband, noted,

The children to this day think he was an absentee father. And he was, but his presence was very much felt, and his interests—even though he wasn't here because his work, I think, almost always came first (M of N-2).

She repeated, "He wasn't the kind of father that would play baseball or football or anything like that with his sons. He didn't want to or [didn't] make the time."

Between the extremes, some neurologists recall that the time spent in discussions with their parents, especially at dinner time, was a very important influence in their lives.

> One of [my father's] favorite games was "Do you know who did so and so?" or "Do you know what happened when?" A lot of that sort of thing. . . . When he was around, there was always a lot of testing . . . (N-12).

Another recalls "fun" conversations about the meaning of words: "the semantic distinction, or the philosophical distinction." "Dinner-table conversations were frequently these very complicated discussions . . . at [age] thirteen we'd been doing this for a while already " (N-4). A third reported,

> My parents were both scientifically oriented, even though they weren't scientists. So we talked a lot about it at dinner. Dinner was a big event at my house. We all ate together. My dad would always talk about something intellectual, and he was always the devil's advocate. . . . You learned how to hold your own in an argument . . . you got to try to think out and say what you thought, and make it logical (N-7).

Still other neurologists recall spending a considerable amount of time with their parents (usually fathers). Some of the parents who were themselves engaged in medical or scientific pursuits shared their work with their children as well as sharing in their children's activities. For instance, one son of a pharmacist remembers spending many hours with his father both in the pharmacy and on fishing trips, and he remembers long discussions about the pharmacy and about how his father came to do the work he did (N-15). Another neurologist noted,

> I would never have been able to do [many scientific activities] if my father hadn't been an organic chemist. I'd come home and say, "Gee, I'm interested in this," and my father would get involved with me. Which was a good thing (N-14).

But, typically, those children who spend considerable time with their parents did so on more commonplace activities.

> We used to do, I guess, the usual things that boys and their fathers do together. We used to play ball together, for example. We used to do various hobbies and things together. We had a stamp collection. . . . He taught me how to play chess. . . . (N-13).

Fathers and sons were equally likely to spend their time together fishing or camping, collecting coins, watching TV, or going to baseball games.

SUMMARY OF THE YEARS
TO AGE THIRTEEN

The first thirteen years in the research neurologists' lives seem to have set the stage for their later work in five important ways. First, almost all the neurologists developed an interest in "things that were scientific or quasi-scientific." "It's an intellectual curiosity to know more about your universe or your environment or things that make things go" (N-13). In their spare time the children were likely to be found working on scientific projects of some sort, or with science kits. These were the kinds of activities their parents supported most.

Second, most of the youngsters developed basic skills manipulating objects and thinking through problems or projects. When given kits of some type they "used the instruction book." They learned to find and follow plans, "[take] the directions and measurements out of books" (N-8). "If I hadn't had a model, I wouldn't have done it" (N-10).[3] In the course of describing the research neurologists' development the theme of following instruction books or written directions will come up again and again.

Third, the neurologists learned the importance and habit of achievement. Working hard and following things through to their conclusion became standard for the youngsters, as they were for the parents. The youngsters learned to make the most of their free time, to do things they enjoyed and to do them wholeheartedly. And they learned to treat school seriously, whether or not they enjoyed all that they had to do in school, because they learned to believe it would be invaluable for their further achievement.

Fourth, the youngsters developed confidence in their ability to achieve—both in school and in whatever activities they chose to pursue out of school. By thirteen they had almost fully internalized a statement they had been hearing from their parents for years: "They always told me that I could do whatever I wanted to do, be whatever I wanted to be . . . it was, 'of course you can do it' " (N-7). Most of their experiences had proved that to be true. The youngsters learned that even initial difficulties would, in time and with perseverance, be overcome.

Finally, and perhaps most important for the work they would do later, the youngsters developed a style of working that was very flexible. The children were encouraged to have several different interests at once. They learned to move from chemistry to biology experiments or vice versa, from reading to sports to science to music, working at whatever they enjoyed in "binges" (N-9), following opportunities, apparently without any sense of discontinuity.

---

[3]This is in constrast to the mathematicians, who engaged in many of the same activities but preferred to do without the instructions or directions.

The Adolescent Years

SCIENCE AS A HOBBY

As the children grew older and their lives became more complex, scientific projects continued to be a part of their activities, and these grew more complex as well. Almost all the neurologists spent some of their free time during their junior and senior high school years on scientific projects. There was an enormous variation, though, in the amount and type of investment the youngsters made in such activities. Some did sporadic experimenting; a few always seemed to have some project in progress.

The adolescents "built radios and sent away for kits" (N-1), "[kept] notebooks for various things" (N-9), and made "collections." One "had my [his] own study, which was way up on the third floor where I [he] had my lab" (N-9). Another "actually set up a lab in a basement, benches and everything" (N-16).

The specific scientific discipline of a youngster's projects seems to have mattered less than the process of investigating.

I chopped up frogs that I found in the backyard . . . had a colony of mice. . . . I tried to do things that were a little different. One of my projects in eighth grade, I tried to figure out how a nuclear reactor worked. . . . Most people go to encyclopedias. . . . I sent away to the Nuclear Atomic Commission for specifications of the local reactor they were building then. I actually had the cooperation of my science teacher, who didn't understand a whole lot more, but at least he gave me some guidance as to what things might mean that were obvious to him . . . that was the kind of thing I did (N-4).

A couple of years it was astronomy. So we got a cheap telescope and I got into that, and then I wanted to take pictures, so I rented a cheap camera. . . . Then it would be, I got interested in microscope work. I would do things like that. Do them for a couple of years, intermixing with sports or other things. . . . I was into growth hormones for a while. Because I got into this in biology. So I started reading about it. And there was this plant hormone . . .

that people were studying. So I sent away for the patent. I synthesized it and started putting it on plants and stuff. I used to enjoy stuff like that. It never went anywhere. I never discovered anything with it, but it was fun (N-14).

A few of the neurologists had parents who would help them with their projects. More had parents who encouraged the activities wholeheartedly and provided materials, but did not actually take part. "We would see that whatever materials were necessary, [for his projects], or reading matter that was necessary, it was available in the house for him" (M of N-6). All of the neurologists had parents who were supportive, although they were not always delighted with a specific project. "My mother was not terribly happy about the mice in the basement" [N-4]. But for the most part, the youngsters carried out these hobbies on their own.

About a third of the researchers mentioned *Scientific American* as an important resource, although none seemed to recall how or why they had access to the material.

I had a book . . . published by *Scientific American* or one of those things, of projects you could do at home . . . and this was one in it. . . . I had to really spend a lot of effort to try to understand it. I had to build a lot of stuff from scratch. I remember I actually had to call the author of the chapter on this thing to really learn about it. . . . It took a lot of initiative to do that. . . . My father worked on it with me. . . . I won a prize for it. . . . It was special to me (N-6).

I'm not sure where *Scientific American* came from. I might have been given that as a present. But that was where, in retrospect, a lot of my interest . . . came from (N-3).

I was reading what would be called lay adult scientific literature. *Scientific American.* I would get my ideas about things [from there] (N-9).

I think a lot of [my ideas] came from looking through things like *Scientific American.* I think *Scientific American* was a major source for me. I used to love the amateur scientist in *Scientific American* (N-16).

The scientific activities were thought of as "hobbies for me" (N-14). Some projects were used to fulfill school assignments, but most were pursued strictly for pleasure when the youngsters had nothing else to do. "I would still rather have gone out and played [with friends] than do that" (N-16). A few of the neurologists reported working on scientific projects with their friends, but that too was sporadic. They were more likely to report, "I didn't share my scientific interest. . . . [Experimenting] was my own hobby" (N-4). The experiments and investigations were typically private, leisure-time activities unconnected to the bulk of the youngsters' lives, which were spent in school and at extracurricular activities.

SCHOOLING

Four of the twenty research neurologists (20%) were sent to private schools beginning about seventh grade. Two of these were able to attend private schools only because they received scholarships. The other sixteen neurologists attended public schools, which they typically referred to as "a well-rated all-around school" (N-17), "a more academically oriented high school than any other in town" (N-8), or "one of the very best schools in the city" (N-4). The teenagers were placed in "honors" or "advanced" classes in the public schools, which used those kinds of tracking systems.

There is a tension in the story that the research neurologists and their parents tell about school experiences through high school. On one hand they have few memories of classes or teachers. It is not that the experience was a bad one; it was reported as inconsequential. On the other hand, they clearly remember being successful at the experience of schooling— whatever that involved.

With only two exceptions, the adolescents were successful students. A few reported on their academic achievement modestly.

It was a big high school. There were about four hundred kids in my graduating class, and I was really not the best student. There were probably ten or twenty kids ahead of me. I'm not sure that I was that much noticed (N-5).

I wasn't by any means among the first twenty students in the class. Of course, it was a class of nine hundred (N-20).

I was known as a very good student. There were a number of very good students (N-12).

Others reported on their academic successes more assertively: "I was the fourth best" (N-19), or "always close to the top" (N-5), and "one of the two or three smartest" (N-11) in classes.

The research neurologists were evenly divided between those who reported working hard for good grades and those who thought they got good grades simply because they were intelligent people.

I think I've always been more hardworking than smart, as far as brain power goes. I don't think I have as much as most, as a lot of my friends in high school or college. I was always close to the top, but I think it was mostly work—working and trying until it clicked—more than brain power (N-1).

I worked hard. I didn't work nearly as hard as my brother. All these . . . scholastic things came easily to me . . . and the schools weren't all that challenging (N-7).

I felt I was an overachiever in the sense that I didn't think I was the brightest. I felt I was about middle. . . . As it turned out, I got very good grades in high school and did super well and was fourth in my class. . . . I could see an insight and brilliance in other people that I didn't think I had. . . . I was always studying from 7:00 [at night] on. . . . I enjoyed it (N-9).

I caught on quicker than most kids (N-8).

Whether the students had to work hard for good grades or whether the good grades "just sort of came" (N-3), all the research neurologists were aware that academic success was important. It was necessary for future success, for day-to-day privileges, and for personal pride. "There was always, I would say, an undercurrent to 'no matter what you're going to do [in life] . . . if you want to do it, you've got to get good grades' " (N-9). "It became perfectly clear that if I didn't do well in school, I wouldn't be able to play football" (N-11).

> I do think you develop certain internal standards by the time you are in junior high school or high school . . . and it was a source of pride to me if [my grades] were good and dismaying if they weren't (N-8).

The importance of good grades was well internalized and accepted, as can be seen in one mother's comment: "In high school I was mostly conscious of his athletic interests. We took for granted his educational accomplishments" (M of N-2). She added, "He did well in both."

Despite the considerable amount of experience the individuals had with science outside of school, they were not necessarily better students in science courses than in other classes. They and their parents report a mélange of interests, including foreign languages, history, mathematics, and especially English classes. The research neurologists did their best work in classes they found "interesting" or "exciting" or "challenging."

The common denominator of the rather small number of classes the neurologists recall getting very involved with had little to do with the subject matter but rather with the way the classes were taught. According to one, "The teachers that really impressed me in general were those that insisted upon excellence and didn't mess around. High-standards-type teachers" (N-2). For another, an English class was especially important because the teacher

> . . . insisted no kid would be in her class without knowing the basic rules of grammar. . . . In a pleasant manner, but with no nonsense about it. There was no slipping through. People were supposed to learn this stuff. It was very helpful. It left an impression on me (N-13).

Best classes were also those with teachers "who most enjoyed their work . . . they were teachers with a lot of enthusiasm . . . really dedicated to making their subjects interesting and fun" (N-6).

Four neurologists found certain high school science teachers exciting for the same reasons just noted.

> I had a biology teacher in high school who never gave an A for this specific lab notebook that he had us make. He never gave one. He refused to give one. He gave me an A−. He would insist on very good work and a high standard of excellence and still to this day he's one of the best teachers. Interestingly, I met him at my high school reunion. He's the only teacher who came. I told him how much he inspired me, and he called me back to give a lecture to his kids. . . . I was president of his biology club. So that was a very big influence on me that made me realize I had talent in biology (N-2).

Another excellent biology teacher

> . . . just went through an entire biology experience, dissecting guinea pigs and we did all kinds of things. We extracted chlorophyll and played with tarantulas. And she was somebody who was enormously interested in what she was doing and knew a great deal about it (N-11).

The same neurologist commented, thinking about this class for which he had to write a paper that was "nearly a thesis," "I think that if I had had an equally impressive chemistry teacher, I probably would have gotten into chemistry" (N-11). One neurologist remembered an exciting physics class:

> [The teacher] expected a lot, demanded a lot. But that's what made it fun. You had to really work too. It was sort of like sports when the coach was really pushing you down the stretch and you were in good shape and it all felt good. I liked that (N-16).

Two of the neurologists had fond recollections of seventh-grade science teachers simply because these teachers recognized their interest in science.

That was the first time, in fact, that I had ever been exposed to a teacher who had a specialized interest. . . . I was labeled as being interested in science and I liked that (N-12).

I remember one experiment I practiced at home. We made a steam engine and it turned a wheel, and at home I had a Bunsen burner and at school we had a Bunsen burner, but it was covered with asbestos. My experiments didn't work when I got to school. I later figured out after class that the asbestos was cooling it down. I remember Mrs. ———— . . . because of the embarrassment. She stuck with me after school until we figured out why it didn't work (N-1).

The neurologists typically worked hard, and certainly did well in school. But neither they nor their parents have strong memories of the coursework. Exciting or stimulating classes were few and far between, and these youngsters had many other things to do and think about. One neurologist seems to speak for many with this remark: "With some exceptions, in retrospect, what was intellectually exciting was what you did on your own. School, to be perfectly honest, was really rather a drag" (N-8).

High school science classes, especially, were dismissed as just another chore of going to school. At best they were referred to as "interesting to a limited degree" or "undistinguished." At worst,

I really have bad memories of school science. Science was really deadly. The science teachers I had . . . I just don't have any pleasant memories of it. . . . Very few experiments for demonstration. I think [the teachers] really didn't know their subjects (N-5).

Nonetheless, the adolescents did take all of the science classes their schools had to offer, often including one or more "advanced" or "college-level" classes. As one researcher remarked, "It was the nature of the high school that if you made good grades and you were capable of it, you were expected to take these [rigorous] courses" (N-5). So they were as likely to take advanced classes in English, for example, as in any of the sciences.

EXTRACURRICULAR ACTIVITIES

The most significant thing about high school to these teenagers was extracurricular activities. Many of the research neurologists did spend some of their time on academically related activities. However, the academic activities were typically given minimal time compared with other opportunities the schools made available.

Almost half the neurologists had one or more experiences with a science or math extracurricular program. These included being president of the school biology club, a leader on the school math team, or attending some sort of special after-school, Saturday, or summer program "for a select group of . . . science students."

About a third took part in one or more science fairs, and one "used to win science fairs all the time" (N-14). Many purposely avoided science fairs, however, even when they were actively doing science projects outside of school. "[I] never [did] anything for the science fair, which I looked upon as a longitudinal commitment. I did short-term projects because of my athletic commitments and things like that" (N-19). "It would have been a little flaky to go to a science fair. . . . A fair for science would have been a drippy thing" (N-7).

The one extracurricular activity that almost all of the research neurologists were involved with was athletics. They played baseball, basketball, soccer, track and field, wrestling; almost anything and everything. "All the time I was in some sort of practice session after school" (N-11). "That's what I was really interested in all through junior high and high school" (N-8). Some were very good athletes, "all-state" in this or that; others were "run of the mill," but almost all spent the bulk of their time on sports.

They played sports "because I enjoyed doing it" (N-13), not because they were pressured to be athletes by their parents. School success always came first in importance in their own minds and in the minds of their parents. But athletic success was not far behind in importance: to their peers, their communities, and their families.

> Sports was what was reinforced. . . . There was very little recognition for what you did academically. There were award assemblies, but what the other kids, and probably the parents too, paid attention to was not academic sorts of things (N-8).

Because the neurologists' parents had always expected their children to be academically successful, and those expectations had been fulfilled for years, the neurologists noted that by the time they were in high school, their parents probably gave "more reward, or interest, in " 'how well did you do in sports? Did you make the . . . team' " (N-14).

The second most mentioned type of extracurricular school activity was school government or social organizations. About one-third of the neurologists were very involved in these (two were "the president of the class"). Other individual interests included debating, foreign-language and philosophy clubs, and music groups.

These were very busy teenagers, involved in a wide variety of school activities. "I was very committed to extracurricular activities" (N-14). "I was a member of tons of organizations" (N-19). "The range of activities was important to me then" (N-11). When asked how they found the time to do so many things, one neurologist summarized what most said in some fashion: "I found my schedule was just about right" (N-9).

Their parents also remember them as "extremely well rounded" (M of N-2) and able to manage busy schedules. "He worked hard, and then when he played, he played hard" (M of N-6).

> He made his own schedule but he always got everything done. . . . [He played] sandlot football, and [was] then into all the sports, and was in debate and took music lessons and was in the band and all these things. But I did not pay attention to the management of his schoolwork. I mean, there was no reminding (M of N-1).

The same mother, commenting further that her son had no trouble juggling his busy schedule, added, "I'd like to think that we had the kind of [home] atmosphere that encouraged it, but it wasn't suggesting or telling."

YOUTHFUL ASPIRATIONS

The research neurologists remember trying out career aspirations for themselves as adolescents, most of which had to do with being successful at something scientific.

> In elementary school I was mainly interested in chemistry. And then in junior high I got interested in electronics and wanted to be an electrical engineer. Engineering at that time was *the* field, right after medicine, as far as what to do if you wanted to be a success. And so, I wanted to be an engineer. And then in high school I switched back to chemistry (N-1).

> By the time I had graduated the sixth grade, I had gotten a book on astrophysics . . . and that had excited me. . . . [When I finished with that book], I was interested in being an astrophysicist or a nuclear physicist, at least my understanding of what they did. . . . I got my chemistry set in seventh grade. . . . I had a bench . . . fifteen or twenty feet long with a huge panel. . . . I began doing experiments. One day I came [upstairs] with singed eyebrows, and my mother said, "That's it." She said, "If you want to do experiments, you find some other field where you're not going to blow this house apart." . . . I had been interested in biology; I had a microscope. So I progressively shifted my interests from chemistry to biology . . . it was a lot safer. . . . [Then] it seemed that I needed to be, needed to do medical research. . . . Sometime before I got through high school, I made the transition. I had more of a concrete idea of what it entailed being a doctor than being a biologist (N-4).

> I think from late grammar school I knew I wanted to go into science. I really didn't have a clear idea what science was all about . . . either as a doctor or researcher. Then I think through high school I leaned more and more to the research end of things (N-16).

When I was in junior high, I think it was at this point that I really thought in my mind that I was going to be a doctor. I was singled out to start taking some college courses at ———. So I started taking chemistry . . . I guess I kind of had the idea that if you made good grades and that sort of thing, then that's what you did [become a doctor] (N-9).

By the time I was in high school, I knew that I wanted to be a biochemist. . . . Why a biochemist? . . . Well, my brother had math and physics sewn up, so I didn't want to try that [laughs] (N-7).

I think it was a TV program called "Medic" [that prompted the decision to become a doctor at age fourteen]. . . . That had a big impression on me. And then I heard people talking about what they wanted to become. It was sort of goal-oriented talk about eighth or ninth grade. . . . I sort of liked the idea of being a doctor. . . . I mean, it was an intellectual endeavor, and you could do science, and you could do things with people, and there were a couple of friends of mine who thought the same thing (N-9).

The research neurologists' recollections of their career aspirations during junior and senior high school seem quite important for at least three reasons. First, they reflect the adolescents' preoccupation with science, and sometimes with medicine as a field that would make their general interest in science "concrete." Second, they indicate the youngsters' pattern of attaching themselves to one aspect of science and then shifting their attachment to another, depending on environmental influences. Third, they reflect the importance placed on being "successful," academically and intellectually, and the assumption most of the youngsters held that this was to be just a natural part of their lives.

SUMMARY OF THE ADOLESCENT YEARS

By the time the research neurologists entered junior high school, they were firmly set on a course of academic success. They knew this was important and they had already come to assume and expect the same high level of achievement that their parents valued. Academic success would be the background upon which all the rest of their endeavors would be superimposed.

The teenagers became active seekers of activities they could find pleasure in. They didn't wait for someone to present an idea or an activity to them. They learned, as their parents modeled, that "doing" was enjoyable, and there is so much that one could possibly do that one should only do what one enjoys. While they certainly appreciated whatever approval or reward was offered for what they did, they also learned to do some things independent of such potential applause. They pursued "hobbies" out of personal interest and for personal satisfaction.

As teenagers they also learned how to juggle activities, doing what seemed most worthwhile at the moment without necessarily having to give up competing interests. They could be successful, although not the very best, at several things. By the time they left high school, they typically had enormous confidence that "when I really want to do something, I can do it, and I can do it extremely well. And when I don't want to do something, I just don't do it . . . that well" (N-2).

During these years the research neurologists also learned to be independent learners. If they got interested in something scientific, for example, they learned that there were instruction books and the like they could use to pursue their interests. They also found that if they got started on their own, materials, physical assistance, and intellectual support would be forthcoming.

Finally, these teenagers learned more math and science than most do. They took four years of math and four years of science and whatever "advanced" or "double" science courses were available in their public schools. They took these classes often in the absence of any special interest in them—typically the classes were not interesting, challenging, or exciting, although science as something done out of school was.

If one were searching for high school students who would

likely go far in the field of medical research, it would have been extremely difficult to identify the research neurologists in our sample who have subsequently demonstrated extraordinary ability. As high school students they were not dedicated to a life of science, working in laboratories singlemindedly pursuing future careers. "[He was] well balanced . . . he wasn't one-sided at all. I've been glad of that " (M of N-1). They were not even the "best" science students in their classes, although clearly they were very good. These were bright, middle-class students, apparently following a pattern their parents modeled: being wholeheartedly engaged in a wide variety of activities (including active involvement with their school communities) and responding most favorably to those teachers who valued their own work and set strict standards for students.

The College Years: A Gradual Narrowing of Vocational and Avocational Interests

There was no question about whether these youngsters would go to college; that they would "was just assumed."[4] The question that did arise, though, was whether they would be admitted to the colleges they were most eager to attend. For the most part, their choices were schools with stiff competition for a place in the freshman class. Because they had done well in school, and because they had learned to believe that getting a good education was the key to a successful life, it was natural that they "wanted to go to the best place" (N-2). "My parents, particularly my father, always wanted me to go to an Ivy

---

[4]One of the research neurologists was an exception to this statement and to all other statements having to do with getting good grades and being successful in school. He had considerable difficulty with his schoolwork until his second year in college. He questioned whether or not he ought to go to college, but his parents and school counselor assured him that it would be worthwhile for him to do so.

League school" (N-3). "I chose ———— because it was a first-rate college" (N-19). "[My friends and I] all went to good-quality schools" (N-4).

Not all the research neurologists were accepted by the college that would have been their first choice.[5] Nevertheless, they all were accepted by, and attended, selective schools. (None, for instance, went to a state or city school required to admit anyone from the area who had a high school diploma.) Only one chose to attend a college that was clearly the least academically prestigious of those that had accepted him, a decision made "for no particular reason other than a couple of my friends were going there" (N-12).

Even as they entered college, eight of the future research neurologists had some idea that medical school would follow. Nine others thought about careers involving science and research, with greater or lesser certainty. "I already knew that I wanted to go into research . . . into science" (N-16). "I was leaning toward something in the science field, and that's as far as it went" (N-6). A few of those interested in scientific research held medicine in the back of their minds as a way of making their scientific interests concrete. "I had left high school winning some sort of award in biology, so I automatically assumed I'd go into biology or medicine" (N-4). Only three of the people we talked with seem not to have thought at all about either science or medicine. Of these, one intended to study mathematics, another architecture, and the third thought he might become a dentist.

As one could expect, the future research neurologists took a lot of science courses while in college. The biological sciences seem to have been more attractive to many of these students than the other sciences, for several reasons. Some of the students enjoyed the liveliness of the department. "Biology was a very big department with a lot of interesting things [going on] as compared to physics, chemistry, or whatever. So I picked

---

[5]This seems to confirm that although the youngsters were clearly good students, they were not, for the most part, extraordinary.

biology" (N-14). That same neurologist added, "If I was going through today, I would probably have been a molecular biophysics major because *that* department has now gotten into things more." Others began to feel that biology was the area where, according to one, "I could accomplish something" (N-10). Another noted, "I began to realize that biology was easy for me and physics was not. I could be a really good biologist, but just a run-of-the-mill physicist" (N-12).

Most often the preference for the biological sciences seems to have to do with finding oneself more comfortable with the "loose" way of working that the biological sciences require than with the "rigorous" quantitative emphases of the other sciences. The research neurologist just referred to explained the difference this way:

> Biology . . . requires a tolerance for a lot more intellectual slop. It's a lot more nebulous [than physics or math]. A lot of the type of people who are attracted into physics and math tend to be very intolerant of areas where there is a lot that isn't known (N-12).

Another neurologist put it this way: "My favorite statement is that in physics the person does the experiment over and over again and takes the average . . . a biologist does the experiment over and over again until it works" (N-9).

Just as had been true during their high school years, however, the college students were attracted to a wide range of subject matter besides science. Three were serious students of philosophy, three others were especially interested in history, four studied psychology, and one was very interested in economics. In two instances, the student's choice of college courses proved troublesome when he belatedly decided to go to medical school. One was required to attend summer classes after his graduation because "I didn't do enough science to go to medical school" (N-3). The other made his decision so late in his senior year that he had to "sit out" a year before he could begin medical school.

In addition to their studies, the research neurologists continued to pursue a variety of extracurricular activities, although none did so with the same intensity they had displayed during high school. In sports, for example, they reported feeling "out of my depth. I had clearly outgrown that as a consuming interest fairly early in college" (N-8). Similarly, another noted, "I very quickly realized that although I was fairly decent in athletics, I was in the minor leagues" (N-14). Many continued to play intramural sports or fraternity games, but, more typically, they turned their attention to fraternity parties, dating, campus politics, playing music or cards, and the like.

SCIENTIFIC RESEARCH

In light of what was to come in their development, one aspect of the research neurologists' college years seems quite important: their introduction to formal research. Three had already been exposed to scientific research-in-progress as high school students working in laboratories of some sort for summer jobs. Ten of the twenty had research experience while in college. They did this in one of two ways.

Sometimes the research was a required part of a science class or honors thesis. Other times it was independent of formal college work. It may have been an after-class or summer job, or a summer fellowship. One research neurologist commented matter-of-factly,

> If you major in science, there are opportunities in the summer to do research. . . . When I was an undergraduate, [my college] had several National Science Foundation summer fellowships for students (N-14).

Either way, the circumstances the college students found themselves in had much in common.

The first research projects were almost always thought of as a lot of fun, even when the experiments failed, as they did most often. "I liked doing the lab work. Great excitement with the unknown" (N-9).

[The project] was a lot of fun. . . . That was excitement. Do the experiment, get the results. . . . Making discoveries . . . figuring out new ways of measuring enzymes to make things easier. . . . It was just a whole lot of fun (N-7).

One neurologist explained his first research project this way:

It was designed to answer some straightforward question that could be approached and studied in some small block of time, learning some simple techniques. . . . I came to some conclusions . . . but nothing came of it. It wasn't published or presented or anything. . . . It was just sort of fun (N-6).

Another reported similarly, "It was not expected that one would solve any major issues, but that you had an opportunity to learn the tools, so that you could ask the questions" (N-11). This researcher was clear, though, that something did come from the experience, although his work also was not published or presented. He reported that the experience was an important one for him because when subsequent research opportunities arose, he "knew how to do things, to choose a problem intelligently and apply the tools to it." Other researchers also noted that subsequent research opportunities often came about because the professor in charge of the first project was pleased with the work of the fledging researcher or because other professors were impressed by the student's work.

The students' introduction to formal research seems to have had two effects. First, it provided some concrete experiences that made the idea of becoming a scientist a "real" possibility. "I had some contact. . . so I had a sense of what basic research was about" (N-4). Second, it allowed the students to develop practical and cognitive skills, to learn techniques with equipment and techniques of asking and answering researchable questions. "I was learning the tools of the trade" (N-11).

The earlier statement that only ten of the twenty had research experience while in college may be somewhat misleading. All but one of the research neurologists did laboratory work for the science classes they took while in college. The distinction they seemed to make between what they reported as research and what they do not think of as such had to do with whether the project was set up to explore something unknown (research) or whether it was an exercise to teach the student about work scientists had already done. Thus one neurologist who had a large number of laboratory experiences as part of science classes reported doing no research in college. "We had fairly didactic labs," he explained. Similarly, almost all the neurologists reported reading scientific research reports and doing literature reviews of scientific research while in college. Because the research neurologists typically took many science classes, they had a good deal more experience with scientific work than might seem to be the case at first glance.

Interestingly, the neurologists' college laboratory and research experiences did *not* transform their earlier "interest in sciences" into a passion or something of that sort. Contrary to what one might have expected of people who have gone on to unusual success in scientific research, while in college the future research neurologists were as likely to become consumed with history, philosophy, economics, and the like as with any particular branch of science. Similarly, they were as likely to be noticed and encouraged by a philosophy professor, for example, as by a biology professor.

APPLYING TO MEDICAL SCHOOL

These were not singleminded college students. They continued to be as flexible about their interests as they had been in high school. "One thing that continually excited me was dealing with teachers who were enthused about their work. . . . That was probably why I got so interested in economics" (N-6). For at least two years of college, sometimes longer, they remained uncommitted to any definite kind of life work. Just as they had been loose about their plans while in high school because they knew four years of college lay ahead, these students seem to have been casual about their plans early in college because they assumed graduate school of some sort would follow.

But postcollegiate education requires a good deal more specialization than college. One can't blithely aspire "to go to the best place." How was it that the research neurologists narrowed their interests and decided to apply to medical school?

Typically, a firm decision to go to medical school was made during the students' junior (third) year of college. It was then that a decision of some sort had to be made; there was no longer an assumed course of action. Medical school was the choice for three different but not mutually exclusive reasons.

The dominant reason (N-11) for choosing to go to medical school had to do with a belief that this would provide "a good education in basic science subjects" (N-1), thus they "had nothing to lose" (N-12) in their pursuit of scientific careers. As another reasoned, "When you get done with medical school, you can go into any sort of science you want" (N-3). The confidence these individuals had that medical school was an appropriate means to a scientific career is perhaps best illustrated by one subject who declined a spot he was offered in a Ph.D. program in one of the sciences. He chose medical school instead because he felt that with an M.D. degree "I could do essentially anything. . . . Research, take care of patients, teach" (N-11). Furthermore, he reasoned, "I knew it would only take me four years to get an M.D. [degree] and five to seven to get a Ph.D." After the fact, he realized that given the time he spent in clinical training and specialty training, his earlier time comparison had not been a very intelligent one.

The eleven people who reported thinking about medical school primarily as further education in basic sciences indicated that although they had maintained their interest "in science" through college, they had not fastened on a particular kind of scientific work to pursue. A few found that their interest had begun to focus on "research in an area that was relevant to humans" (N-7). According to one, "My interest was never in practicing medicine, although after I left medical school, I realized it was an option. . . . My inspirations were from the world of medical research" (N-4). Another reported,

> Medical school seemed to be a reasonable step in my education because it would give me a very broad exposure to all of medical science, which to me was most relevant about science. . . . And so I decided to go to medical school just to leave open all options (N-10).

The second explanation for the decision, one that six people emphasized, was that it was merely formalizing years of "aiming toward medical school" (N-9) or being "sort of pre-med since kindergarten" (N-2). Taking medical boards, thinking about which schools one might like to attend and all of the rituals associated with formally deciding to go to medical school made a reality of what had been an assumption for years. One neurologist explained the assumption he held this way:

> I guess I kind of had the idea that if you made good grades and that sort of thing, then that's what you did. In fact I got to the point that I don't know if there was anything else I could do. I don't think I've ever really regretted it, but I think I could have been doing something else (N-5).

Although the decision to go to medical school was a naturally evolving one for these six students, three or four were uncertain about whether they would actually practice medicine or would do medical research exclusively.

The third and final reason, one that is dominant in only three histories but is also part of some other explanations, is, apparently, the lack of anything else as appropriate to do. In the absence of knowing what one wanted to do, and feeling disenchanted with other avenues they had been pursuing, these college students opted for the possibility of flexible, respectable careers, toward which they saw their friends aiming.

> I thought this [previously assumed direction] was ridiculous. I just can't do this. . . . [So I] decided, "Why don't I try medical

school?" I thought I might enjoy it. And it seemed like a logical thing. Medicine struck me as having a lot of flexibility (N-13).

For the first two years of college one of the two things that I was [as] interested in [as] science was in the field of economics. And actually for some period of time I thought about doing that . . . as a career. I became disenchanted with that somewhere along the line. . . . I enjoyed [science classes] and I did well in them. And I think I wound up almost by exclusion in a crowd of people who were equally enjoying those kinds of courses and doing well in them, and perhaps that had some force. . . . They were people whom I stayed friendly with throughout the rest of the time, and they were all pre-med (N-6).

For two of the research neurologists medical school was actually a second choice. One was not admitted to a favored Ph.D. program. The other discovered just how important it was to his parents that he go to medical school when he made a serious move in another direction.

Sometime in my third year I decided I was going to go to grad school in philosophy. That was the only time that my parents indicated strongly that they had considered other professional options for me. It was a real problem (N-4).

This individual applied and was accepted to a Ph.D. program in philosophy, which he never attended. He felt, for the first time, that "there was no question that there was a lot of pressure exerted" by his parents.

Another research neurologist, the one who was quoted earlier as becoming disenchanted with economics and then following his pre-med friends to medical school, also remembered discovering during college how important his medical career was to his parents.

In retrospect, financially that was a major concern of theirs—to be able to have enough money to send me through medical school. And that was probably an important goal all the way through (N-6).

The research neurologists' comments about their relatively late discoveries of the aspirations their parents had for them seem important for two reasons. First, they reflect a long-standing pattern in the children's interactions with their parents. Behaviors that the parents valued were assumed and seldom talked about; only those behaviors that were in conflict with the parents' values were noted and quickly stopped. This was most clearly demonstrated when the research neurologists talked about their elementary and high school achievement. The only time grades were important or even talked about, the neurologists typically reported, was when they came home with a grade below the A that was expected.

The second reason for highlighting the comments is that they indicate how quickly and easily the youngsters learned to share family norms. They did this so quickly and easily, it seems, that most often it wasn't even noticed. Parents served as models throughout the child's development and provided resources, opportunities, and suggestions. They seldom pressured their children in any way—because they didn't have to.

We see in our data that the research neurologists moved continuously in the direction of scientific achievement, even, as was often the case, when they were not consciously doing so. For example, although less than half were planning to go to medical school during their early years of college, all but one shared this experience: "My interests had me take all the courses that were prerequisites [for medical school]" (N-1). This was as true for the previously mentioned student who received a fellowship to do graduate work in philosophy as it was for the others.

However, even while in college the research neurologists typically did little to suggest that they would attain unusually high levels of achievement.[6] With only two exceptions they were not the hand-picked, favored students of their science

---

[6]In fact, one research neurologist was initially rejected by all the medical schools to which he applied. After a year of graduate school in psychology, during which he reapplied, he was admitted.

teachers, encouraged to work for a Ph.D. One who atypically had a fairly specific goal of studying neurosciences reported, "If what I had understood was that you learn about neuroscience by being a graduate student in physiology, I probably would have done that" (N-8). But, as he continued, "I had just very meager counseling. I chose medical schools by flipping through their catalogues and seeing how many courses they offered in neurosciences—which is a terrible way to do it."

SCIENCE VERSUS MEDICINE

The research neurologists did study a lot of science while in college—something that sets them apart from many college students. But this does not distinguish them from those students who go to medical school or from those who earn Ph.D.'s in one of the sciences. There are certain aspects of their development, however, which may distinguish them from future clinical doctors and future basic scientists.

Unlike many "pre-med" students, the research neurologists were typically more interested in the study of science while in college than in the practice of medicine. Because science courses are often prerequisites for medical school, the research neurologists took many classes with pre-med students. Thus they were academically prepared to apply to medical schools when they decided to do so toward the end of college, and they were socially prepared to do so. However, psychologically they were primed to think of medical school as a step in the direction of a scientific career. As respectable as the role of doctor is in American society, research was thought of even more highly by the individuals we interviewed.

> It was quite clear that discovery and invention was a very exciting thing to [my father]. That's what I saw as very rewarding—being able to invent or discover something important that would be recognized (N-10).

This was supported to the extreme by one of our subjects who, although aiming toward medical school even when he entered college, believed that practicing medicine could just never be enough.

> I was raised to think that research was the beginning, middle, and the end. Somebody was either good or bad, worth something or not worth something, based on how much research he did (N-2).

Our subjects were also different from college students who subsequently work for a Ph.D. in one of the basic sciences and thus opt for the life that goes with research almost exclusively in a laboratory. They did not seem to have the obsession that we understand is necessary to be a Ph.D. physicist, for example. They could be tempted away from scientific pursuits by many aspects of life outside a laboratory. They also tended to think of themselves as "doers" as much as "thinkers." For instance, one explained his fascination with chemistry during college this way:

> The more you do it, the more you get intuition. . . . It's almost like cooking . . . and I was always a good cook in that sense. You get an idea, a feel for putting things together. I could see that as something I could do well. Some of the theoretical and physical concepts I always thought some people could do better than I could. I always saw myself as a practical achiever and not so much as a theoretical achiever (N-9).

Medical school seems to have been a very appropriate choice for the individuals we interviewed for several reasons. First, it gave them time to continue exploring a variety of disciplines. Four years of college had typically left these individuals faced with new options rather than focused on anything in particular. For one, "it was really a combination of those biology and psychology courses that I remember being very excited by" (N-8). In other instances the research neurologists reported being intrigued with the mesh between biology and chemistry, chemistry and psychology, or psychology and physiology. Something about "nervous-system things" was exciting, but very few could be more specific than that. Medical school seemed enough like studying science, and there was enough science in medical school to make it an appropriate choice at this stage of the research neurologists' development.

Second, medical school appealed to the research neurologists' interest in people. Almost all had always enjoyed being with their peers—whether on a sports team or a debating team, engaging in long talks with a group of like-minded individuals, or "partying." Many had become very curious about what makes people tick, especially in college, exploring human behavior through literature, philosophy, psychology, and history. Medical school was an appropriate choice for students of science who realized, as one put it, "I liked people and I didn't like the image of someone huddled in their lab all the time" (N-1).

Third, going to medical school fit well with the values and ambitions the research neurologists had learned from their parents. A medical degree would ensure financial security and autonomy over one's work. It was also prestigious—intellectually and socially.

SUMMARY OF THE COLLEGE YEARS
The research neurologists were well prepared for college classes in the sciences. They were not only knowledgeable about sciences, their interest in them had developed predominantly *outside of* school. The latter point seems important to remember because it suggests that it would be difficult for the individuals simply to abandon science in favor of a subject they might encounter for the first time in college. They couldn't merely trade an interest in science for an interest in another subject because the study of science was more than a school subject for almost all of these individuals.

The research neurologists also entered college experienced in juggling several different interests at once. They continued to do that during college. They studied science and humanities, for instance. They also played sports, got involved with politics and "partied." Studying, of course, was the first priority for these individuals, who had, years before, internalized a strong belief in the importance of academic achievement. Thus, as coursework became more demanding than it ever had been, the research neurologists gradually narrowed their interests, not entirely sacrificing sports and the like, but limiting them as was necessary.

The research neurologists spent their college years pursuing whatever subject was taught by teachers who seemed to them to be most excited or fascinated with their own work. They were able to get involved in thinking through the intricacies of whatever subject matter caught their fancy, apparently without concern about where the studies would lead. Only when it became clear that the students were really not likely to be successful, financially or otherwise, if they pursued a certain subject did they gradually lessen their involvement with that subject. When one abandoned philosophy because of the difficulties such a career would pose for the lifestyle he aspired to lead, and another abandoned mathematics because he realized he would never make any great discoveries, they seem to have been eliminating choices rather than defining what they really did want to do with their lives.

During college many of the research neurologists had their first experiences working in scientific laboratories. These experiences were not major turning points in the neurologists' careers; they did not ignite a fire of excitement so strong that it required intense, continuous, passionate involvement in that type of work. But these "fun" experiences did several things that the research neurologists noted as very important for their subsequent development. First, they made the work of a scientist something real in these college students' lives. They saw people doing scientific research and realized that they could do the same; science became somewhat more concrete and practical. Second, they developed both competence and confidence with equipment and procedures, which would make any subsequent opportunities seem more possible and perhaps even more intriguing.

The research neurologists left college with much the same

general interest in science as when they entered, but with far more expertise. Since no particular kind of scientific research had become a preoccupation, and no other subject seemed more fascinating than science, the neurologists chose to do what seemed to be the most flexible way to continue to study science until they fastened on something in particular: go to medical school.

Learning Research Neurology: Medical School

Again, as was their pattern, the research neurologists spent at least a year or more in medical school sampling courses. They entertained thoughts about being a hematologist (N-4), for instance, or being a pediatric oncologist (N-17). They also weighed the alternatives of practicing medicine and of concentrating on medical research. They typically stayed uncommitted for as long as it was possible to do so.

Sometime between the middle of their second year in medical school and the end of their third year almost all fastened on neurology as an area of sustaining commitment. In part, as one put it, "I eliminated everything else" (N-12). More accurately, it would seem, the students discovered the field that matched the ways of behaving and thinking they had been mastering for more than twenty years.

The neurosciences provided an intellectual challenge. Neurology was said to be "*the* greatest mystery that confronts man" (N-10), "a more intellectual field than [internal] medicine" (N-12), attractive for "the complexity and intricacies of it" (N-2). It also provided the kind of intellectual challenge that was especially well suited to the style of working the students had developed. Flexibility and the ability to juggle several different ideas at once matter as much as singleminded persistence. "It's a lot of game playing. . . figuring out what the problem is" (N-12). To figure out the problem, the neuroscientist typically needs knowledge of several science disciplines and needs to be able to shift his thoughts easily from one way of working to another. A broad example of this would be the way one research neurologist explained his current work:

> What I'm doing now isn't a field, it's a conglomeration. And I think that's what I find most attractive about it. I can go into the lab and do something at the molecular level. . . . And then if I feel this is too basic, it's not answering pertinent questions, I say, well, I have to go see some patients and I have a longitudinal study. . . . And I can do different things at different times in the week. I can be a statistician. . . a molecular-biologist, a doctor, an administrator. . . a writer at night. . . . I like the diversity (N-9).

The students were also attracted to neurology because "it was relatively current, a hot area" (N-18). As another put it, "Neuroscience was where it was at" (N-16). This seems to have been important for several reasons. First, as one scientist explained, "If one wants to do discovery or what have you, you want to have it in an area that people think is important" (N-10). Second, and perhaps more significant to many of the individuals we talked with, this particular "hot area" was one "we were just barely starting, as opposed to some areas that were halfway worked out already" (N-16). The newness of the area seems to have important consequences.

One physician-scientist explained that neurology is "the area in which the most is being learned about something important. Every day there's new and fundamental information" (N-11). Another carried that explanation a little further: "Neurology seemed like an area that nobody knew anything about. A good area to go into research. It would be easier to break into" (N-18). With a lot to be learned, the chances of making one's mark—of finding something significant and becoming successful—were very good. The chances were better still because not that many people were studying the neurosciences when the research neurologists in our sample discovered the area.

One research neurologist explained that part of what he liked about the field was being able to "be in a kind of area where I could be by myself, keeping the number of people that I would be in direct competition with as low as possible" (N-12). Another compared neurology with pole-vaulting, a sport he spent a lot of time on while in high school and in college. He "was pretty good," he explained, because "there are barely more than three entries [in a pole-vaulting competition]. So if you can make the first height, you've got yourself a prize" (N-10). Elsewhere in the interview the same neurologist elaborated:

> Obviously my whole life has been spent trying to find something that I could excel at, and pole-vaulting would be a specific example of that. A very focused activity, where you can measure your progress in terms of inches. So I guess that . . . is what made me tick, trying to find something. I suppose all those years of drifting were trying to find something I could focus on (N-10).

THE INFLUENCE OF TEACHERS

How the physician-scientists found neurology is one of the most interesting aspects of this part of their story. Many were simply attracted to the people they saw working in the area. One summarized it this way:

> It turns out that it was pretty much the same idea of people, the best teachers swayed me. . . . So those people who were the most dedicated to their work, the most exciting, that's the field I became interested in (N-6).

The same neurologist spoke at length about the four or five neuroscience professors at the medical school he attended "who all interacted" and "loved their work." "These were very outstanding people . . . [and] outstanding teachers and the residents in neurology were [also] all high-caliber people" (N-6).

Some of the research neurologists met specific teachers

who became important role models and, sometimes, mentors. According to one,

> I never before had attached myself, sort of, to one of the science teachers and said, "Hey, this is it." . . . But I did in my freshman year in medical school. . . . I would consider myself, and my parents might feel somewhat that way too, sort of a late bloomer (N-20).

Several others talked about experiences like this:

> In the middle of my junior year in medical school a neurology department was created, and one of the guys that came is a guy I still work with. And he took an interest in me. . . . It was very fortunate. He had time. He had interest in me. And after a year or two I got the hang of doing research and learning methods. . . . In addition to thinking straight [he] was a role model of somebody who really worked hard and enjoyed it. . . . If I'd gone to medical school or another residency and had someone who wasn't as talented as [he is], I don't know that I would be as happy with what I'm doing, which is one measure of success (N-3).

One research neurologist summarized his experience this way:

> My scientific growth and career involved a group of mentors. . . . It's very important to have people to look after you. It means giving you advice. It means steering you in the right direction. It means having someone you can trust. It means [someone] saying, "Don't go to that conference. . . . Read this, don't read this." It means [their] wanting to do whatever they can to help you in your career (N-19).

For still others, the influence of a specific person wasn't as important as the influence of an environment filled with excitement and challenge. These individuals didn't point to any one person as having a major impact on their development; instead, they talked about working with "bright and enthusiastic" residents and attending physicians, and studying in schools where "the neurosciences program was the strongest" (N-9). They watched their teachers working in one of the newest of medical sciences and decided, "I guess I really wanted to be more like these people I saw leading what I viewed as exciting lives" (N-5).

DOING RESEARCH

As would be expected of students who were in medical school as a means to learn more about sciences, the best remembered and most talked about medical school experiences were those involving research. The research neurologists report an interesting progression of such experiences. Most began doing projects that were laid out for them by a teacher, or by the scientific literature, during medical school elective periods or during the summer.

> You come to the lab because you have a vague idea of what's going on, and you try to pursue something along the same lines. . . . In medical school, the professor . . . showed me a variety of fascinating mutations, altering nervous function, and I could see how I could go about exploring those. So I just took one and did it (N-11).

> He laid out a project for me, and I thought that was good (N-13).

> The first year I was essentially a technician. He taught me things to do, and I just did them (N-1).

> I'll tell you how I got started on day one. He gave me the lab and and he said, "Here, I want you to work on this sort of area". . . . So I spent probably the first six months of my year repeating everybody else's work. Because I didn't know how to do the experiments. I didn't know how to use the equipment. So what better way of knowing than to duplicate what other people had already done. When you duplicated it, then you were familiar with the experiments and you could do them (N-10).

The research neurologists typically enjoyed the work and were proficient. "I had a lot of fun with it. . . . There was no pressure on me to produce results. There was pressure on me to understand what I was doing and do it properly" (N-12). The same researcher added, "There was a lot of emphasis on critical thinking."

Each experience seemed to lead to another opportunity to work in a professor's lab, and with each opportunity typically came a more responsible role in the research.

I took a tutorial in developmental neurobiology and I found it fascinating. . . . I got along very well with [a teacher]. So she agreed to be my preceptor on a physiological psychology problem. That was the entrée (N-4).

[I] approached one of the professors there to work with him . . . on one particular aspect of immunology that his lab was engaged in. . . . [I] really spent the first summer learning about things and by the second summer was able to design some studies that were asking specific questions that were of interest to me at the time. That turned out to be fairly profitable. I put the material together and learned a lot of new techniques. I was able to publish it (N-6).

The second year I was much more independent, and we found an interesting thing to study, so I was allowed to study it. We got a paper out (N-1).

[Another professor] liked the work I was doing with [Prof. A], and he said he thought he had a project that was a surefire winner. . . . And he asked me if I wanted to work with him. We did . . . a very nice project, we really did it very well. We got along very well also. And I got to present it at [a medical convention] (N-13).

Even the projects that did not work out as intended and did not lead to papers or presentations were usually viewed as important experiences. According to one of the research neurologists who worked for a while in a very unsuccessful lab, "what you really learned was how *not* to do research" (N-8). He then explained how that was valuable to him:

You got very good at troubleshooting experiments, going back and reviewing literature and figuring out where things worked and where they didn't. I also got fairly facile with . . . the manual kinds of things (N-8).

Another reported somewhat different consequences from a similar situation:

> The professor didn't know anything. He was quite ignorant . . . but in the process of this great frustration of trying to get an experiment going I had to go and read some stuff and that's when I found these two books by ——— . . . . They were the most earthshaking thing I had ever come across (N-10).

Subsequently the same researcher interrupted his medical studies for a year to work in another lab.

> [The director] was very good, and I'm amazed that he wanted to have some student there. . . . He essentially gave me a room with all the equipment and everything and said, "Go to it." And then I spent a year doing just that. I spent probably eighty to one hundred hours a week. . . .I was there day and night. . . . By the time I went down there, I had read extensively in the area. . . . So I was certainly more knowledgeable than anyone in the lab in terms of background (N-10).

Four of the research neurologists were enrolled in five-year programs designed to prepare medical researchers (M.D./Ph.D. programs). Five others, including the researcher referred to in the preceding paragraph, decided to spend an extra year or more in medical school doing research (typically inserted between the second and third years of clinical education). The medical schools they attended encouraged this and helped the student find an appropriate lab in which to spend the time.

Most of the other eleven students were planning alternate ways of learning to do research by the end of their third year in medical school. This was relatively easy to arrange given the structure of medical education. Instead of spending an extra year in medical school, several of the research neurologists applied for internships and residencies intending to do research with professors they admired or in certain sorts of labs.

By the end of their junior (third) year in medical school the research neurologists had typically settled on what they wanted to do. "I was really a changed person" (N-13), reported one who remembered his haphazard decision to go to medical school. They were committed to medical research, typically in the neurosciences, or, at least to neurology as their area of specialization. (Three only discovered their desire to do research *after* medical school.) The combination of their research and clinical interests was built from many different bases, including child neurology, pharmacology, psychiatry, and virology. Neuroscience research seems to require knowledge in at least one specialty in addition to neurology.

SHARPENING ONE'S SKILLS

The next four or five years were busy ones. The students had to build technical skills. They had to learn how to define and tackle important questions on their own. They also had to learn the ins and outs of the high levels of the science world: how one gets grants, from whom, and so on.

The research neurologists typically went to study with people recommended to them by their favorite professors, or followed their professors to different universities to continue their work together. They spent much of their time on a series of research projects, but also took "time out to learn good medicine—scientific clinical medicine" (N-20). They reported working with "very strict scientific thinkers" and "very supportive and interesting teachers."

Nine of the twenty spent some time either studying at or working for the research laboratory of the National Institute of Health (NIH).

This was a high-powered lab with a lot of bright young people. . . . A lot of important people in science were coming through there all the time. A lot of the best people in my field had trained there (N-12).

For this researcher, and most of the others who spent time there, it was "a couple of the best years of my life." One expressed disappointment:

> My experience there was not the greatest because my supervisor was not someone who I admired. . . . That was not a terribly productive time at all for me, but it was productive for me in the sense that I met a lot of other people (N-20).

Experiences at NIH were more typically thought of very positively. "It was pure research in a hardworking lab. . . . It was an important part of my research training" (N-11). The same researcher compared his work at NIH with that done by students during their last year in a graduate school program and reported that he learned so much, so well, "It's widely presumed I have a Ph.D."

CONCLUSION

At NIH and labs of that sort the research neurologists ended their formal education in an environment much the same as they had inhabited for years. They studied the process of defining and conducting research in "a high-powered academic environment" (N-14). They were surrounded by models of excellence, by high standards and high expectations, and even by a tradition of high performance. They watched people who were "hardworking" and who were excited about what they were working on, people with the qualities their parents had modeled for them years earlier.

The richness of their scientific environments seems to have been especially important to the research neurologists but not very intelligible to them. Just as they were unable to recall how or why material such as *Scientific American* was available to them when they were youngsters, they were unable to say much about how they moved from one "high-powered" research environment to another. The scientist-physicians also talked about a learned ability to delay gratification and about the importance of luck.

I can remember as a child sort of toying with the idea of discovery, at the level of alchemy. Creating and discovering. It was totally in a vacuum. . . . I dreamed about discovery, but it never happened. Because you have got to have the ingredients there. . . . You have to have an environment rich in ideas, and then being driven to clarify a problem in the midst of all these ideas. . . . Doing it because you think this is the most important way to go (N-10).

I think that . . . first you need a basic intelligence, you don't have to be super bright. . . . Have to gather lots of facts before any kind of imagination can work. You can be tremendously imaginative, but if you don't have the facts, you can't work with it. I think you have to have a willingness to put off some gratification. To take a fellowship . . . [and] just enjoy the science . . . enjoy doing it for its own sake, just fun. And I think recently I've just gotten lucky (N-18).

I look at academics as sort of like athletics. In other words, you train, you spend a lot of time in the laboratories, it's sort of like you're in practice. And then the big game is when you publish your papers and people evaluate what you're doing, or when you go to a meeting (N-14).

One of the research neurologists commented quite accurately, it would seem:

I would think that if you had seen me ten years ago, you would not have guessed that you would be interviewing me today. You would have thought that I was bright . . . but it wasn't clear that I could focus myself on anything (N-3).

We, and he, cannot begin to guess what he will be doing ten years from now. But today, as their colleagues clearly acknowledge, the research neurologists we have interviewed are extremely talented individuals. They have demonstrated the ability to

take a series of observations and look at them in a certain way, to recognize they are all interrelated in a certain way, so our level of understanding is advanced. . . . Something that never existed is now known, and that's the most rewarding (N-10).

The research neurologists have varying commitments to science and the practice of medicine. At one end of the continuum, one is exclusively a scientist. Although "the medical education was extremely valuable for me because it gave me a very broad perspective" (N-10), he doesn't consider himself to be a very good clinician. He isn't interested in working with patients and so he hasn't even kept up his medical license. At the other end of the continuum, one who enjoys the clinical medicine enormously told us, "I still don't think of myself as a researcher. . . . I consider myself a physician who does research" (N-13). He says his career at the moment is in medicine rather than in research per se, the role of which is to bridge the gap between research and clinical practice. One placed himself squarely at the point where medical research and clinical medicine meet:

> There's lots of people who can do good science, and . . . lots of people who can be good clinicians, but there are very few people who can have an overview. . . . I'm not the best scientist around, and not the best neurologist around, but I'm the best at the interface (N-12).

Most of the research neurologists spend about 75% of their time on their research and 25% working with patients and teaching. All seem to enjoy their varied work enormously.

> I'm doing now precisely what I wanted to do as a child. My image of what I wanted to do as an adult was precisely what I'm doing now, although I had no idea what kind of area it would be in or exactly what kind of job it would be, what the details were . . . [teach a little, a bit of clinical work, and mostly research] . . . beautiful stains, fancy microscopic tools that you use, and the kind of intellectual activity . . . putting together a puzzle for which you can find hints, postulate hypotheses and test them (N-4). Things

are going out in nine directions at this point. It works. . . . It's probably all that I could ever dream about because I say, "What shall I do today, what puzzle should I try to figure out?" (N-3).

Basically, I've always wanted to do it all [laughs], and that's what I've ended up doing. So, I don't have to leave too much out of my life. Well, I knew I was interested in certain things, I just didn't know how to [bring] it together (N-1).

11

★ ★ ★ ★ ★ ★

Phases of Learning

Lauren A. Sosniak

The concert pianists invested an average of seventeen years studying, practicing, and performing before they reached the exceptionally high level of learning that qualified them for this study. The sculptors, swimmers, tennis players, mathematicians, and research neurologists also spent prolonged periods learning to be as accomplished as they are today. Time is a critical factor in the learning process, although it alone is not sufficient to ensure successful learning. We are reminded daily that people do spend many years engaged in an activity (cooking, typing, or teaching, for example) without ever learning to do it well. What a learner does, how he or she does it, and how things change as the years pass, are certainly more important variables than the absolute amount of time spent at an activity.

An unexpected finding from the interviews with the concert pianists—the first group of individuals we talked with—was the structuring of the lengthy process of learning into three broad phases. The early, middle, and later years of learning are divisions that the pianists and their parents made clear as they talked about changes in behaviors, perceptions, and experiences over time. These divisions are not neat and exact, but they are identifiable by looking at the following: (a) the learners' relationship with the piano and the world of music; (b) the parents' and teachers' roles in the process of development; and (c) the motivators, rewards, and symbols of success. The transition between one phase and the next may be dramatic or it may be so gradual that an observer would not notice, until long afterward, that the shift had been made.

The purpose of this chapter is to discuss the structure of learning suggested first by the interviews with the concert pianists and their parents and later evidenced in the experiences of the other groups of successful learners we studied. What are the dominant themes of each phase, essential features, and apparent effects? What did the parents, teachers, and pianists *do* that seemed to create these qualitatively different periods of learning? How did the pianists make the transition from one phase to another?

This chapter will focus on the concert pianists' experiences. This is to avoid confusing the discussion of the phases by introducing profound differences in the substance of what is learned. However, the pattern of the three distinct periods of learning is substantially the same for the sculptors, athletes, mathematicians, and research neurologists. Some readers may find themselves readily translating the general themes into the specifics of the talent fields that they know best.

In the final section of this chapter we will suggest some markers a reader might use to recognize similar periods and the transitions between them in the learning experiences of the other groups of exceptionally accomplished people discussed in this book. In that last section the reader will also find a brief discussion of some of the differences in the pattern peculiar to the different fields of accomplishment. The comparison of the pianists' experiences with those of the athletes, mathematicians, and research neurologists will be brief. The authors of the chapters describing the experiences of the different groups of learners also make use of this framework as they find it appropriate to do so.

The First Phase of Learning— The Early Years

The early years of learning were playful and filled with immediate rewards. "Tinkering around" at the piano, "tapping out melodies" was "fun." Musical activities were games that could be played over and over again. One pianist recalls

> plunking on the keys as much with the palms of my hands as with my fingers, and then running to Mother and saying, "Was that a nice song?" and then going back and doing it some more (P-2).

Another pianist was given a toy piano at the age of three and a half, and her mother "always put the piano in the area where [the child] was playing . . . always kept it handy" (M of P-28).

The pianists' parents encouraged their children to sing songs, identify notes, or pick out tunes. Some parents played children's records, others kept the family radio tuned to an FM classical music station. Much attention, praise, and applause was given in response to the children's musical efforts. When the children developed skill, they played duets with their parents and entertained family and friends who came to visit. In the early years, music was an amusement for the parents and the child. It was an interest parents could share with their child and an opportunity for parents and children to play together and feel a closeness with one another.

Most of the pianists began taking lessons by the age of six, and these were also "fun" experiences. "It was an event" (P-4). "I looked forward to them" (P-28).

First teachers were said to be "very kindly, very nice" (P-10) and enormously patient—"just pointing out my carelessness . . . in a very unconstricting way" (P-28). Lessons were filled with smiles, positive reinforcements, and rewards. One teacher "carried a big bag of Hershey bars and gold stars for the music, and I was crazy about this lady" (P-24).

Instruction during the early years was informal and per-

sonal. Both teachers and students seem to have been uncon-
cerned with objective measures of achievement. Exploring
possibilities and engaging in a wide variety of musical activities took precedence over how right or wrong or good or bad
the music making. One pianist noted, for example, that when
he would play a high note, his teacher might say, "Doesn't that
note just feel so good that you'd just want to hold it a little
longer?" (P-2).

The students responded to the teachers' warmth and affec-
tion and to the possibilities presented in each lesson. "[He]
must have been a real hero to me. I was enamored of him. He
would occasionally come over to dinner, and those were the
highlights of my life" (P-15). They got involved with their
teacher, and through the teacher they got further involved
with music and the piano.

The playful, enticing phase of learning and the effects of
such an experience can perhaps be seen best in an instance
where a child did *not* begin with such an experience. One child
(P-7) took lessons for almost three years simply because his
parents insisted that he do so. He would skip lessons or show
up late, and avoid practicing—whatever he could do to make
it clear to his parents and teacher that he did not like studying
the piano—but his mother would not let him quit. When he
was about nine and his mother "was just about to give it up
and say 'Okay, we'll quit it,' " a set of experiences took place
that encouraged the development of an almost romantic involvement with music. In a music class in public school

> the teacher played the first movement of a Grieg piano concerto on
> a recording. . . . This was the first time I'd heard classical music,
> and I never realized that piano could sound that way. . . . That had
> a tremendous effect on me. . . .

He went home "remembering all the tunes, whistling the
opening theme" and mentioned it to his mother.

> And wisely she contacted the teacher in school, found out what the
> piece was. The next time she was over in the city, she picked up

that recording. . . . I'll never forget the scene . . . [she came home] and she put that recording on. The only recordings I'd heard were these little 78 things that lasted four or five minutes. This was 33 1/3. It went on for twenty-five minutes, this piece. And I didn't even bother to play the other side of the record for over a year. . . . I became very ambitious. I wanted to learn important pieces.

He then picked a very hard piece of classical music and told his piano teacher that that was what he wanted to learn to play.

She thought to herself, "He'll never be able to play it. It's in four sharps. . . . But maybe since he's having such a bad time, it wouldn't be good to discourage him." So she gave me the first movement. And I struggled through. I couldn't sight-read at all. It was just awful [he said with a smile]. I had to pick out the notes one at a time. . . . I couldn't really handle it. But at least I was . . . practicing and playing the piano with some kind of enthusiasm.

Piano lessons started to seem like fun. "I think it was play time. It was fun time. I'd just play my [important] pieces. I'd play them badly. She'd make some suggestions. I'd try them again."

This pianist got caught up in the excitement of it all. For a period of three or four years he toyed with possibilities in music making. He played "important" pieces, joined two record clubs, listened to all kinds of classical music, and found rewards from his parents, his teacher, and others for his enthusiasm with music making.

The playful phase of learning came later for this pianist than for many we interviewed, but it had the same qualities and effects as the play of the three- to seven-year-olds. Learning was enjoyable and enticing. There was no particular pattern to the learners' activities. They were pursued out of curiosity, for fun, with surprising rewards and continuous excitement or challenge. For relatively little effort the learner got more than might be expected. The effect of this first phase of learning seemed to be to get the learner involved, captivated, hooked, and to get the learner to need and want more information and expertise.

As would be true with most games, the more the pianists played at the keyboard, the more skilled they became. In the process of exploring, they discovered some principles, which made subsequent work somewhat more systematic and disciplined. These discoveries also heightened the pianists' awareness that music making was not just play, it was also something that could be studied seriously.

Some of the pianists recall dramatic moments that led to a sudden shift from an emphasis on fun to an emphasis on study. These moments included having a memory slip during a performance and hearing an outstanding musician perform in a symphony hall.[1] Other pianists gradually found themselves spending more time at the piano working more carefully than they had before. All were prodded, prompted, encouraged, and supported by parents and teachers who had, themselves, already decided that it was time for the child to think and act more seriously about making music.

Parents and teachers skillfully managed the pianists' transition from playful to more serious attention to music making. The most obvious way they did this was by arranging the move from "nice" teachers to teachers who were recognized for their expertise and were well connected in the local music community. In nine instances out of twenty, first teachers told parents that the children "needed someone who knew more than I did" or "needed a really top-quality teacher." This, after six months, a year, or two or three years of instruction. If the teachers did not decide the pianists needed better instruction, the parents eventually did.

The move from easygoing to more disciplined instruction is an obvious sign of change in the learning process. But the pianists' willingness and ability to work at music making more

---

[1]The phrase *memory slip* was used rather than the more common phrase *slip of the memory* because that is how it was referred to by several of the pianists.

seriously were set in motion long before such a move took place. During the years of play and exploration parents and teachers set conditions that would facilitate later development of systematic and disciplined learning.

Some parents went to lessons with their child to learn exactly what to help the child with during the week. All the pianists had parents who monitored at least the quantity if not the quality of daily practice, typically in very unthreatening ways. Sometimes parents sat on the piano bench with their children, "because it's pretty hard to just sit down and practice without someone there beside you" (M of P-4). More often they listened from another room and praised, encouraged, and instructed as they saw fit. Parents helped children develop the habits of practice, discipline, and attention to detail while the activity was still predominantly "fun."

Teachers kept notebooks for the students, outlining practice schedules and recording weekly accomplishments. Piano pieces were marked with gold stars or check marks when they had been played satisfactorily from beginning to end. Teachers arranged small recitals several times a year, and the child was "taught to perform right along as I was taught to play" (P-29).

The Second Phase of Learning— The Middle Years

Somewhere along the line, the child must become possessed by music, by the sudden desire to play, to excel. It can happen at any time between the ages of 10 or so and 14. Suddenly the child begins to work, and in retrospect the first five or six years seem like kinderspiel, fooling around (Isaac Stern, *The New York Times Magazine*, December 23, 1979).

The pattern that Stern identifies seems consistent with the pianists' reports.

The dominant theme of the middle years, which typically

began when the pianists were between the ages of ten and thirteen, was precision.

> I would take more care with how I prepared things. Do it right from the very beginning. Learn it slowly. Put in the right fingering. Just do things with care (P-28).

This period was marked by a tremendous amount of time spent on details. The pianists did the same thing over and over, now consciously making slight variations each time. They were busy looking for flaws in their own playing as well as in the music making of great performers. There was a belief that all flaws could be corrected, and a dream of doing as well or better than the examples being set. Knowledgeable criticism from teachers and juries of musicians at adjudications and competitions became as rewarding as applause and adulation had been earlier.

Lessons changed dramatically.

> [They] were very long. Very, very detailed. Always working on the shape of my hand and all these little tiny things. She had me phrase things, had me do things over and over to make them as beautiful as possible. With great attention to detail (P-13).

"The training was fairly thorough. He gave me basic technical studies I still use" (P-10). "The minutest movement would be discussed. Just how you held your hand" (P-26). The teacher "expected perfection of me constantly" (P-6) or "wanted everything just so" (P-15).

In the second phase of learning, instruction became more rational and less informal and personal than it had been earlier. Technical skills and vocabulary were the core of lessons. The rules and logic of music making were dealt with in a very disciplined and systematic way. Objective measures of achievement—the results of adjudications and competitions—provided both a personal sense of accomplishment and a means of planning subsequent instruction. The personal bond between teachers and students shifted from one of love to one of respect.

Most of the pianists learned "technique" by working through the music they were assigned. Each new and more difficult piece was approached as a new set of problems.

> Like this would be . . . my first piece that had octaves, or a lot of double notes of some sort, or a certain kind of digital problem. So we'd work on that, and he'd give me exercises or suggest ways of practicing (P-25).

Many of the pianists talked about working on one piece of music for as many as eight or ten lessons, going over it note by note, phrase by phrase, "until I got it right."

In addition to technical mastery, a new musical dimension was gradually made available to the pianists.

> We talked about when this composer lived, and what kinds of things were going on. Cultural attachments and the like in the other arts. What this represented, what this went along with, or what was parallel to this. Significance on the very spiritual level. Very detailed. Very intense (P-25).

> He continually stressed that there was something behind the notes or underneath the notes that one must respect. That there's something bigger than respect for just the literal facts on the page and that's the heart of the matter, what the music has to say, the content (P-7).

Parents began to consider what other activities they could allow their child to engage in without the possibility of harming his or her music making. And they thought about how much of an investment they could allow their child, or themselves, to make in music without hurting the child's broader development. Their actions, whether consciously decided upon or spontaneous, generally were strongly supportive of musical development.

Parents began making large sacrifices of time and money to

get the child to a better teacher, buy a better piano, and travel to competitions. They rearranged life in their homes to accommodate their children's musical activities. Parents and children willingly began to sacrifice all other extracurricular activities, and sometimes to sacrifice a general education as well, to concentrate on piano practice.

What keeps a child at monotonous and boring tasks? How did the pianists stand the drudgery involved in some of the mastery they were working toward? In part, perhaps because technical mastery was taught "intelligently," in the Deweyian sense, not mechanically. Instruction seems to have been designed to "stimulate intellectual eagerness, awaken an intensified desire for intellectual activity and knowledge, and love of study" (Dewey, 1933, p. 262).

Most of the problems to be solved in lessons were determined by the teacher, as were the subjects for the intense conversations. But the students didn't seem to mind their relative impotence in deciding what they wanted to work on or talk about. It was as if both the teachers and the students knew that the students needed to be set in a direction that they weren't likely to be able to find on their own. After all, the students were only *learning* the path to musical accomplishment. Although the teachers set the direction for the students, the pianists were expected to take an active role in solving technical problems and thinking about musical issues. Together, the students and teachers worked at precise, disciplined, technical mastery and the beginning of broader understandings.

There was a reciprocal respect between the teachers and their students. The teachers found themselves working with students who could, perhaps, become fine musicians, youngsters with reasonable ability and an intense involvement (fostered earlier) with music. The students found themselves working with teachers who were dedicated to music and who appreciated ability and commitment.

The student/teacher relationship was carried well beyond the once-a-week lessons. The teachers encouraged, enticed, and prodded the students to take part in public musical activities. They told students about competitions and adjudications, spent extra hours helping the students prepare for these events, and sometimes went so far as to drive the students several hundred miles to take part in these activities. The teachers arranged recitals, negotiated auditions with important local or visiting musicians, and wrote the letters or made the phone calls that gave the pianists the opportunity to spend summers at special music camps and eventually to study with the best musicians in the country. These experiences were all important for learning about and becoming part of the world of music.

Part of the answer to the question of why the pianists would work so hard at such serious and demanding tasks may also have to do with the rewards accrued for doing so. Recitals and competitions, played before increasingly larger and more musically sophisticated audiences, were exciting and challenging experiences that broke the monotony and demonstrated the worth of the tedious practicing. Seeing one's name in the newspaper, being invited to perform for a variety of organizations, going to special summer camps for musicians, and being encouraged to dream about life as a professional—onstage, with an orchestra, in front of an audience—were tremendously energizing experiences.

Over a period of four to six years, the pianists developed skills, a sense of competence, and an identity as musicians, although they were still just good amateur pianists. Some developed such a strong commitment to music making in the middle years of learning that there was no question about doing whatever was necessary to become professionals. Some resisted making the psychological commitment. But regardless of whether the commitment was firm or not, all continued working in ways that were important for eventual accomplishment. Between the ages of sixteen and twenty, the pianists typically began to make the transition to the third phase of learning.

The Third Phase of Learning— The Later Years

The emphasis in the third phase of learning was on making music personal and making personal music. Like the previous transition, this one from technical precision to personal expression was again sometimes gradual and sometimes abrupt. One pianist found,

> All of a sudden my ear is telling me something is not quite right about the way I'm playing. There are certain kinds of technical things that are sounding very harsh. And the more I'm listening to recordings of great masters, I think, "Gee, their tone is so wonderful, what's wrong with mine?" (P-23).

The question that all the pianists and their teachers faced was: Given all the students knew, could they go beyond that knowledge to understand, appreciate, and finally bring something of themselves to the experience?

According to more than one of the master teachers we interviewed, youngsters sometimes "sound remarkable . . . and suddenly they stop dead and they go absolutely no further." One teacher told us,

> Often after teaching a young person quite a number of years even, and they play very well, you suddenly find a ceiling when they have to do something by *themselves*. There's sometimes a lack of imagination, or a lack of intellectual grasp.

Some students are simply great imitators. Another teacher commented,

> That's fine, if it's a stimulant [to creativity], but not if it remains as a product. . . . We all learn by imitation of a sort. But we have [to have] a way of making it our own.

The pianists learned to take charge of their music making while working with master teachers—teachers who were among the most respected faculty members at professional schools of music and who were, or had been, renowned concert pianists themselves. They were able to study with these teachers because of arrangements made by previous teachers or someone they met at a competition or summer camp. The pianists, their parents, and their teachers share the conviction that "you can't teach someone an experience that you haven't gone through yourself." The theme that emerges clearly in this third phase of learning was that the teacher "didn't want to teach me as a pianist so much as to become a musician" (P-4).

During special summer programs and other meetings with professional musicians the pianists had inklings of what would be involved in the third phase of learning. Nevertheless, most were surprised, stunned might be a better word, by the demands that would be placed on them.

At first the interaction between student and teacher in this phase was akin to that between slave driver and slave, since the pianists clearly became slaves to music making. One described the experience that almost all had in this way:

> He was an impossible taskmaster. It was incredible. He would just intimidate you out of your mind. He would sit there. . . . You played a concert, you didn't play a lesson. You walked in prepared to play a performance. . . . You would get torn apart for an hour (P-5).

The pianists were "expected to practice anywhere from four to seven hours" (P-23) a day. The teachers did not tolerate sloppiness or laziness. The work they assigned required a tremendous amount of time and attention, and the teachers were quick to let their disappointment be known when a student did not meet their standards.

Some of the pianists remember being terrified before lessons or in tears afterward. But they also remember the esteem they felt for their teacher, which was often enough to carry them through some very trying months as they acclimated themselves to this new way of working. The pianists spoke with awe about the opportunity to study with such outstanding musicians. "The idea that this man was willing to teach me, to give me his time, overwhelmed me" (P-5). "What she said to me was like the voice of God" (P-13).

> One was studying with the whole composite musician, not just a piano teacher. His way of looking at a piece of music was therefore much broader than probably most other people's. . . . His whole attitude about music was very special. It was a great privilege to work with someone like this (P-22).

During this third phase of instruction, the pianists learned to sacrifice some of the details of music making that had been so important earlier and to search instead for feeling, meaning, and expression. Instead of watching each step they took, the pianists were helped to see the "hills and valleys" (P-23), the broader, more generalized aspects of different pieces and styles of music.

> We tried to become more intellectual about how phrase structure [worked] and what it meant and what you were trying to say, rather than how do you accomplish this at this instrument (P-4).

The master teachers tried to impress upon their students the notion that no two musicians should ever play a piece the same way. A performance must reflect the pianist and should represent his or her most careful thoughts and strongest emotions.

> It was not so much a question of his teaching me how to play the piano. He couldn't teach a beginner. . . . You would have to be relatively accomplished. . . . He doesn't teach you how to play the piano, he teaches you . . . integrity, devotion, and a complete dedication to music making and being an artist (P-6).

Practice began to take place as much in the head as in the hands. Even more time than before, perhaps eight or ten hours a day, was spent working at and thinking about music. Models were now studied more for their strengths than for their flaws.

In this phase of learning, the pianists were usually living with other young musicians like themselves, people who shared the same commitment and provided stimulation and challenge. The pianists were entering competitions that they knew were very important for the development of a career. These competitions required rigorous technical preparation. They also gave the pianists chances to meet and get to know some inspiring and internationally important older musicians, as well as the best musicians of their own age. The connections the pianists made in these years would turn out to be useful for years to come.

The third phase of learning was the time to make the "learned" an integral part of the learner; the time to find the meaning and emotion of the larger experience, and to make music one's own. The pianists learned to make personal decisions about expression and interpretation based on technical knowledge, historical understanding, and deep and close personal associations with other musicians. One pianist summarized work with her final teacher this way:

> He made me think and he made me experience and he made me understand that you have to find your own way. You have to know what's right [and] what's wrong, but the possibilities and tonal color are absolutely endless (P-24).

Over a period of years the pianists began to identify and develop personal musical styles. They began finding and solving their own problems and satisfying themselves rather than the teacher. Eventually, according to one, "you reach the point where you must become your own critic. You know yourself when you have [given a solid performance] and you know when you haven't" (P-1).

The following three sections are written especially for the academic reader. They provide historical and theoretical perspectives important for educators or social scientists whose interests are to interpret and generalize from the specifics of the pianists' experiences, and to continue research in this vein. Some readers may choose to skim this more technical discussion, or to bypass it entirely and continue instead on page 434.

Historical Views
on Phases of Learning

There are certain kinds of changes that take place during the process of learning that are not only well accepted by educators and laymen alike but also assumed to be inherent in the process. There are, for example, "aha!" moments, growth spurts, plateaus, regressions, and peak experiences. These words convey an impression of learning as serendipitous or whimsical. They are sometimes given some order by framing them within an episodic view of learning, the importance of which, according to Jerome Bruner, a noted education psychologist, is reflected in the almost universal division of school curricula into units. But even episodes imply an irregular, discontinuous, generally unpredictable view of learning. The pianists' experiences seem much more systematic than that.

Educational research and practice rest on the premise that systematic, lawful changes *do* take place over an extended period of learning. Two groups of educators—educational psychologists and curriculum specialists—have worked for years developing orderly views of change over time. Educational psychologists have typically been concerned with lawful changes that take place in the learner. Curriculum specialists have worked to understand logical development of subject matter.

The psychologists' contributions include the enormous body of literature on Piagetian stages of cognitive development (and related work on language development or moral development), and the practices of grouping students for instruction by age and of designing curricula specifically for "adolescents" or other psychosocial stages. But the systematic changes the psychologists have been concerned with are developmental changes that take place in children's general ways of thinking or behaving, not those that take place in the acts of learning.

David Feldman, a cognitive psychologist studying universal and unique human development, points out that most of the research on the development of the mind begins with assumptions that are in conflict with what learning is all about. In *Beyond Universals in Cognitive Development* (1980), he summarizes four assumptions that current theories of psychological development share: universal achievement, spontaneous acquisition, invariant sequence, and hierarchical integration of steps or stages in the developmental process. Feldman notes that

> these assumptions reflect the fact that developmental psychology has concentrated on understanding those changes in the child's behavior that occur without special environmental intervention (p. 7).

In contrast, learning is that portion of human development that results expressly from environmental intervention—from study, instruction, or experience.

Curriculum specialists who have studied the structure of science and knowledge in general have attacked problems of teaching most directly—what, when, how, and why. The assumption underlying their work seems to be that learning will follow teaching. But an understanding of the structure of the disciplines is far removed from an understanding of the order that might exist in the experience of learning, in the "doing." The question of whether there are important developmental changes in the process of learning—found in the interaction of a learner with some subject matter within some environment (e.g., an "instructional situation")—has been given little attention beyond brief mention by a few historic figures in education.

One of the most famous attempts to describe the longitudinal development of learning is that of Alfred North Whitehead (1929). In "The Rhythm of Education" (pp. 15–28) and "The Rhythmic Claims of Freedom and Discipline" (pp. 29–41), Whitehead defined three stages of learning: romance, precision, and generalization.

> The stage of romance is the stage of first apprehension. The subject matter has the vividness of novelty; it holds within itself unexplored connexions with possibilities half-disclosed by glimpses and half-concealed by the wealth of material. In this stage knowledge is not dominated by systematic procedure. Such system as there must be is created piecemeal *ad hoc* (pp. 17–18).

"In the stage of romance the emphasis must always be on freedom, to allow the child to see for itself and to act for itself" (p. 33). Romance is an awakening or arousing stage. It sets in motion the possibilities, through continued engagement, of the acquirement of precision and subsequent fruition.

In the stage of precision,

> width of relationship is subordinated to exactness of formulation. It is the stage of grammar, the grammar of language and the grammar of science. It proceeds by forcing on the students' acceptance a given way of analysing the facts bit by bit. . . . Precision is barren without a previous stage of romance. . . . (p. 18).

Precision is the stage of technical mastery. It is learning the rules and the exceptions of the language of the field. It is coming to terms with the discipline at its current level of evolution.

> The final stage of generalization is. . . .a return to romanticism with the added advantage of classified ideas and relevant technique. It is the fruition which has been the goal of the precise training (p. 19).

This "is the stage of shedding details in favour of the active application of principles, the details retreating into subconscious habits" (p. 37). As R. S. Peters (1966) explains,

> [The students] are on the inside of the activity and have mastered both its established content and the procedures by means of which it has been developed. They are now in a position to revise and develop it for themselves, to invent and cut new pathways in their exploration (p. 57).

Whitehead notes that his stage theory is based on a vision of life in general as periodic and cyclical, "yet always different as we pass from cycle to cycle, though the subordinate stages are reproduced in each cycle" (p. 17). He asserts that if life is this way, education should be this way as well.

> Education should consist in a continual repetition of such cycles [of romance, precision, and generalization]. Each lesson in its minor way should form an eddy cycle issuing in its own subordinate process. Longer periods should issue in definite attainments, which then form the starting-ground for fresh cycles. We should banish the idea of a mythical, far-off end of education. The pupils must be continually enjoying some fruition and starting afresh— if the teacher is stimulating in exact proportion to his success in satisfying the rhythmic cravings of his pupils (p. 19).

John Dewey described similar "Stages, or Levels" very briefly in a discussion of curiosity (1933, pp. 37–40). Before Whitehead and Dewey, G. Stanley Hall suggested such periods and described them in some detail in a paper entitled "The Ideal School as Based on Child Study" (1901). Hall's address before the National Education Association was a speculative account of what education would be if based on the nature and needs of childhood. Whitehead's stages of romance, precision, and generalization are strongly foreshadowed by Hall.

According to Hall, between the ages of two or three and six or seven "the child needs more mother, and less teacher" (p. 117). Early education must respect "idleness and the intermediate stage of reverie" (p. 117). "In play, and in play only, life is made to seem real" (pp. 117–118).

A new period of education begins when the child is eight or nine, and will last nearly four years. "Child nature suggests very plainly that this period should be mainly devoted to drill, habituation, and mechanism. . . . Discipline should be the watchword" (p. 119). "Accuracy, which when out of its season is fraught with so many dangers for mind and body, is now in order" (p. 120).[2] In this period, "[t]he ideal teacher will be a stern disciplinarian, genial withal, but rigorous and relentless in his exactions, and intolerant of all scamp work" (p. 127).

A final period of education begins when the students are thirteen or fourteen and lasts about ten years.

> The drill and mechanism of the previous period must be gradually relaxed, and an appeal must be made to freedom and interest. Individuality must have a far longer tether. . . . [We] must lead and inspire (p. 130).

> [The student] is all insight and receptivity; he has just entered the stage of apprenticeship to life; he has awakened to it as at a second birth, and has found all things new and glorious (p. 132).

> The teacher must teach more, and know more; he must be a living fountain, not a stagnant pool. He should not be a dealer in desiccated, second-hand knowledge, a mere giver-out and hearer of lessons (p. 135).

Relating These Views to the Study of Talent Development

After five or six interviews, the pattern in the pianists' development, described earlier, began to emerge so strongly that we went in search of theories that might help us understand

---

[2]Of special interest within the present context, Hall wrote: "If the piano or any other musical instrument is to be learned, this is the time for drill, especially on scales and exercises" (p. 120).

the findings. The longitudinal nature of learning has been so neglected that it seemed one could only turn to theories of learning built on theories of human development. Whitehead's rhythms of learning seemed to represent an outline of the pianists' experiences best; Dewey and Hall added some details; but all seemed inappropriate in some ways and inadequate in others.

One of the more troublesome aspects of relating the work of Whitehead, Dewey, and Hall to the pianists' experiences is that those men all argued from a position of biological imperative. This is troublesome for two reasons. First, it is difficult to understand why they ground their arguments in the biological nature of man. Education is *not* a normal and naturally occurring phenomenon. Whitehead, Dewey, and Hall are clear that education can, and often does, proceed in an order other than the one they recommend, although in such instances, for them, it is no longer good or proper education. They also note that all children are not necessarily always going to experience the phases of learning as they outline them.

Second, despite the fact that the themes they propose for phases of learning have much in common, their observations of human nature and child development differ from one another in some important respects. For example, Whitehead envisions a period of romance through the ages of thirteen or fourteen, precision between fourteen and eighteen, and generalization from eighteen to twenty-two. Hall asserts a four-year period of precision beginning at eight or nine. Both seem to assume that people older than twenty-three are no longer classifiable as learners—at least not in any systematic fashion.

Part of the problem of making sense of Whitehead and Hall may be that they were trying to incorporate too much human development, learning, and the process of schooling. Their theories of learning are mixed up with theories of curriculum: Both men give special attributes to particular subject matter and prescribe not only the appropriate way to teach children of different ages but also the appropriate subjects to teach. Just as they assign different ages to similar phases of learning,

Whitehead and Hall also assign different subject matter to each phase.

Despite the inconsistencies and the incompleteness in the writings of these two men, they cannot be dismissed. The nature of the different periods of learning each describes is strikingly similar to what the pianists and their parents described in great detail. This similarity contains a message, and that message is twofold. First, we need to bring a long overdue long-term perspective to studies of learning; to recognize that learning takes place over long periods of time and to study learning as it builds over time. Second, a systematic pattern to successful learning may well exist, but in order to identify it we need to disengage the concept of learning from the much broader one of human development.

Learning is distinct from human development, and the distinctions are such that our understanding of the latter may not tell us as much about the former as we think. John Gardner (1961) reminds us,

> the process of learning through life is by no means continuous and by no means universal. If it were, age and wisdom would be perfectly correlated, and there would be no such thing as an old fool—a proposition sharply at odds with common experience (p. 139).

If we are ever to help people learn better than "average" or even better than what they would do without any intentional effort, we have to raise our understanding of learning beyond the limits imposed by age-related laws of spontaneous and universal human development.

When we do, we will still have a temporal dimension with which to contend. This belongs as much to studies of learning as to studies of any kind of growth, although it is typically ignored in the former. The better we appreciate the time involved in learning something (especially learning it well), the greater the likelihood that we will improve our ability to create conditions that encourage long-term, nontrivial growth.

Phases of Learning, Not Human Development

With an enormous amount of prompting, guidance, encouragement, support, and structure from their parents and teachers, most of the pianists seem to have moved through three qualitatively different phases of learning in an easy progression. They did so at different rates and in very different ways, but without too many long pauses or discontinuities. We might say that there was a rhythm to their learning.

However, several of the pianists who appear to have been without enough guidance and support at certain times did not move easily through the phases. There are points in particular cases when the individual was not working in the manner that the typical pattern suggests. It was clear to the pianists that these were points where the learning process was breaking down and was in danger of falling apart entirely.

An earlier illustration (see pp. 412–413) revealed how one of the pianists who had been studying music arduously needed to go back and have fun with it before he could really begin the process of successful learning. The process of learning seems just as likely to falter if the learner remains in a particular phase for too long—either playing with music long beyond the usefulness of this enticing period or working at precision longer than the student could stay interested without being given a glimmer of something beyond technical mastery. The pianists provide examples of both of these situations, examples that become clear because of the "corrections" that took place.

Two pianists were encouraged to move from early playful learning with local teachers because the teachers reported to parents that they had "reached the limit of what I can do for him. It's time for him to move on." Unfortunately, although their second music teachers were definitely more knowledgeable, they were not extremely systematic or disciplining. One pianist reports that after he had been studying with his second teacher for a while,

My father and mother apparently got into a very big argument because they felt that my training was inadequate. [The teacher] would be giving me concertos and things without proper technical exercises to go with that. . . so at some point that reached a crisis and I auditioned for ——— [whom] I consider my first piano teacher, because he did give me the technical foundations and a really excellent repertoire. I started with [him] about age thirteen, I'd say (P-10).

The pianist had been enjoying his lessons with the second teacher, but subsequently came to believe that he could never have become an exceptional pianist if he had not made the switch to the man he now considers his "first" piano teacher. "I didn't know what I was missing as far as technical training was concerned."

Another pianist also found himself "playing" too much and studying too little while working on basic technique. "And there were a lot of good things that came out of that. But also I missed some of the more permanent foundations of just taking time to solidify things" (P-23). When he moved to his next teacher, he had to "regress," as he put it, in order to master the principles and foundations of piano playing.

The final example that demonstrates the importance of the sequential phases of learning and how they are shaped by the environment is one where the learning almost stopped at the phase of precision. One pianist (P-20) spent about nine years being taught technical skills (after about four years of "romance" with music). He was growing quite weary of this and was looking forward to giving up piano lessons after he graduated from high school and entered a liberal arts college. During his senior year in high school he began studying with a new piano teacher.

The main thing I got from him was inspiration. . . . He allowed me tremendous freedom to grow and express myself. . . . He did say to me, when I played, "That's very individual. I've never heard it done before that way. I think you could play that in Carnegie Hall." . . . That was exactly what I needed.

This pianist registered at, but never attended, a local liberal arts college. Instead, he went to a school of music and "became a pianist."

These examples of phases of learning gone awry and then corrected somehow, in order that the learning process continue, are suggestive in two ways. First, they imply that the type and amount of previous experience a student has had with a subject matter may be at least as important a guide for instruction as the age and psychosocial status of the learner. Second, they hint that the sequence of the phases may be pedagogically important, although not psychologically or biologically determined.

Though the typical ages at which the pianists were working in each phase were as stated, the ranges varied enormously. This seemed to reflect the skills of the teachers the pianists studied with and the different kinds of home involvement with music. The difference between phases of human development and phases of learning is further supported by research on strategies for understanding melody carried out by Jean Bamberger (1981). She found that the

> qualities that are associated with the behavior of young children [according to Piaget's schema] seem to reappear in the . . . strategies of older children and even adults when they are confronted with a specific problem in a domain that is new to them (p. 11).

Although not biologically determined, the phases empirically derived from the pianists' experiences, like those outlined by Whitehead and Hall, may very well be logically necessary for successful learning. Together, they seem to reflect the entirety of a learning experience—from getting involved; through mastering skills, techniques, understandings, and ways of tackling problems; to finding the larger meaning, making the learning personal and worthwhile, and becoming educated about something. Furthermore, that which can be gained from each phase seems to be prerequisite for being able to make the most of the subsequent phases.

Whitehead and Hall note, for example, that learning may begin at the second phase, although it would be "barren" or "feeble and intermittent." This seems to be the way the pianists experienced being expected to work at technical mastery before they were able to play with, and become captivated by, music making. Moving to the third phase without adequately working through the second would leave the learner forever limited by too poor an understanding of the rules of music making to know when the rules could be profitably ignored.

The Phases in Other Fields of Development

The phases that have been identified cover spans of years with dominant themes, years in which there is an emphasis on a particular view of the "to to be learned" and a particular attitude toward learning. The first phase, of play and romance, is a period during which there is an enormous encouragement of interest and involvement, stimulation, freedom to explore, and immediate rewards. The second phase, of precision and discipline, is a period during which skill, technique, and the habit of accuracy are dominant. The third phase, of generalization and integration, is a period during which the development of individuality and insight and the realization that music can be a significant part of one's life come to the fore.

The phases are not innately determined, nor do they arise from the subject matter of lessons or the curricula for a course of study. They emerge from the interaction of the learner, the teacher, and some subject matter—in the doing or the act of learning. Most subject matter could probably be rendered into material appropriate for any phase, and most material could be presented in such a way as to entice, teach basic skills or understandings, or encourage generalizations beyond the specifics. Moreover, it is likely that a learner of any age could be guided through these phases, in fact may have to move through them if he or she is to learn something to the limit of what is possible.

This has been an attempt to outline a systematic pattern to the process of learning, one that makes sense empirically, logically, and pedagogically. The exact timing of the three periods was different for each of the pianists, as were the specific details to which the three broad ways of working and thinking were attached, but the nature of the periods and their sequence were essentially the same in all the pianists' histories.

Each period of learning serves important functions in the learning process. The pattern is dependent on opportunities available to the learner, and on the skills, responsiveness, and intuition of teachers, parents, and others involved with the learner. The same pattern may not be universal throughout all of education; sometimes precision alone or romance with a variety of subject matters may be all that is necessary and desirable. But when we seek to help students develop high levels of ability with broad sets of skills, this way of understanding the process of learning may be more useful than most.

The phases of learning just described have been useful to researchers studying talent development in fields as far from music making as Olympic swimming or research mathematics. The reader will find many references to the patterns in the chapters in this volume that describe the development of the swimmers, tennis players, sculptors, mathematicians, and research neurologists. Here I will briefly discuss how the periods of learning seem to relate to those other fields.

First, the reader should know that although the chapters in this volume have different authors, this study of talent development has been a team effort. Each of the researchers brought different interests and areas of expertise to the project and focused his or her work on a specific part of the study, but all of us worked very closely for more than three years. We not only held formal staff meetings, studied one another's interviews, and read the most tentative drafts of one another's papers, we also shared the same office space and daily conversation. The ideas in this chapter were shaped and framed by the findings and speculations of the other researchers, as their work was shaped by mine. The following brief thoughts about how the periods of learning relate to the other fields of talent development are drawn from this collaboration.

On the face of it, the athletes' experiences seem very similar to the concert pianists'. The athletes' initial involvement in their fields came about in very matter-of-fact ways. It was the thing to do because others around them were doing it. Typically they learned a good deal about their fields before they ever met an instructor. And their early instruction was also informal. Their lessons, the practice, and so on were initially child's play.

We see the athletes being enticed into working harder and more seriously by applause from their parents, the excitement of some public events they were witness to, and their own small successes. We find parents being drawn to increase their interest and involvement in the child's activity by the same things, as well as by their child's enthusiasm. And as will be demonstrated in other chapters, child's play turned to very serious work.

Apparently it is only after the athletes have firmly committed themselves to the day-in and day-out regime of fine-tuning their bodies and their conceptions of what they are trying to do that they raise their horizons to the limits of what is possible in their sport. At first the discipline of their work seems almost an end in itself: to perfect one skill after another. But eventually, as the athletes master the separate parts of their sport, they have to learn to put them together into a whole that is different from the parts. And for all the dedication of their coaches and parents, eventually the athletes have to do this work by themselves and for themselves.

The mathematicians' and research neurologists' development also followed periods of learning similar to the pianists', perhaps more closely than the athletes' did. Those two fields, however, do not allow for as ready a comparison as was possible with the sports. Part of the problem of trying to determine if the patterns of learning are similar, especially with the mathematicians, is that there is so little about their development that can be seen. One can't watch mathematicians doing their work or learning to do it; almost all of the action takes place in their minds. Even the parents' and teachers' roles in the process, the motivators, rewards, and symbols of success are less visible than for the pianists or athletes.

Nonetheless, the mathematicians' and research neurologists' histories show the same pattern of changing involvement with their work, as described in this chapter. They, too, seem to have experienced a period of great freedom to explore, with encouragement and immediate rewards, followed by a period of digging in, repeating problems or experiments again and again, trying to make things work, and trying to understand the principles underlying the successes. Again, as more tasks were accomplished correctly, the individuals apparently began to see a much greater meaning to what they were doing. And again, they had to bring their individuality to all the rules and order that they had learned in order to reach the levels of accomplishment they have.

Another limitation in trying to compare the mathematicians', neurologists', and sculptors' experiences with the pattern found in the pianists' development is that one has to be able to suspend age-related comparisons. The mathematicians', neurologists', and sculptors' development is elongated compared to the pianists' and athletes'. The former spend many more years getting ready to learn the field they will later become accomplished in than the latter. The pianists, for example, begin their formal studies by about the age of six. The mathematicians don't encounter the formal study of mathematics until high school. If the amount of experience the learner has had with some subject matter is one way of trying to demonstrate what period of learning he or she is working in, the mathematicians' early years of learning would take place around the age at which the pianists or swimmers are entering the third period. Part of what is peculiar to the development of the mathematicians, research neurologists, and sculptors is that they spend many years developing skills, habits, and attitudes they will use in a field that is unknown to them at the time they are being well prepared for it.

The phases of learning derived from the concert pianists' experiences do reappear in the experiences of the five other groups of accomplished people we studied as part of the development of talent research. Whether they are relevant to the host of fields in which people develop high levels of competence is a matter for further investigation. The test of an idea of phases of learning, however, will not be in how well it explains learning after the fact, but rather in how well it can be used to help more students learn more successfully than they would have otherwise.

REFERENCES

Bamberger, Jeanne. "Growing-up Prodigies: The Mid-Life Crisis." *Developmental Approaches to Giftedness and Creativity*, edited by D. H. Feldman. San Francisco: Jossey-Bass, 1982.

Bruner, Jerome S. *The Process of Education*. New York: Vintage Books, 1963.

Dewey, John. *How We Think*. Chicago: Henry Regnery Company, 1933.

Feldman, David Henry. *Beyond Universals in Cognitive Development*. New Jersey: Ablex Publishing Corporation, 1980.

Gardner, John W. *Excellence*. New York: Harper and Row, Publishers, 1961.

Hall, G. Stanley. "The Ideal School as Based on Child Study." In *Health, Growth and Heredity*, edited by Charles E. Strickland and Charles Burgess, pp. 114–136. New York: Teachers College Press, 1965.

Peters, R. S. *Ethics and Education*. London: George Allen and Unwin Ltd., 1966.

Whitehead, Alfred North. *The Aims of Education*. New York: The Free Press, 1929.

Winn, Marie. "The Pleasures and Perils of Being a Child Prodigy," *The New York Times Magazine*, December 23, 1979.

12

★ ★ ★ ★ ★ ★

Home Influences
on Talent Development

Kathryn D. Sloane

T his chapter focuses on the home environments of the
swimmers, tennis players, pianists, and sculptors. The
previous chapters described the typical patterns of development for each of these groups of talented individuals. Descriptions of the roles of the parents and other family
members in the development of talent were included in these
preceding chapters. The purpose of this chapter is to discuss
the typical pattern of parental support and encouragement of
talent development by pooling the information on the home
environment across four of the talent groups (swimmers, tennis players, pianists, and sculptors).

The generalizations in this chapter were drawn primarily
from the interviews with the parents of the talented individuals. Information on the home environment was also obtained
in the interviews with the talented individuals. Rarely was the
information from the two sources contradictory. The interviews with the parents, however, provided more information
on the early years of talent development and on the context
and rationale of decisions throughout the process.

In this chapter, information from each of the four talent
groups will be analyzed.[1] The aim is to identify processes and

patterns of home support and encouragement that are similar across these four fields of talent development. Examples from each of the talent groups will be provided to illustrate these processes whenever possible. When a pattern or process does not apply to one of the talent groups, the discrepancy will be noted and discussed.

Family Values

VALUE OF ACHIEVEMENT

Reports of the families' routines of daily living, work habits, and leisure time revealed parents who were hardworking, active people. A variety of activities filled their days. These parents wanted to be involved in something, learning about something, working on something, as often as possible.

Doing one's best—whatever the task—was very important in these homes. It was not enough to stay busy. Emphasis was placed on doing the best one is capable of. Once goals were attained, there was pride in achievement, the reward for a job well done. Some of the parents were known as "perfectionists"; nearly all set high standards for the successful completion of a task.

The parents organized their time and established priorities as a means of pursuing a variety of activities while expressing the belief that "if it's worth doing, it's worth doing well." Work was completed before play. Wasting time or idling away the hours was cause for disapproval in these homes, as was doing a sloppy job or shirking responsibilities.

Even in their leisure time, the parents chose activities that

---

[1]This chapter focuses on the psychomotor and aesthetic areas in the study. The processes of home support and encouragement for talent development described in this chapter also apply to the cognitive area. The reader is referred to the chapters on research mathematicians and research neurologists for specific descriptions of the role of the home in the development of talent in these fields.

required practice and learning. Favorite hobbies or avocations were rarely passive, nonparticipatory activities such as
watching television. The parents were more often attracted to
avocations that involved active participation, such as carpentry, gardening, sewing, sports, reading history or literature,
playing musical instruments, travel, photography. When they
were spectators instead of participants, as in attending concerts or sporting events, they studied and discussed the performances of others to increase their own knowledge, skill, or
appreciation of the activity.

The parents' commitment to the productive use of time and
doing one's best was evident in the values they taught their
children. The parents expected all family members to learn
this code of conduct, and the models the parents provided of
working hard and setting high standards of performance were
clearly recognized by the children.

> [Father] was just a very honest, hardworking person. . . . When I
> say hard worker, I mean hard. . . . When he came home at night,
> he would just keep working . . . he has to be constantly busy (A-14).

> I can remember my dad working around the house—I can't give
> you a specific example—but if something wasn't right he'd just rip
> it up and redo it (S-5).

> The whole family's attitude . . . you can see their work ethic. . . .
> Work is the goal of life (P-15).

In addition to providing role models, the parents explicitly
discussed with their children the importance of trying hard
and doing well.

> I was always the one who sort of drummed it into them that you
> always have to do the very best you are capable of and anything
> less than that is not enough (M of P-25).

> We always stressed that anything that is worth doing is worth
> doing well. No matter how many times you do something, you al-
> ways try to do it as well or better than the time before (M of S-14).

We always stressed that what he should do with his life is always do his best, that nobody could expect more (M of A-5).

The parents put these discussions and maxims into practice. The parents checked the children's homework, or at least glanced over it for neatness and blatant errors. The children's extracurricular lessons and practice were supervised by the parents. Responsibilities and household chores were shared by all family members and were performed under the watchful eyes of the parents.

> I think theoretically we work with the idea that everybody should have a specific chore. I don't think actually we really ended up with any one person being responsible for emptying wastepaper baskets and everything else, but everybody participated, believe me. . . . I just originally believed that everybody should participate, that everybody has a responsibility in this world, whether it's at home or anyplace else (M of T-7).

> I didn't want a son who didn't do a thing. He was taught at the very beginning that he had to do his share . . . the kids had to help clean, and boy, did they hate it. We'd work until twelve or one o'clock, until the job was done, then they were on their own (M of P-28).

The parents guided and monitored the children's time in the early years, since "little children couldn't judge time. They would intend to do something but wouldn't do it unless they were guided into it" (M of P-13). Over the years, the children learned to juggle family responsibilities, homework, practice, and other activities. They learned to abide by the family's code that "work had to be done before I could go out and play" (S-19).

The children's play, or free time, was also monitored by the parents to a certain extent. While the general rule was that once responsibilities were taken care of, the children were "on their own," the parents disapproved of idling away free time. So they arranged "constructive" activities for the children to pursue. They read to the children, or played games, or introduced the children to hobbies. Or, they took advantage of local facilities or neighborhood activities to channel their children's energies. As an example, a swimmer's mother recalled joining a local sports club

> to have something to do with the children in the summer. I spent the whole summer there with them. You have to have something to do with the kids, they can't just float around all summer. I knew where they were all the time (M of S-1).

It is interesting to note the extent to which the parents' own interests and preferences influenced the children's "free time" activities. For example, parents who cited sports as their own favorite pastime were more likely to encourage their children to play outdoors and be physically active than to read or draw or listen to music. Parents who were interested in music or the arts tended to do the reverse.

In summary, the parents of the athletes, musicians, and artists believed in the importance of working hard and doing one's best. They organized their time, established priorities, and set standards for the completion of a task. They were proud of their achievements and skills. This emphasis on self-discipline, the importance of doing one's best, and the satisfaction of accomplishment may be termed "value of achievement."[2]

The parents' value of achievement was applied, at first, primarily to short-term goals and was focused on daily activities in the family's routine. Few of these parents had specific career aspirations or lifetime goals for their children when the children were young. Most made it clear, however, that "whatever it was, I wanted him to do it well" (M of P-4). Initially, they felt that education was important and that their children should work hard in school.

---

[2]The *work ethic* is a common term that aptly describes these parents' views. *Achievement-oriented, goal-oriented,* or *getting-ahead philosophy* also apply.

The parents expected their children to learn and to live by this value of achievement. They were models of this value and they conveyed their expectations to their children through discussions and through the organization of the family's daily routine. They monitored the children's efforts to make sure the children worked well and thoroughly completed certain tasks. These codes of behavior were an integral part of family membership; this was just the way things were, the family's "style."

> It's a family situation where people finish what they start and do the best they can. General self-discipline, and if everyone in the family has it, then I think the assumption is that that is what one does [M of S-6].

VALUE OF THE TALENT AREA

The parents in our sample reported a range of interests, but one type of activity generally stood out as a special interest in each home and a favorite for vacations and free time.

In some of these homes, sports and physical activity (athletics) were favorite pastimes. Only a few parents were involved in athletics as a profession (three were tennis coaches). The majority were avid amateurs and spectators.

> We both tend to be athletic (M of S-5).

> I have pursued some type of physical activity all my life (M of S-1).

> I was interested in every sport going. . . . During school years I, for a long while, paid much more attention to sports than I did to books. I did everything. Field hockey, baseball, riding, some tennis, and I didn't take up golf until I was about thirty. . . . Then took that up and really pursued that very competitively until I went to work (M of T-7).

These parents joined sports clubs and made frequent use of neighborhood recreational facilities. Their friends tended to be people who were also "sports-minded." The family played sports together, attended sporting events, and discussed the achievements of local athletes. Their children were more often encouraged to run and swim and play catch than to stay inside and read, for example.

Other parents preferred to spend their time enjoying music, literature, art, and "cultural" events. Two parents were members of symphony orchestras and one parent was a commercial artist, but the majority enjoyed these activities as hobbies or preferred avocational interests.

Some of these parents were considered fairly proficient amateur artists or musicians. They practiced regularly, read books on art techniques or the history of music, and were familiar with the great names and current development in the field.

> [I] started practicing [a string instrument] at age ten, played sonatas or whatnot with my mother [and still practice regularly] . . . music is a daily diet in terms of listening; it was one in my childhood. My wife . . . loves music, but she has not practiced piano since she was a kid. But we both love music and go to concerts, and listen to music somehow a little bit every day of our lives (F of P-8).

Others were not as knowledgeable or proficient, but they appreciated and were impressed by others who were. They knew people who were professionals or accomplished amateurs and enjoyed listening to or talking with these friends about the field.

> I had a friend who was very good on the piano and organ. . . . I loved her music and I loved to hear her play. . . . She was doing what I would have liked to have done (M of P-4).

> I can't say that [husband] is particularly creative. He likes the arts and we go to plays, operas, and concerts. We both like those things very much (M of A-4).

In most of the cases in our study, the parents' special interests were highly related to the field in which one of their children became an outstanding achiever. In other words, the parents of the swimmers and tennis players tended to be people who particularly enjoyed sports and physical activity. The parents of the musicians and artists tended to prefer music, the arts, and literature.

These different groups of parents conveyed to their children their belief that athletics, music, or the arts were important. They viewed these activities as valuable and enjoyable because of their own interests and positive experiences, and they wanted their children to enjoy these activities, too.

> I wanted them to have the experience of music and literature, but even *more* fully [than I had]—things I knew of because of my experiences in college [M of P-25].

> I am a sports-minded person myself. I just think everybody should be interested in sports. . . . I tried to expose them to everything. I went through each sport and made it available to them so at least they would know the specifics of each sport . . . all my children were taught to swim, play golf, play on Little League baseball teams (M of S-8).

To summarize briefly, the parents in our sample had preferences for specific types of activities. Leisure times—evenings, weekends, and vacations—were frequently devoted to these special interests. The parents varied in the degree of their skill and expertise in athletics, music, or the arts, but they considered their special interests valuable and enjoyable. They modeled a value of the talent area (athletics, music, or the arts) and wanted to share their experience and interest in the area with their children. The parents drew from the types of activities they themselves enjoyed when planning family interactions, outings, and vacations, and many of the activities the family participated in together were related to the talent area.

The children's introduction to the talent area during these family activities and the subsequent initiation of formal instruction are described in the following section.

The Early Years of Talent Development: Parents Initiate Instruction

INTRODUCING THE CHILDREN TO THE TALENT FIELD

Most of the individuals in our sample were first introduced to the talent area—sports, music, or the arts—by their parents, relatives, or family friends. Vacations, weekend outings, or interactions among family members frequently included activities in the talent area.

> [Music] was a natural part of our life, even when we didn't have [outside] exposure to it. We performed it to the best of our ability. . . . I had a lot of music in the house, and I sang. So they were exposed to my singing. We also had a piano . . . (M of P-29).

> [We went to art museums] quite a lot and we usually took the children with us. . . . They would walk around the room very quickly, while we were standing in front of one picture . . . then they'd come back and point to a picture and say, "We like that the best." A lot of times it turned out to be a very good one. They liked going with us, I don't know whether it's because they liked going with *us* or because they enjoyed the art (M of A-6).

> We always kidded that [daughter] woke up in a car bed, next to the tennis courts, hearing the *ping-pong* of tennis balls—that was one of the first sounds she recollects probably . . . we belonged to a club and played tennis all weekend (M of T-11).

> Even when he was real tiny, I'd take him to a pool and put him in a playpen. He was still just a baby. . . . We'd get him in the water with water wings, so he was used to the water (M of S-4).

It was in the context of these activities in the homes or with the family that the children began developing simple skills in the talent area. Parents, or older siblings or relatives, taught informal "lessons" whenever the child showed an interest or when the family was involved in the activity. For example, if the child gravitated toward the piano, the parents played a simple tune or "showed him how to do a scale" (M of P-2). If the family was at the pool (or lake or beach), the parents taught the child to float or kick and paddle.

In most families, this introduction to the field and initial, rudimentary skill development occurred in the following way. Parents (or other family members), in pursuing their own interests, created situations that intrigued, interested, or involved the child. The parents responded to this interest favorably, by allowing the child to participate or by arranging special opportunities specifically for the child. Thus, the child's interest was rewarded or encouraged, and the child did learn some simple skills.

> When [son] must have been around four years old, my husband had a [tennis] match and started playing and [son] picked up a racket and said, "Can I play?" and my husband said, "Sure." And since that time, he's always had a racket in his hand (M of T-10).

> When he was four, his musical interest really became obvious. He wanted me to practice all the time. He learned to tell time because I told him, "If you'll tell me when it's 10:00 every morning, then I'll practice for an hour." He would always tell me, and then he would stand by the piano the whole time I was practicing and then he would sit down and play (M of P-25).

The parents encouraged the children's interest and provided opportunities for the children to learn in other ways as well. For example, they provided resources and materials specifically for children—records, toy instruments, sketch pads, watercolors, and sports equipment. In some instances, these resources were provided to entice and to interest the child in the talent area.

> I always put the [toy] piano in the area where she was playing, always kept it handy for her. . . . If you have an instrument where they can get at it, they'll learn it (M of P-28).

In other cases, materials were made available in response to behaviors the parents perceived as interest. One three-year-old "was going around the house tapping out rhythms on the furniture." His parents' response was to buy a toy drum, "just so he could have an instrument to play with" (M of P-7).

The children's participation in these activities and the subsequent development of skills were seen as "natural" or "normal." Few parents (or older siblings or adults) were teaching the child these skills with any goal in mind other than helping the child participate in family activities or entertaining the child.

> [Water] didn't scare her. It didn't scare any of the other children. It was just the way we started them out. She tried to follow her brother out. She spent more time under the water than on it—not unusual, because I grew up around water and so did my husband, so it was just a continuation of the way we learned to swim. It was a natural thing as far as I was concerned (M of S-3).

> [Grandmother] would take the newspaper and have me copy things from the newspaper. She would draw certain things too. . . . It wasn't like Grandma Moses or anything like that—they weren't finished drawings or on canvas . . . she'd just take butcher paper or something and just draw. . . . I really never imitated her, but I'd pursue that and she'd help me with something like that . . . just spending time with your grandmother (A-14).

It is important to note that it was not always a parent who taught the child rudimentary skills or sparked the child's initial interest. Relatives, family friends, neighbors, older siblings, peers, or friends of older siblings were sometimes responsible for introducing the child to the talent area. The parents, however, usually responded favorably to these experiences the child had with others and began providing resources and learning opportunities for the child.

In summary, opportunities to become familiar with the talent area were available to most of the individuals in our sample from an early age. These opportunities occurred through: (a) watching parents, older siblings, or family friends participate in and enjoy talent-related activities; (b) access to resources and materials, which were available because of the parents' activities or were provided by the parents specifically for the children's use; and (c) listening to the parents discuss the positive benefits of such activities, either with the children or with friends or relatives.

In the context of these family activities, the children developed an interest and learned some basic skills in the talent area. Their interest was encouraged by positive responses from the parents. Skill development occurred through informal lessons and the use of available materials and resources.

Sports, music, or the arts were certainly not the only experiences these children had in the family. Athletes' parents listened to music, and pianists learned to swim. But in each home there were clear preferences for specific types of activities, and these were pursued more frequently. The children's interest and participation in these preferred activities received more attention and response from the parents than did other activities the child may have enjoyed.

PROVIDING FORMAL INSTRUCTION IN THE TALENT FIELD

The parents in each of the four groups demonstrated a willingness, perhaps even an eagerness, to provide educational opportunities in addition to school.

> I felt that educational opportunities were so narrow. Whatever they were going to become, whatever they were going to develop out of their own curiosity, would have to come from their home environment. I did not feel that the public school gave that to the unusual child. Of course, I didn't know if my children would be unusual, but I wanted to give them the opportunity to have more. So we did more things than the family might normally do—things I thought were stimulating. We took them to concerts when they were very young, for example (M of P-25).

The parents were selective, however, about what type of early lesson to provide. Some experiences that they thought would be important could wait. For example, many of the athletes' parents wanted their children to have music lessons, but they assumed that opportunity could be pursued at a later time. In the meantime, their sports club offered swimming or tennis lessons, so they took advantage of these. In contrast, the pianists' parents thought of music lessons much earlier.

The athletes and musicians began lessons in their respective fields by age six or seven, on the average.[3] Swimming, tennis, or piano lessons were not generally available through the school system for children entering elementary school. The parents decided to hire a teacher for their children on a one-to-one basis or to enroll their children in special classes. The parents provided the tuition, transportation, equipment, and materials needed for formal instruction in the field.

The parents enrolled their young children in lessons in the talent field because they believed the experience would be a valuable one. Some parents were eager to enroll the child in special classes as soon as a teacher would accept the child. Others found teachers when the child asked for them (usually because other siblings or friends were taking lessons) or when the child demonstrated interest in other ways.

Occasionally, the parents were aware of the child's interest but waited for "external validation" of their perceptions before actually finding a teacher. One father said he knew his son enjoyed playing musical games, but he waited because parents "can be so prejudiced. I didn't trust myself" (F of P-22). When the neighbors began encouraging him (" 'He's coming into our house and he's banging around, and some of it sounds pretty good for a little kid and you sure ought to get him a piano.' "), he found a teacher for his five-year-old. Other parents were encouraged by kindergarten teachers or the instructor at the local sports club or public park to get the children started.

---

[3]The sculptors did not take special classes in their talent area as early or as consistently as did the musicians and the athletes. Only a few had formal lessons outside of school, and these lessons generally lasted only a few weeks or a year or two. The homes of the sculptors, therefore, are not included in this discussion. See the special note at the end of this section.

It was important to these parents that their children take lessons in sports or music as early as possible. The choice of the specific sport or musical instrument was, to a certain extent, arbitrary. Piano seemed a logical first choice of musical instrument, but the parents assumed the child could switch to another instrument later if he or she wished. The choice of swimming was most often determined by the availability of facilities and a coach. The parents of the tennis players were more directive, wanting the child to learn tennis because they were avid players themselves. The availability of courts and tennis programs was, of course, a necessary prerequisite.

Although accessibility and availability played a large part in the selection of a beginning teacher, the parents did choose this first teacher with care. The parents asked friends for recommendations or, in some cases, were attracted to instructors who had reputations for being particularly good with young children. The criterion at this point was the teacher's ability to work with children. The parents wanted the beginning teacher to teach the fundamentals of the field in an enjoyable way. They wanted the children to learn, but the children's interests were to be encouraged, not squelched by a teacher who was too "harsh" or too "demanding."

The parents tried to find teachers who had the "right" personality and who would take an interest in their child. Sometimes they narrowed their choice to two or three reputable teachers and then selected the one who could best provide the attention and encouragement they felt their child needed. Again, being "good with children" was more important than the teacher's technical expertise.

[The first coach was] a very athletic person, very good at instructing the whole group at a time, not just one child. He coached with emotion and explained things to them—even I understood him. He got some very good results with the groups he had. He was good with the children and a good instructor (F of S-2).

He wasn't a great teacher, but he knew the fundamentals and he was pretty musical and he and [P-22] got along fine, which is pretty important. It's important for the student to understand the teacher (F of P-22).

The parents usually attended at least the first few lessons with the child to be certain they had selected the right teacher. If the parents did not approve of the teacher's techniques or personality, another teacher was found very quickly.

So I started to investigate teachers for her. I got the advice of people who had used several teachers. . . . There was one woman across the street about a block down and we tried her. . . . And she had a canary that sang all the time, that she kept right over the piano . . . [P-24] always looked at that bird. She couldn't concentrate on her lessons, so [the teacher] really didn't think too much of her. And I thought, well, I'll have to find someone else. We investigated one woman who I didn't think would fit the bill. I didn't think their personalities were right for each other. The second choice was Mrs. ———, and we went to her right away. And she liked [P-24] from the very beginning (M of P-24).

THE PARENTS' ROLE
IN LESSONS AND PRACTICE

Although the instructor's responsibility was to provide good instruction in a positive atmosphere, the parents did not believe their child's progress was solely in the hands of the teacher. They felt it was their responsibility to make sure their child was well prepared for lessons, practiced regularly and thoroughly, worked hard, and did his or her best. As one mother said, "We were never parents who dropped the kids off and expected the club to take care of them" (M of S-9).

The parents made explicit efforts to learn the requirements and standards set by the child's instructor. Some of the parents who attended the first lessons continued to attend lessons regularly with the child. They did this because they "thought it would be fun just to see" (M of P-15) and to help the child with practice. At the lessons, these parents began to learn the specifics of instruction in the talent field.

We sat there . . . while he took a lesson, so we learned as well as he did, and then you know what to look for (M of T-18).

I think I learned everything I know about it from [child's first coach]. . . . I just remember all the instruction—how to hold your head, how to put your arms in the water, your kick, your breathing (F of S-2).

Occasionally, the parents took lessons themselves "to help him, because we wanted to do everything we could" (M of P-4) and to better understand what was required of their child. Those who did not attend lessons themselves had frequent discussions with the child and with the teacher or coach. Parents also bought books and subscribed to magazines to learn more about the details of instruction and performance in the specific talent field.

The parents learned that to advance in a talent field, daily practice was important and not to be neglected. In sports, practice at the swimming pool or tennis court was scheduled and supervised by the coach. The parents arranged the family's routine to conform to this schedule. They drove the child to and from practice, spent their weekends at swimming or tennis events, and rearranged mealtimes. When practice was in the home (especially in music), the parents helped the child schedule and plan practice time. They scheduled a regular time and made sure other family activities did not interfere.

Most of the pianists' parents monitored the amount of daily practice in the home. They listened or watched to ensure the quantity of time spent. The children were not allowed to "play around," skip drills, or quit before the designated time. Practice had priority and was to be done every day, despite the inconvenience of schedules. Consistent with the "value of achievement" philosophy, the parents taught their children that practice

. . . had to be done. If you didn't work nothing would be accomplished. Lessons won't be ready and so on. And also I think another thing would be brought up—that there would be something else come up tomorrow and you want to do that, too, and you won't get it done tomorrow, so why not get it done today (P-4).

In addition to monitoring the amount of practice time, these parents did whatever they could to make the practice productive and enjoyable. Those parents who had sufficient expertise corrected mistakes and offered advice.

I was working around in the house and I had half an ear on what he was doing, and if he was doing something wrong, I would correct him (F of P-22).

I would go down when he was practicing and if I didn't like something, I would scream. If he was having trouble with something, we'd go in and figure it out. He wasn't allowed to [practice] mistakes. My ear was good enough, so I'd know if something was wrong (M of P-29).

The parents also applauded and encouraged the child's efforts and tried to convey to the child their interest and involvement. Even those who could not offer advice or corrections would help in other ways. For example, one mother remembers "walking across the room at a certain pace, like a walking metronome" when her son practiced particular pieces (e.g., a funeral march).

He would say, "You've been to funerals, do you think this is a good speed?" [So she would play along,] thinking, oh my god, the potatoes are overcooking. But he always came first. The potatoes could burn, but if that's what he wanted, that's what it would be (M of P-15).

The parents' involvement in daily practice helped the child prepare for lessons. It ensured the amount of practice time and prevented the child from practicing mistakes or "playing around" instead of concentrating on the task. But the parents' involvement also served as motivation and encouragement for the child's efforts.

The children love it because they don't feel they are being forced. [She] loved it when her father stayed with her or I stayed with her (M of P-1).

I would always sit down with him [to practice]. . . . And I think that helped, especially when they're young. Because it's pretty hard just to sit down and practice without someone there beside you (M of P-4).

The parents of the athletes and musicians learned to judge their child's progress and assess his or her strengths or weaknesses. In addition to the frequent discussions with the instructor, the parents also evaluated the child's progress by attending meets or tournaments or recitals. And they attended *all* of them. They knew what the instructional goals were from their involvement in daily practice. They were learning more and more about the field—the rates of progress that were reasonable to expect and what the child's next goals would be. At the "public" events, the parents could judge the child's progress relative to the previous event and to the child's peers.

[We] didn't need [the coach] to tell us how all the children were doing. We could tell ourselves when we went to meets. Their times were progressively better, and they had a better outlook on what they were doing (M of S-12).

[He] was always the hit of the show [recital] because he was so far advanced than the other children who had been taking lessons (M of P-15).

More resources and opportunities were provided to promote and encourage the child's learning in the field. The parents subscribed to talent-related magazines, bought books about composers, took the entire family on trips to weekend competitions, or attended concerts—all so the children could learn more about the field and observe the performance of the more advanced person in the field. Birthday gifts and special rewards became increasingly focused on talent-related materials and supplies.

The child's efforts in the field became a central part of the family's life. Discussions at the dinner table often focused on practice, the child's progress, future competitions, or the performance of other talents in the field. Musicians' families learned to accommodate the ever-present piano and the resulting distraction. In the athletes' homes, family vacations were planned around meets and tournaments, and workout schedules determined mealtimes. Close bonds were also developed with other families who had similar interests.

In these early years of talent development, the talent field provided ample opportunities for the family to enjoy activities together. In the car to and from practice, parents and children had the time to talk and they had topics to discuss. Meets, tournaments, recitals, and concerts became family affairs. Over and over we heard parents describe how enjoyable and rewarding these early experiences with the children were.

> We used to go to the meets with the little kids, and you never got so excited when he was in the Olympics as you were when he was nine and ten and eleven years old (M of S-10).

> He loved to play duets [with his mother], that was a big item. It was just more fun than anything (M of P-4).

> I loved driving the youngsters around to the tournaments. . . . I really enjoyed taking them around. It was a great pleasure for me (M of T-11).

In addition to providing an opportunity for the family to pursue activities together, the talent field also became a means of translating the value of achievement into specific behaviors. The importance of goals and self-discipline were evident in the rules and expectations surrounding lessons and practice. The parents saw to it that the child worked consistently toward the goals set by the teachers or coaches. Progress was monitored by the parents at practice and at public performances. In some families, goals and progress were recorded on charts or in notebooks. When progress faltered, the parents discussed possible causes with the child and/or the teacher and sought solutions to the problem immediately.

Doing one's best was stressed continously, with respect not only to public performances but also to daily practice. "Slacking off" during practice or repeating mistakes were cause for reprimand. As might be expected, the parents had different methods of handling this situation. Some appealed to the child's professed love of the field or reminded the child of goals and accomplishments that lay ahead. Others emphasized the time, energy, and resources already committed. Still others threatened to discontinue their support and provision of resources if the child was not dedicated to working hard.

Along with self-discipline and doing one's best were rewards and praise for a job well done. Ribbons and trophies decorated the family room; scrapbooks were filled with newspaper clippings. The joys and pride in winning were stressed, as was the satisfaction of doing your best even if you weren't first—this time. The parents were there with applause and verbal praise when goals were attained, with solace and encouragement when goals were not quite reached.

SPECIAL NOTES ON THE SCULPTORS

Like the musicians and athletes, the sculptors learned to value the talent area (for the sculptors, this means the arts and cultural activities) from their parents, relatives, or family friends. They were encouraged by these adults to draw, paint, and experiment with model building and carpentry. Resources and materials were provided for them, and in many instances these adults taught the children specific skills.

Unlike the musicians and athletes, however, few of the sculptors were involved in formal instruction in the field during the elementary school years, other than art "periods" offered in public school. The degree and type of parental involvement in "practice" also contrasted with that of the athletes' and musicians' parents. There was an emphasis on independent learning and working alone in the sculptors' homes. Children were expected to define and pursue projects on their own. There was no scheduled time for artwork or related activities, such as building or working with models. The child was allowed to pursue this type of activity whenever he or she wished. Further, while the parents taught the children carpentry skills or some drawing and painting techniques, these "instructions" were provided primarily to help the child get started on a project. The parents were then available to help with problems, encourage efforts, and applaud accomplishments.

The Middle Years of Talent Development:
Parents Adapt to Changes in
the Child's Talent Development

After a few years of formal instruction, and with the support of the parents, the individuals in our sample were doing well in their talent lessons. As students in the talent field, these individuals were well prepared for lessons, were highly motivated, and were steadily improving.

The parents, and the individuals themselves, were encouraged by this early progress. The children found learning the basics in swimming or tennis or music fun and enjoyable. Listening to practice or watching local competitions were seen by the parents as pleasant ways to share experiences with their children. There came a time, however, when higher levels of attainment were envisioned. The parents no longer viewed the child's lessons in the talent field simply as exposure to an interesting and rewarding type of activity. They began to wonder what could be accomplished with more time, better teachers, and more challenging competition or material.

The change into the next period of talent development, termed the middle years in previous chapters, was frequently signaled by the switch from the beginning teacher to a more advanced instructor.[4] With a new instructor, lessons were more difficult and intense. Practice was longer and more arduous. The child was now in competition with a more able group of children who had also worked hard to develop their talents. The goals to be attained at this point were higher. Few were aspiring to the "limits of learning" in the field as yet, but they were working to become more accomplished, more serious, and more dedicated to the field. The child entered a new phase of education in the field. The family entered a new phase as well, one of focusing more attention, time, and resources on the child and his or her development in the talent field.

The catalyst for changing instructors varied from family to family. Winning an important competition sometimes convinced the child and/or the parents and teachers to consider the child's potential more seriously. Success in competitions or adjudications also opened doors and presented opportunities. The child, parents, teachers, relatives—or any combination of these—may have noted the need for a change for any number of reasons.

The new teachers did not need to be warm, supportive individuals like the beginning teachers. The instructors sought at this level of the child's development were those who had the technical expertise, the knowledge, and the "connections" necessary to expand the child's education and opportunities in the talent field. Usually the parents had to seek advice from teachers, coaches, or experts in the field to get information on prospective teachers.

Finding a more advanced teacher was one indication of the parents' commitment to the child's talent development. Advanced instructors were not as common as beginning teach-

---

[4]The middle years is defined slightly differently for the sculptors. This period for the sculptors is marked by an increased "seriousness" toward art, just as the athletes and musicians became more serious about their studies in their respective fields. For most of the sculptors, however, this period marks the beginning of their formal instruction in art in high school or other art classes.

ers. Advanced instructors were also more expensive, often farther away from home, and took only a limited number of students. The parents arranged auditions, paid the additional fees, and accommodated the longer and more frequent commutes to lessons and practice. In some instances, which will be discussed later in this section, major sacrifices were made by the parents and family members in order to provide quality instruction for the child.

CHANGES IN THE PARENTS' ROLES
IN LESSONS AND PRACTICE

On the surface, the parents' participation in the child's lessons and practice decreased, as compared with the degree of involvement in the early years of talent development. The child had advanced beyond the parents' level of expertise in the field, so parents could no longer help with practice. Earlier motivational tactics, such as playing duets and marching in time with the metronome or devising little rewards for a good workout, were no longer appropriate for a child whose goals were to master a field of study and to compete against the standards set in serious competition.

Nonetheless, the demands on the parents' time and their financial and emotional resources increased. Supporting and encouraging the child during this second phase of talent development meant making the child's work a high priority in the family. These parents had tremendous respect for the child's efforts and achievement and were willing to do whatever was necessary to continue this support.

The increase in the time the child spent working in the field translated into greater demands on the family's time, and the family routine was again arranged to accommodate the child's practice schedule. The parents chauffeured the child to and from twice-daily workouts or to the nearby city for music lessons. They juggled mealtimes to conform to practice schedules or postponed family activities that interfered with the piano.

If he had to be at the Steinway upstairs, we just found someplace else to do what we had to do. . . . Hearing the piano at all hours, it was just part of our lives (M of P-7).

It was the early morning [practice schedule] that made it tough on the family . . . [but] I could get over there and back before the rest of the family was tearing around. . . . But it worked out . . . your dinner would be later, breakfast might be a little rushed . . . (M of S-5).

The child's lessons, practice, and competitions in the field dominated the family's routine. Family vacations, weekends, and social activities were increasingly centered around the child's work in the field. Other interests were gradually eliminated. The families became "swimming families" or "tennis families" or "music homes," with the majority of time outside of school or jobs being spent in field-related pursuits.

Most of our vacations were frankly tennis-oriented (M of T-7).

The whole family revolved around the music, and unfortunately, I think that's what it takes (M of P-13).

Swimming was our way of life. All our vacations and extra money went into swimming weekends—that was our recreation (M of S-1).

The cost of equipment and supplies increased dramatically. The pianists, for example, needed a grand piano. As a teacher told one pianist's parents, "If they were going to be serious about his studying the piano, they had to do something about providing him with an instrument worthy of his lessons, of his commitment" (Brother of P-26). The cost of a grand piano was awesome, given this family's budget. But the parents

deprived themselves for him, they really did. Because they couldn't afford the $10 weekly lessons, and the $3000 piano that they bought . . . that $3000 was earmarked for a new car for my father (Brother of P-26).

Travel expenses to national or regional competitions also became a part of the family budget. To continue to improve, athletes needed the experience of competing with more advanced talents. Pianists needed the experience of performing publicly and of being critiqued by experts at workshops and adjudications. The expense of sending the child or traveling with the child (which was more often the case, since these parents felt it was important to do things as a family) could run into thousands of dollars a year.

In addition to the financial and emotional support, and the time involved in lessons, practice, and attending competitions and adjudications with the child, the parents found ways to be involved in the field themselves. Athletes' parents became timers at meets, tournament officials, fund raisers for the team, assistants to the coach. Some of the musicians' parents became beginning teachers, using the skills they had learned while helping their own child.

> I just took beginners. If they showed any real talent, I'd send them to another teacher, because I don't think they should be held back (M of P-4).

The parents did whatever they could to remove obstacles, soothe failures, help the child over humps. They placated school officials or made special arrangements when the child had to miss classes for practice or travel. They threatened, cajoled, listened sympathetically, sought remedies to problems, cried and laughed with the child. Note, for example, the ways two of the swimmers' parents treated problems associated with moving up through the ranks of age-group competition.

> At ten and under, she was one of the top ten-year-olds in the country. At eleven years, she was at the bottom of the heap. She'd say, "Mom, what's wrong with me?" and we'd talk about "Well, you've grown, and it will take you a while." It took her close to two years to become accustomed to that extra height (M of S-9).

When he changed age groups, I remember he had been at the top of his age group, the ten-year-old, and he was winning first place. . . . Then when he turned twelve, he was at the very bottom, and all these other kids were getting ready to go into the fourteen, and naturally he was losing then, and he would say, "I think I'll quit swimming." And I would say, "There's just one thing. If you decide you want to quit swimming, I want you to quit while you're a winner. You just be a winner again. If you want to quit, quit, but don't quit while you're a loser." Then by the time he was a winner again, he didn't want to quit (M of S-10).

Providing emotional and motivational support was not a new thing for these parents. They wanted their children to work hard and achieve, they enjoyed spending time with their children and being involved in the children's activities, and they valued and respected the talent field.

However, the increased demands on their time, the family's life-style, and their financial resources required them to make difficult choices and decisions. The parents sometimes had doubts about the decision to make the child's efforts in the talent field a main priority. They did not always know if the choice of instructor or the timing of the competitions would be best for the child's progress in the talent field. They worried about the activities the child missed out on, "normal" activities that other adolescents pursued or activities the child enjoyed but had to eliminate.

She used to enjoy playing tennis, but the problem was that what was good for tennis is not good for the piano. She was told by her teacher not to play tennis, and she resented it. She's well coordinated and could have been a good tennis player, but she didn't pursue it (F of P-8).

I guess [he] didn't have a normal childhood, because it took so much out of him to play the tennis. He didn't have time when he came home, after the tennis he had to do his homework, it was late so he didn't have the time to run around in cars or go partying or get into drugs. . . . We felt it was a good choice. . . . He's met so many nice people and he's done a lot with his life (M of T-10).

[He] gave up quite a lot. . . . Parties, social life were greatly curtailed. Swimming had to come first, in our house, too, if you
wanted to be good (M of S-12).

As illustrated in the foregoing quotes, the benefits of the
child's involvement in the field outweighed the sacrifices, according to these parents. Using time productively, setting
goals and doing one's best to attain them, and establishing
priorities were a way of life. "You can only excel in one thing
at a time," they believed, and defining a task and sticking with
it was the way to excel. As one mother said,

When you finally get dedicated in preparing for a national competition, you have to put that first, because if you start putting it
second, pretty soon it slides down the way-side and gets lost. Our
house runs on a workout schedule. . . . We were all in training the
summer of '76, before the timed trials (M of S-12).

ONE CHILD
One consequence of the parents focusing on the one child's development in the talent field was that they had less time to
spend with other family members. Working to help the child
learn and achieve often resulted in a closer relationship with
this child than with the others.

[S-17] never went through a rebellious period like most children
[e.g., the sister] do. But I think that was because we were so close.
After she started swimming, we were with her all the time. It has
left us with a very close relationship—sometimes it worries me—
in fact we worried that it may be a little too close (M of S-17).

Other family members realized that one child was "special" in
the family and received more time and attention from the parents.

[My other daughter] says, "Everytime it's my birthday, you're
never home, you're at a swimming meet with [S-4]." She was
swimming, but she'd be at another meet somewhere else and she
would go with friends (M of S-4).

My daughter says we favor [P-23]. [And do you?] Yes, I guess it does happen. We were very proud of him—his performing and all. It's not that we weren't proud of the others. But because we like music and we understand more about music [than] that of what our older son is doing, that makes a difference (M of P-23).

When the individual in our sample was an only child, or the youngest by several years, this focusing of the parents' time and resources did not create a problem. But in a few extreme instances, the parents feel that the attention was too one-sided.

I'd like to give advice to those who have younger children. Don't give all your attention to the star, because there are other ones down there in the background. I wouldn't say that's all of [my younger son's adjustment problems], but I think that's part of it. I'm sure that had an effect on [my younger child], but you can't go back . . . (M of S-4).

Some families faced decisions that illustrated their commitment to one child and his or her development in the talent field in ways extreme even for our sample. These were the instances in which an advanced instructor was not available in the immediate vicinity. Major changes in the family were therefore necessary in order to provide the child with high-quality instruction. In a few instances, the family moved to another city or state so that the child could study with a respected teacher or coach. In other cases, the family split into two households. Families who chose this option did so in one of two ways: Either the child moved nearer to the desired instructor and lived at a boarding school, with friends, or relatives; or the father became a "weekend parent," living within commuting distance of his job during the week while the mother and children lived within commuting distance of the instructor.

At this period in the children's development, no one was sure the child would "make it," or even what the final goals would be. So why were the parents willing to increase their commitment, to focus on one child's development in the talent field, and to adapt to the demands this increased commitment entailed? Even in those families in which extreme changes were not necessary, there were major sacrifices, doubts, and difficult decisions to be made.

One reason the parents gave was the pleasure and enjoyment they derived from watching the child develop in the talent field. Those children who progressed rapidly, who were consistent winners, provided consistent encouragement to the parents for their efforts.

Another reason for the parents' increased support for the one child was a sense of responsibility to develop the child's talent. For some, this feeling of responsibility derived from their perceptions of the child's specialness or potential in the field. Others listened to teachers, relatives, or friends who were impressed with the child's abilities and progress and who urged the parents to provide even more opportunities for the child.

In addition, a small percentage of parents were highly skilled in or knowledgeable about the talent area and were aware of the length of time and the changes implicit in the development of one's abilities in the field. These parents knew that reaching higher levels of accomplishment in the field depended on getting the right teachers at the right time, and spending long, arduous hours of practice. Because they valued the field themselves and could understand the child's needs, they were willing to adapt to the changes in the family during this period of the child's development.

The homes of the musicians and athletes are similar in the extent to which the family's time and resources were focused on the child's development in the talent field. The specific behaviors involved in this focusing were different. A swimmer's home, for example, had a different set of priorities, activities, discussion topics, even books and magazines, than did a pianist's home. In each of the four talent groups, however, resources, encouragement and support, models, and instructional opportunities were available in the environment.

In the sculptors' homes, this environmental support was ex-emplified in attitudes and behaviors that were different from those found in the pianists, swimmers, and tennis players. As discussed in the "Early Years" section of this chapter, the em-phasis in the sculptors' homes tended to be on independent learning. These parents were less likely to monitor and guide their children's work than were the musicians' and athletes' parents.

The sculptors signed up for art, architecture, or mechanical drawing classes in high school. Thus, the parents were not usually involved in finding a teacher or the scheduling re-quirements of special classes. When the sculptors did enroll in special programs, the parents paid tuition and arranged for transportation and supplies.

Much of the sculptors' art education during this period took the form of visiting museums, reading art books, or experi-menting with art tools and materials. These were solitary pur-suits, and the parents by and large respected and encouraged these activities.

The parents' support and encouragement took many forms. Some parents converted areas of the home (e.g., basement, at-tic) so that the child would have the space and privacy to work. They provided material and supplies—torches for weld-ing, canvas, paints, wood, and tools. A few prominently dis-played the child's work in the home. Perhaps the most important form of support, in the sculptors' memories, was simply leaving the sculptor alone to engage in art and art-re-lated activities.

Modeling, discussions of conceptual and technical issues, and the introduction to new ideas and skills were rarely the domain of the parents in the sculptors' group. Those sculptors who had these opportunities in their high school years (many did not until college) gained them through other adults. Fam-ily friends, neighbors, and relatives were often the ones who played these roles.

Some of the sculptors' parents were initially concerned when the child began speaking of art as a possible career. An art interest was fine, and should be encouraged, but the financial security of an artist left much to be desired. Some parents hinted at architecture or commercial art, or mentioned acquaintances who pursued art interests avocationally. Others were more explicit about their concerns, but all parents eventually reached the point where they agreed to continue their support for the child's art education.

The Parents' Role in the Later Years of Talent Development

During the later years of talent development, the individuals in our sample typically studied with a master teacher in the field. The individual's education in the talent field was now under the guidance and tutelage of experts. As adolescents or young adults, the individuals in this study assumed the primary responsibility for pushing, driving, and motivating themselves. They had to make the talent field their own.

The parents were no less supportive, having resolved—or at least reduced—whatever doubts they may have had about their child's aspiration to strive for the highest levels of accomplishment. The parents, however, knew little about the requirements and demands of lessons and practice at this point in the adolescent's education. They were no longer in a position to open doors for their child; others who were experts or had "connections" in the field took on that responsibility.

The parents helped the adolescent make the transition. They consulted with teachers and experts to find the best teacher and/or school. They discussed the options with their child, weighing the benefits of a music school as opposed to a liberal arts college with a strong music department, for example. They visited colleges, talked with potential master teachers, and ultimately trusted the decision made by their child and his or her advisers.

Generally, the parents paid the tuition and living expenses for their children's final stages of formal education and training in the talent field. Many of the athletes received scholarships for their college years, although there were major expenses if they were coached by specialists not working in a college setting. The musicians and sculptors particularly needed financial assistance, as few individuals in these groups won scholarships or were sponsored by a specific group or patron. In these two groups, many parents continued to provide financial support after college while the young adult was becoming established as a promising young star in the field.

The complexities involved in these later years of talent development usually made it impossible for the parents to play a leading role in their child's decisions and progress. They remained a strong force in the background, however, as providers not only of financial support but also of emotional support. Perhaps most important, they offered a nurturant, understanding environment for their child to retreat to, if necessary. From their years of involvement in the child's talent development, they could share and appreciate the successes and lend a sympathetic ear to the failures.

The parents in our sample continue to enjoy and support their children's work. The swimmers' careers as swimmers ended with the Olympics, but the pianists, sculptors, and, to some extent, the tennis players anticipate long-term careers. The parents continue to attend competitions, concerts, and art shows. Many of the parents in each of the groups have continued their own involvement in the talent field, utilizing the skills and experience they gained from their participation in their own child's talent development.

Discussion of the Findings

The preceding sections of this chapter summarize the typical pattern of parental support and encouragement throughout the many years of talent development. Many more detailed aspects of the values, attitudes, and behaviors these parents reported could be further analyzed and discussed. An extensive

analysis of many subtle differences among the home environment processes of these four groups is beyond the limits of this
chapter. Three points are worthy of special attention, however. These generalizations emerged very strongly in the pianists', swimmers', and tennis players' homes, but were not as
strong in the sculptors' homes.[5]

First, we were struck by the degree to which the athletes'
and musicians' families were "child-centered." The vast majority of these mothers did not work outside the home, which
was not unusual in the 1950s. Many of them, however, reported rarely, if ever, leaving their children with baby-sitters.
The parents were also willing to channel their own interests
into the child's activities, to rearrange their schedules to conform to the child's activities, and to devote awesome amounts
of time to monitoring practice and attending meets, workouts,
and tournaments.

Shared family activities were encouraged. The talent field
proved to be an excellent way for the parents and children to
enjoy and benefit from family interactions. The parents
placed great importance on spending time with the children
and becoming involved in the children's activities. They saw
shared experiences as a foundation for close relationships, and
the family's involvement in the talent field provided a mutually attractive situation around which to share these experiences. One mother spoke for many when she said, "As far as
I'm concerned, [the talent field] helped our family become a
family, because we were spending all this time together" (M of
S-12).

The second point is the degree of concentration on the
child's development in the particular talent field. The child's
progress in the talent field was clearly important to the parents, but lessons and practice in the field were not the child's

---

[5]In the sculptors' homes, resources were available, values and attitudes
were supportive of the eventual career decisions, and ample opportunities
were provided for the child to develop skills and interest in art activities.
The focusing on one child and one special talent field, however, were not
as pronounced in these homes.

only activities. The parents expected their children to have opportunities and experiences in other areas as well. Cub Scouts or Brownies, dancing lessons, baseball, class plays, and summer camp were as likely to be a part of the athlete's childhood as they were a pianist's or artist's. The parents admitted, however, that they were not as involved in these "extra" activities as they were in the child's lessons in the talent field. They did not apply the same standards of time or performance to these other activities.

It was not always clear why the parents focused more heavily on one of the child's activities. Their own interest in the talent area played a part. They enjoyed some activities more than others and were willing to spend time participating in activities related to their special interests.

The parents' value of achievement also seems to have played a role in making the talent field a priority. The parents placed a great deal of emphasis on doing one's best and achieving. For any number of reasons (for example, the degree of parental supervision and provision of resources, the early introduction to the field, or the parents' value of the talent area), the child did very well in early lessons in the talent field. The parents were well aware of the child's progress, through their own involvement, and less aware of the child's other accomplishments. When the time demands of lessons and practice in the talent field increased, the parents encouraged the child to drop other competing activities in favor of the talent field. They believed the child had a better chance of becoming a high achiever in the talent field. *This* was the field the child was doing best in and was, therefore, the field that should have priority.

The individuals who eventually attained the limits of learning in their respective fields were seen as "special" in the family. The parents not only focused their attention on one area of the child's development, they also focused more of their attention and resources on this particular child.

Typically, more than one child in the family was involved in lessons in the particular talent field. These were family activities, and most of the children in the family were exposed to the talent area as a consequence of family membership. But in only a very small number of the cases did one of the siblings come close to the level of accomplishment in the talent field that the individual in our sample attained.

The child who "made it" was not always the one who was considered to be the most "talented." Many parents described another one of their children as having more "natural ability." The characteristics that distinguished the high achiever in the field from his or her siblings, most parents said, was a willingness to work and a desire to excel. *Persistence, competitiveness,* and *eagerness* were other often-used terms.

During the period of early instruction, these "characteristics" were noted by parents in the child's approach to lessons and practice in the field. This child more readily submitted to the regime of daily practice. He or she followed instructions, concentrated on the task, and seemed to enjoy practice instead of considering it a drudgery. The parents appreciated the child's responses to lessons and practice. Working with this child—taking him or her to lessons, discussing progress, helping with practice—was pleasant because the child was willing to do the work and was enthusiastic.

While the parents did not necessarily feel that this child was more "gifted" than the other children in the family, they did believe that this child showed more promise for excellence in the field. As the parents learned about the number of hours of practice needed to master certain skills, they realized that the child who was more willing to "work at it" was more likely to do well. In the early instruction period, we began to see evidence of this child gaining a special status in the family as the one with the most potential for success in the talent field.

The indications of the "specialness" were, at first, subtle. There were rarely explicit pronouncements in the family that this child was to be given special consideration and privileges. Rather, it seems to have been a gradual process. Parents made small concessions at first. For example, these children were excused from household chores and responsibilities because "we felt homework and practice were making enough demands on his time. . . . We let him have full rein of time [for practice] and [did] not force him to do things that other children have to do" (M of P-15). As long as the child was practicing, which was considered a constructive activity, the parents felt that the child was working and learning. They also understood that the child could not excel in everything at once. So, we see some of these extremely achievement-oriented parents being satisfied with average, or sometimes mediocre, school grades, for example, as a trade-off for the talent development.

Our data suggest that the parents spent more time working with this child on the talent field than they did with other children who were also taking lessons. Most parents reported making conscious efforts to distribute their time and attention as equally as possible, but it became increasingly difficult to do this. Even when all of the children were swimming, for example, the parents often had to make choices about which meets to attend. Recall the sibling's complaint cited earlier, that " 'everytime it's my birthday, you're never home, you're at a swimming meet with [X].' "

IN RETROSPECT

The parents see their child's development in the talent field as an important part of their family's life. They feel strongly about this, despite some of the problems previously discussed. There were comments such as, "The whole family revolved around music. And, unfortunately, I think that's what it takes." But the field also provided "a common interest and a common goal. As far as I was concerned, it helped our family become a family, because we were spending all this time together."

Looking back at their role in the process, the parents are pleased, but still a little dazed, by the results. They recall, as young parents, having had initial ideas about experiences they would like their children to have and standards they would like them to attain. They wanted to do whatever they could to give their support and to promote achievement. But gradually, accomplishing these seemingly innocent goals required more and more of the parents' time and resources. Almost without realizing the cumulative effects of their involvement, the parents found themselves caught up in the process of one child's development of talent. As one parent said,

> . . . all of a sudden it was big business. It was too late to back out. I suppose if we had gone into it with our eyes open, we would have done the same thing. But I had *no* idea of what we were getting into—at all (M of S-9).

Another mother mused, "Funny how you get into these things before you know how much work it's going to entail" (M of S-10).

At the conclusion of each interview, we asked the parents if they would do anything differently. Most thought not, believing their decisions and courses of action over the years were necessary for their child's success. The choices were not always easy.

> We did feel an obligation to provide opportunities, and that made it hard—not knowing if you were making the right decision. We still wonder what would have happened if we had made different decisions (M of P-5).

A variety of "different decisions" could have been made. The parents could have been less involved with their child's development. They could also have promoted the development of different talents. We have some ideas why the parents chose to focus their commitment on one child and one area of talent. What would have happened had the parents been less involved in sports or music is something we, and the parents, can only speculate about. As one mother said,

> I often think that with ourselves and with these children that there are so many possibilities of talent that lie undiscovered and "Did you develop the right one?" I ask that of myself (M of S-13).

We believe, as do the parents, that the parents' interest and participation in the child's learning contributed significantly to his or her achievement in the field. We find it difficult to imagine how these children could have gotten good teachers, learned to practice regularly and thoroughly, and developed a value of and commitment to achievement in the talent field without a great deal of parental guidance and support. The role of the home in supporting the long process of talent development is only one piece of the picture, but it is a crucial one.

13

★ ★ ★ ★ ★ ★

A Long-Term Commitment to Learning

Lauren A. Sosniak

I n the preceding chapters we have seen that successful
learning required years of hard work. We have also seen
that successful learners and their parents typically invested the necessary time and energy without realizing, for
many of those years, exactly where they were headed. Becoming concert pianists, Olympic swimmers, research mathematicians, and so on were ambitions that developed after the
individuals had done considerable work leading in those directions. What was it that kept them engaged in their fields before they developed such ambitions? How were they able to
maintain their interest through the many more years it took to
achieve unusual levels of excellence? How can we account for
their willingness to work continually at one type of activity for
well over a dozen years?

The purpose of this chapter is to explore the process of creating and maintaining long-term commitments to learning.
The concert pianists' experiences will provide the details in
the chapter. The broad themes to be discussed, however, are
applicable to all six groups of people interviewed for the Development of Talent Research Project. Some of the subtlety of
creating and maintaining long-term commitments to learning

in the fields other than music making will be lost in such an approach. But the hope is that in this way we will be able to present clearly what seem to have been among the most salient features of the process. Readers may find themselves readily translating the broad themes into the specifics of the talent field they know best.

THE BEGINNINGS OF INTEREST

The earliest "work" at the piano, "plunking on the keys" as toddlers and picking out little tunes with one finger as five-year-olds, seems relatively easy to understand. Benjamin Spock (1976) and Arnold Gesell (1946), among others, note that these activities are part of the normal development of a child—at least in homes where pianos or the like are available and parents are willing to live with the noise that these activities create. They are examples of exploring, manipulating, and controlling the environment that child psychologists regularly find in the actions of young children. If some thing or way of working is part of a child's environment, it will probably be tried out in some fashion. Playful activity with a musical instrument of one sort or another is likely to be part of almost any child's life, unless it is discouraged.

But studying something systematically, with a teacher, at a set time and place, and practicing daily in preparation for lessons, are not activities arising spontaneously from normal physiological or psychological development. Years of persistent work at one type of activity is rather unusual in today's society, especially for people between the ages of five and twenty-two. Listening to the pianists talk about what kept them at the piano, one is immediately struck by the multitude of motives and rewards for their efforts.

At first it was typically the family interest in their activity that kept the young children engaged. The decision to begin piano lessons, and to practice daily in preparation for the weekly lessons, was made for the pianists by their parents. Parents took the children to and from lessons and made sure the children practiced every day. Whether or not the pianists enjoyed studying and practicing, they really had little choice in the matter at the start.

Parents did make a serious effort to try to find a piano teacher with whom their child would be comfortable. They looked for someone who had a reputation for being good with children. They monitored their child's early experiences, some by sitting in on early lessons, to make sure that the child and teacher were "getting along." A quick change in first teachers was made by several parents when they sensed that their child was uncomfortable or just not getting what he or she needed.

Most of the children enjoyed their lessons. Their teachers were warm and nurturing. "It was an event" to go to lessons, and the event was often filled with rewards of smiles, gold stars, candy bars, or sodas. Several of the pianists quickly began to think of their teacher as "a second mother."

Nevertheless, a few of the pianists were very unhappy about the predicament they found themselves in. "I hated it. . . . I did what I was told to do" (P-8). "I always regarded the piano lessons as something I wanted to get out of the way. . . . It was part of an obligation that I had to do, but I really didn't look forward to it" (P-20). "My parents would insist. You have to go to your lessons" (P-7).

It was fortunate for the majority of the budding pianists that their teachers were the kind of people with whom they could feel comfortable, who could make beginning lessons seem like fun. Initially, however, the pianists' parents were insistent that all of their children have at least a minimal level of exposure to musical education. Music was important to them; it was something they intended to offer their children in the hope that it would enrich their lives. Musical instruction was simply part of belonging to the family.

These parents were perhaps a little more committed to musical education than average. They were firm not only about lessons but also about daily practice. Again, some of the children enjoyed practicing while others disliked it, but none had much choice about whether or not to do it.

In some homes there was a set time every day for parent and

child to sit together at the piano. These were often, but not always, pleasurable times for both parent and child. Several of the pianists who were not excited about practicing recall that if they didn't practice, or didn't practice well enough, parents threatened to stop the lessons. Most of the pianists report having practiced matter-of-factly, although perhaps not as much as a parent or teacher would have liked or not without a little prompting by an adult.

The monitoring the parents did when the children were beginning their studies seems to have had enormous consequences. By trying to ensure that child and teacher "get along," the parents were, in effect, providing the kind of instruction that would in itself provide further motivation for learning. By insisting on daily practice, the parents were helping teach discipline and establish a habit. The pianists report that later on the habit was hard to break. Finally, the parents ensured that their children would learn something from lessons, and would learn faster than might others who were left on their own.

BUILDING A SENSE OF SPECIALNESS

Not long after the pianists began studying and practicing daily, they also began developing reasons for doing so that were stronger than mere necessity. While talking about their early interest in the piano and music making, a repeated theme seems to be: What else could I be doing with my time that would be as exciting or offer as many rewards? For a few of the pianists, the planned nature of the activity and the rapport they quickly developed with their teachers were motivation enough for their involvement. "It was new and fresh and exciting" (P-25).

All of the pianists discovered immediate rewards for their efforts. Most frequently mentioned were approval and attention from parents.

> My mother liked to hear me play. I knew it gave her pleasure. So when she would come home, I would sometimes run over to the

piano as she was coming in the door and play her favorite pieces (P-20).

[The pianist] loved to play duets. That was a big item. It was just more fun than anything. And of course [father] loved to hear us play together. That brought the family together (M of P-4).

The children were asked to play for friends and relatives who came to the house.

There was an awful lot of praise and an awful lot of attention. Play for the family, play for this one, play for that one. There was so much reward for performing that I've always loved it (P-24).

The youngsters learned that musical activity was something special in their homes, something worthy of applause. All of the notice meant that there was much to be gained from paying attention during lessons and practicing daily, and much to be lost if they did not do these things.

Over a period of time the children also learned that playing the piano was their chance to be special—different from and somehow better than other children their age or in their families. "I think I knew I was special. . . . There wasn't anybody my age who played, that I knew" (P-24).

I became identified with the piano. That was the only way I could stand out and be someone special. Even though I resisted it, it was part of my identity very young (P-8).

"I must have liked it, being special" (P-10).

The children learned to feel special in their homes, at first. But soon their sense of being special was reinforced by responses from people outside their homes. Many of the pianists reported being told by their teachers that "I was her favorite student" or "I was his best pupil."

The teachers seem to have enjoyed working with these students and to have offered a little more attention and care than most students get from their teachers. The children were given extra instructional time, special encouragement, carefully selected material, and choice spots on recital programs.

> I think I became her most promising student. So she showered a lot of attention on me. I would come in for an hour lesson, but it would always be like an hour and a half (P-1).

> I knew he was very delighted with me. I got lots of approval from him, and lots of approval from my parents after they talked to him (P-15).

Family friends and relatives contributed to the pianists' developing sense of being special. One father, comparing the experiences of his older child who became a pianist with those of his younger child who has pursued an entirely different career, noted that the pianist "received so much of the limelight" and the younger child "was often a 'me, too' person." This parent reported trying to bring the younger child into the limelight, but

> people were always asking about [the pianist]. People can sometimes be cruel without realizing it. . . . Only interested in one thing and that's all they care about (F of P-22).

The children were invited to play at elementary school assemblies. They earned distinction among schoolmates, which, although in certain instances was something of an embarrassment, was always a way of asserting one's uniqueness and unusual value. "The playing was the only thing I felt that gave me something for [my peers in school] to look up to me" (P-24). Another pianist reported how important it was to him when a third-grade teacher suggested that he play in the end-of-year talent show:

> I said I'd be embarrassed, and this and that. She said, "No, you wouldn't. People would like it and people would like you for it."

And I risked it. And of course I was nervous. And the kids went wild because they had no idea. . . . They just stomped their feet and screamed and howled and hollered. And suddenly I felt welcome. It was like this great thing (P-15).

The pianists were told, again and again, how valuable they were for their ability to play the piano.

I was a little kid, and here were my parents and all the teachers in my school and the principal of my school. . . telling me that I was going to be great and famous and how unusual I was (P-13).

How unusual were these children as a group? Recitals and competitions provided some objective evidence that a few of the children were quite good. Six of the pianists had notable success before they reached their teens. These youngsters either had an opportunity to perform with a symphony orchestra—the result of a prize-winning performance in a children's competition—or else they had the opportunity to audition for an outstanding pianist and teacher who then decided to work with them.

The other fifteen pianists did not begin to approach this type of confirmation of their sense of being special until their late teens or early twenties. Nonetheless, they found their own equivalent of such success and specialness in local recitals or performing opportunities, in their acceptance by the most respected local teacher, or in their "star" status in school or in the neighborhood. At the very least they gained esteem from being better than their brothers or sisters or neighborhood friends who were also taking piano lessons. Affective consequences, it would seem, do not depend on national norms, but rather on where a person stands in his or her own locale.

A child who is labeled "special" in a community, or even in a state, is not necessarily "special" at the national or international level. The child and those doing the labeling are not likely to recognize the gulf between these levels of achievement, but those who have crossed into the national or international arena know it well. The effects of the labeling are important nonetheless in keeping the learner at a task and in ensuring that the learner gets the best educational opportunities available. In her studies of families as educators, Columbia University professor Hope Jensen Leichter finds that "if family members define situations as real, they are real in their consequences" (1974, p. 37).

By the time most of the pianists were about eleven or twelve, there was no longer any question at all about the distinctive treatment they were being given at home.

I got out of a lot of chores. . . . I was really indulged because I was the pianist. And so I got away with murder (P-28).

There was no question that I was the big star (P-5).

We did give him special privileges. . . . We didn't feel that he should have little chores around the house because it cut into his music time. When we realized he did have this talent, we let him have full rein of time and did not force him to do things that other children have to do. We realized that he was special and that he should not be asked to wash the car (M of P-15).

For the most part, the pianists responded eagerly to all the attention and adulation. Their sense of being special reinforced their desire to learn more about music making.

I think that I had to be the center of attention. Performing gives you that platform and sets you apart from everybody else. If you look at the way a typical performance is structured, typically a solo piano recital, there's only one person on that stage and maybe a thousand, maybe two thousand people in the audience, all riveted on that one performer. I think that was probably, without my ever even being aware of it, what made me want to do that (P-26).

As the children were labeled "special" for their musical involvement, music became more important not only to the youngsters but to their parents as well. What had once been "a good thing for the child" or "fun" became something serious. Perceptions that the children were special for their musical abilities led to actions that would increase the children's opportunities to learn and to succeed.

DEVELOPING FEELINGS OF COMPETENCE
The days of playing the piano turned into years—and "Christmas was the only day off" (M of P-13). Practice became a routine part of the youngsters' lives.

> I would get up and practice just like you would get up and wash your face in the morning and brush your teeth. It was a very natural thing to do, and you just accepted it as something very normal (P-4).

> When you're studying four or five years, or three or four years, habit has taken over quite strongly, I think (P-10).

The pianists report that although initially they worked more for attention and the chance to be regarded as special than out of any burning desire to learn particular things about music making, that was to change. As months and years passed, the pianists found that playing was no longer simply fun, it required a lot of work. The work, however, was becoming much more than a requirement or an obligation the pianists might have had to fulfill for their parents. The pianists began to realize that they were becoming skilled at music making. It was something they could do, and do well. "I could do one thing that nobody else could do. I could play circles around everyone at the piano" (P-29).

Competence consciously became as important for the youngsters as applause had been earlier, mastery as stimulating as attention and approval. "[The piano] was something I was good at, and that was important to me. I had to be good at something" (P-8). Being good at something, and being better at something than others their age, became strong incentives for intensifying their work. "I was so ambitious. I felt I had to prove something, and the best way to do it was through the piano" (P-7).

One way of understanding the pianists' continued involvement with music is provided by Robert White's work on *competence effectance*. White defined competence in a broad biological sense as "an organism's capacity to interact effectively with its environment" (1959, p. 297).[1] The reports of the pianists' experiences are very much like the examples White used to illustrate his theory. From the toddler banging on the keyboard and then running to Mommy for confirmation that he had played a nice song to the adolescent practicing a passage many times over in search of the exact sound he heard on the recording of that piece of music, one can see the active pursuit of seeking to affect the environment if not the actual need to do so. And as White explained, the pianist "does not have to do it wholly for mother; as an active living being he has his own stake in growing up" (1960, p. 114).

The pianists' parents and teachers created the context within which musical accomplishment became a way to interact effectively with the environment. And they provided conditions necessary for the learners both to become increasingly more competent and to recognize that competence in themselves.

Some parents actually began studying music themselves after their children had developed minimal levels of competence.

I remember one period of a year or two when both of my parents decided to take lessons on other instruments so that they could play along with me in a chamber situation (P-5).

---

[1]Robert White wrote of *competence effectance* as a biological motive. "It's adaptive significance lies in the promotion of spare time behavior that leads to an extensive growth of competence" (1960, p. 103). Since this investigation only focuses on the specific adaptations that have led to such growth, it would be inappropriate either to accept or to reject the biological underpinnings of White's work.

According to one mother, "We could appreciate what she was doing, and she had a sense of support" (M of P-8). According to another pianist,

> I think that as a youngster it made a great impression. One, that they would take that kind of activity—I mean real activity—themselves. And two, they also directed a great deal of interest toward my work (P-4).

Parents began building large classical record collections and attending musical performances regularly. "We did it [attend weekly concerts] for him. And of course we enjoyed it, too, so that was one thing the family would do together" (M of P-15).

Parents also began watching closely for progress and using a variety of different achievements or lack thereof as reasons for finding a better teacher for their child. It became as important to the parents that the children excel as it was to the children themselves.

> My father and mother apparently got into a very big argument at one point because they felt that my training was inadequate . . . so at some point that reached a crisis, and I auditioned for ——— (P-10).

> My mother, quite rightly I think, deduced, and my father too . . . that I was the biggest fish in the conservatory and that I was playing better at thirteen than most of the students and most of the faculty there. . . . And she figured that there comes a point where you outgrow the teacher (P-15).

> I got to the point (about age eleven or twelve) where I wasn't making any progress at all, and my father felt that if he's going to be paying for the lessons, even if it's not going to go anywhere, I've got to be doing better than I was doing. I needed somebody to teach me how to practice, for example. [So my father found a new teacher] (P-22).

Teachers were equally important for helping the students develop competence and the feeling that musical competence was valuable. The teachers were serious about music making and held the students to high standards.

> I never felt that there was an opportunity to skip over anything. In other words, if something was not quite to a point, they didn't say, you know, "Well, we'll go on and catch that next time." I never felt that was a possibility. I always felt it had to be finished, whatever met with their approval (P-4).

Every time the pianists were assigned a new task, they knew they had completed the previous one well, and they knew very specifically what they had accomplished. The pianists also gained a sense of their cumulative accomplishments and their progress in general when they were asked to play in the choice spot in the teachers' recitals, invited to play a solo recital, given free or extra instructional time, encouraged to enter a youth competition, and so forth.

Recitals, competitions, and adjudications were also powerful means of developing actual competence and feelings of efficacy for music-making abilities. These events gave students and teachers something very specific to work for and provided a means of evaluating one's progress over time. They also brought the children's solitary work into a public arena. All the fanfare that went along with these activities helped the children view their work as something that was real and important in the larger world.

Although winning a competition or receiving a top score in an adjudication was certainly a stimulus for continued work, the failure to win a prize or be judged best did not seem to be exceptionally discouraging for the pianists. Teachers and parents helped the youngsters use these opportunities to appreciate both progress that had been made and the road still to be traveled. The teachers, especially, seem to have emphasized that the events were most important for learning what one had to work on next, in order to be better next time.

According to White, motivation subsides "when a situation has been explored to the point that it no longer presents new possibilities" (1959, p. 322). The pianists, with the help of their teachers and parents, never reached the point of exhausting the possibilities in music making. With each experience the students developed some competence and uncovered still more to be learned. As the pianists' "fitness to interact with [their] environment" grew, so too did the challenges within their environment.

The pianists began by "playing the piano"; they moved to a study of technique and later, still, learned the art of interpretation. They performed first for their parents, then for members of their community, and eventually for increasingly larger and more diverse audiences. The pianists first mastered pieces of music, then full programs; they played solo recitals and then with the full orchestra. The music they played changed, as did their interpretations and performances.

The pianists offer a set of reasons for their continued efforts, many of which had to do with their success in dealing with their environment through music. They used music in their search for parental and teacher approval and reward, personal meaning, and a place for themselves in society.

ACCUMULATING ADVANTAGES

Feelings of specialness and competence seem to play significant roles not only in keeping the youngster at the piano but also in ensuring optimal instruction and further opportunities in the process of learning. It seems that the more special and accomplished the pianists felt themselves to be, the more willing they were (often even eager) to invest time and emotional commitment in musical activities. Similarly, the more special the parents and teachers thought the child to be, the greater their investments toward the students' eventual accomplishments.

It is important to remember that these feelings increased in intensity and breadth over perhaps a dozen years. It may be expressly because of this extended period of time that the commitment to music seemed to become so natural; neither the children nor the parents quite realized the enormity of the decisions and choices they were gradually making in favor of musical development. The children, who had practiced daily for months and years and who were well rewarded for their effort, eventually found it hard to stop working at music making. There was nothing else at which they had worked as long; there was nothing else at which they were as good. Their parents, who over time had invested more and more of their time, money, and emotional resources in the child's musical career, also seemed to find it more natural to continue doing so than to stop.

The work of sociologists such as Merton (1968), Cole and Cole (1973), and Zuckerman (1977) provides yet another way of understanding how the pianists were able to maintain the lengthy commitment necessary for their eventual accomplishments. These researchers have been interested in how scientists, especially Nobel Laureates, achieve success. Learning is but a small part of that process, and of the sociologists' analyses. But the chain of events their work reveals, and the "accumulative advantage" they propose, seem useful stepping-stones for understanding the pianists' lengthy commitment, as well as their eventual successes.

Robert Merton (1968) postulated a "Matthew effect" in science:

> The accruing of greater increments of recognition for particular scientific contributions to scientists of considerable repute and the withholding of such recognition from scientists who have not yet made their mark (p. 58).

He found that eminent scientists "are given disproportionate credit in cases of collaboration or of independent multiple discoveries" and that their contributions to science have heightened visibility compared with less-well-known scientists. The self-assurance of these eminent scientists,

> which is partially inherent, partially the result of experiences and associations in creative scientific environments, and partially a

result of later social validation of their position, encourages them to search out risky but important problems and to highlight the results of their inquiry (p. 62).

Cole and Cole (1973) proposed the "accumulative advantage" hypothesis, a generalization and expansion of the Matthew effect: "Those who are initially successful have greater opportunities for future success" (p. 119). The Coles note social advantages for positional and reputational success and visibility, as well as concurrent and increasing advantages in distribution of resources and competition for rewards. They find a labeling process and tracking system that have many of the features of a self-fulfilling prophecy. They describe the process this way:

> In graduate school, certain students are labeled as being "bright" and "promising." They usually become the students of the most powerful and eminent professors. As graduate students, they are given access to greater resources and often have the opportunity to publish papers with their mentors. Perhaps even more important, they pick up self-confidence and the belief that they have what it takes. The "knighted" students of the most eminent professors are also most likely to receive first-job appointments to prestigious academic departments or research laboratories. At these research centers they again have resource advantages and find it easier to publish.

> At this point another step in the process of accumulative advantage may take place. A young scientist at a leading research center publishes a paper which is labelled "interesting." He then has even greater resources made available to him as he becomes more integrated into the establishment. It is now true indeed that he has great advantages over his colleagues at graduate school who were not labelled as "bright," were not fortunate enough to be sponsored by an eminent professor, and who did not pick up the self-confidence needed to do high-quality research. The probabilities of the favored young scientists receiving support for their research, working in social and intellectual environments that are conducive to new discoveries, and collaborating with other im-

aginative scientists, are now no longer the same as for their less-favored colleagues. The chosen are given an advantage over the others (pp. 237–38).

There is clearly a labeling and tracking system in the development of concert pianists. It may be even more critical in the development of musicians than in the development of scientists because it begins in childhood, not in college or graduate school. In some instances, advantages begin to accrue for two- and three-year-olds when parents label the child "musical."

Whether a child singing in a crib is unusual or not, parents of some of the pianists we interviewed, who thought it was, began to provide social and material resources not normally available to most two-, and three-, or four-year-olds. The parents sang to their children, played musical games with them, bought them musical toys and records, spent time helping them identify different pieces of music that they listened to together, and so forth. One father recalled this experience with his daughter before she began school: "She started to sing beautiful songs—like Christmas songs. . . . So we bought her, for Christmas, a piano. An upright, small piano" (F of P-1).

The intensity of the musical experiences the pianists had in their homes before they began lessons varied widely, as did the parents' perceptions of their child's musical sensitivity. But all the pianists had some informal musical training before going to their first "real" piano lesson. "He knew the notes and everything before he started taking lessons" (M of P-23). "Just like in preparation," one pianist reported. "She just wanted me to have a little head start" (P-15).

The early experiences the pianists had with music in their homes gave them the head start their parents hoped for. Most of them began lessons with an interest in, and ease with the piano, a belief that learning more might be fun, and a little more knowledge and skill than many beginning students have. Teachers typically distinguish between "fast" and "slow" learners and from among the former identify their "best" pupils. The pianists we interviewed were so identified rather quickly. As select students they were given extra teacher time and attention, special encouragement, carefully selected material, and choice spots in recital programs. Small wonder, under these circumstances, that the pianists were motivated to play.

At least when it came to performing musically, the pianists developed enormous self-confidence. This was visible in the way they walked out on stage and performed in early recitals. Recitals are risky ventures for performers of all ages. But these pianists, who had been playing for their family and family friends from the first, met the challenge with aplomb. Their ability to do so added to their stock of advantages in two ways. First, the pianists received additional social validation of their position as good young musicians. Second, these experiences extended the pianists' visibility in the local music community.

We also find substantial pedagogical advantages during the pianists' early years of learning. In effect, the pianists were doubly instructed because of the congruence between their parents' and their teachers' values and behaviors. Although lessons were only once a week, the six days between each lesson were spent practicing under supervision. Parents and teachers rewarded the same behaviors. Each appreciated and advanced the work of the other, even though the teachers were sometimes unaware of the help they were getting from the parents.

During their early years of piano lessons and recitals the children were recognized as being talented and were so informed. Figuratively, and sometimes quite literally, they moved to the head of the class. The flow of resources important for musical development, from parents and teachers, grew stronger. We speculate that the combination of the naturalness with which the child was exposed to music and the feelings of specialness the child derived from playing the piano gave the pianists a decided advantage over their agemates almost from the start.

Parents became more convinced of their child's potential

with each recital or comment from a teacher or neighbor. Teachers joined in "recognizing" the student. A concerted effort was made to find a better teacher for the child, one who was more musically knowledgeable, a recognized expert in his or her part of the country and well connected in the local music community.

These new teachers set high standards, were very disciplined, and demanded precision and attention to details from the students.

> I would bring the same piece nine, ten, eleven, twelve weeks in a row sometimes. [Lessons were] very intense. Very, very detailed. Lots of technical things (P-25).

> I remember one time she said, "You've got to practice two hours a day." I thought, my goodness, that was just a lot. But I remember doing two hours a day (P-23).

By setting high standards, insisting they be met, and showing the students how to do so, these teachers offered instructional opportunities that would be of great advantage in years to come.

The teachers also made sure that the pianists had many experiences outside of weekly lessons that made music making a real and vital part of their lives. The pianists were introduced to competitions, adjudications, and other events that were challenging, rewarding, and stimulating for further learning. Working with the best teachers in their part of the country and taking part in public events frequently helped the pianists develop a name for themselves.

As they became better known in the music community, opportunities and rewards came more easily. Getting their name in the local newspaper as a participant in a regional competition, for example, might lead to an invitation to play for a local social club. Of course each chance to perform in public helped the pianist do better in competitions.

By the time the pianists reached their teens, so many opportunities for successful learning had been presented and taken advantage of that it would have been extremely difficult for a less-advantaged child—a late beginner or a student with less family and teacher interest and support, for instance—to break into the system and catch up. Furthermore, so many opportunities had been taken advantage of that it would have been extremely difficult for the pianists to stop studying music and begin working at something else.

The pianists were well aware of their skill as musicians and their relative lack of skill at doing anything else. This made it difficult for them to find any activity as rewarding as music. They could already do something well. Though they may not have appreciated how long it took them to get where they were, the pianists gradually began to feel as if there wasn't anything else they could do, even if they wanted to, or at least not nearly as well as they played the piano.

The pianists and their parents made so many sacrifices in favor of music making that both psychologically and practically they closed doors behind them. Typically, they treated music more seriously than they did their schoolwork. The youngsters missed opportunities for developing in other areas—such as science or athletics. Of course all of this did not occur overnight. Changes such as those described developed slowly, building one upon another, over a period of more than a dozen years.

By the time the pianists reached high school, most had developed personal identities as musicians. Over a period of years they had been labeled and given special treatment for their musical abilities—first from their families, then from their classmates, and ultimately from their communities. After a while it became impossible for the pianists to separate what they did at the piano from who they were. They thought of themselves as belonging to a special group of people—musicians. The more experience they had with other musicians, at special summer programs, for example, or at competitions, the firmer this identity became. As one father noted, by the end of high school his son "had won lots of competitions, and everyone thought that there was no other field for [him] other than music" (F of P-22).

The most critical step in the transition from being a talented teenage pianist to becoming a professional performing soloist seems to be that of moving to a master teacher (see chapter 2). The pianists were able to work with these teachers because of the advantages they had accumulated in the process of learning. They were in the right positions to be noticed by the master teachers—at summer programs or at competitions—or to be recommended to the teachers by the network of people who channel the "best" pupils to the "best" teachers.

It is important to know the right people, schools, and events in order to succeed in the music world. But our interviews revealed that an individual or a family doesn't have to be born knowing the right people or places. We found that if they started early enough, worked hard enough, and cared enough, they could and did learn to master the system.

Advantages were not easily gained. They were acquired in exchange for a lot of hard work. Someone had to be willing to act at every opportunity, to be persistent, and to make sacrifices. In the early years most of the action was taken by the parents. Later, teachers and the pianists themselves became more involved in creating and building the advantages that helped the students maintain their commitment.

Music making seems to have become almost a religion for some of the pianists.

> I just remember being aware of . . . this sense of mission as it were
> . . . some role that I would play, important, significant role in musical terms. That *I* would have something special to say with specific works (P-5).

They report experiences that "I think I blew [it] . . . up in my head and I said this is a sign" (P-8). It became necessary "to get the music the way you want it to sound. And while you've heard other people play it, better than you can play it, still they never did exactly what you wanted" (P-2).

One pianist explained why some built a mystique around music making:

> I think there's a tremendous force. The psychological effect that operates when you've done something for so long. You feel that it must have incredible value to you simply by virtue of spending so much time. . . . It would take, I think, a trauma to break that and have something else take precedence (P-10).

But whether or not there were religious undertones to the pianists' commitment, all realized their attachment to music making—if not by the end of high school, certainly in the two or three years that followed.

> There was nothing to take equal interest with music, which I had been doing so much longer than anything else (P-10).

> It's the easiest way I know to make a living. It's what I know how to do. It's what I've been trained for. I don't know how to do anything else as well (P-24).

INTERPERSONAL INFLUENCES

There is yet another way of understanding how the pianists were able to maintain the lengthy commitment to learning as they did. One theme, repeated by pianist after pianist, has to do with the emotional support and inspiration they received from other people while they were learning to be musicians.

In the conduct of this study we assumed from the start that learning is typically an interpersonal activity, not something done in isolation. Families, teachers, peers, and others play a critical role in what an individual learns, how well he or she learns it, and how long he or she continues the learning process. Thus, the interviews were designed to uncover who the pianists worked with, how they worked with these people, and what parents, teachers, and others did in the service of the pianists' development. We did not anticipate, however, just how important the emotional contributions of all these people would come to be viewed.

As has been well acknowledged by now, it was often the pianists' emotional responses to their first teachers—"[She] did make me feel appreciated and loved" (P-28)—that helped them get involved with the work they would eventually make their livelihoods. What has been passed over too quickly, perhaps, is that it was similar bonds with subsequent teachers that helped the pianists maintain and expand their commitment to learning the art and science of music making. Some examples will help to make this point concrete.

One pianist (P-20) "started making a lot of progress" when, at the age of twelve, having studied piano lackadaisically for seven years, his parents found a fourth teacher for him. "I realized that this woman was very sincere. She was not someone to just take my money. She was very, very interested in seeing me develop. The woman was a very dedicated teacher. She would keep me for two or three hours a lesson when she was just paid for one. She worked so hard with me that she was sweating when she worked."

The teacher died less than two years after he began working with her, but she continued to be an important force in his music making for many years to follow. It wasn't until college that he found another teacher he could admire as much. This teacher, too, "made me want to do well, so I started to practice." The pianist reports that as he increased his daily practice time, "of course I started making progress." Then, "I saw he was responding, so I started practicing four hours a day, then five hours a day, then six . . ."

The pianist just described was far from an isolated example, although the story of his development was among the more dramatic. Another pianist explained,

> I've always had ambitions. Before I hooked into the piano, it was mathematics. For a short period of time it was being an explorer.

I mean, when I decided I want to be an explorer, I wanted to be a world-famous explorer. Then it was tennis when I was ten. . . . And I really worked and practiced hard. . . . It wasn't until I was thirteen that I really decided it was music I wanted to do. And that could have been a temporary thing also except at the same time I latched on to a really fine teacher in another town. An inspirational guy (P-7).

His ambitious energy was unfocused until he found a teacher whose presence was so powerful that the issue was decided once and for all. This pianist added, "I knew he really believed in me. . . . I was somebody really special with [him]."

Still another pianist explained the great increase in the time he spent practicing this way: "Because I liked my teacher . . ." (P-8). Yet another told how he decided to choose among the several master teachers for whom he had auditioned. It was, in part, because "I also felt the great interest on his part in my own talent" (P-4). Over and over the pianists made reference to the impact of teachers for whom they felt love, admiration, and respect, and from whom they felt dedication to music making and to their students' development. Several said they felt they were "going nowhere" when they worked with teachers who lacked such qualities.

Teachers alone would not have been able to provide all of the emotional sustenance the pianists needed to continue at their work year after year. Fortunately, the pianists' parents and a number of other people—schoolteachers, family friends, and established musicians—provided similar support. Always there was someone who listened and got involved, thus helping the pianist maintain the persistence necessary for his or her development. The parents and teachers especially seem to have created, with the pianists themselves, an interdependent and self-sustaining system of mutual encouragement and support.

The pianists' parents made it clear to their children that, as one put it, "They believed in the value of what you were doing, and always had the money to support [anything related to music]" (P-10). "We just had to sacrifice, that's all," a parent reports, "because we wanted him to have another piano. He was progressing and doing very well" (M of P-23). "I think they were so supportive and so behind me, without pushing me into it" (P-15).

> They were openly encouraging. . . no question about that. They were vitally interested in what I was doing. And encouraging. And listened. But I don't remember any sense of a stick being held over my head. Anything like that (P-5).

One of several pianists who had patrons[2] for a portion of his student years reported that people who helped him "just liked me and they felt that I had potential, and they wanted to help me" (P-29). That same pianist succinctly expressed what almost everyone said, each in his or her own way: "There was always a person somewhere who took an interest in me and helped me get from one point to another" (P-29).

One pianist summarized it this way: "I got the feeling from others that it was worth trying" (P-23). The perceptions that they were capable, that they could become outstanding musicians, and that such a goal was worth working for, pervaded the pianists' histories.

John Gardner (1961) writes,

> Excellence is not an achievement of demoralized or hopeless individuals. I am not suggesting that those who achieve excellence are more cheerful or optimistic or carefree. They may be suffering. They may have moments of despair. They may lack self-assurance in many dimensions of their lives. But deep within them they have a hard core of conviction and self-trust that makes their achievement possible (p. 104).

---

[2]These were persons who paid for lessons and travel expenses for competitions or who arranged special performances for the student.

The pianists were not born with such conviction and self-trust, but they do seem to have developed both. They did so in the context of supportive and encouraging adults who often had confidence in them before they had confidence in themselves.

BUILDING AND REBUILDING A COMMITMENT

The pianists' motives and their commitments changed over time, and were forced to do so for at least three reasons. First, age influenced what they could do with their time, what motivated them, and how some things motivated them. Gold stars and candy bars, for example, were appropriate for the young children, but would have been scorned by the adolescent and thought meaningless by adults. World fame appealed to the imagination of teenagers and older students, but hardly ever occurred to the young student for whom praise from family and friends was quite sufficient. Also, as the pianists grew older and moved into worlds beyond the family and even the community, options and choices about what to do with their time became much more complicated.

Second, as instruction changed and demands on the learners increased, the nature of the activity changed. They had to recommit themselves again and again to a new activity. Each new commitment went beyond the one before because the amount of time and effort involved made it impossible to do other things. What kept the six-year-old at a piano for forty-five minutes a day was hardly the same as what kept the same student at the piano for two or three hours a day at the age of thirteen. Neither explanation is adequate for understanding why the eighteen-year-old worked six or more hours a day at music making. Even the satisfaction of playing a piece of music from beginning to end differed for the six-year-old, the sixteen-year-old, and the twenty-six-year-old. What constituted doing something well was also different for each.

Third, the time spent doing something, the experiences the learners had over time, and the expertise they developed altered their motives and how they reacted to subsequent experiences. Maintaining a commitment was different from developing one to begin with. Building an increasingly more intense commitment was different still and was a function of an accumulating history of experiences.

Most of the pianists reported that they did not think they were "born to be a pianist" (P-7). They told humorous stories about how musically unsophisticated and unappreciative they were for many years.

> I remember hearing Horowitz . . . when I was about nine. I remember nothing about the performance except that he played "The Stars and Stripes Forever" (P-5).

With a few exceptions, the pianists' parents did not push their children into musical careers. In fact, it typically took the parents years to realize that their youngsters were headed in that direction.

> I just thought this is a nice thing for someone, to have music as well as other things, so I know I never planned this or pushed for it. Never in my wildest dreams did I think he'd be a concert pianist. . . . I thought he'd be something like a physicist or an engineer (M of P-15).

> Now that I think back, I think I would have started him with a better teacher—at a conservatory—if I had known he was going to become [a concert pianist]. . . . At that time, I didn't think it was important (F of P-22).

A pianist reports,

> I came from a kind of family background that was not very intellectual. We sort of did things with common sense, and if it worked, it did, and if it didn't, we tried to find another solution. You made a plan, but it wasn't a grand plan with a great deal of forethought for the next ten years like you were an administrator. You just sort of did it, and if you didn't do so well, then you talked about how you could alter it. So that's the way it was for a long time (P-23).

The mother of another pianist reported, "I don't think I did too much planning. I operate on instinct, on what's good at the moment" (M of P-29).

But the pianists were born into homes where music and music making were valued. They were also born into what might be called child-centered homes: homes where children were special; homes where trying to do the best for one's child was a matter of daily practice, not just ideology; homes where no sacrifice was too great for a child's potential success.

The pianists were also fortunate to work with teachers who went out of their way to try to help the student succeed. With only two exceptions, all of the pianists worked with at least one teacher who saw that pianist as more than just another student, as a very special student indeed. These teachers worked aggressively to provide the pianist with whatever opportunities were necessary to move the student ahead to the limits of his or her potential.

The pianists became immersed in an activity that was supported by family, friends, and teachers. They thrilled in feeling competent and special. They lived in an atmosphere where there was unlimited belief in their potential and almost unlimited resources to make that belief a reality. They got caught up in the process of learning, and they learned very well indeed.

CONCLUSIONS

Merely spending hour after hour at an activity for many years will not ensure successful learning. Time invested in learning must be well spent, of course. But there are no shortcuts to excellence.

A central problem in the development of any kind of excellence, then, is the problem of keeping a student at an activity for the many years necessary to learn unusually well. Although our interviews with successful learners did not uncover specific ways to solve this problem, they did reveal recurrent themes that helped account for the lengthy commitments of the individuals who are now so accomplished. We have presented these themes with examples from only the concert pianists' experiences, but they are just as prominent, with appropriate variations, in the histories of the five other groups of people studied.

The individuals were introduced to the area in which they would subsequently excel as a matter of course. Activity of that sort was ongoing or valued in their environment. The natural way of life in the home often encouraged interest in the area. Certainly any interest the child did show was well rewarded.

The youngsters realized soon enough that the talent activity was something special in their home. Toying with it earned them a little more attention than almost anything else they tried. Over a period of time they also learned that pursuing the field was their chance to be special—different from and somehow better than other children their age or in their families. The sense of being special was a stimulus for work throughout the individuals' development, but especially so in the early years of learning, when many other reasons had not yet come to the fore.

At first there was not a lot of work involved in staying with the activity. Even when formal instruction began relatively soon after the child's introduction to the field (in piano, swimming, and tennis), the playful aspects of the activity were emphasized for quite some time. As the demands on the students increased, so did their reasons for persevering. Foremost among these, the individuals began to realize that they were developing considerable skill. The activity, then, was their avenue for demonstrating their competence; it was their way of fitting into and having an effect on their environment. (This was only possible, of course, because the activity was valued by people who mattered to the students.)

The fact that the talent area became an integral part of the youngsters' lives throughout their years of learning may well be critical for reaching unusually high levels of accomplishment. There are both obvious and subtle ways in which this helped the students develop and maintain their long-term commitment. One set of these has to do with the parents' involvement in the activity and in the child's learning.

Initially, the parents made the talent field accessible and desirable to their children, provided the structure for the early learning, and helped the children develop the habit of emphasizing one kind of activity over others—all because they themselves valued the activity. The early and easy access the children then had to the talent field allowed the children to develop skills that may be prerequisites to the kinds of learning at which they would excel, skills that are typically overlooked in early formal instruction. (For example, for the artists, developing one's "ear" or "eye"; for the athletes, learning to use one's body comfortably; for the mathematicians and neurologists, making logical connections between the observable and the abstract, and then between different ideas.) Certainly the individuals gained a head start over other children whose parents knew less or cared less about the activity.

Furthermore, because the activity was valued by the parents, the children were typically doubly instructed (at least during the early years of learning). In addition to their formal instruction, they were taught skills and attitudes at home, informally, often without conscious awareness of the teaching on the part of the parent-teacher or the child. Most important, it seems, the parents were willing to make the necessary changes in *their* lives in response to their child's development and to promote further growth. The parents' substantial involvement in the child's learning helped the student to accumulate considerable advantages in the process of learning over others of the same age who did not have similar support.

There are other notable consequences of the mesh between the learning and the learners' lives. Although successful learning involves considerable solitary work, the individuals we interviewed had access to public arenas where they could demonstrate their skills, test themselves, derive rewards for their past efforts, and find reason for further work. Also, the students had adult models for the activity, exemplars they could use not only for inspiration but also for clues about what had to be learned next.

The very accomplished individuals we talked with do not credit their achievements to any single force. Instead, their reports reveal a combination of motives for their work. Creating and maintaining a long-term commitment to learning means simultaneously developing a day-after-day perseverance and an appreciation for the year-by-year context for each day's work. It involves both a narrowness of attention and a very broad vision. Although educators know a good deal about keeping students at a task for a short period of time, the same methods are not likely to be as useful for helping students develop the extended kind of commitment that successful learning involves. At the very least, it seems difficult to conceive of creating and maintaining such a commitment unless the learning is a vital and valued part of the students' lives.

REFERENCES

Cole, J. R., and Cole, S. *Social Stratification in Science.* Chicago: University of Chicago Press, 1973.
Gardner, John W. *Excellence.* New York: Harper and Row, Publishers, 1961.
Gesell, A., and Ilg, E. L. *The Child from Five to Ten.* New York: Harper and Brothers, 1946.
Leichter, Hope J., ed. *The Family as Educator.* New York: Teachers College Press, 1974.
Merton, Robert K. "The Matthew Effect in Science." *Science* 5 (1968): 56–63.
Spock, Benjamin. *Baby and Child Care.* New York: Simon and Schuster, 1976.
White, Robert W. "Motivation Reconsidered: The Concept of Competence." *Psychological Review* 66 (1959): 297–33.
———. "Competence and the Psychosexual Stages of Development." In *Nebraska Symposium on Motivation*, edited by M. R. Jones, vol. 8, 1960.
Zuckerman, Harriet. *Scientific Elite: Nobel Laureates in the United States.* New York: The Free Press, 1977.

14

★ ★ ★ ★ ★ ★

Generalizations About Talent Development

Benjamin S. Bloom

hroughout this book the major emphasis has been on the development of individuals within a particular talent field. In each of these talent fields we selected approximately two dozen individuals who had reached particular criteria of excellence in the talent field before the age of forty. We interviewed the majority of these individuals, their parents, and in some cases their outstanding teachers.

In chapters 2 through 10 we described particular aspects of the development within each talent field. We pointed to common features of this development as well as to some of the differences within each group. In three of these chapters (chapters 3, 6, and 9) we described single cases. Our special concern has been to represent as accurately as possible the major features of the development of talent *within* each talent field. We checked each other to be certain that the descriptive material was representative of the interviews with the individuals, their parents, and in some instances their teachers. There is no doubt that to some extent each of the talented individuals had unique experiences. However, with the exception of the three case studies, our major concern in the other chapters was to find both the common features and the exceptions in the development of talent within each field.

In chapters 11 through 13 we have concerned ourselves with the attempt to find common features within particular talent areas *music and art, swimming and tennis,* and *mathematics and science* as well as common features across the entire range of talent fields. There we have sought to find generalizations about talent development that transcend the individuals we interviewed as well as the talent fields we studied. The accuracy of these general characteristics, processes, and generalizations will be determined by the extent to which they are eventually supported by further studies of these and other talent fields. We hope the readers of this book will read chapters 11 through 14 as a series of perspectives on and generalizations about the talent development process.

In this final chapter, common features of the teaching and learning conditions for the development of talent are described and some additional generalizations are suggested. Some of these ideas about the process of talent development may be summarized briefly in the following statements. These ideas are developed in greater detail in this chapter as well as in chapters 11, 12, and 13.

• Talent development is initially viewed by the young child as play and recreational. This is followed by a long sequence of learning activities that involve high standards, much time, and a great deal of hard work. Finally, there are special learning experiences that strengthen dedication to an activity that eventually becomes a combination of work and play—an avocation, a calling, or a lifelong career. (See also chapter 11.)

• The home environment developed the work ethic and the importance of the individual's doing one's best at all times. This was initially applied to most activities in the home and the school. Later, this value was most directly related to learning and participation in the chosen talent field. (See also chapter 12.)

• Each group of parents strongly encouraged their children's development in a particularly highly approved talent field and gave much less support to other possible talent fields and activities. (See also chapter 12.)

• No one reached the limits of learning in a talent field on his or her own. Families and teachers were crucial at every point along the way to excellence. The role of the home changed greatly over time, as did the qualities of the teaching and the qualifications of the teachers. What the families and the teachers do at different times and how they do it clearly sets the stage for exceptional learning in each talent field. (See also chapters 11 and 12.)

• Clear evidence of achievement and progress over more than a decade of increasingly complex and difficult types of learning was necessary to maintain commitment to a particular talent field. (See also chapter 13.)

Teaching and Learning Conditions for the Development of Talent

The individuals we studied attained very high levels of talent development after many years of study and practice. Although each individual and each talent field has many unique characteristics, in this section we will describe characteristics and processes generally present in much of the talent development reported in this book. Although we cannot prescribe the ideal conditions of teaching and learning for the development of talent, we can describe some of the positive conditions we found in the different areas of talent development. Here we attempt to point to the conditions or processes present in the three broad areas of talent development (artistic, cognitive, and athletic) we have studied. The reader interested in a particular field will find much the same conditions described in the relevant chapter on the specific talent field.

In describing the positive conditions we will concern ourselves with the role played by the talented individuals, the parents, the teachers, and others at each stage of the talent development process. For the purposes of brevity we will use illustrations from only three of the fields (swimming, piano, and mathematics), but many of the same processes also apply to the other three fields (tennis, sculpture, and neurology).

THE HOME ENVIRONMENT
AND EARLY LEARNING

The parents of the talented individuals varied greatly in the level of education they had completed, the type of work they engaged in, their economic level, and their avocational interests and activities. However, they were all genuinely concerned about their children and wanted to do the best for them at all stages of their development. To a large extent they could be described as *child-oriented* and willing to devote their time, their resources, and their energy to giving each of their children the best conditions they could provide for them. Almost no sacrifice was too great if they thought it would help their children's development.

In the majority of these homes we found that the parents placed great stress on achievement, on success, and on doing one's best at all times. These parents were *models* of the "work ethic" in that they were regarded as hard workers, they did their best in whatever they tried, they believed that work should come before play and that one should work toward distant goals. They expected their children to learn the same values. They taught these values to all their children and reminded them frequently when they strayed from these values.

The children were expected to share in household chores and responsibilities and to do them well. They were expected to do their chores and their schoolwork before going out to play. The family routines, including meals, bedtimes, family interactions, and recreation, were structured to give the children appropriate responsibilities and to help them become "self-disciplined." When a child became interested in a talent field, he or she was expected to make use of the same values as they applied to the particular field. To *excel*, to *do one's best*, to *work hard*, and to *spend one's time constructively* were emphasized over and over again.

Where the parent groups differed most was in their interest, involvement, and valuing of different areas of talent development. The parents of the athletes (tennis and swimming) were interested in athletics, they encouraged their children to do well in one or more sports, they believed their children would benefit greatly from participation in sports, and they tended to know a great deal about sports. Some of these parents had been very actively involved in sports, while others were still actively involved as participants or as observers of one or more sports fields.

In these homes, the children were encouraged to participate in sports activities at a very early age. They learned about various sports from family talk as well as from watching their parents. In some cases, the parents were members of tennis or country clubs, and the entire family was involved in the sports activities as the preferred type of recreation. Many of these children learned to swim or play tennis at an early age with or without formal instruction in the field.

In the homes of the concert pianists and sculptors, there was an emphasis on music and/or the arts. These parents enjoyed music or art, attended concerts or art exhibits, and expected their children to become interested in these fields. Some of these parents were quite expert in one of the fields, while most of them had a strong interest in one or more of the aesthetic fields.

In these homes the children became knowledgeable about music or art at an early age. They observed their parents' interest, they became involved in music or art on an informal basis, and they learned to talk about the field and to enjoy it with their parents. Most of these children acquired an early interest in these fields and accepted them as a natural activity shared by family members.

In the homes of the mathematicians and neurologists, the parents were strongly interested and involved in intellectual activity. In these homes, the parents had a strong vocational commitment to one of the learned professions or at least a strong avocational interest in some field of intellectual activity. These interests were a matter of family talks, of parental example in work or hobbies, and quite frequently they were emphasized in discussions of school learning and long-term educational planning. In most of these homes, the children were expected to do well in school, and to go on to college and professional or graduate school was believed to be the "birthright" of the children in these families.

In these homes, the parents encouraged the *curiosity* of their children at an early age and answered their questions with great care. When the questions became too complex, the parents looked into the matter before giving the child an answer. Reading was a central family activity, and the children were read to a great deal until they could read for themselves. Many of the young children in these homes were encouraged to engage in model building and to do independent science and technical projects at increasing levels of complexity.

In the early years, most of the parents found it natural to encourage their children to participate in their (the parents') favored activities. They were good teachers for the children's early starts in the field, they were patient in helping the children learn very simple skills, and they praised or applauded each child for small efforts in these fields. While none of them regarded any of their children in these early years as likely to become a great achiever in a talent field, they did encourage an interest in the talent area for all of their children.

The Early Years

As we have pointed out, the Olympic swimmers, the concert pianists, and the research mathematicians, came from families that were especially interested in sports, music, or intellectual activity, respectively. As young children they had already learned something about the field from parents, older siblings, or friends of the family. Most of the swimmers had already learned to swim before this period, many of the pianists could pick out a tune on the piano or read notes and play them in the home (usually helped to do this by a member of the family), and many of the mathematicians had already done small projects that emphasized science or related topics and had heard and participated in home discussions about intellectual activity.

A beginning regular teacher began to give the pianists lessons by an average age of six, the swimmers got their first systematic lessons in competitive swimming by an average age of eight, and the mathematicians were introduced to mathematics in junior or senior high school. Typically the initial lessons were given in swimming and piano for about an hour each week, while the mathematics was taught about four hours each week. All of the lessons included instruction on specific points and observations of the learners' performance (or work) with frequent correction. In addition some learning tasks (or homework) were assigned to be practiced and perfected before the next lesson.

THE SWIMMERS' AND PIANISTS' TEACHERS

In the case of swimming and piano the beginning teacher was typically a person chosen because of proximity to the home of the child. The initial lessons cost very little, and where facilities were used, such as a public swimming pool or the country club (to which the parents belonged), there were few or no extra costs for the lessons.

The initial teachers were largely determined by the chances of proximity and availability. Only rarely were the beginning teachers chosen for their special qualities as teachers. In most cases, these parents had relatively little teaching experience in the field and rarely understood, at this point, what criteria might be used to select an outstanding first teacher. The teachers selected were probably the best for teaching beginners in a field. Rarely were they outstanding persons in the talent field, and in no case was the first teacher as good a performer in the talent field (concert pianists or competitive swimmers) as these students eventually became.

However, in most cases the teachers (in piano and swimming) were almost perfect for the young people. They liked children and rewarded them with praise, signs of approval, or even candy when they did anything right. They were extremely encouraging. They were enthusiastic about the talent field and what they had to teach these children. In many cases, they were well known by the family and they treated the child as a friend of the family might.

Perhaps the major quality of these teachers was that they made the initial learning very pleasant and rewarding. Much of the introduction to the field was as playful activity, and the learning at the beginning of this stage was much like a game. These teachers gave much positive reinforcement and only rarely were they critical of the child. However, they did set standards and expected the child to make progress, although this was largely done with approval and praise.

These teachers were especially skillful in helping the child make progress over relatively short periods of time. They were good at finding flaws in the child's performance and helping the individual correct them. They set tasks to be accomplished each week and checked the child on his or her progress. They also found ways of praising and encouraging the child for what he or she had accomplished.

The piano teachers had relatively good relations with the parents and would commonly instruct the mother in what had to be done during the week, usually obtaining her help in monitoring the young child's practice. In the case of swimming, the coaches monitored the practice activities in the swimming pool.

THE MATHEMATICIANS' TEACHERS

The initial teachers of mathematics for these students were those assigned to particular high school (or junior high school) classes. Some of these were good teachers of initial mathematics. The most successful ones (in the eyes of our mathematicians) were the ones who helped them grasp the larger patterns and processes in the subject and who encouraged them to "discover" the underlying ideas and processes. Such teachers would allow the students to find and use alternative procedures for solving particular mathematics problems.

In some instances when the teacher was too pedantic and insisted on a standard set of procedures for solving particular problems, the students we studied had great difficulty until someone intervened to permit the young student to learn from reading mathematics textbooks on his own outside of the classroom.

MOTIVATION FOR LEARNING

Typically the initial instruction in piano was about one half hour a week. However, during the week the teacher expected the child to practice about an hour a day. Frequently, the mother, at the beginning, monitored the practice and occasionally reminded the student of points made by the teacher.

In swimming, the teaching and practice were several hours each week done at the pool under the supervision of the coach or his or her assistant. Here the practice and the perfection of strokes, breathing, and strengthening of particular muscles was done on a schedule set by the teacher, with frequent observation, monitoring, and suggestions by the teacher. Practice time was usually scheduled during hours when the pool was free for this activity, so there were frequent informal competitions among the swimmers as well as suggestions about techniques from other swimmers.

For most of the mathematicians, the joy of discovering a new way of solving a problem was more important than a high test score, receiving a good grade, or getting the teacher's approval for their work. They were able to do some of this on their own, with occasional help from a fellow student or the support of family members.

In all the fields most of these young students were regarded as fast learners by their first teachers. They came to the next lesson well prepared and typically had mastered the tasks set for them by the teachers. Whether or not they were really faster learners than others is not known, but it is clear that most of them showed good progress from lesson to lesson.

However, the attribution of "fast learner" to them by the initial teacher was one major source of motivation. The teacher soon regarded and treated them as "special" learners, and the students came to prize this very much.

The teachers typically praised them for their progress, and this was an important motivation for further practice and further progress. Many of the teachers kept records of the child's progress (especially in piano and swimming), and this typically helped prove to the children that they were progressing and that if they kept at it, they would make even more progress.

There were some local public events, such as piano recitals, swimming contests, and mathematics contests. These contests provided incentives to the young people to do intensive practice and to become as good as they could for the public event. For many of the young students in our study, winning, or even doing very well in the event was a major source of reward and praise by others.

PRACTICE ROUTINES
AND THEIR MOTIVATION

As was already pointed out, in piano the practice routine took place in the home and, at least initially, was monitored by the mother. In mathematics, the homework was done in the home, but only rarely did the young mathematicians need or seek help from parents or others. In swimming, the practice was done at the pool and was monitored by the coach or his assistant.

The amount of practice during the initial year was about an hour a day. This typically increased during the next year or two to as much as one and a half to two hours daily. The acceptance of the practice routine and its use to solve specific learning problems enabled them to become very good in particular skills, routines, or performances. The practice period became a high-priority task, taking precedence over play, television, social activities, and almost everything else.

The parents played a very important role in helping to establish the early practice and homework routines. They helped to give it high priority over other activities, they praised the child for his or her progress, and they helped make clear to the child that such continued progress was expected. When there were difficulties—and there were many examples of this—the parents insisted on the practice, helping the child set up a schedule for it and keep to this schedule. In extreme cases, they threatened to cut off the piano lessons (or sell the piano). In swimming, the threat was to drop the child from the team or cut off further lessons by the coach. In the case of the mathematicians, the somewhat older students got so much pleasure from their math or science assignments (or projects) that little parental pressure was needed to get them to do their homework.

In part the practice routine was adhered to by the child because of the rewards for progress provided by parent and teacher approval and acclaim from fellow students and the audience for good performances. Sometimes tangible rewards and prizes served this function as well.

As they began to receive recognition for the talent in the early years of instruction, the children's investment in the talent became greater. No longer was the prime motivation to please parents and teachers. It now became the individual's special field of interest. The child became more capable and outstanding in this talent field than he or she was in other areas, such as particular school subjects, other social and extracurricular activities, or other talent fields. The child was identified by others as having special qualities in the talent field and became known to himself as well as to others in terms of his involvement in that field.

SUMMARY OF THE EARLY YEARS

What we saw in this period of beginning instruction was a child who more by circumstances than personal choice began instruction in the field. The child made relatively rapid progress in a few years, in part because of an excellent teacher who made the field interesting and very rewarding and also because of parents who gave approval and helped the child to set up practice routines and to use the instruction and practice in very effective ways. Rewards and recognition by siblings, peers, and sometimes a wider public also provided motivation. There was a relatively good fit between the child's physical and personal characteristics and the talent field. This period of instruction in the early years went well; the child put in the time and effort required and increasingly became identified with the talent field.

During these early years much of the teaching and learning was playful. The child enjoyed the learning because it was so rewarding. With very little effort one could do interesting new things. There was much to discover and explore on one's own or with the aid of the teacher. In most cases, the children enjoyed these early years of learning and needed little or no prodding to take the next lesson or to demonstrate to others what he or she had mastered.

In the first period of formal instruction it is evident that motivation and effort count far more than do the particular gifts or special qualities in the child. It is the motivational support and encouragement by the home and the teachers as well as other rewards by siblings and peers that made the learning of the rudiments of the talent field so good and the devotion of the child to the practice routine and other requirements so great. Within two to five years, most of the individuals in our study began to see themselves in terms of the talent field and became less identified with alternate talents or other aspects of school and social life. They began to become "pianists" and "swimmers" before the age of eleven or twelve, and "mathematicians" before the age of sixteen or seventeen.

The Middle Years

FINDING A NEW TEACHER

Most of our talented individuals had very good experiences with their initial teacher(s), and many of them had developed a very comfortable relationship with them. However, after a number of years during which they had made relatively good progress in the talent field, someone—a parent, a friend of the family, an expert in the field, or even the teacher—thought that the child could make even greater progress if a new and more expert teacher was chosen.

At this point the parents began the search for the best teacher available in the area. While the first teacher typically lived in the neighborhood, the second teacher rarely did. During the search for the second teacher, experts and other informants were consulted to determine what expertise was necessary at this stage. A short list was compiled of the teachers who could satisfy these requirements. Frequently, the initial teacher participated in the selection process.

Typically, the second teacher had a good reputation for developing talent in the field, lived some distance from the student's home, charged much more for the lessons, and was careful in selecting the students he or she would teach. In most cases there was an audition or tryout before the student was selected. The teacher sought evidence of the student's capabilities to date, the seriousness of his or her intentions in the field, and the evidence that there was a strong interest in the talent field.

In the case of the pianists, the new teachers were regarded as being very good or even outstanding. Each was recognized as one of the best teachers in the geographical area and was highly respected in music circles. In some cases the new teacher was also recognized as a good concert pianist. In all cases the teacher expected much more from the young pianist than had the previous teacher.

In the case of the swimmers, the new teacher was usually the coach at a major swimming pool in the area and had a very good reputation for training outstanding swimmers. The swimming teams they trained were usually among the most successful in the geographical area. Here also, the teacher expected a great deal from the young swimmers—more than had been expected or demanded by previous teachers.

In the case of the mathematicians, the new teachers were usually connected with a college or university department of mathematics. In many cases, these math teachers also taught advanced or graduate courses in mathematics and after a short time encouraged the undergraduate student to enroll in their graduate courses in mathematics. Frequently, the student had been referred to them by friends or colleagues they respected.

THE TEACHING

The new teachers had a larger perspective than the previous teachers had. They usually taught only the outstanding students in the talent field and they expected some of them to reach very high levels of attainment. They were perfectionists who insisted that the student reach the highest level of capability possible for him or her. They demanded a great deal of practice time from the student and looked for much progress in a relatively short period of time.

For the pianists, the teachers emphasized such technical qualities as fingering, phrasing, and sound quality as well as a deeper sense of the music the composer intended in a particular composition. Teacher and student discussed varying interpretations of the music and the influence of the composer's attitude toward the music on the music itself. The student was expected to practice as much as two to three hours a day in order to be well prepared for the next lesson. During these years there were many recitals and other public events, which the teacher used in order to note the student's progress and identify flaws or difficulties to overcome.

For the swimmers, the new teachers emphasized precision in strokes, endurance, and the planning and execution of a particular tryout or race. The coach and the swimmer set very specific goals and worked over a period of time to achieve them. During these years, the coach used the swimming tournaments and other public events in the field to note progress as well as to determine specific aspects of the swimming that needed further work and appropriate changes in procedures and attitudes. The talented student was expected to practice as much as three to five hours a day during these middle years.

For the mathematicians, the new teachers taught classes of students and only rarely gave the talented student more attention than he or she gave to other students. The undergraduate students in our sample typically did very well even when compared with graduate students. However, there was still a great deal of independent learning on their own from books and other writing on these subjects. Sometimes the students discussed these ideas with other mathematics students. The teachers encouraged these students, discussed mathematics topics with them, or pointed to the work of an outstanding mathematician on a particular topic. At this point, the math students were putting more time into their mathematics than into other aspects of the college work they were taking.

THE PARENTS

The parents had been much involved in the talent development of their children during the early years. However, during the middle years the major role in setting expectations and demands was assumed by the new teacher. The parents helped their children set schedules and plans for the practice, but by this time they did not need to monitor the practice, since the students had already developed the appropriate habits. The parents (or other sources of funds) had to provide the extra money for the new teachers, the costs of special equipment (such as a grand piano), and the costs of participation in public events such as tournaments. In addition, since there was usually much greater distance to the new piano teacher's studio or to the swimming pool, the parents of the pianists and swimmers frequently had to put a great deal of time into chauffeuring the talented students to and from lessons and practice periods. They also made changes in family schedules, meals, and other routines as needed to accommodate the special needs of these students.

Perhaps the major point about the middle years is that most of the talented individuals became fully committed to the talent field and needed less and less emotional support from parents to maintain practice schedules and to give so much time and involvement to the talent field. They did need help in scheduling school and other activities around their great involvement in the talent field. However, much of the external motivation and direction was provided by the teachers during these middle years.

INCREASING COMMITMENT
TO THE TALENT FIELD

During the middle years most of these students became increasingly committed to the talent field. The influence of the teacher or coach during these years was very great in that they helped them set long- as well as short-term goals in the field. These teachers gave them a perspective on the field, including the meaning and purpose of the field in its largest dimension. The teachers also helped them see where they could fit into this larger view of the talent field.

During the middle years most of the students' close friends and associates were also involved in the talent field, and these peers helped them view themselves in relation to it. They were frequently aspiring to the same goals and they became friends as well as competitors for these goals.

There were many public events (recitals, contests, tournaments, team activities) in which they were involved. As the individuals in our sample gained recognition and became more successful in these public events, they increasingly developed a view of themselves as "swimmers," "pianists," and "mathematicians."

As these talented individuals moved through the middle years, they developed the long-term goals of becoming an "outstanding swimmer," a recognized "concert pianist," or a "research mathematician." Now more and more their motivation for effort in the field and their aspirations for developing particular qualities, skills, and performance in the talent field became "internal motivation." That is, although these young individuals still responded to external pressure and encouragement from teachers, peers, parents, and others, much of their motivation for effort and progress in the talent field became their own. They became their own critics of their "work in the field " and they accepted their own role as the primary motivator for their further progress.

SUMMARY OF THE MIDDLE YEARS

The emphasis in the middle years was on precision and accuracy in all aspects of the talent field. The teachers at this stage typically worked only with outstanding students in the talent field and they expected much from their students. They were businesslike in their teaching and demanding of great perfection in what the student was to do.[1]

The student was expected to put the talent field above all competing activities, and the typical student at this time put approximately twenty-five hours per week into practice and preparation for sessions with the teachers. Only individuals almost fully committed to the talent field could make the progress expected of these students.

Most of these students were highly motivated to learn in the talent field by this time and depended less on encouragement and support from the family. They received much of this motivation from the evidence of their progress and from the support of their teachers and peers in the talented field, as well as from their relative success in public events such as tournaments, contests, and recitals. Although their parents were very supportive in many ways, increasingly the talented stu-

---

[1] We speculate that if these had been their *first teachers* in the talent field, many of these talented individuals might have dropped out of the field in a few years. On the other hand, if these talented individuals had remained with the very comfortable, highly rewarding, and playful first teachers, they would not have reached the levels of talent development that were necessary by the end of this period.

dents became more responsible for their effort and progress in the talent field. And they were now working toward the highest goals in their fields.

The Later Years

FINDING A NEW TEACHER

During the middle years, the talented individuals had become relatively successful in their field under the guidance and instruction of an outstanding teacher. The success so far and their strong interest in the talent field led the talented individuals, their parents, their teachers, and other experts in the field to begin to plan for further instruction for them under a master teacher. A great deal of time and effort and many expert informants were consulted to determine which of several possible teachers (or schools) would be most appropriate for the talented individual.

It should be noted that there are only a small number of master teachers in the country in a particular talent field—perhaps about eight to ten in each field. Some of these teachers have gained a reputation for their role in developing young concert pianists. Others are known for their coaching of Olympic swimmers, while still others are noted as the teachers of remarkable research mathematicians. A great deal of information is usually available about these master teachers, their record for successful talent development of their students, and their personal characteristics—at least from the key people in each talent field.

These master teachers are very careful in selecting the advanced students with whom they will work. Gaining acceptance from them usually requires a great deal of correspondence and support from previous teachers and other experts in the field. Typically, much effort was expended by the student and others in order to get an interview, audition, or tryout with the master teacher. These meetings were planned with even greater care and preparation than the students had previously made for the major public events in which they had participated.

The master teacher's willingness to accept the individual as an advanced student conveyed the expectation that the student could go far in the talent field. However, this was conditional on the student's giving himself or herself fully to the instruction and the teacher's demands for perfection. Both students and teachers speak of this as "putting oneself in the hands of the teacher without reservation." Whatever initial expectations were communicated to the student at the beginning of the relationship, these expectations and demands were constantly raised until they were at a point where the student was expected to do virtually all that was humanly possible— and in some cases this was greater than any other human had done before. This was especially true of the Olympic swimmers, who were expected to exceed records beyond that ever previously accomplished by any human being. So, too, was it true of the mathematicians, who were expected to solve problems that had never been solved before.

THE TEACHING

The pianists were now learning from the master teachers in their field. They were trying to give meaning and purpose to their music. The role of the teacher was to find flaws in their musical performance and to help them to overcome particular difficulties. Before each meeting with the master teacher, they prepared as though for a concert before an entire audience. The master teacher listened, found flaws, and expected a major improvement at the next meeting. The pianists were also learning the history of their field and to search for their own personal style and work. The details were less important than the larger conception of the music. Here again, the talented individuals were spending almost all their time on the perfection of their style and performance.

They related to critics and teachers primarily as a means of further developing their personal style and approach to the music. Their contacts with their fellow students were also important as a way of exchanging ideas and observing how others attack related problems of style and meaning in music.

Under the teaching regime of the master teacher, the swimmers developed a set of strategies and the ability to analyze the major features of their opponents' race. They perfected the fine points of their talent field, developed great endurance and strength, and were able to analyze their own performances to determine needed changes. They devoted increased attention to studying the process (by observing as well as by analysis of motion pictures of themselves) to determine small changes that could improve their performance. Their master teachers expected almost complete commitment to the field, great investments of time in practice, and quick learning of new or changed details in the performance. Both teachers and students were working toward ways in which the talented individual could reach the highest level of competence possible and successfully compete with the top swimmers in the world.

The mathematicians worked with their master teachers, consulted with them, and observed the ways in which these master teachers do creative research in this field. Mainly they were learning research strategies and ways of finding and solving problems that are in some respects different from those that have ever been solved before. They became committed to the talent field in terms of the amount of time they devoted to the field and their almost complete identification with it. They were also learning much from their contacts with their outstanding fellow students in the field and from the written work of the greats in the field. Much of their learning was from their research—it was learning by doing what research mathematicians do. Their aspirations were now to do what no one had been able to do before.

MOTIVATION

During the later years, the students increasingly became responsible for their own motivation. With the master teachers they set goals for themselves and noted their progress toward these goals. They participated in public events—recitals, contests, and seminars—and compared themselves with their fellow students. They took on projects or tasks and, with the master teachers, determined their success in accomplishing what they had set out to do.

The students' performances in these semipublic or public events were analyzed by the master teachers as well as by the students in order to perfect particular aspects of the performance. These events were very effective as a basis for bringing the student emotionally as well as technically to the highest level possible at the time. The student was motivated to prepare as well as possible for these events, and these competitions or performances became ways of heightening the preparation and securing the best effort possible.

These public events also brought the students into contact with some of their outstanding peers in the field as well as with the top people in the field. Each student studied these models and determined what he or she must still do to reach the highest level of attainment possible.

SUMMARY OF THE LATER YEARS

The emphasis in the later years was on the perfecting of the talent to the highest level, on the development of the individual's personal style, and on the larger purpose and meaning of the talent. The master teacher was important in helping the individual find his or her own way of expressing the talent.

During these years almost all of the individual's time was spent in the talent field, much of it in preparation for each new session with the master teacher. In these sessions, the master teacher searched for small changes in the performance and ways in which the individual could express his or her own interests and style.

Much learning took place in the relationships and comparisons with the other advanced students who were studying with the master teacher. These relationships were both competitive and instructive in seeing how others attacked related problems.

During these years the student was completely committed

to the talent field. Now most of the motivation was internal and related to the larger goals and purposes of the student in the talent field. The public events such as concerts, recitals, contests, and seminars were important as evidence of progress and achievement in the talent field.

Chance and Purpose in the Talent Development Process

There were some chance elements in the talent development process. These include securing positive initial learning experiences in a talent field, the support of a patron or sponsor when essential, and especially the extent to which an individual's physical, intellectual, and personal characteristics were matched with qualities that were of special value in a given talent field. Quite frequently there was a trial-and-error process in which, for example, the child entered a number of different sports before finding the one he or she liked most or where success was most assured. Many of the mathematicians and neurologists had explored other academic fields before they settled on these fields. Most of the sculptors made drawings and paintings before they specialized in sculpture. Similarly, a few of the pianists had tried other musical instruments before they found the piano to be most satisfactory.

As we have seen throughout this book, the values and behaviors of the parents had a large deterministic effect on whether the children were encouraged in sports, music, the arts, or intellectual activities. However, the specific talent field finally chosen had to do with the availability of particular facilities such as swimming pools or tennis courts, the availability of particular musical instruments or art materials, and the ease with which the child could secure the necessary materials, teachers, and support from parents. Frequently a child became involved because an additional swimmer or tennis player was needed for some event, because a teacher of piano was available at little cost, because there was an unusually able schoolteacher who interested students in a particular science or mathematics course, or because siblings or friends had already entered the particular talent field. The talent *area* was much encouraged by the parents, while the specific talent *field* chosen was frequently dependent on particular chance events at the time.

Only rarely were the parents very knowledgeable about how to get the child started in a talent field or how to find a good first teacher. Typically, first teachers were chosen because they lived close to the child's home, because they were available (in swimming or tennis) in the public parks or country clubs, or because they were the teachers assigned to the children in the neighborhood schools. Sometimes the first instruction was provided by a parent, a friend, or a relative in a very informal way.

However, once the instruction had started, we find (in our successful samples of talent development) that chance events played only a minor role, while purposive responses to situations played a very large role in the talent development process.

Although most of the parents knew little about what was required in the introduction to the talent field, they did watch to see that their child was getting involved in the learning. They carefully monitored the child's progress and came to know when things were going well or poorly. When things were going badly, they looked into the matter and reassured the child, got special help when this was possible, or sought a replacement teacher when they were convinced that this was needed. The parents followed the child's progress and did much to ensure that the child developed good practice habits, that the child arranged his or her schedule so that the training and practice were given high priority over other activities, and that the child was much encouraged in these early years for his or her efforts in the talent field.

The first learning emphasized simple tasks and short-range goals with which the children could be very successful. There was also an emphasis on initial learning that could be enjoyable for the child. As the child succeeded in the simple tasks, the complexity of the tasks was increased, and the child was helped to reach for longer range goals. There were public events such as recitals, contests, and art showings in which the child could get a sense of success as well as demonstrate to the parents, teachers, and others that he or she was making progress in the talent field. Gradually there were more important public events as the child made further progress. Where teachers were involved in these first learning steps, there was excellent communication between these teachers and the parents. The learning with the teacher was supported and encouraged by the home in a variety of ways. Also, problems and difficulties perceived by the parents were taken into consideration by the teachers and "solved" before they became too big or too emotional.

As the individual progressed in the talent field, it seemed to the parents and to others that the child had gone as far as possible under the present conditions and that a new and different set of experiences, teachers, or situations were now needed. Where a new teacher was needed, the parents sought advice from previous teachers and from other informants as to the best possible teachers for this stage of learning. The process of bridging the transition to the new teacher was effectively negotiated by the parents, who by now had learned much more about the process of talent development than they knew at an earlier point.

The new teacher was typically an outstanding teacher in a large geographical area, and the parents had to provide for larger financial costs, better instruments or equipment, and transportation to and from the teacher. Since the new teacher placed greater demands on the child in terms of higher standards, more rapid learning, and increased practice time, the parents were especially needed to help the child meet a difficult schedule of talent development as well as maintain school and other responsibilities.

During these middle years of talent development the child

was expected to participate in many public events such as recitals, contests, or showings, which made heavy demands on
being well prepared. Here, both parents and the teachers were
extremely supportive of the student in terms of encouragement, planning for the events, as well as seeing to it that the
child was well prepared both technically and psychologically
for these difficult events. When there were letdowns after such
events, especially when the child did not do as well as expected, both teachers and parents did much to provide emotional support to help the individual take it in stride.

During the middle years, the talented individual became increasingly independent and participated to a greater extent in
making decisions and planning next steps in the talent development process. Although the parents were still important in
providing emotional and financial support, the talent development process became much more technical and complex
such that few parents could keep up with the learning requirements of the field. More and more it was the teacher and the
student who had to make these decisions, with the support of
informants who were well versed in the talent field.

When it came time for the talented person to move to a master teacher or a finishing school program, there was a great
deal of time invested in deciding which of several possible
teachers (or schools) were appropriate. The student was
largely responsible for choosing the final teacher with the aid
of informants such as previous teachers, experts in the field,
other students, and sponsors. While the parents played a supportive role here, it was largely to help the student make the
emotional commitment to stay in the talent field.

The final teachers were very careful in selecting the advanced students with whom they would work. Gaining acceptance from these teachers required a great deal of support
from the previous teacher(s) and from other experts in the
field. Typically there was much effort expended by the student
and others to get an interview or audition with the master
teacher and to demonstrate one's capabilities for the next
level of learning. These meetings were planned with even

greater care than the previous recitals, contests, and other major public events.

Once the students had been accepted by the master teacher, the parents' primary role was to help provide the financial resources needed. The student was now under the tutelage and support of the teacher. While other students frequently provided both competition and emotional support, it was largely the student and the teacher who determined the next steps in the learning process. In addition, these final teachers were important in helping the students make the contacts and arrangements to enter the talent field as a professional, scholar, or researcher.

At each stage, the parents strove to improve the situation and to secure the best of learning and developmental conditions for the next stage in the talent development process. However, few of the parents knew enough about the long-term process of talent development to provide a master plan for the different learning stages. Even some of the first teachers rarely knew enough to make such a plan. For most of the talented individuals, the planning in the early years was on a short-term basis. As additional teachers, special experiences, and resources were required, other informants, teachers, and experts were consulted until the transition was completed. When this went beyond the competence and resources of the parents, other experts and resources played a larger role. Gradually it was the talented individual (with the aid of teachers, peers, and other informants) who played an increasing role in making major decisions.

There must be many errors in the talent development process, and this must be especially so in the transition from one stage to the next. While one gets a glimpse of some of these errors, even in our talent sample, it is evident that the errors were corrected quickly for the individuals we studied. Chance and error may help explain why so few individuals who start in a particular talent field stay in that talent field over the many years required for its full development. Without the purposeful step-by-step talent development process, it is unlikely that even the individuals we studied would have reached the high levels of talent development reported in this study.

A Longitudinal Perspective

Although our sample of one hundred twenty talented individuals includes the outstanding achievers in each of the six fields, only a few of these individuals were regarded as child prodigies by teachers, parents, or experts. Even those few who were regarded as unusual at an early age were not perceived to be able to do things in their talent fields that would compare with mature talented persons in these fields (or to be able to accomplish what they would many years later). Two of the pianists had won *child competitions,* which gave them the opportunity to play with a major symphony orchestra by the age of ten. One of the swimmers was a national champion in his *age group* by the age of eleven—after only two years of intensive training in the field. One of the mathematicians was enrolled in advanced college mathematics courses by the age of thirteen. While these were remarkable early developments, none of these had reached mature stages of development in their field by the age of eleven or twelve.

Although we cannot be certain of this, we believe that only a small percentage (10% or less) of these talented individuals had progressed far enough by age eleven or twelve for anyone to make confident predictions that these would be among the top twenty-five in the talent field by the ages of twenty to thirty. Why was it so difficult to identify these highly accomplished individuals by the beginning of adolescence? Why couldn't more of them have been predicted to reach very high levels of accomplishment ten years later? Even in retrospect, we do not believe that the perfecting of aptitude tests or other predictive instruments would enable us or other workers in the field to predict high-level potential talent at these early ages.

We believe it is so hard to predict because what the individuals have already learned by ages ten or eleven is very different from what and how they will learn at a later age. There is so much to learn and develop to reach the heights of talent development that no matter how much the individual has learned by these early years, it is only a small portion of what he or she must learn before reaching the extreme levels attained by the individuals included in this study. Being very good in one phase of the learning may not have a high relation to being very good at a later phase, even though both phases of the learning are in the same talent field. The motivation to learn in an early phase is not necessarily related to the motivation to learn in the more complex and difficult later phases. And finally, the continued support of parents, teachers, and others is necessary to help the individual move from the initial learning process to the increasingly difficult and demanding learning processes at the later stages.

Our interviews have helped us to understand some of the sharp changes in the talent development process from the age of seven or eight to ages twenty to thirty. There are changes in the substance and style of learning and instruction as well as changes in what is to be learned. In the specific chapters on the development of talent in each of the fields we have described the changes in learning and the teaching that take place in the early, middle, and later years.

THE EARLY YEARS
The early years of instruction deal with the basic kinds of learning in the psychomotor, music and art, or cognitive fields. For example, the tennis players are developing a good stroke in the early years while the swimmers are learning the basic swimming strokes. Both groups are learning to enjoy the talent field and the competition with their age-mates. In these years the young athletes lack the strength, endurance, skills, and styles of performance that they will develop in later years.

The pianists are learning to play relatively simple music while the artists are learning to draw and paint relatively simple objects and scenes. However, both are finding great interest and even enjoyment in the learning. This is especially true of the pianists who have highly rewarding and encouraging teachers. In addition, parents and others are giving much approval for their first efforts in these fields. In these early years the pianists and artists are developing technical skills and a feeling for the music or art, but they are far from the complete involvement in the process and the insights into the music or art they will develop over many years.

The mathematicians and the neurologists are learning relatively simple mathematics and science concepts and are developing some skill in learning these ideas on their own. They are becoming fascinated by the ideas and are enjoying the opportunity to make relatively simple discoveries on their own in these fields. The mathematicians, especially, are interested in their own ways of learning, with a minimum of help or interference from teachers or other adults. Here also both groups are learning some of the fundamentals of mathematical and scientific thinking, which are still far from the great insights they will later develop for attacking the new problems in these fields.

THE MIDDLE YEARS
During the middle years there are major changes in what is to be learned and how it is to be learned. The tennis players are developing great precision in the placement of the ball, overcoming particular weaknesses in their game, and acquiring great competitive skills. The swimmers are perfecting their swimming strokes to be more efficient and learning how to plan a competition so as to have the speed and stamina necessary to win against their age-mates. More and more they are getting satisfaction from competing against others rather than from the approval of their teachers or even from their parents. Their teachers at this stage are making heavy demands on these athletes in terms of practice, training, endurance, and the perfecting of particular aspects of the sport.

At this stage, the pianists are learning to play the piano with technical excellence under a teacher who makes great demands for practice and accuracy in fingering, timing, and phrasing. Here the artists are also developing greater technical excellence in their painting and sculpture with teachers who are rarely satisfied that they have done full justice to the subject or to the media being used.

Similarly, the mathematicians and the neurologists are now being introduced to mathematical and scientific concepts that are more complex and abstract. Their teachers are making greater demands on them and they are improving in their ability to learn many of these ideas on their own. In some cases, they are beginning to explore new ideas or innovative methods in these fields from their reading and from their discussions with some of their teachers. In many instances, they are learning with much older students and are becoming recognized by their teachers as being especially outstanding in their understanding of relatively complex ideas in these fields.

THE LATER YEARS

During the later years what is to be learned and how it is to be learned are again very different. The tennis players and the swimmers are developing a set of strategies and the ability to analyze the major features of their opponents' game or race. They are now perfecting the fine points of their talent field, developing greater endurance and strength, and can now analyze their own performance to determine needed changes. They are working with master teachers who expect almost complete commitment to the field, great investments of time in practice and the perfection of various aspects of their game or race, and quick learning of new or changed details in the performance. Both teachers and students are now working toward ways in which the individual can reach the highest level of competence possible in these fields and can successfully compete with its top leaders.

The pianists and sculptors are also learning from the master teachers in their field. They are trying to give meaning and purpose to their music and art. The role of the teacher is to find flaws in their music or art and to help them overcome them.

They are also learning the history of their field and to search for their own personal style and work. The details are less important than the larger conception of the music or art. Here again, the talented individuals are spending almost all their time on the perfection of their style and work and they refer to critics and teachers primarily as means of further developing their personal style and approach. Their contacts with their fellow students are important as a means of exchanging ideas and observing how others attack related problems of style and meaning.

The mathematicians and neurologists are now learning from some of the outstanding teachers in their field. They are in many instances working with these teachers, consulting with them, or observing the ways in which these teachers do creative research. Mainly they are learning research strategies and ways of finding and solving problems that are in some respects different from those that have ever been solved before. Now they are almost completely committed to the talent field in terms of the amount of time they devote to it and their almost complete identification with it. In some ways they are learning as much from their contacts with their outstanding fellow students and from the written work of the greats in the field as they are learning from their major professors. Much of their learning is from their research—it is learning by doing what neurologists and mathematicians do. They now aspire to do what nobody has been able to do before.

SUMMARY

Although we describe these changes in terms of stages—early, middle, and later years—these are only signposts along a long and continuous learning process. It typically takes these individuals ten to fifteen years to move from the relatively simple beginnings to the complex and difficult processes that characterize the later learning in each of the fields. And as long as they remain in the talent field, the learning is never complete—even when they no longer have designated teachers or coaches.

The outstanding young student of mathematics or science (or music, art, tennis, or swimming) is a far cry from becoming an outstanding mathematician, neurologist, pianist, and so forth. And being good as a young student in the field is only in a small part related to the later development. In between is a long process of development requiring enormous motivation, much support from family, the best teachers and role models possible, much time, and a singleness of purpose and dedication that is relatively rare in the United States at present.

Precociousness in a talent field is not to be dismissed, but it can only be realistically viewed as an early stage in talent development. There are many years of increasingly difficult stages of talent development before the mature and complex talent will be fully attained. No matter how precocious one is at age ten or eleven, if the individual doesn't stay with the talent development process over many years, he or she will soon be outdistanced by others who do continue. A long-term commitment to the talent field and an increasing passion for the talent development are essential if the individual is to attain the highest levels of capability in the field.

Only One Child in a Family Is Treated as Special

We remind the reader that each of the one hundred twenty talented individuals we have studied were selected for this project because they were considered to be among the top twenty-five individuals in the United States in terms of their attainments in a particular talent field. In only two families were there two children who attained this recognition in the same talent field. In about ten more families another sibling came close to the level of accomplishment demonstrated by the talented individual in this study. In general, the talented individuals in this study represent such a small and rare group that it is surprising that other siblings even came close to demonstrating similar levels of development in the same talent field.

The point of this section is that these children came to be treated as special by their families, teachers, and immediate acquaintances long before they were recognized as special by some of the experts in their particular talent field.

The majority of parents were strongly committed to the work ethic. They raised their children to believe in the importance of doing something well, to place work and duties before pleasure, to believe in the importance of hard work, and to strive for future goals. The parents were typically models of the work ethic and applied it to their own work and lives. The parents expected all their children to live by these rules and, of course, took great pride in their children who learned these lessons well. Typically, the talented individuals we studied tended to be good exemplars of the work ethic, and this was especially true in their talent field.

The parents were also to some extent involved and even committed to the talent area—sports, music and the arts, or the cognitive fields. And they especially prized any of their children who showed promise in particular talent fields related to the parents' area of special interest. They did much to encourage their children's progress in "appropriate" talent fields (with less support for other talent fields). The parents did a great deal to help the children get excellent instruction, motivate them to practice, and monitor their progress. They devoted much of their time and the family's resources to the children's learning in the talent field.

Although most of the parents did not, at the beginning, have a plan for the long and costly process of talent development, they participated in it on a daily basis and over time became more knowledgeable about this process. They learned with their children by observing each child's development and by maintaining frequent communication with the teachers. They found experts who could give them advice and they came to know other children (and their parents) who had already progressed further in the talent development. Many of the parents learned from the teachers and others what was needed at each new stage of the process and what they could do to help their own children (and especially the talented individuals we studied) to negotiate this long and difficult process of talent development.

At the beginning, the investment in terms of time and resources spent on the talent field was minimal. The first teacher was not expensive, and a child was not expected (or encouraged) to spend a great deal of time on practice. As a child demonstrated some progress and interest in the talent field, he or she was given greater attention and support from the parents. Typically, the first teacher noted the child's progress and communicated this to the parents. And if the teacher didn't note the signs of progress, the parents frequently noted it and checked their appraisal with that of the teachers or other informants. It should be pointed out that at this point the child was being compared with a few other children taking lessons from the same teacher or in the same class. Most of the comparisons were local and confined to other children who were known by the family or the teacher. At this beginning stage of the learning no one was likely to view the child as likely to become one of the outstanding persons in the talent field.

When the teacher, parents, and other informants thought the child was ready for more advanced activities in the talent field, they searched for new types of learning experiences. Typically, these included a more advanced teacher, more demanding learning situations, placement with other more advanced learners, and more complex processes, procedures, and learning materials. All of this required much more practice and learning time from the child and a greater commitment to the talent field. Especially when a new teacher was involved, there was emphasis on higher standards of performance. The child, now nearing adolescence, was expected to reduce time devoted to competing activities such as other talent fields, social activity, or other extracurricular activities in order to become more fully devoted to the particular talent field.

If other children in the family were also involved in the same talent field, the child who later became the talented individual in this study was already showing greater promise than the others. If there was sibling rivalry, the "talented" child was beginning to do better than the others. As the child received greater recognition for his or her progress, the parents devoted more of their time and attention to the "special child." More and more they dwelt on the special characteristics and attainments of this child.

The parents also devoted more of the family's material resources to the special child, and this child became very central in the family constellation. The parents expressed special pride in this child's progress and rewarded increased devotion to the talent field by excusing this child from family chores and duties (frequently required of the other children in the family) in order to increase the time spent on the talent field. They also required less of this child in school or other activities and made other allowances for the increasing demands of the talent field.

It was especially in the middle years of talent development that the child became regarded as special. As the demands of the talent field increased with regard to time, costs, and attention, the other children in the family frequently suffered in comparison and undoubtedly suffered in terms of bruised egos. The sacrifices made by the family for the special child and his or her talent needs were in part borne by the other siblings in the family. The biblical story of Joseph and his brothers seems to have parallels in talent development.

It is also true that during this stage of talent development many of the school peers and adult acquaintances of the child began to regard him or her as special. Especially was this likely to be true when the child was recognized for his or her attainments in competitions, recitals, and other public events relating to the talent field. The child came to have a reputation for being unique in the talent field and gradually became something of a local celebrity.

Even more sacrifices, especially of money, were typically required of the family as the talented person entered the final years of talent development. The costs were very great for master teachers, special programs, and special institutions in order for the young person to devote almost full time to the talent field. While frequently some of these costs were borne by scholarships and special grants, the family sacrifices tended to be quite great. During these later years of talent development, the young persons in this study were regarded as among the most outstanding students in the talent field by their teachers and by some of the experts in the field. Now they were regarded as special in the talent field not only by the family but also by a wider public.

In sum, the individuals in our study were regarded as special by the families and by some of their first teachers for their early progress. Later they gradually became special for the fulfillment of their earlier promise as they studied with subsequent teachers and as their capabilities in the talent field developed and came to the attention of experts in the field and of a wider range of people.

The process of talent development requires great time and money. The process also involves great psychological costs for the talented individual as well as for the other members of the family. During many of these years, the family life and resources revolved around the development of this one child. Few families were able to provide the psychological, time, and material support for more than one member of the family to attain the heights of talent development. Although most of these families did not foresee the great costs and sacrifices necessary for the talent development over the many years, their view of the child as special motivated them to do whatever was necessary to help the child at each step in the process.

The talented individuals included in this study have reached a remarkable level of excellence in their fields. They are clearly members of a small world-class group in these talent fields. Over many years they devoted enormous effort and time to this development. And during many of these years they made the talent field central in their lives. Such development also involved great costs and sacrifices by parents and siblings. At least from the parents' point of view such sacrifices were necessary if one of the children was to attain outstanding talent development.

Human Potential and Talent Development

We have studied only six fields of talent development. Although these are important and distinct fields, they are far from a sample of all the possible fields of talent development. It is our hope that other researchers will extend this type of research to other fields of talent development. Undoubtedly the picture of talent development and what is necessary for great talent development will change as further research increases our understanding of a wider variety of fields.

Our present findings point to the conclusion that exceptional levels of talent development require certain types of environmental support, special experiences, excellent teaching, and appropriate motivational encouragement at each stage of development. No matter what the quality of initial gifts, each of the individuals we have studied went through many years of special development under the care of attentive parents and the tutelage and supervision of a remarkable series of teachers and coaches. All the talented individuals we interviewed invested considerable practice and training time, which rivaled the time devoted to school or any other activity. And this time was in many ways more intense and rewarding than the time they put into almost anything else.

Only rarely were the individuals in our study given their initial instruction in the talent field because the parents or teachers saw in the child unusual gifts to be developed more fully. They were given the initial instruction and encouragement to learn because their parents placed very high value on one of the talent areas—music and the arts, sports, or intellectual activities. The parents wanted all of their children to have a good opportunity to learn in the talent area they preferred.

We speculate that if the talented individuals we studied had been reared in a very different home environment, it is probable that their initial instruction and encouragement to learn would have been very different. And it is not likely that they would have reached the level or type of talent development for which they were included in this study.

It was the child's small successes and interest in the early learning in a talent field that teachers and parents noted. It was these small successes that resulted in the child's increasing interest and greater commitment to the talent field, the parents' increasing encouragement and support for the child, and the search for better teachers and better learning experiences in the talent field. These early minor achievements, rather than evidence of unusual gifts and qualities, were the basis for providing the child with the further opportunities to develop in the talent field.

GENERAL QUALITIES

In each of the chapters on a particular talent field we noted some of the general as well as the specific qualities (specific to the talent field) that appear to be related to talent development in that field. The general qualities that appear to be present in all talent fields include the following:

- Strong interest and emotional commitment to a particular talent field
- Desire to reach a high level of attainment in the talent field
- Willingness to put in the great amounts of time and effort needed to reach very high levels of achievement in the talent field

These general qualities appear again and again, even though in each case they are related to a particular talent field.

In some of our cases, particular aspects of these general qualities were learned in the home in the early years before the individuals received formal instruction in a particular talent field. Subsequently, the combined efforts of parents and teachers enabled the individual to make excellent progress in the talent field. It is believed that the early development of these general qualities is related to the child-rearing practices in these homes (see chapter 12) as well as to the strong interest of the parents in the talent area.

Such qualities, for us, represent socialized qualities learned in the home, learned from teachers, and sometimes learned from peers and siblings. Theoretically, they can be learned by a high proportion of individuals if the appropriate socializing conditions are available in the home and/or the school, if they are encouraged and supported by teachers, and if there is support for them by peers and siblings. We believe they can be learned more easily if they are valued in the individual's immediate environment, and only rarely can they be learned well if parents and other significant persons in the individual's environment devalue or scorn them.

Another general quality that was noted in each of the talent fields was the *ability to learn rapidly and well*. This ability to learn rapidly and well was especially pronounced in these individuals by the middle stage of talent development. This characteristic was especially important as a basis for selection for more advanced instruction in each talent field. The master teachers or coaches looked for this quality when they screened prospective students for further development. Some of the teachers we interviewed enthusiastically described individuals who best exemplified this quality and spoke about particular instances where it was demonstrated.

This facility in learning appears to be most directly related to a particular talent field in that the individual who learns rapidly in one talent field may or may not have a similar facility in learning in other talent fields. Many of the talented individuals we interviewed expressed regret that they could not learn in other talent fields or school subjects with the same ease.

We believe this facility in learning is in part a result of the earlier learning experiences where the individual was expected to learn something to a high standard before proceeding to a more advanced task. In general, our earlier research (Bloom, 1976) has demonstrated that mastering the *prerequisite earlier learning* before proceeding to the more advanced learning has a positive effect on both the quality of the learning as well as on the rate of the learning.

SPECIFIC QUALITIES RELATED
TO PARTICULAR TALENT FIELDS

The development of an *effective tennis or swimming stroke* appeared to be an early requirement for progress in these fields. In our chapters on these fields we noted the emphasis on this in the early years by the coaches and the great amount of practice time devoted by these young athletes to the perfecting of their basic strokes in tennis and swimming. Other specific qualities, such as *physical conditioning, endurance,* and *strength,* were developed to some extent by the training programs in tennis and swimming.

In these sports, additional qualities such as *motor coordination, speed of reflexes,* and *hand-eye coordination* were regarded as important by the coaches. Some of these qualities are likely to be inborn. However, we believe these may, in part, have been developed to some extent in the early years. These qualities may be especially difficult to develop after certain ages.

Sensitivity to sound and *good pitch discrimination* were regarded as valuable assets in the early learning of music. Some of the pianists had these qualities to a high degree at a very early age, while in other cases these were learned to some extent at a later age under appropriate conditions in the home or from excellent teachers.

Sensitivity to form, line, color, and texture were regarded as special assets in art. These were especially emphasized and learned to some degree in the middle and later learning experiences of the artists.

In the two cognitive fields we studied, mathematics and neurology, Ph.D. degrees were required for entrance into the special field. The level of *academic aptitude* (as well as prior *academic achievement*) required to satisfy the entrance requirements for the Ph.D. is usually high, and it is likely that many of the talented individuals in our study were unusually high. Whether these academic aptitudes and abilities were largely inborn or learned to some extent in the home and school is not clear.

DIFFERENT QUALITIES NECESSARY FOR DIFFERENT TALENT FIELDS

As we review the different fields of talent development we have studied, we are impressed with the fact that the specific qualities that appear to be necessary for talent development in music and art are very different from those that appear to be necessary for talent development in swimming and tennis. Also, the specific qualities that appear to be necessary for talent development in mathematics and neurology are very different from those that are essential in the other talent fields. Some of these qualities may be inborn, while others, as we have pointed out, may be qualities developed over a number of years by the parents and teachers.

We have also noted throughout the book (and especially in chapter 12) that the values of parents, their interests and activities, and their methods of child rearing differ greatly from field to field. Although there are common threads in these child-rearing patterns for the two sports fields, these differ in some respects from those found in the homes of the mathematicians and neurologists, and these were different in other respects in the homes of the pianists and sculptors.

Thus, we find specific qualities in the individual as well as particular child-rearing practices and teaching practices in the different talent areas: sports, the aesthetic fields, and the intellectual or cognitive fields. What works well and appears to be necessary in one set of talent fields seems not to be essential in another set of talent fields.

We have only studied six talent fields. We conceive of the possibility that there could be as many as several hundred fields in which talent could be developed. For example, if we limited our sports fields to the Olympic sports events, there would be more than two hundred different sports events. In each of these Olympic sports, there are likely to be different qualities of body build, strength, types of coordination, specific skills, endurance, and so on that are necessary for an individual to have or to develop if he or she is to qualify for the Olympic team.

Similarly, there may be many types of intellectual qualities necessary to excel in the many different academic and professional fields. Also in the arts, music, and literary fields many different types of interests, skills, and special qualities need to be present or developed. All of this is to suggest that there are many fields of talent development that are so distinct that an individual who possesses the particular qualities (inborn or learned) that enable him or her to excel in one field may even be at a great disadvantage in another field.

The characteristics required for a broad range of talent fields in modern society are such that a large proportion of individuals could learn well in one or more talent fields—if the conditions for their development are available in the homes, the schools, and other learning opportunities. This is not to say that each one could reach the extreme level of talent development (the best two dozen in the nation in each field) that was the criterion for each field we studied.

What is likely in most societies is that human potential for talent development is very great, probably much greater than any single society can support. For example, few societies could provide financial support for ten thousand outstanding concert pianists or an equal number of tennis stars or research mathematicians.

In the chapters of this book we have described the conditions and the process of talent development over a decade or more for each of six talent fields. In this study, we have concentrated on the individuals who attained the highest levels of talent development in each field. It is likely that lesser levels of talent development can be and are attained with fewer years of commitment and with support and instruction at a lesser level. The talent development that enables one to be outstanding among one's immediate peers and friends, is less than that required to be outstanding in a small community. As the population increases to the city, the state, the nation, and the world, the requirements for the level of talent development become greater and greater.

All of this is to point to the enormous human potential available in each society and the likelihood that only a very small amount of this human potential is ever fully developed. We believe that each society could vastly increase the amount and kinds of talent it develops. We hope that this book has provided some clues as to the positive conditions necessary for such talent development.

REFERENCE

Bloom, Benjamin S. *Human Characteristics and School Learning.* New York: McGraw-Hill, 1976.

INDEX

About the Authors

Dr. Benjamin S. Bloom is a Charles H. Swift Distinguished Service Professor Emeritus at the University of Chicago and a professor of education at Northwestern University. A faculty member and researcher for over forty years, he has written seventeen books, many of which have been translated into over ten languages. As a founding member of the International Study of Educational Achievement, his ideas on curriculum and evaluation have formed the basis for educational methods in more than forty countries.

Dr. Bloom's research on human growth and learning was instrumental in creating the Headstart Program in the United States and spurred the great rise in Early Childhood Education in many countries. His work has demonstrated that the learning potential of most students is far greater than is evidenced under the usual classroom conditions, and points to the profound effects of the home environment on the early learning of the child.

Dr. Lauren A. Sosniak was the Research Coordinator for the Development of Talent Project, and has written a number of articles about the study. Currently she is interested in successful learning as it takes place in public schools. Dr. Sosniak received her Ph.D. from the University of Chicago and has taught at both the elementary and college levels.

Anthony G. Kalinowski received his Ph.D. in Measurement, Evaluation, and Statistical Analysis from the University of Chicago's Department of Education. He planned and carried out all aspects of the study of the Olympic swimmers. In addition to writing the two chapters on swimmers in this book, Dr. Kalinowski has written on the personal influence of the family and the coach as well as freedom and responsibility in the development of talent. He is currently a psychometrician working on licensing and certification examinations.

William C. Gustin is a Ph.D. candidate in the Department of Education at the University of Chicago. His major interest is in curriculum development. Mr. Gustin has been a teacher of mathematics and science. He is currently involved in evaluation and research in mathematics for the Charleston County School District in Charleston, South Carolina.

Judith A. Monsaas is a Ph.D. candidate in the Department of Education at the University of Chicago. She is an adjunct instructor in the Department of Education of Roosevelt University. Her major interests are evaluation, measurement, and statistical analysis. Currently, she works for the American Society of Clinical Pathologists on the development and analysis of certification examinations for medical personnel.

Kathryn D. Sloane is a Ph.D. candidate in the Department of Education at the University of Chicago. In her dissertation, and in other professional writings and presentations, she has analyzed the methods families use in creating home environments which promote and encourage exceptional talent development. She plans to do further studies on the influence of environmental conditions on the development of specific values, attitudes, interests, and abilities. Ms. Sloane is currently involved in measurement and evaluation research as an evaluator of special programs in mathematics and medical education.